D1710329

# NAFTA's Second Decade
## Assessing Opportunities in the Mexican and Canadian Markets

# NAFTA's Second Decade
## Assessing Opportunities in the Mexican and Canadian Markets

Louis E. V. Nevaer

THOMSON

SOUTH-WESTERN

Australia · Canada · Mexico · Singapore · Spain · United Kingdom · United States

THOMSON
———★———™
SOUTH-WESTERN

NAFTA's Second Decade: Assessing Opportunities in the Mexican and Canadian Markets
Louis E. V. Nevaer

**Vice President/**
**Editorial Director**
Jack Calhoun

**Vice President/**
**Editor-in-Chief**
Dave Shaut

**Acquisition Editor**
Steve Momper

**Channel Manager,**
**Retail**
Chris McNamee

**Channel Manager,**
**Professional**
Mark Linton

**Production Manager**
Tricia Matthews Boies

**Production Editor**
Alan Biondi

**Manufacturing Coordinator**
Charlene Taylor

**Sr. Design Manager**
Michelle Kunkler

**Cover Design**
Beckmeyer Design
Cincinnati, OH

**Cover Images**
Digital Vision and CORBIS

**Compositor**
ATLIS Graphics & Design

**Printer**
Phoenix Book Technology
Hagerstown, MD

International Division List

**ASIA (Including India):**
Thomson Learning
60 Albert Street, #15-01
Albert Complex
Singapore 189969
Tel 65 336-6411
Fax 65 336-7411

**AUSTRALIA/NEW ZEALAND:**
Nelson
102 Dodds Street
South Melbourne
Victoria 3205
Australia
Tel 61 (0)3 9685-4111
Fax 61 (0)3 9685-4199

**LATIN AMERICA:**
Thomson Learning
Seneca 53
Colonia Polanco
11560 Mexico, D.F. Mexico
Tel (525) 281-2906
Fax (525) 281-2656

**CANADA:**
Nelson
1120 Birchmount Road
Toronto, Ontario
Canada M1K 5G4
Tel (416) 752-9100
Fax (416) 752-8102

**UK/EUROPE/**
**MIDDLE EAST/AFRICA:**
Thomson Learning
Berkshire House
168-173 High Holborn
London WC1V 7AA
United Kingdom
Tel 44 (0)20 497-1422
Fax 44 (0)20 497-1426

**SPAIN (includes Portugal):**
Paraninfo
Calle Magallanes 25
28015 Madrid
España
Tel 34 (0)91 446-3350
Fax 34 (0)91 445-6218

For my mother

Sibila Concepción
1943–1967

# TABLE OF CONTENTS

# Introduction

As the North American Free Trade Agreement (NAFTA) embarks on its second decade, it is an opportune moment to assess the progress of this free-trade accord and the opportunities in the Mexican market that are looming on the horizon as NAFTA builds on the accomplishments of its first decade. More than $1 trillion worth of business opportunities exist in the Mexican market in the course of NAFTA's second decade. A significant proportion of these opportunities depend on mitigating the limitations evident during NAFTA's first decade, such as in wastewater management and the environmental industries.

To be sure, the successes of NAFTA have been so seamless, and the new opportunities hold such promise, that is imperative to evaluate strategic thinking about business opportunities throughout North America. The integration of the American and Canadian markets has progressed further along simply because the U.S.-Canada free-trade accord predates NAFTA by three years. It was, in fact, the success of free trade between the United States and Canada that emboldened expanding free trade to include Mexico. Despite concerns expressed by critics that including a developing nation in a free-trade agreement with the United States and Canada would prove disastrous, quite the opposite is true. The United States, Canada, and Mexico are stronger than they were before NAFTA. As NAFTA's second decade begins, moreover, the most exciting—and promising—opportunities are found in the Mexican market. Assessing these opportunities is imperative to sustain growth over the next ten years. The need to understand the Mexican market is the more urgent, particularly in light of four developments that now impact the nature of business life as the first half of the twenty-first century unfolds.

"NAFTA," for all practical purposes, is a polite way of saying "integrating Mexico." And savvy Canadian companies, from Scotia Bank to Bombardier, have secured significant market share in the "NAFTA" marketplace at the expense of corporate America during NAFTA's first decade. Indeed, as we examine in Chapter 2, Mexicans hold Canadians in high esteem, and on many occasions would rather do business with Canadians than Americans. This has given corporate Canada a remarkable competitive advantage. Corporate Canada, in fact, has identified Mexico as its largest growth market, with the more lucrative business opportunities expected there during NAFTA's second decade. For corporate Canada, growth lies south of its "south of the border": Mexico. That 80 percent of the more than $1 trillion worth of business opportunities discussed in this book is in Mexico is a reflection of where corporate Canada is focusing its energies during NAFTA's second decade.

North of Mexico's border, the most compelling economic development is to be found in the changed demographics of America. Foremost is the ascendance of Hispanics in the United States. "Hispanics have edged past blacks as the nation's largest minority group, new figures released today by the Census Bureau showed. The Hispanic population in the United States is now roughly 37 million, while blacks number about 36.2 million," Lynette Clemetson reported in January 2003.[1] The socioeconomic consequences of this seismic demographic shift are breathtaking in scope. "African-Americans and the African-American leadership community are about to enter an identity crisis, the extent of which we've not begun to imagine," Henry Louis Gates Jr., of Harvard University, told African-American academics who gathered in Harlem to discuss the state of black studies in America. "For 200 years, the terms 'race' or 'minority' connoted black-white race relations in America. All of a sudden, these same terms connote black, white, Hispanic. Our privileged status is about to be disrupted in profound ways," he told the attendees, who were shaken by the new Census figures confirming America's new demographics.[2]

Of equal, political, importance was the unprecedented terrorist attack on the United States on September 11, 2001. Prior to this date the United States believed itself invincible. Thus it was easy for American officials to dismiss the Mexican and Canadian proposal in the second half of the 1990s for the establishment of a "North America Security Perimeter," or NASP, out of hand—and with a roll of their eyes. With the urgent establishment of a

Cabinet-level Homeland Security office, headed by former Pennsylvania Governor Tom Ridge, it is clear that Washington, Ottawa, and Mexico City must now embark on a comprehensive and coordinated security plan to safeguard the integrity of the continental neighbors. NAFTA facilitates the kind of law enforcement, security intelligence, asylum policies, and immigration reforms required to protect all the borders that unite more than separate the three national economies.[3]

Another ominous development was how free, or at least freer, trade—and the capitalist market system that makes it possible—was discredited by the meltdown of the Argentine economy during the 2001–2002 and by protectionist measures of the Bush administration.[4] Within a few months of the White House announcement that the establishment of a hemisphere-wide free-trade zone was a foreign policy objective, Argentina's default on its foreign obligations and the dreadful manner in which the Argentine peso was devalued have given fresh ammunition to critics of the market economy.[5] Of greater concern remains the willingness of the Bush administration to capitulate to domestic politics and undermine free trade, whether it is unfair duties on steel imports or increased farm subsidies. These decisions, as outrageous as Argentina's default on its foreign debt, discredit the United States, anger allies and undermine the market system and globalization alike.

These setbacks in this hemisphere stand in sharp contrast with the fourth development: the stunning ease with which the adoption of the Euro has occurred bodes well for the future of the European Union as a single economy. The fact that other nations, such as the remnants of the former Yugoslavia, have adopted the Euro as their own currency strengthens arguments that the NAFTA partners should begin to think about the adoption of the U.S. dollar as the legal tender in all three nations. This objective becomes more suggestive as the three nations move from being mere trading partners to a working economic bloc.[6]

For executives in all three nations, NAFTA has been remarkable in both opening up new markets and the absence of significant conflict. This absence of conflict, which is to say economic and political stability through a period of significant and radical transformation, is necessary for nurturing the confidence for business to prosper. Apart from the catastrophic devaluation of the Mexican peso in December 1994, it is a testament to the important role governments can play in protecting the integrity of market economies from financial shocks.[7] Whether it was the overheating of the Mexican economy that resulted in a deep, though abbreviated, recession; or the undisciplined correction in the stock valuations as the dot-com mania came to an end with the bursting of the speculative bubble on Wall Street; or the quiet, but perplexing, continued and sustained devaluation of the Canadian dollar; it is clear that the governments of the United States, Canada, and Mexico are destined to play pivotal roles as the business of integrating the economies of North America accelerates.

However much many in the business community may be loath to admit it, governments do exert considerable influence on the kinds of business opportunities in the marketplace. When Ronald Reagan first articulated his vision of a "common market" between the United States, Canada, and Mexico that would stretch from "Yukon to the Yucatán" on the presidential campaign trail in 1980, for instance, it would take his two terms to convince Mexico to abandon its six-decades-old import-substitution development model. It would then take the entire administration of George Bush *père* to negotiate NAFTA, and it was under Bill Clinton's watch that the United States Congress approved it before it went into effect a year later on January 1, 1994.[8]

In the first decade that NAFTA was in effect, moreover, trade between the United States and Mexico tripled, and the U.S., Canada, and Mexico all experienced a period of sustained economic growth. That growth, however, was threatened in September 2001—not by the familiar economic crisis, but by the failure of the political leaders in the three countries to provide the requisite stability and security upon which business depends. Whereas in the past, business crises were of an economic nature— the 1982 devaluation of the Mexican peso that resulted in a "lost" decade, or the 1973 "oil shock" in the United States that resulted in a period of "stagflation"—by the end of 2001 the threat to the business of the North American economy was political. It was the failure of governments in Washington, Ottawa, and Mexico City to coordinate and integrate their policies to fulfill the obligations to the 500 million people living in North America that plunged the three economies into recession.[9] A well-coordinated attack confined to specific urban centers, however, was enough to shake the confidence of people "from Yukon to the Yucatán" so completely that the viability of scores of businesses, from the airline industry to tour operators, from clothing retailers to homebuilders, was threatened.

In retrospect, a strong case can be made that it was the failure of the three nations to move forward to establish NASP that intensified the effects of recessions in the three nations by the end of 2001. This security "perimeter" consists of safeguarding the people of North America.[10] This, in turn, requires that Washington, Ottawa, and Mexico City coordinate their security, intelligence, economic and immigration policies.[11] The result is a misguided continental immigration policy, one in which people needed for economic growth encounter obstacles, while enemies of North America are free to enter and leave at will.[12] While known terrorists have entered the United States by car from Canada and known al-Qaeda members have been monitored on holiday near Acapulco, legitimate labor and business activities have been encumbered by misguided policies in all three nations.

Calls to "seal off" the borders are doomed to fail, if not due to the expense of militarizing the border, then because of the economic harm that would be done to the economy when the flow of trade is slowed.[13] Jeffrey Davidow, then the American ambassador in Mexico City, described the paradox of sealing the borders without undermining economic growth well when he noted, "you have industries in the United States saying, 'Look, we really depend on the use of these people we used to call illegal immigrants. We cannot really run the hotel industry in Las Vegas without them. Agriculture in California would be a lost cause if it weren't for them.'"[14] And as a matter of law, the Posse Comitatus Act of 1878 makes it a criminal offense to use the military for the purposes of complying with U.S. law.[15] Of equal concern, of course, are the physical demands that make sealing the border impossible.[16]

National security and the labor required for sustained economic growth are therefore linked in the minds of officials contemplating what shape the NASP takes.[17] In fact, the tenuousness of that interdependence became clear when an ill-conceived state of heightened scrutiny at the borders between the U.S., Canada, and Mexico in the wake of the terrorist attack precipitated an unintended economic crisis to all three North American economies.[18] "In the aftermath of the terrorist attacks on the United States, North America's borders have been battened down and toughened up as officials try to keep out terrorists and prevent future attacks," Anthony DePalma reported as the border economies of North America encountered an economic meltdown. "Passports still are not required, but a comprehensive combination of heightened surveillance, intensified scrutiny, and a general wariness on the part of border officials in all three countries means that traveling to America's nearest neighbors now definitely seems like entering another country, perhaps even another world."[19]

This is bad for business everywhere throughout North America. Within days of heightened security measures being implemented, national airlines in all three countries suffered staggering economic losses, forcing emergency bailouts to protect the integrity of the air transportation industry. Some members of Congress who represented communities along the border compared the economic consequences of interrupting the flow of trade along the border analogous to the effects of a natural "disaster"—one requiring immediate emergency federal aid.[20] "Some years in Laredo, the amount of the city's total retail sales is greater than the city's total personal income," Keith Phillips, the chief economist for the San Antonio branch of the Federal Reserve Bank of Dallas, told the *Wall Street Journal.* "Those extra sales dollars come from Mexico."[21] Moreover, with the economy of the United States dependant on more than 300 million annual border crossings, millions of American jobs were threatened as Canadians and Mexicans, fearful that the United States was no longer safe because it might come under attack again, stayed away and not just for day trips along borders.[22]

It is worth noting how in the early 1990s, in anticipation of the passage of NAFTA, prescient managers throughout corporate America began to consider how their business would change as freer trade became the order of the day. This is how a bureau chief for the *New York Times* reflects on how his employer prepared itself for the passage of NAFTA. "The prelude to the agreement was already changing the ways the *Times* treated Mexico," Anthony DePalma writes. "The newspaper's editors had not traditionally thought of Mexico as part of North America. . . . 'We know as much about Pakistan as we do about Mexico,' Joe Lelyeld, the *Times*'s executive editor, told me when we first discussed the assignment. He felt the impending trade agreement dictated that the time had come to change that. One *Times* correspondent, Tim Golden, was already in the Mexico City office redirecting his extensive knowledge of Central America toward Mexico. And when I arrived, for the first time in memory, the *Times* had two correspondents exclusively dedicated to covering our most populous neighbor."[23]

In the second half of the 1990s and throughout the 2000s, this expanded coverage of Mexico gave way to a different way of seeing the role of Canada and Mexico in the life of the United States. As Anthony DePalma, the first correspondent to be bureau chief in both Mexico City and Toronto for the *New York Times,* describes the change:

> From 1993 to 2000, North America evolved from being defined solely as three separate nations divided by two borders on one continent to being recognized as a community of shared interest, common dreams, and coordinated responses to problems that have no regard for borders. . . . Our borders will not disappear, not any time soon. But what may fade away are the misunderstandings and ignorance that have plagued North America for so long.[24]

This foresight has a significant role to play in NAFTA's second decade. Indeed, one of the more persistent misunderstandings has been that our nations are engaged in a zero-sum contest. That one country's success would be at the expense of another was a charge falsely made during debates about NAFTA.

Ross Perot's notorious accusation that NAFTA would result in a "giant sucking sound" was proved demonstrably false as the trade among the three nations prospered without a mass exodus of industry from the United States to Mexico.[25] That more sensible and reasoned voices prevailed is comforting, particularly for the people who happen to live in the United States, Canada, and Mexico who continue to benefit from the efficacy NAFTA fosters. It is a testament to the success of NAFTA that, in less than a decade, when Canadians stay in Canada and Mexicans stay in Mexico, American lawmakers compare the consequences to a natural "disaster" for the American economy. The bottom line of pure economics—in dollars and pesos—means that NAFTA, by virtue of being a success, is here to stay.[26]

The natural competition in the quest for status among nations, on the other hand, means that with the European Union's monetary and economic consolidation, the priorities for the second decade of NAFTA are different. This economic partnership now must entail not only an expansion of economic integration but also the political and security requirements for protecting the integrity of North America. What then-American ambassador to Mexico Jeffrey Davidow pointed out was consistent with the overarching consensus that, blessed with abundant natural resources, phenomenal investment capital, and tremendous human ingenuity, the potential of the integrated economies of North America can be used to create a sustainable period of robust—and sustained—economic growth.

As NAFTA commences its second decade, then, the discussion

presented here is an assessment of the business opportunities in Mexico and an examination of the political requirements business leaders in the U.S., Canada, and Mexico must meet to cultivate those opportunities. While the polemics surrounding the "globalization" are oftentimes passionate, what is a fait accompli is the simple reality that the economies of the North American nations are in the process of economic and cultural integration.[27] The future of the United States, Canada, and Mexico is indivisible. Also undeniable is that the business community is at the forefront of propelling this economic integration. In essence, the emergence of a united Europe and the terrorist attack on the United States give greater currency to the proposition that NAFTA, having proved itself as an economic arrangement, must now become a common market.

This book sets out to provide the business, economic, and intellectual wherewithal to enable American and Canadian executives and policy makers alike to analyze their strategic thinking as the economic integration of North America accelerates.[28] The success of NAFTA remains a widely unrecognized achievement. "If Americans don't trust government, if Canadians don't trust democracy, and if Mexicans don't trust anyone, not even themselves, how could the three nations possibly have had anything in common?" asks Anthony DePalma.[29] The answer to that question is beyond the scope of this book. What is undeniable, however, is that one consequence of NAFTA's success is the proliferation of exceptional business opportunities in Mexico. As we shall see, infrastructure, energy development, financial markets, and consumer markets are areas of tremendous opportunities that are stronger, anticipating NAFTA's second decade. Along with these business opportunities, others are emerging in the wake of both the terrorist attack of September 11, 2001 and the challenge Europe's monetary integration represents. As Anthony DePalma argues in *Here: A Biography of the New American Continent*, our ideas about our continental neighbors have to be updated to reflect the more sophisticated economies and interdependent politics that characterize the North America of the twenty-first century.

To this end this book is divided into four sections. Part I examines NAFTA's first decade. Chapter 1 provides a brief overview of why the North American Free Trade Agreement was established in 1994. Chapter 2 reviews how and why NAFTA became a quiet success story. While the world's attention was diverted by other problems—chaos in the Balkans, failed peace initiatives in the Middle East, an unending recession in Japan—NAFTA exceeded expectations in industry after industry, often ahead of schedule, and at times accelerated timetables—to allow governments to catch up with economic growth.[30] Indeed, in less than a decade Mexico's economy, which could once be dismissed as a "developing" economy of an "emerging" nation, managed to topple Japan as America's largest trading partner after Canada.[31] Chapter 3 examines how Mexico and Canada have forged close relations during NAFTA's first decade, to the surprise of American observers. In this process, Mexicans and Canadians have established unusually close bonds. As nations, they respect each other, and as individuals, Canadians and Mexicans like each other. Not unlike friends who realize, unexpectedly, that they share the same demanding boss—or difficult in-law—Mexico and Canada realize that each shares a border with the United States. This affords both a knowing intimacy, and a common bond that forms the foundation for bilateralism. The nature of the Canada-Mexico "alliance," in fact, is powerful; it limits the range of options the United States has over some of its domestic policies, as the failure of Prohibition demonstrates. As NAFTA matures, moreover, there are common characteristics of both Mexicans and Canadians that affect the business environment, particularly relevant since corporate Canada now enjoys a considerable competitive advantage over corporate America in the NAFTA marketplace.

Part II examines five industries with tremendous potential: infrastructure, financial, energy development, education and environmental. The first decade of NAFTA was devoted to an initial transition—opening borders and business, whether in the form of a McDonald's franchise in Mexico City or the acquisition of an American cement manufacturer by Cemex®, was straightforward enough. It consisted of bringing down barriers and opening up trade. Thus goods flowed across the borders and services were offered by new subsidiaries, joint ventures or enterprises that sought to increase the number of options businesses and consumers alike had available to them. This proliferation of choices, whether in the form of gigantic Wal-Marts® or boutique financial services companies, proved, at times, almost overwhelming to Mexicans.[32]

Other opportunities require longer development times, and thus only now fuel sustained economic growth. When the United States embarked on the creation of the Eisenhower Interstate Highway System in the 1950s, for instance, that process took two decades—and continues to this day. After the successful conclusion of NAFTA's first decade, now that markets are open and business is thriving, the second phase, continental economic integration, can accelerate. It is clear that where highways, railroads, seaports, and airports are concerned, the United States, Canada, and Mexico have to embark on improvements and expansion that will last decades and cost in excess of $3 *trillion* dollars in NAFTA's second decade.[33] How basic infrastructure dilemmas are resolved will shape the future of the North American economies throughout this century. Whether it is the construction of a new airport for Mexico City; or the manner in which railroads link Canada, the United States, and Mexico; or how highway congestion is dealt with in major urban centers throughout the United States, the three governments have to consult one another to ensure that the integrity of the continental infrastructure system is rational and evolves into a master continental plan.

Infrastructure of another kind—financial—looms large. The acquisition of Mexican banks by, primarily, Spanish and American interests has ushered in a new era in banking and finance. Though specific deals, such as Citigroup's acquisition of Banamex®, are stories unto themselves, that significant investments are being made is a measure of the opportunities. Whether it is in the area of remittances—an $11 billion industry in 2003 characterized by aberrant profit rates—or offering long-term retirement savings and investment plans, financial opportunities abound.[34]

One aspect of the changes brought about by economic growth and political reform is seen in the energy sector. That the three North American economies have prospered for the better part of a decade means that the demand for energy has grown. And as the energy crisis in California in the early part of 2001 and the collapse of Enron at the end of that year demonstrated, there are times when public policy can create problems. Whether deregulation was misguided or simply mishandled is immaterial; the problems it created were real enough. This is not to say that deregulation was wrong per se, for, as we analyze in Chapter 6, the Mexican case is one where regulation stifles growth. How Mexico is able to resolve the paradox its Constitution creates—oil production (Pemex) and electric power generation (CFE) are state monopolies—will have to be addressed in short order. The Mexican economy, quite simply, has outgrown the protectionist barriers created in the first half of the twentieth century. Creative solutions are urgently needed; without tens of billions invested in production capability, the growth of the Mexican economy cannot be sustained.

Another kind of power—brain power—needs to be nurtured through reform and expansion. Compared with Americans and Canadians, Mexicans have not enjoyed the privilege of as many educational opportunities. Mexican families routinely send their children to the U.S. and Canada to pursue college education. How Mexico's youth and young adults are educated needs to be reformed from within. Though efficient enough in teaching basic skills, far too often Mexicans are taught to recite facts by rote without being taught how to analyze, interpret, and understand these facts. These educational shortcomings, of course, are not unique to Mexico: American high schools graduate students who are functionally illiterate every year. The consolidation of a democratic middle class in Mexico, however, now requires the founding and expansion of institutions of higher learning similar to what the United States experienced at the end of the nineteenth century, when world-class universities were founded throughout the nation. The business of education, from teaching English as a second language to the establishment of liberal arts colleges and technical universities, is poised for strong growth.

The final chapter in Part II examines the moral authority of the quiet but powerful green revolution precipitated by NAFTA that has taken hold in Mexico. Environmentalists in the U.S. and Canada were among the most adamant critics of NAFTA, but NAFTA, ironically, has nurtured the growth in Mexican *environmentalism as an industry*. The forces galvanized to oppose NAFTA created a public consciousness receptive to environmental issues. It also propelled an entire class of Mexicans into professional activism. Whereas in the United States this has resulted in a constant conflict between industry and environmentalists, Mexicans, who are culturally less inclined to be confrontational, are proving more successful at working out solutions and avoiding societal conflict than their American counterparts.[35] As a business culture, then, industry actively solicits the participation of environmental consultants, simply because the environmental despoliation in the Mexico City metropolitan area is a constant reminder of the importance of protecting natural resources. While lagging in their ability to protect the environment, Mexicans are cognizant of the threat pollution represents to society. Though environmentalism as an industry is still in its infancy, it would be cynical to think of business's interest in the issue as an attempt to co-opt environmentalists; it is often enough a sincere attempt to learn from America's experience, particularly since contemporary sensibilities are cognizant of the fragile nature of the environment.[36]

Part III examines how Mexican Paternalism has been dismantled—and assesses what remains to be done. In an economic development model that limits the role of money, fundamental changes in the institutions that encapsulate organized labor are necessary. Chapter 9 examines how wages must rise while nonpecuniary subsidies provided to workers (as a way of subsidizing business) have to be dismantled. This means several things. Foremost, unions are coming into their own as they are being weaned from state control; for the better part of the twentieth century Mexican labor unions were the means through which the ruling party dispensed patronage in exchange for support on election day. This arrangement was the reason American labor unions looked upon their Mexican counterparts with disdain, since Mexican labor unions were seen as a mechanism by which Mexico's ruling party maintained a stranglehold on political power. "For decades, U.S. unions have looked at Mexico with suspicion and hostility, condemning the country's low-wage policies, while Mexicans accuse U.S. unions of protectionism and racism," David Bacon reports, summing up decades of animosity across the border.[37] That American labor unions now are working to strengthen their Mexican counterparts is the beginning of the standardization of independent labor rights and obligations across the borders, and it speaks volumes of the sea change in labor relations ushered in by NAFTA.

This process of dismantling and revamping social and economic relations to conform to the expectations of contemporary market systems is far easier when there are existing institutions or traditions in place. How Mexican labor unions become "upgraded" is relatively straightforward. The success of NAFTA, however, poses two challenges. One concerns the introduction of new mechanisms for dispute resolution and arbitration when conflicts arise. The other is more challenging, for it deals with reining in of rogue elements and illegal practices. Government has a significant role to play in providing a mechanism to resolve disputes, protect the interests of public and private parties, and build a judicial framework through which the nations of North America can enjoy a level playing field.

Chapter 10 addresses the question of dispute resolution. As NASP takes on a greater urgency, the institutional structure for dispute resolution among the NAFTA partners needs to be strengthened. When conflicts arise, absent a fair system for protecting the interests of all parties, tremendous economic losses can be incurred. An absence of a cost-benefit analysis in the conflict involving the failure of the Mexican fishing industry to protect dolphins resulted in a boycott by American activists that, in turn, resulted in an inferior societal outcome in both Mexico and the United States. The disputes arising from NAFTA provisions allowing truck companies to operate on both sides of the border were another instance in which matters of economics and practicalities were politicized and distorted by rhetoric. Both these instances demonstrate that it is in everyone's interests to have nonpolitical, nonpartisan arbitration systems in place that consider cost-benefit analysis in balancing the rights of private parties and society. The final two chapters address the most unpleasant aspects of closer relations: corruption and drug interdiction efforts.

Chapter 11 examines corruption. Is Mexico inherently a more corrupt society than either the United States or Canada? In an unconventional analysis, we discuss how, by limiting the role of money, Mexican Paternalism fostered a culture where petty corruption suffused daily interactions. That otherwise ordinary bureaucratic transactions are lubricated with the routine dispensing of "tips" pales in comparison with system corruption on an institutional level. But because the average citizen encounters demands for "tips" from cops, public officials, or other authorities on a daily basis, the *perception* that the whole of society is corrupt is given greater currency. In contrast, corruption in the United States, for the most part, takes place behind closed doors, oftentimes leading to subpoenas that, ultimately, arrive to find trails of shredded paper.

The last chapter in Part III examines the most challenging business activity that takes place in North America—renegade entrepreneurs trafficking in illicit drugs. While the United States has traditionally sought to focus on the supply aspect of drug consumption to the exclusion of the demand side, entrepreneurs in the drug business are far ahead of officials in all three countries. How new problems—sophisticated production of narcotics in the United States and Canada, the emergence of substance abuse in Mexico—are to be addressed poses challenges for North America. It also offers opportunities, opportunities that can capitalize on the implementation of NASP.[38]

A conclusion summarizes the megatrends that demand attention and that are transforming the business landscape of all three

North American nations as NAFTA enters its second decade. Finally, a note about how this book is written is in order. Because of the broad topics covered in this discussion, an Executive Abstract appears at the beginning of each chapter. This is followed by a Discussion that makes the case for the position presented or analyzes the reasons for the market opportunities described. This is followed by a Summary or Market Investment Opportunity assessment of the size of the potential market during NAFTA's second decade and the major policy points to take away from each chapter. This presentation is intended to assist the reader in understanding the appropriate lessons, even if, at times, there are digressions here or there.

## ENDNOTES

1. "Hispanics Now Largest Minority, Census Shows," by Lynette Clemetson, *New York Times,* January 22, 2003.
2. Gates quoted in "New Topic in Black Studies Debate: Latinos," by Felicia R. Lee, *New York Times,* February 1, 2003.
3. The idea of a North America Security Perimeter reemerged on the radar screen of America's political life when the *Los Angeles Times* published an op-ed piece by Frank del Olmo. "The negotiations with Mexico aimed to legalize the status of 3 million to 4 million Mexican workers in this country, [is] an admirable goal sought both by Bush and his Mexican counterpart, President Vicente Fox. Given all that has happened in the last month [of September 2001], those talks would now have to be conducted differently," he opined in "Border Politics Just Shifted in Three Countries," October 14, 2001, October 14, 2001. "For a start, Canada should be included. And with all three signatories to the North American Free Trade Agreement at the table, the goal should be what the new U.S. ambassador to Canada, Paul Cellucci, calls a 'North American security perimeter.' Precisely what this security perimeter entails varies, depending on who you talk to. Some hard-liners envision a Fortress America, self-sufficient in food supply, Mexican oil and Canadian water (Canada has one-fifth of the world's fresh water supply). But Cellucci and other specialists would be satisfied with harmonizing the immigration laws and regulations of all three North American nations. Ardent nationalists in Mexico and Canada will surely raise a fuss. Fox already is under pressure to fire his controversial foreign minister, Jorge Castañeda, because of his outspoken support of the United States. And shortly after the terrorist attacks, Canadian Prime Minister Jean Chrétien rejected calls to tighten his nation's liberal immigration and political asylum laws." It astounds that exactly five months before the terrorist attacks on New York and Washington, Adolfo Aguilar, Mexico's National Security Adviser, met with American officials to propose "a master plan for the fight against organized crime, drug trafficking and violence." Rejected out of hand at that time by Attorney General John Ashcroft, National Security Adviser Condoleezza Rice, and officials from the FBI, DEA, State Department,

and the Pentagon, the Mexican delegation returned to Mexico City frustrated. Sergio Aguayo, a respected professor at the Colegio de Mexico, told reporters that Mexican intelligence and law enforcement officials were routinely treated like "servants" by their Washington counterparts. "Servants are not allowed to ask questions. They are only supposed to follow orders. That attitude has to change," he told the *New York Times*. That attitude did change, in fact, but only after the World Trade Center and the Pentagon had been attacked, and another jetliner had crashed in Pennsylvania. See "Mexico Seeks Closer Law Enforcement Ties with Wary U.S.," by Tim Weiner and Ginger Thompson, *New York Times*, April 11, 2001.

4.  It is important to note that the growing opposition to "globalization" is best seen as a backlash not against the market economy itself, but of the problems that arise when market imperfections and market failures are not corrected.

5.  "The idea that the neoliberal model of the Washington consensus is dead is something heard not just in Argentina, but being repeated throughout Latin America," Felipe Noguera, a political consultant based in Buenos Aires, told Larry Rohter of the *New York Times*. "There are a lot of people out there right now who are looking for an alternative and have concluded that Argentina offers one." See, "Argentina's Crisis: It's Not Just Money," by Larry Rohter, *New York Times*, January 13, 2002.

6.  It is not uncommon in both Canada and Mexico to have business contracts written to include the U.S. dollar as the legal tender for the transaction into which the parties enter.

7.  Mexico rebounded from the December 1994 currency collapse in record speed, making its payments ahead of schedule, "prepayments" that effectively silenced critics of the emergency loans orchestrated by the Clinton Treasury Department over objections of Republican leaders in the Congress.

8.  The Mexican debt crisis of 1982, months before José López Portillo left office, prompted his successor, Miguel de la Madrid, to work closely with the White House and international lending agencies to revamp Mexico's development model. This culminated in 1988 when Mexico formally joined the General Agreement on Tariffs and Trade, or GATT. As the 1980s became the 1990s, two new administrations worked to expand trade throughout North America. George Bush, galvanized by the success of free trade between the U.S. and Canada, enlisted Canadian Prime Minister Brian Mulroney to move forward on Mexican President Carlos Salinas' overtures. The agreement that resulted, however, would not be implemented until new leaders governed each nation: Jean Chrétien in Ottawa, Bill Clinton in Washington, D.C., and Ernesto Zedillo in Mexico City.

9.  Though the three economies move in sync, there were signs that each economy has its own internal rhythm and resilience. "Mexico's fragile recovery could still be derailed, especially if the U.S. economy dips back into recession," Brendan Case reported in the summer of 2002. "The recent losses in U.S. stock indexes, along with the weakening of the dollar against the euro, have some economists fretting that the recovery in the United States could lose steam." See "Mexico Seeing Economic Upturn," by Brendan M. Case, *Dallas Morning News*, July 8, 2002.

10. As we shall see, the white paper promoted by Tom Ridge at the White House in 2002 raised serious problems, for its implementation would usurp functions and authorities dispersed among various agencies, from the INS to the Coast Guard. But that NASP was inevitable was not debated. The white paper noted that "our borders today are porous and highly vulnerable to penetration by foreign terrorists." As a remedy it proposed to combine functions of the Coast Guard, the Customs Service, the Immigration and Naturalization Service, and the Department of Agriculture's quarantine inspection program into one agency with oversight authority.

11. Consider the implications of current Canadian laws which allow anyone arriving in Canada to request political asylum and be granted an automatic temporary visa, after which the person is allowed to move freely. Under Mexican law, anyone who produces a return ticket and demonstrates enough funds to pay his way is granted an automatic 30-day visa, which can be extended to six months upon request. U.S. law, likewise, allows for "student" visas to be granted to individuals without anyone following up to check to see if, for instance, the person granted a visa to learn English at an American college ever showed up for class and instead enrolled in aviation flight school.

12. The *Wall Street Journal* endorsed Fox's vision of North America. "What makes Mr. Fox so intriguing as a leader is his ability to blend theory with reality," Judy Shelton gushed. Fox, she wrote, "has a bold plan that will create free movement in people as well as goods across North America. This would be good for Mexico, and us too." See "North America Doesn't Need Borders," by Judy Shelton, *Wall Street Journal*, August 29, 2000.

13. Because the United States occupies such a large geographic mass, militarizing the borders would entail costs so high that it would be impossible. Consider that the Air Force suspended patrolling the skies over New York and Washington, D.C. about three months after the September 11, 2001 attack, citing costs exceeding $300 million and wear on the F-15 fighter jets. If the cost is $100 million per month to protect adequately the New York-Washington corridor, it is clear that a continuous state of high alert is unsustainable, simply because it would bankrupt the nation.

14. Quotation appears in "An Effort to Lift the Gate a Little," by Tim Weiner, *New York Times*, September 9, 2001.

15. This complicates any attempt to have the military assist the Immigration and Naturalization Service, whose agents are under federal command. The same applies for using the National Guard to enforce immigration laws at the borders, ports, and airports.

16. "They are absolutely getting weary. The body can take only so much physically. The guys are working 16-hour shifts in heat that'll knock you down," Rudy Santos, a Customs chief in Laredo, Texas who oversees 36 inspectors, told the *New York Times*. The amount of work is staggering: "A quarter of the [Customs] service's more than 20,000 agents are deployed at the border posts. Every day they see roughly 1.3 million people going in and out of the United States. They peer into 350,000 cars, trucks and buses a day. With the help of their sniffer dogs, they seize more drugs than any other arm of the government. They collect more revenue— about $22 billion a year in duties and fees—than anyone but the tax

man," Tim Weiner reported. See "Border Customs Agents Are Pushed to the Limit," by Tim Weiner, *New York Times,* July 25, 2002.

17. "North and south of the U.S., old phobias and nationalist sensibilities are resurfacing and restraining Canada and Mexico from giving unconditional support to the U.S. campaign against terrorism," James Smith and Maggie Farley reported. "In Canada, that has led political foes to accuse Prime Minister Jean Chrétien of excessive caution for trying to resist being swept into a U.S.-led coalition. In Mexico, meanwhile, Foreign Minister Jorge Castañeda has faced calls that he resign for his unequivocal declaration of solidarity with Washington after the Sept. 11 attacks on the World Trade Center and the Pentagon. The two countries' responses reflect their long-conflicted relationships with their powerful neighbor—and their desire to be an ally without sacrificing their ability to act independently. They also share a preference for caution over confrontation." See "Canada, Mexico Responses Reflect Conflict," by James Smith and Maggie Farley, *Los Angeles Times,* September 26, 2001. Canadians expressed exceptional solidarity with the United States. "In small towns and cities, from Atlantic Canada through the prairies to the Pacific coast, many Canadians are saying what Washington would like to hear, if it could hear them," Barbara Crosette reported. "Give the Americans what they need to make North America safer, they say, even if that means a loss of Canadian sovereignty and tougher immigration and asylum laws." See "Support for U.S. Security Plans Is Quietly Voiced Across Canada," by Barbara Crossette, *New York Times,* October 1, 2001.

18. That economic development through NAFTA was overtaking the movement of people across the borders could be seen in one city: New York. The 2000 Census reported that almost 300,000 Mexicans from Puebla and Oaxaca were now living in the New York greater metropolitan area. That most of these people are of Zapotec descent means that this arguably constitutes the largest voluntary migration of one group of Native Americans since the Ice Age, raising tantalizing cross-cultural questions best addressed by anthropologists in the decades ahead.

19. "Slow Crawl at the Border," by Anthony DePalma, *New York Times,* October 21, 2001.

20. "Tight new security restrictions at crossings with Mexico are choking the economic life out of border towns in California and the Southwest, congressmen from the region say," Greg Winter wrote in "Tightening of Border Pinches Local Economy," in the *New York Times* on October 16, 2001. "Some lawmakers have begun pleading with the Bush administration for low-interest loans or grants until the crisis subsides, calling the situation a 'state of emergency' comparable to that posed by a hurricane or an earthquake."

21. "Mexican Customers Lift Texas Retailers," by Joel Millman, *Wall Street Journal,* November 7, 2000. "In 1998, the latest year for which the bank has Mexico-based sales statistics," Millman writes, "shoppers spent almost $700 million in Laredo, out of a total of $1.8 billion."

22. What is often overlooked by Americans is the role international tourism plays in the economic life of the United States. Though more Canadians visit the U.S. than Mexicans, Mexicans spend more than Canadians. And together, it is Canadians and Mexicans that are the engines that drive the

U.S. tourism industry, according to figures provided by the Department of Commerce.

23. Anthony DePalma, *Here: A Biography of the New American Continent*, page 25. The unintended irony, of course, was that, by the end of 2001, Americans knew a great deal about Pakistan that they found frightening. Concerning the revolution in how the *New York Times* covered Mexico, consider the fanciful story on street names. "The map of one of the world's largest metropolises is a kind of literary masterpiece. The street guide reads as if a writer from the school of magical realism had translated the encyclopedia, cut his work into confetti and sprinkled it over the city," begins "In a City Where Good Luck Meets Hope, Signs of Magic," by Tim Weiner, *New York Times*, August 7, 2000. Loving articles about Mexico are a rarity in American media. "Good Luck crosses Hope, then hits a dead end. . . . And Comprehension ends in Silence," Weiner noted.

24. DePalma, *Here*, page 354.

25. In what became the most celebrated exchange in the 1992 presidential election, Ross Perot claimed that the passage of NAFTA would result in a "giant sucking sound" as American manufacturing jobs went south of the border. The only sucking sound, however, has been caused by an explosion of trade. American exports to Canada more than doubled from $179 billion in 1993 to $350 billion in 2000, while imports from Canada more than doubled to $229 billion in 2000 from 1993's $111 billion. Greater growth has been registered on the Mexican front. American exports to Mexico rose from $42 billion in 1993 to $112 billion in 2000, while imports from Mexico more than tripled from $40 billion to $136 billion during the same period. This increase in trade was accomplished without significant disruption in employment patterns among the three nations; moving traded goods is more reasonable than moving laborers.

26. In the United States and Canada, by comparison, economic growth was so robust that some commentators wondered if the boom of the 1990s meant the "death" of the business cycle. The exuberance may have been irrational at times to be sure, but the underlying observation remained valid: through the expansion of trade and technological innovations, the integration of the North American economies was well underway.

27. Former Mexican president Ernesto Zedillo, in fact, coined the phrase "globophobia" to describe the irrational fear of increasing free trade in a series of addresses in March 2001.

28. Though the discussion presented in this book concentrates on the U.S.-Mexico side of NAFTA relations, it is intended to assist Canadian executives in understanding how opportunities throughout the Mexican economy are emerging. Canadians, no doubt, need no reminders that America's neighbors oftentimes end up giving more than they receive in their "bilateral" relations.

29. *Here: A Biography of the New American Continent*, by Anthony DePalma, page 277.

30. The Mexican banking industry, for example, opened up to foreign competition years ahead of schedule. In other areas, from private companies being able to have disputes settled satisfactorily through NAFTA arbitration, to American and Canadian environmentalists working with their Mexican counterparts to influence public policy, to the

"rationalization" of air travel services among North American airlines, NAFTA continues to confound critics and surprise supporters.

31. If in the 1980s the specter of Japanese "domination" of business world— and the global economy—prompted an avalanche of business books analyzing the how and the why of Japanese economic ascendance, there has been a dearth of books that examine the transformation of the business landscape of the integrated North American economies.

32. Critics often pointed to "excessive" consumerism as an affront, arguing that Mexico, by entering into NAFTA, had sacrificed its spiritual life for the materialism of the Home Shopping Club. Then again, anyone who has misgivings about how "local" firms are "threatened" by Wal-Mart should see how such a company is portrayed in the 2002 film *The Good Girl.* If ever there was a community in desperate need of a Wal-Mart, this is it. As we shall examine, the proliferation of unwanted choices is a market imperfection arising from a discrepancy between Stated Preference and Revealed Preference, and is not an indictment of the market economy.

33. It is estimated that the United States needs to spend $1.3 trillion to *repair* existing infrastructure. These are the findings of a study issued by the American Society of Civil Engineers (ASCE) after analyzing the nation's infrastructure it graded as "D+." "As dismal as these grades seem, many of the downward trends can be reversed with increased funding and a renewed partnership between citizens, local, state and federal governments," ASCE Executive Director James E. Davis told CNN when the report was made public. (See "Report: $1.3 Trillion Needed to Rebuild the Nation's Infrastructure," by Julie Vallese, *www.cnn.com/2001/US/03/08/crumbling.infrastructure/index.html.*). Mexico needs to spend almost $1.1 trillion to upgrade and expand its infrastructure across the board and around the nation. Canada's total bill is estimated at $650 million. Thus more than $3 trillion is required over the next decade if the NAFTA nations are to establish a competitive advantage over the European Union.

34. In the case of remittances, this is an instance in which politics conspires against consumers. By virtue of their legal status, many Mexican workers in the U.S. do not have access to the American banking system, forcing them to use expensive alternatives to handle their personal and family finances. At the same time, the saving rates among Mexican consumers lag far behind those of Americans and Canadians, signaling that personal retirement as an industry is a fertile market, particularly as the Mexican middle class continues to grow in numbers and strengthen in financial clout.

35. Unlike the United States where radical activists from Earth First! have booby-trapped trees in the Pacific Northwest, maiming or killing lumberjacks, or PETA extremists who vandalize research laboratories, Mexican society has no tolerance for this kind of activism within its borders.

36. In no small measure it is the realization of how disregard for the environment can threaten people that has gone far in raising the level of awareness about environmental issues among the Mexican public. That Mexico City has among the world's worst air pollution is a constant reminder to policy makers and the public at large about the

consequences of environmental despoliation. In many ways, Mexicans are eager to learn from Americans about restoring an environmental equilibrium. Mexican government officials, for instance, want to clean the air in Mexico City by studying how Los Angeles, in a two-decade program, has made stupendous strides in cleaning the air over the greater Los Angeles basin.

37.   "New Players - New Game? Guest Workers or Amnesty," by David Bacon, Pacific News Service, August 7, 2001, Pacificnews.org.

38.   "The new American war on terrorism has scored an unintentional victory, though it may be temporary," Fox Butterfield reported in "Officials Report Drop in Drug Smuggling," *New York Times,* September 28, 2001. "Tightened security along the border with Mexico since the terrorist attacks on Sept. 11 has helped reduce the flow of illegal drugs, as cautious smugglers from Mexico have cut back on their shipments to avoid having them seized, Customs officials say." Thus the paradox of how complex relations have become becomes clear. Though seizing more drug shipments is consistent with law enforcement objectives, one has to bear in mind that during the same period, the same increased "security" and "scrutiny" had an unintended effect: So many law-abiding Mexicans were frustrated by the inconveniences and delays at the border that they stayed away entirely. The result was a decline so catastrophic in so many American communities along the border that lawmakers sought emergency federal aid, declaring the situation a "disaster."

PART I

# THE DISCREET CHARM OF NAFTA

# 1

# An Overview of the Establishment of the North American Free Trade Agreement in 1994

$T$he North American Free Trade Agreement came into existence for three reasons. The first was to expand the success of the U.S.-Canada Free Trade Agreement that resulted in tremendous strides in integrating the economies of the United States and Canada. The second was to address the perceived threat of a unified European trading bloc, facilitated by the stunning success of the European Union, by creating one, unified North American trading bloc. The third was to integrate the Mexican economy into that of the United States and Canada in such a way that it would foster sustained growth in Mexico, implement fundamental capitalist reforms, and provide an engine to lift Mexico's workers out of poverty.

The weakest link in North America was, of course, Mexico. Pursuing an import-substitution economic development model for decades, "burdened" by millions of indigenous people who were poorly educated and whose lifestyles were incompatible with the acquisition of material goods, and confronting the challenges of meeting the democratic aspirations of an electorate frustrated by the continued dominance of a single ruling party, Mexico would have to implement sweeping reforms that challenged the quasi-socialism it had fostered for NAFTA to succeed. One consequence of a paternalistic government is that it inculcates risk adversity in the population. From Russia to Mexico, the transition to capitalist market systems and democratic institutions has instilled, largely along generational lines, as much apprehension *of* the future by elders as excitement *for* the future by youth.

Mexican Paternalism, after all, had proved itself to be an effective way of filling in the sweeping broad strokes of the nation's political and economic landscape. But it was not very efficient in providing the wealth of choices that a nation's consumers demand over time. While getting television for the first time is thrilling, in short order consumers want a variety of viewing options. While having fundamental consumer goods on grocery shelves is a sign of progress, it's not long before consumers want to be able to choose between Coke® and Pepsi®—or some other brand. And so it goes for every aspect of life, from airlines to denim jeans, from brands of toothpaste to video games available at the nearest mall. As the Soviet Union demonstrated in stark terms, a command economy is able to impose discipline on its people, but it cannot provide the kind of incentives that translate into consumer choices; providing hand soap was an accomplishment in itself, with matters about "brand" being superfluous.

The "macro" successes of paternalism inevitably fail to meet the "micro" demands of a nation's consumers. In a mixed economy there are no hard and fast rules; pragmatism is the order of the day, the only thing that closely resembles an ideology. Consumer (and voter) dissatisfaction, however, is a slow process of revelation after revelation. If the cell phone has not been invented, there is no consumer demand for it. Until there are enough people walking around with beepers, there's no one to beep. Taking the kids to Disney World™ is not a consideration until Disney transforms the Florida wilderness into Disney World. It could be argued that these changes in consumer demands are the result of demonstration effects: people want what people see. This is true enough—provided paternalism does a credible job of providing for everyone. It is only when it fails to meet society's expectations that questions arise. An airline whose flights depart and arrive on schedule goes unnoticed; only when there are delays do people begin to wonder why this should be so.

Mexican Paternalism became ever more important in the struggle to lift people out of poverty by providing them with health care, education, and employment opportunities. As the Mexican economy grew, there were significant social dislocations—rural poor moving to the cities in search of better lives— that further taxed government institutions. "For the poor, the government can be central to their well-being, and for some even to survival. For the rich and the comfortable, it is a burden save when, as in the case of military expenditure, Social Security and the rescue of failed financial institutions, it serves their particular interest," John Kenneth Galbraith observed.[1] The very success of the PRI in providing fundamental social services, then, undermined its very viability. The PRI's fundamental success made it obsolete; the Mexican nation simply outgrew the natural limitations of Mexican Paternalism as a development model.

To be fair, "Mexican Paternalism" as envisioned by Mexico's PRI did a credible job of building a "nation" during the 1930s, 1940s and 1950s. By the 1960s, however, when a consumer culture emerged around the world, people began to take note of the limitations and shortcomings of the Mexican economy. As we go through this book, it will become clear that Mexican Paternalism encountered two obstacles it could not overcome. The first one was a byproduct of its own success. It managed to create a social welfare system that was ambitious—providing not only medical insurance and instituting price controls on food, pharmaceuticals, and consumer products but also offering workers subsidized housing and fanciful schemes that provided subsidized furniture and vacations—but that could not encompass everyone.

As Mexico's population and economy grew, so did the number of people excluded from the warm embrace of Mexican Paternalism. Mexican Paternalism, in effect, could accommodate the needs of an economy comprised of about 60 million people. This means, quite tragically, that the remaining 40 million people (of which 10 million are the disenfranchised indigenous peoples) are left out in the cold. As a result, there was an embarrassed admission of these limits, one in which Mexico spoke of the "formal" economy in its official statistics and rhetoric, while lamenting the existence of a "parallel" economic reality that was "informal." Mexico's formal economy, in essence, refers to the 60 million Mexicans who are taken care of by Mexican Paternalism. Mexico's informal economy refers to the 40 million who are left out.

This was the second consequence of Mexican Paternalism, the division of the Mexican people into two opposing groups: those in the formal economy and those left disenfranchised in the informal economy. Those who are part of the formal economy have access to health care, public schools and all the other benefits of a modern welfare state. Those who are left behind in the informal economy simply languish. Of these 40 million Mexicans, approximately 10 million are impoverished indigenous peoples scattered throughout the thousands of hamlets and towns that litter the Mexican countryside. Another 10 million Mexicans have been forced to abandon Mexico for the United States in order to improve their material lives.[2] These are, correctly, economic immigrants seeking a better life in the United States who, until the election of Vicente Fox in July 2000, did not officially exist, for their very existence was a reminder of the human consequences of Mexican Paternalism.[3] This was made the more stark in 2003, when the last tariffs protecting Mexican farmers were eliminated, which was not without controversy in Mexico and Canada given that the U.S. passed $100 billion in farm subsidies the previous spring, giving American farmers an unfair competitive advantage.

Then there are another 20 million Mexicans who are not indigenous people, but are nonetheless disenfranchised, comprising two-thirds of Mexico's poor. Mexican Paternalism, under increasing stress, saw a barrage of criticism. With demands for democracy from leftists and decentralization by conservative businessmen, the political and economic shortcomings of Mexican Paternalism came under attack. This was not unique to Mexico, of course. As Cornell University economist Robert Frank explains:

> Paternalistic laws are often attacked on the grounds that they unjustly abridge individual freedom. . . . True individual sovereignty implies that people have not only the right not to be restricted by others—as the libertarian position stresses—but also the right not to be subjected to behavior they consider harmful. If the concept of individual sovereignty is to have any intelligible meaning at all, there can be no distinction *in principle* between the legitimacy of these two subsidiary rights: The right not to be offended is just as worthy of our respect as the right not to be restricted. Yet these rights cannot be exercised simultaneously. . . . The libertarian who insists that the right not to be restricted cannot, as a matter of principle, ever be negotiated away, shows contempt for the rights of people to resolve such issues for themselves.[4]

Throughout the 1960s, 1970s and 1980s, Mexicans wanted to do just that. Official Mexico was assailed, but lacking a Plan B, the PRI could not bring itself to recognize that its paternalism had, by failing to provide for everyone, divided the Mexican nation into two segments. Other nations, however, could—and did. NAFTA further complicated matters of Mexico's social engineering elite. "As much as NAFTA ignited an economic evolution," Ginger Thompson reported, succinctly describing the socioeconomic consequences of the economic revolution that unfolded during NAFTA's first decade, "it has also set off a kind of social landslide as the government struggles, in the span of a decade, to move millions of people from farming into other ways of life."[5]

The United States, for its part, found great utility in Mexican Paternalism. Under the guise of national security, it sought to certify which Mexicans properly belonged to the formal economy— and were therefore "good" Mexicans—and which were members of the informal economy—and therefore to be shunned. Consistent with the same segregationist policies pursued at home, where the fiction of separate but equal in reality meant separate and *not* equal, American diplomats found useful the way Mexican Paternalism efficiently created similar categories for Mexicans.

When dealing the Mexicans—whether in Mexico or in the United States—American officials looked to see if the individual in question was part of the formal economy or not, in order to determine if he or she was a "good" or "bad" Mexican. This was the great tragedy of the limits of Mexico's Paternalism, the creation of two classes of Mexicans, one that transcended race as the point of demarcation in Mexican society. It created a public fiction in which the failures of Mexican Paternalism were seen not as a question of public policy, but as the individual shortcomings of those left out. Here, then, lies the fundamental tension and conflict, one that spills over the border. By this I mean that from the early 1940s through the year 2000, the governments of Mexico and the United States participated in a collusion designed to turn their backs on the poorest Mexicans, a concept that will be discussed in greater detail.

What is important at this juncture, however, is to understand that the persistence of poverty speaks to the limits of paternalism itself. Mexican Paternalism had, quite simply, exhausted itself by the end of the 1980s as a development model and a political system. If a more equitable distribution of wealth was to be achieved and the democratic aspirations of the Mexican people realized, market reforms had to be introduced, borders had to be opened, and a process of economic integration had to be launched. Mexican Paternalism resulted in a series of bad economic decisions that would otherwise have been remedied by an unfettered market.[6] The mere existence of millions living in poverty challenged the inherent justice of the sociopolitical institutions of both the United States and Mexico, for they were evidence of the human consequences of unchecked market imperfections.[7]

The economic crisis of 1982 changed all that, and a few years later, Mexico was ready to commit to the kinds of reforms that made NAFTA possible. Since Mexico joined the General Agreement on Tariffs and Trade, or GATT, in 1988, corporate Mexico has undergone structural changes as significant protections of more than half a century of Mexican Paternalism have been eliminated. During the 1990s Mexican companies have been forced to get up to speed, perish, or establish alliances with foreign companies; corporate Mexico is emerging more sophisticated and resilient in its ability to compete. On the political front, the Mexican government has struggled to deal head-on with one unintended consequence of Mexican Paternalism: the socioeconomic stratification of Mexican society. Not unlike segregation in the United States, this approach has divided Mexican consumers into two distinct economic markets as outlined above, with approximately 60 million Mexicans enfranchised within the formal economy of Mexican Paternalism and 40 million others disenfranchised, relegated to the informal economy. Mexican demands for immigration reform are designed to recognize the de facto ebbs and flows of workers across North America, and to ameliorate the dislocations that continue to characterize Mexico as continental integration accelerates.

## ENDNOTES

1. John Kenneth Galbraith, *The Good Society: The Humane Agenda*, Boston: Houghton Mifflin Co., page 8.
2. The trade-off, often ignored, is that for millions of Mexicans in the United States, the costs are great. While they do improve their material well-being, their spiritual and family life suffers. Consequently, millions of Mexicans "commute" across the border for several years, many returning to Mexico once they have saved enough to start their own businesses in their hometowns.
3. Vicente Fox's victory resulted in all manner of hyperbole. During the presidential campaign, for instance, Fox predicted he would be the "Neil Armstrong of Mexican politicians—the first opposition candidate to set off in [the presidential palace] Los Pinos."
4. Robert Frank, *Choosing the Right Pond: Human Behavior and the Quest for Status*, pages 224–225.
5. "NAFTA to Open Floodgates, Engulfing Rural Mexico," by Ginger Thompson, *New York Times*, December 19, 2002.
6. This is not to say that the market provides immunity from the consequences of irrational individual or collective choices. "The stock-

market bubble led to bad political decisions as well as bad business decisions; and we'll be paying the price for many years to come," Paul Krugman noted of the Internet "frenzy" of the mid-1990s. See "Damaged by the Dow," *New York Times,* September 2, 2001.

7.   Canadian Judith Alder Hellman offers an intriguing Marxist analysis of the persistence of economic crises in *Mexico in Crisis,* which underscores the frustrations encountered by individuals of all political beliefs concerned with the question of how people can best be lifted out of poverty.

# 2

# Mexico After NAFTA: A Market Economy Flourishes—As Does Ambivalence Towards Paternalism

## EXECUTIVE ABSTRACT

The transition from a paternalistic development model to a market economy has been challenging, but successful. Unlike other nations, Mexico has been able to maintain political stability through two economic crises and the political ascendance of a powerful opposition.[1] The legacy of authoritarianism, and the social welfare state that it nurtured, however, holds sway in the imaginations of millions of Mexicans. As we shall examine later in this book, limiting the role of money under Mexican Paternalism necessitated an array of government agencies that dispensed economic benefits—and political patronage. The remarkable fact remains, however, that Mexicans, who have cultivated markets since pre-Columbian times, have embraced modern capitalism. The benefits of NAFTA have been many, and Mexican leaders have been sensitive to the pace at which social welfare programs are reformed, privatized, or dismantled. The result is an almost seamless transition from a closed development model to the vibrant market economy that is strengthening Mexico with daunting speed.

## DISCUSSION

"There will no longer be a paternalistic government, but one that shares responsibility," Vicente Fox proclaimed in a televised speech that set out his administration's six-year plan in May 2001.[2] How "responsibility" is shared between government and the public, including business, remains to be seen, and the process likely will evolve over decades.

What is certain, however, is that Mexico has had several defining moments. The first was the successful implementation of NAFTA. The second was the transition to an opposition government when Vicente Fox assumed the presidency of Mexico after 71 years of uninterrupted rule by the PRI. Within the span of a decade, then, a series of changes have unfolded that have changed how Mexicans see themselves and their place in the world.[3] It has also changed the way Mexicans conduct their business lives. "When I first arrived in Mexico," Alain Giberstein, a Frenchman who moved from Paris to Mexico City more than a decade ago, said, "people were very, shall we say, informal. They arrived late, or cancelled appointments. It was very difficult for them to make commitments. Shipments were late, or incorrect. Payments were not timely. It was a struggle, simply because there was a certain lack of professionalism about how business was conducted. It was very frustrating."[4]

It was a droll observation that the twin evils of fawning over foreign customs (French and Spanish) and procrastination were epidemic in Mexico. If so, that was the Mexico before NAFTA. "Now, it is remarkable to see how attitudes have changed. People are so much more professional. There is a, shall we say, 'first world' approach to business. After the peso was devalued in December 1994 I seriously contemplated moving back to France. But I always believed in Mexico and the Mexican people and decided to remain. It wasn't easy, but I am glad I stayed. Throughout the 1990s, Mexico has changed in so many ways. The emergence of a business ethic is remarkable. Mexico before and after NAFTA is two different countries. It is night and day, it is that dramatic."[5]

Observations by foreign businessmen living in Mexico are borne out by American economists and officials. "People thought that we would see an invasion of U.S. companies into Mexico [after NAFTA] and Mexican companies disappearing. It's going both ways now," José Felipe Garc´a, an economic development specialist at Tucson-Mexico, a project to increase trade between Mexico and Arizona, told the *Los Angeles Times*.[6] What has occurred in Mexico, of course, is not a miracle but the natural process when sweeping economic reforms are introduced—and a nation is ripe for assimilating change. Indeed, what Henry Fielding wrote of the English of 1751 applied to the Mexicans after

NAFTA took effect: "Nothing has wrought such an Alteration in this Order of People, as the Introduction of Trade. This hath indeed given a Face to the whole Nation, hath in great measure subverted for the former State of Affairs, and hath almost totally changed the Manners, Customs and Habits of the People."[7]

More than 350 years later, this process is seen in Mexico—as well as other nations that have not enjoyed as seamless a transition to a market economy. Even in Russia, for instance, echoes of NAFTA's success are representative of what happens the world over when nations are afforded market opportunities. Consider how Bill Keller describes the emergence of "new" post-Soviet Russians:

> Drop into a McDonald's here [in Moscow], and you find Russians who scarcely existed a dozen years ago—Russians with decent clothes and healthy teeth, Russians with jobs that give them spare time and cash for a family splurge, Russians with, polls show, a flicker of optimism. You find Russians who have more or less achieved their plaintive ambition to be "normal people."[8]

Academic careers have been made comparing and contrasting the most famous revolutions of 1917—Mexico's and Russia's. Though the course each one took was far different, it is interesting to note that neither lasted more than an average life span: seven decades. For the Russians, the end of the Soviet era, as Bill Keller notes, "begins in the Gorbachev era, when the abject failure of the Soviet economy became clear to all but the most deluded."[9]

Delusions swirl the globe like the weather, indifferent to international borders. The clouds that loom over how Mexicans see their nation after a decade of NAFTA reveal anxiety about the social welfare system, fear about the inability of market economies to end poverty, concern about how market economies create unexpected competitors, and ambivalence about the ideological flows of American policies. Consider each in turn to understand how, behind robust economic growth, there are lingering misgivings that must be addressed in NAFTA's second decade. Mexican labor law, for instance, provides for low monetary wages, of course, but it is rich in benefits. There are ministries that provide health care to every worker, administer housing programs, regulate price controls, and offer subsidies on basic foodstuffs. There are generous maternity leaves and mandated vacation pays; retirement savings programs are guaranteed by the state; severance compensation is mandated by law. American workers by comparison are entitled to a minimum wage with no benefits. In the United States, there are millions of people who work full-time jobs and remain below the poverty line. Mexico's welfare state, a legacy of the PRI, has spared millions a similar fate.

Ambivalence about how the dismantling of Mexican Paternalism will affect these social programs is natural, simply because there are no guarantees. Consider the situation in the United Kingdom, where a similar transition, though on a far more modest basis, has been uneasy. *Wall Street Journal* reporter Mark Champion describes it thusly:

> Britain hasn't decided whether it wants to be a high-tax welfare state, with the government ensuring high-quality services in the style of the Continent, or a U.S.-styled capitalist bastion, with lower taxes and services left largely to local authorities or private enterprise.
>
> As a result, the government can't afford schools and hospitals of the same quality as those in Germany and France. Yet, even after cutting taxes substantially below the European average and freeing its labor markets from a union armlock, Britain hasn't seen nearly the sort of payoff the U.S. gets in terms of productivity or the private-sector provision of high-quality services.[10]

Making sacrifices without realizing the expected gains is a strong rebuke to such reforms.

Then there is the untidy issue of mixed results. "In 1994, the Conservative government privatized British Rail in an effort to rid itself of the huge expense and responsibility of running trains," Champion continues in his report. "The track is now owned by one private company, Railtrack PLC, while 25 other companies operate various routes, and scores more handle maintenance and other chores formerly done by British Rail. Marketing has improved; punctuality and safety have suffered."[11]

Excesses of capitalism need to be checked, and rightfully so. For Mexican officials, the issue of credibility lingers, often in disquieting ways. Though Americans are quick to think of Mexico as a corrupt place, an idea that angers Mexicans, the truth is that the United States fails to adequately police corruption, with excesses in corporate America the most startling example.[12] That American officials deny a systemic problem infuriates both Mexicans and Canadians, particularly since both our neighbors feel that their American counterparts too often affect a sanctimonious manner when wrongdoing comes to light in either Mexico or Canada. Indeed, consider that when George W. Bush told reporters on July 9, 2002 that "there's no 'there' there" when questioned about his alleged insider trading in 1990 when he was a director of Harken Energy Corp., credibility was strained. The facts are clear, however. On June 22, 1990, Bush sold 212,140 shares at $4 each; he did not report this to the SEC for 34 weeks; an SEC investigation concluded that at the time of the sale Mr. Bush knew that Harken was in financial trouble; in subsequent months it was forced to amend its financial statements; and as a result of these disclosures and restatements of finances, the stock closed the year trading at $1 a share. Perhaps George W. Bush is right and there's no "there" there, but his credibility was indisputably questioned by the appearance of there being some "there" there.

To make matters worse, his entire administration's credibility was further undermined by their perceived callousness. Rather than acknowledging problems at Enron, for instance, Treasury Secretary Paul O'Neill famously—and flippantly—said on national television in January 2002 that "companies come and go. It's part of the genius of capitalism." So do Treasury Secretaries, and so did Paul O'Neill. It's part of the genius of Washington.

Mexicans, recovering from seven decades of government mismanagement, malfeasance, and corruption, do not automatically have confidence that those in the private sector will behave in a more trustworthy manner, or demonstrate greater competence. Revelations that Gerardo de Prevoisin siphoned off millions of dollars from the then-newly privatized Aeromexico®, for instance, was a stunning reminder that powerful business executives can collide and conspire with whoever is in political office, using capital markets for unseemly ends. That other, more sophisticated nations encounter the same problems bolsters Mexican skepticism of the market economy. The troubles at Deutsche Telekom®, privatized by the German government in 1996, and which faced monumental problems under the leadership of Ron Sommer, underscored the potential pitfalls.[13] Mexicans' debates about the wisdom of privatizing this or that are replete with horror stories of market imperfections becoming market failures from abroad.[14]

Critics of the dismantling of Mexican Paternalism, in essence, are asking, What's the point of trading a set of public-sector crooks and mediocrities for a set of private-sector crooks and mediocrities? What's the point of privatizing something that might very well need to be nationalized down the road? Why should the United States, in the name of market "reforms," decry

Mexico's intervention in the economy when the United States is quick to bail out its own industries?[15]

There is also the problem of tautological arguments. "Capital markets do not work effectively unless people believe in their essential integrity," Jean Strouse opined in the *New York Times,* commenting on the rash of corporate accounting scandals. "Investors will only take risks if the game isn't rigged."[16] This line of reasoning sounds like the tautology that Ayn Rand offered as her Objectivism progressed: true capitalists act with character, and if they don't act with character, then they weren't true capitalists in the first place, but only some degenerate version of capitalists.[17] It's facile to make the blanket statement that the "vision" of the 1990s was replaced by "verification" in the 2000s, but conceding this point reaffirms the business cycle.

American officials continue to express their frustration at the measured pace of economic reforms. While when it comes to wastewater management, electric power generation, and the oil sector, criticism is in order, in their defense it has to be pointed out that Mexicans fear repeating America's mistakes. If one accepts that capitalist markets are the most efficient economic model—and they are—it is equally important to concede that how markets are permitted to operate determines their success or failure. Strong arguments can be made that how deregulation has been introduced in the United States has been ill-advised, causing unnecessary turmoil. Recall the turmoil and confusion that arose in the airline, banking, and telephone industries when they were deregulated. Consumers are dissatisfied by the inherent volatility in airfares, resentful of how banking mergers and acquisitions have done away with personalized customer service of a bygone era, and confused by the duplicitous (if not fraudulent) charges on incomprehensible telephone bills. How Americans began to deregulate utilities alarms, simply because the California energy crisis in 2000 and the market abuses of firms like Enron demonstrated how vulnerable consumers are to abuses by industry.

Mexican officials wince at the thought of walking away from their perceived duty to prevent this kind of turmoil. Fostering competition without harming the airline, banking, telephone, and utility industries is one thing society expects of its officials. In this regard, then, Mexicans remain as ambivalent as the British about balancing the efficiency of unfettered market economies and the need for safeguarding their nation's social welfare. In terms of dismantling Mexican Paternalism, for instance, Mexicans are cautious. They fear that if wages do not rise fast enough to compensate the dismantling of price controls and consumer subsidies, their purchasing power will be insufficient to secure these goods and services at fair market prices, which would result in an unjust market failure. Mexicans understand that low wages have been, to a large extent, a way for the government to subsidize business by lowering the costs of labor necessary to compensate for higher capital costs.[18] They are concerned that what they take for granted—health care for their families, subsidized mortgage rates, assistance for the purchase of domestic durable goods—will vanish, leaving them as impoverished as America's working poor. They fear that they will bear the burden of the mistakes of public officials charged with "engineering" these changes in a seamless manner. Those concerns are shared by Wall Street analysts who fear that if wages rise too quickly as Mexico's social welfare benefit system is retooled, it could interfere with economic growth.[19]

## The Persistence of Poverty

The greatest disappointment of NAFTA's first decade is the failure to eradicate poverty. Critics charge that by putting the interests of business first, working people, the environment, and social issues have suffered. The continuing uprising by the Zapatista rebels in Chiapas best embodies the hostility of disenfranchised Mexicans to NAFTA. "To divert the poor from the siren call of terrorists, America and its allies must appeal to their entrepreneurial interests. It is not enough to appeal to the stomachs of the poor. One must appeal to their aspirations. This is, in a way, what the terrorists do. But their path leads only to destruction," Hernando de Soto wrote in the *New York Times,* mindful of the fundamental cause of armed conflict.[20] In all fairness, when the rhetoric quiets down, the Zapatistas, their egalitarian proclamations notwithstanding, are insincere benefactors. "The Zapatista rebellion in 1994 had a certain positive effect on Mexican society," Sergio Sarmiento argued in the *Wall Street Journal.* "It drew attention to the extreme poverty of Indian communities and to the racism that has affected Indians for centuries. But the solutions that Subcomandante Marcos proposes would merely accentuate the poverty and isolation of Indians."[21]

"Rights" bills aimed at appeasing indigenous people are often unworkable. "Lawmakers and political analysts—left, right and center—have raised questions about the [Indian Rights] bill, which would amend the Constitution to give indigenous communities the power of 'free determination' and 'autonomy as part of the Mexican state,'" Ginger Thompson and Tim Weiner reported.[22] The Zapatistas would be well advised to look south of the border for an understanding of what "autonomy" for communities of impoverished and illiterate residents produces. "Autonomy was supposed to give [Miskito Indian] residents a say not only in how they were governed, but also control over abundant natural resources," David González reported. "Instead, it has resulted in neglect, with most people barely surviving on farming and fishing."[23] Mexico's Zapatistas "rebels," in essence, are little more than a raggedy band of self-serving outlaws engaged in petty acts of terrorism, who espouse highfalutin ideals while vainly attempting to hide their true intentions.[24]

Neglecting the standard of living of working people, as Henry Ford understood, undermines the inclusive impulse of capitalism. "The difficulty is that for the past 30 years the poor in most places have been more interested in becoming entrepreneurs than revolutionaries. To improve their lives, they have migrated by the millions to the cities. You can see these migrants in the streets of the Middle East or Asia, selling what they manufacture in their shanties, from carpets and books to tools and engines," Hernando de Soto argues, reaffirming Ford's observation.[25] Indeed, most poor people are more concerned with earning a living than joining insurgencies. At the Summit of the Americas held in Quebec in April 2001, protestors demonstrated against the proposed Free Trade Area of the Americas (FTAA), arguing against the potential for environmental despoliation, diminished purchasing power of workers, and social convulsions as people abandoned their communities in search of jobs. Paradoxically, as David Moberg reported in *Salon*, "nearly everyone on both sides of the fence voices support for more trade—but the terms of trade and, most important, the rules of investment that are at the heart of 'trade' agreements. The real issue, according to the Peoples' Summit of the Americas, a shadow gathering of citizens, environmental, labor and peasant groups from the Americas . . . is whether democracy and human rights will be trampled as an FTAA protects the rights of corporations and the mobility of capital."[26]

Perhaps, but poverty at present imposes considerable hardships on the poor—and more. That poor people have always had difficult lives, of course, is no comfort to Mexico's poor, who were sold on NAFTA with the argument that free trade was a ticket out of poverty. That barely a dent in the poverty has been made after a decade of NAFTA continues to frustrate.[27] America's War on Terror, furthermore, has precipitated diminished expectations, proving more frustrating still. "The terrorist attacks of September 11th gave President Fox an excuse for not achieving his promises. Now he has to accept that his friendship with President Bush has great limitations," Jorge Montano, a former Mexican ambassador to the United States said at the meeting of world leaders in Monterrey in March 2002.[28] These "limitations" discredit the market economy, and have repercussions across the hemisphere. "Across Latin America, millions . . . are also letting their voices be heard," Juan Forero reported. "A popular and political ground swell is building from the Andes to Argentina against the decade-old experiment with free-market capitalism. The reforms that have shrunk the state and opened markets to foreign competition, many believe, have enriched corrupt officials and faceless multinationals, and failed to better their lives."[29] Reducing poverty, which would bolster the credibility of the market system—and create more affluent consumers by definition—is the greatest human challenge in NAFTA's second decade.

## Ideologies in Conflict

If the ghost of paternalism lingers in the minds of Mexican policy makers as NAFTA enters its second decade, in no small measure this is the result of confusing signals from the United States. Consider the simple question of the troubling recession following the September 11th terrorist attacks. Louis Uchitelle, a business and economics writer for the *New York Times*, reported on March 21, 2002 that an "unexpected surge" in government spending helped "explain why the recession, to nearly everyone's surprise, has been so mild and may be ending."[30] But it was precisely increased government spending—consistent with Keynesian economics—that was ridiculed by Paul Krugman, one month before the recession ended. "The only clear force for recovery I see is the administration's military splurge. After all, even useless weapons spending does create jobs, at least for a while," he wrote in the *New York Times*. "Japan props up its economy by building bridges to nowhere."[31] Krugman thus argues that the idea that government should implement public works projects simply to create jobs is not enough to spend an economy out of recession.

Is hiring engineers to develop a weapon system any more "useless" than another "useless" job creation program designed simply to protect other kinds of workers' dignity?[32] "Useless" job creation programs alleviated the suffering of the Great Depression: having one set of workers dig ditches that were filled in by another set of workers and having artists paint unnecessary murals in public buildings were common "useless" job-creation schemes. Mexican policy makers, unfamiliar with American politics, are understandably confused. If liberal economist Paul Krugman decries the implementation of a liberal Keynesian policy, and if a Republican administration forsakes a monetarist policy and torpedoes a recession by going on a wild spending splurge, then what is one to make of this?

How the Bush administration has faltered in its commitment to forging closer ties to Mexico and how it has conducted itself on the world stage has disappointed Mexico—and discredited America's commitment to "free trade." Worse than the disputes over steel tariffs, or the failure to comply with the Kyoto environmental treaty (presumably to spare corporate America the expense of complying), was the approval of a $180 billion farm bill in June 2002 proved stunning.

It proved incredible that the most protectionist policies were being implemented by a Republican administration, one that professed the superiority of the market system and demanded other countries to knock down their trade barriers and open their markets.[33] Confusion yields to ambivalence, and as reformists advocate the further dismantling of Mexico's paternalism, questions emerge about how the market economy may be held hostage to the ideological whims of their politicians. Mexicans furthermore remain concerned that their economic development will be held hostage to the *realpolitik* of Washington's domestic politics.

## Unexpected Competitors

If one had "perfect knowledge," one would have tomorrow's closing stock prices today. "Perfect knowledge," an academic conceit used by economists in theoretical models, however, is extraordinarily rare in real life. Its power, indeed, is undermined by the dynamic nature of market economies. NAFTA's first decade underscores this dramatically. As the economies of the NAFTA nations have become integrated, unexpected markets have developed and unforeseen conflicts have emerged. While the "tomato war" between American and Mexican farmers is legendary, one unexpected result of NAFTA has been the emergence of Canada as a contender in this market. While Florida and Texas farmers have long complained in Washington about Mexican tomato growers—and have successfully lobbied for Mexican growers to be subject to antidumping duties—it is now Canadians who have been attacked by American farmers. Mexicans, so accustomed to finding themselves alone in disputes over agricultural complaints from Florida and Texas, have been delighted in their newfound alliance with Canadians, a comforting camaraderie.

"As Canadians see it, Washington uses antidumping and countervailing duties unfairly to hobble foreign goods that compete successfully against American products," Bernard Simon reported in the *New York Times*.[34] "Notwithstanding efforts to bring about economic integration, it's galling that [Americans] still have these issues," Alan Alexandroff, a Toronto trade attorney, is quoted in the article. The sustained devaluation of the Canadian dollar throughout the past decade, rather than unfair pricing, is the economic reason Canadian farmers are more competitive.

Evidence of this competitive advantage is seen in other Canadian industries that have emerged as fierce competitors. It would be absurd, for instance, to argue that Canadian tomato growers and, say, clothing manufacturers, colluded to "dump" their respective goods in the American market. "Canadian manufacturers have [apart from trade pacts] also benefited from the steady weakening of the Canadian dollar from 80 American cents in the early 1990's to just 63 cents now, effectively making their labor and other costs cheaper in American-dollar terms," Bernard Simon explained haltingly.[35] One Canadian firm illustrates succinctly how unexpected markets can flourish. Jack Victor Ltd., of Montréal, exported merely 5 percent of its production to the United States in 1994, the year NAFTA went into effect. Less than a decade later, it was exporting more than 75 percent of its total production to the United States.[36]

This can be called a crisis of confidence. Mexicans and Canadians, who live in so many ways in the shadow of Americans, at times lack national self-esteem. "The first three or four years of NAFTA, [Mexican] companies were protecting their local turf," Carlos Vaaderrama, of the Carlsmith Ball law firm in Los Angeles, explained. "As they began to get efficient competing with imports, they said, 'Now we can go abroad.' "[37] Mindful of this crisis in confidence, particularly among smaller Mexican companies, Luis Ernesto Derbez, Mexico's Economy Minister, argued at the World Economic Forum in February 2001 that "We've got to extend the benefits of the free trade agreement to small and medium-sized businesses. We cannot continue having a relationship of big Mexican, American or Canadian companies alone."[38] Quite right, for this is properly an important part of the agenda for NAFTA's second decade.

While many Mexicans wax poetic about life under the PRI—the way older Russians long for the security the former Soviet Union offered that is now missing in capitalist Russia—most Mexicans embrace NAFTA as part of the future.[39] They like the choices the economy now offers them. The strengthening of their nation's democratic institutions has encouraged Mexicans about the path upon which their country has embarked. They welcome how democracy protects and expands individual civil rights, and makes government more accountable to the electorate. They look forward to greater integration with the United States, and how a vibrant culture fusion is unfolding on all sides of the multiple borders of North America.

The ambivalence about the dismantling of Mexican Paternalism remains, part socialist nostalgia, part romantic imagining of what never was. "Socialist impulses will always linger in the air, because they grow directly out of the human experience of capitalism," Michael Lewis wrote in *Next*. "The neurotic, high-strung relationship between the outside and the inside was the market's new and improved way of dealing with the problem. Socialism hadn't been killed by capitalism. It had been subsumed by it. The market has found a way not only to permit the people who are most threatening to their rebellious notions but to capitalize on them. Gnutella was one of this [sic]; the Internet was another."[40] There is also the appeal of charitably remembering the past. The PRI's leaders, nevertheless, still mocked as "dinosaurs," are increasingly seen not as threats but more like older relatives who have strange ideas and habits, amusing as they are harmless. *The New Yorker* once published a cartoon that sums up the Mexican state of mind. An older man, fully dressed in his military uniform adorned with medals, admires himself in a full-length mirror. His wife also looks on approvingly. "Just look at you!" she says beaming with pride. "How many ex-dictators can still fit into their dictator suits?"[41]

How many PRI leaders can say they still fit into their discredited ideological suits of Mexican Paternalism?

## SUMMARY

1.  As NAFTA continues to accelerate the integration of the North American economies, wages in Mexico must rise to compensate for the dismantling of social welfare benefits of Mexican Paternalism.

2. The persistence of poverty remains the greatest challenge to the continued success of NAFTA.

3. Mexican ambivalence about the United States grows when Washington allows domestic politics to interfere with its commitment to free trade, and this discredits the market economy as a development model.

4. Though Mexico will not return to the authoritarianism of the PRI, the material lives of millions more Mexicans must be improved, thereby giving them a stake in the success of a market economy.

## ENDNOTES

1. The devaluation of August 1982 ended the protectionist development model, forcing Mexico's entry into GATT. The stunning devaluation of December 1994 at first threatened the implementation of NAFTA, but subsequently demonstrated the ability of market forces to correct themselves. In the political realm, economic prosperity proved to be a catalyst for the political maturation of the Mexican electorate. This resulted in the defeat of the PRI, which, remarkably, was the longest-reigning political party of the twentieth century.

2. Fox's speech, delivered in a national address on May 29, 2001, set out a 25-year projection consistent with developing a post-paternalistic modern nation, fully integrated into NAFTA. His lack of political experience, however, resulted in a treacherous learning curve, one that was anticipated by European observers. "Alongside slick marketing, what is needed is the skilful choice of priorities, the nurturing of alliances for change, and persistence as well as popularity-seeking," the London *Economist* observed when Fox took office. See "Fox's Political Challenge," the London *Economist,* December 2, 2000.

3. American fans of Vicente Fox embarrassed with their praise: "He strikes me, in some ways, almost like a poet. He's speaking metaphorically, I think, and he's something of a visionary and he's trying to establish a long-term objective to move toward, to redefine and recast the nature of thinking with respect to U.S.-Mexican relations," gushed Frank Bean, director of the Center for Research on Immigration, Population, and Public Policy at the University of California, Irvine. Bean is quoted in "California Shouldn't Fear Fox's Mexico," by Dana Parsons, *Los Angeles Times,* March 25, 2001.

4. Personal interviews, March 2000 and June 2001.

5. Ibid.

6. "Mexican Businesses Push North of the Border," by Lee Romney, *Los Angeles Times,* February 19, 2001. The list of Mexican companies includes Grupo Bimbo® (baked goods), Gigante® (supermarkets), Grupo Sanborns® (department store that acquired CompUSA), Cemex (cement), and FAMSA® (copper). Some Mexican companies are going global. Bimbo acquired the western U.S. division of Canada's George Weston, Ltd.® for $610 million in 2002. This, an attempt to build

shareholder value through acquisitions in North America, means that Bimbo's five bakeries in California bake such popular brands as Boboli®, Entenmann's®, Oroweat®, and Thomas' English Muffins® west of the Mississippi. Bimbo, the world's third-largest bakery, launched a $1.1 billion international expansion in 1990, with a presence in 16 countries, from the Czech Republic to Canada to Chile; its worldwide sales in 2001 were $3.8 billion.

7.  Henry Fielding, *An Enquiry into the Causes of the Late Increase in Robbers, with Some Proposals for Remedying This Growing Evil,* London: A. Miller, 1751, page xi.

8.  "Arise, Ye Prisoners of Starvation!" by Bill Keller, *New York Times,* February 23, 2002.

9.  Ibid.

10. "Britain Feels Pressure as Public Services Continue to Decay," by Mark Champion, *Wall Street Journal,* March 9, 2001.

11. Ibid.

12. A quick guide to corporate scandals in 2003 includes the following: Enron, 18 indictments; WorldCom, 5 indictments; HealthSouth, 10 indictments; Adelphia Communications, 5 indictments; Tyco International, 4 indictments. These ongoing investigations will take years to complete, and do not include scores of others,

13. When Germany privatized Deutsche Telekom in 1996, the German government retained a 43 percent stake. As a result, when, a mere six years later, the stock had fallen by more than 90 percent of its peak under the crushing debt accumulated under Ron Sommer's leadership, it created an embarrassing crisis for German Chancellor Gerhard Schroder.

14. A measure of how passionately people care about the social safety net is seen in how Spaniards reacted when, though transformed into a prosperous nation, the government proposed changes in Spain's welfare laws. When the European Union met in Seville on June 20, 2002, millions of Spaniards participated in a work stoppage to protest proposed changes in welfare laws, the first general strike in Spain in almost a decade.

15. Here are arresting examples of the U.S. government bailing out private industry: the Savings & Loan rescue, which to date constitutes the largest nationalization of private sector obligations in the history of the world; the airline loan guarantees after September 11th, which was denounced by other carriers, such as British Airways, for creating market distortions since it was a brazen attempt to keep afloat companies (USAirways®, America West®) that would otherwise not survive in a market economy; and the unilateral imposition of steel tariffs and farm subsidies, which protected inefficient domestic producers, undermining the efficacy of supply and demand on a global scale.

16. "Capitalism Depends on Character," by Jean Strouse, *New York Times,* July 7, 2002. In addition to tautologies, of course, is the problem of platitudes: "Arthur Andersen is out of business, Enron is in court, WorldCom is toast. Punishing losses have made it clear that investing entails real risks. But the deposed miscreants made off with millions while company employees and ordinary investors were wiped out." Alas, this is the way of the world.

17. For more information on Ayn Rand, see *Virtues of Selfishness: A New Concept of Egoism* and *Capitalism: The Unknown Ideal.*

18. Subsidized electricity, of course, is another way for the government to make business more competitive. Selling electricity below cost is a contentious issue for the Fox administration, particularly given that Mexico's electrical needs are fast exceeding the ability of the country to generate power.

19. "While Mexicans have only recently begun to see real wage gains after years of steep losses—wages remain 10% below 1994 levels—those gains are now rising at their fastest rate in more than a decade, threatening the centerpiece of Mexico's economic recovery: the central bank's anti-inflation fight," Joel Millman and David Luhnow reported. "In the past, this was never much of an issue. Under the departing Institutional Revolutionary Party, or PRI, wages were set in the government's back rooms in collusion with PRI-friendly unions and employers." See "Mexico's Rapid Wage Gains May Threaten Its Recovery," by Joel Millman and David Luhnow, *Wall Street Journal*, November 20, 2000.

20. "The Constituency of Terror," by Hernando de Soto, *New York Times*, October 15, 2001.

21. "Fox's Zapatista Bill Will Leave Chiapas Even Further Behind," by Sergio Sarmiento, *Wall Street Journal*, March 9, 2001.

22. "Zapatista Leaders Make Their Case to Mexico's Congress," by Ginger Thompson and Tim Weiner, *New York Times*, March 29, 2001.

23. "For Nicaragua's Atlantic Indians, Autonomy Means Neglect," by David González, *New York Times*, September 28, 2001.

24. The tragedy about the Zapatistas is that they are a group of misguided individuals who, thinking they are champions of social "justice" for the marginalized multitudes, are in fact dupes of the brooding solipsism of Subcomandante Marcos.

25. "The Constituency of Terror," by Hernando de Soto, *New York Times*, October 15, 2001.

26. "Will Free Trade Kill Democracy?" by David Moberg, April 23, 2001, *Salon.com*.

27. In all fairness, one has to consider that eradicating poverty continues to frustrate humanity. The United States, which has more material resources and access to the most educated minds on the planet, has met with consistent failure. Since President Lyndon Johnson declared a "war" on poverty as part of his "Great Society," millions of Americans languish in poverty. One measure of this failure is seen in a public service advertisement in New York. It features three children, with the tagline "Would You Like to Eat?" The program, which provides "food for kids when school is out," is testament that in the wealthiest city in the United States, thousands of children risk going hungry during summer vacations. (For more information, see *www.opt-ofns.org*.)

28. Apart from the fracas resulting from Fidel Castro's tirade against his host and the United States, the Monterrey summit underscored the little progress in achieving immigration reform, let alone a general amnesty for Mexican nationals illegally in the United States.

29. "Still Poor, Latin Americans Protest Push for Open Markets," by Juan Forero, *New York Times*, July 19, 2002. Few challenge the efficacy of market economies. "The formula helped give Chile the most robust economy in Latin America. In Mexico exports quintupled in a dozen years. In Bolivia, poverty fell from 86 percent of the population in the 70's to 58.6 percent

today," Forero noted. But it has not been either uniform or equitable. "It's an emotional populist attitude people have. It may not be reasoned, but it's real, and it's explosive and it's not going to be easily contained by coming up with arguments that free trade is the wave of the future," Larry Birns, director of the Washington-based Council on Hemispheric Affairs, is quoted in the article. The repercussions are serious. Consider how a demagogue like Hugo Chávez has divided Venezuelan society. "For decades, Venezuela had plodded along as perhaps the dullest and least fantastic country in the region," Deborah Sontag summed up. "An oil nation with the largest reserves outside the Middle East, it had boasted a relatively dependable, although flawed, democratic system since 1958. Then just as Latin America began stabilizing, democratizing and catching up to staid Venezuela, along came Chávez with his camouflage pants and his talk of revolution. Finally this spring, the Venezuelan president, a throwback in so many ways, provoked an equally retrograde reaction: a coup. And the events in Venezuela raised unsettling questions in the region as a whole: Could epaulets come back in style? Was democracy securely anchored? Could Latin America slide backward into old, familiar patterns?" See "In the Time of Hugo Chávez," by Deborah Sontag, *New York Times,* July 2, 2002.

30.   "Sharp Rise in Federal Spending May Have Helped Ease Recession," by Louis Uchitelle, *New York Times,* March 21, 2002.

31.   "The W Scenario," by Paul Krugman, *New York Times,* February 22, 2002.

32.   Which is less "useless": paying an engineer $100,000 to work on a defense system, or paying ten people $10,000 each to greet people who walk into an Old Navy® store? Who can say with complete moral authority?

33.   C. Fred Bergsten, director of the Institute for International Economics remarked, at that time, that "American farmers have shot themselves in the foot [by lobbying successfully for this bill]. The long-term growth of U.S. agriculture is clearly in foreign markets, particularly the rapidly growing emerging markets. That requires liberalization and access to those markets. The farm bill undercuts our ability to reach those markets."

34.   "U.S.-Canada Tomato War Heats Up," by Bernard Simon, *New York Times,* December 7, 2001.

35.   "In Men's Clothing, More and More on the Labels Say 'Made in Canada,'" by Bernard Simon, *New York Times,* March 23, 2002.

36.   During this same period, its labor force increased from 300 to 800 by 2002.

37.   Quoted in "Mexican Businesses Push North of the Border," by Lee Romney, *Los Angeles Times,* February 19, 2001.

38.   Mexico hosted the World Economic Forum in Cancún on February 26, 2001. It opened with frank remarks from Mexican officials that while poverty remained one of the greatest challenges for NAFTA, ways must be found to make the advantages engendered by NAFTA trickle down to everyone, especially the poorest. For a profile of Luis Ernesto Derbez, see "Helping Manage Transition in Mexico," by Ginger Thompson, *New York Times,* July 21, 2000.

39.   George W. Bush, incidentally, formally recognized Russia as a "market" economy on June 6, 2002. This change in semantics carries considerable benefits. "For Russian companies, this means more possibilities to enter

the American market, and for the Russian people it means the creation of new jobs, and for the Russian economy it means new opportunities and new production of domestic goods," German Gref, the Russian minister for economic development said at that time. Russian officials estimated that they lost $1.5 billion in annual sales to the United States by being denied recognition as a market economy.

40. Michael Lewis, *Next: The Future Just Happened,* New York: W. W. Norton, 2002, page 135.

41. Cartoon by Donald Reilly, *The New Yorker,* June 11, 2001, page 74.

3

# Canada in NAFTA's Second Decade: Aggressively Pursuing Mexican Opportunities

## EXECUTIVE ABSTRACT

It is imperative that American managers realize that Canada and Mexico have a vibrant and complex bilateral relationship that has nothing to do with the United States. Prior to NAFTA this relationship had cultural and diplomatic overtones. Since NAFTA it has an economic and environmental character. It is often defined by the deliberate exclusion of the United States. How Ottawa and Mexico City deal with each other—and the arresting affection Canadians and Mexicans hold for each other as people—constitutes a "white noise" against the more prominent relations between Americans and their neighbors to the north and south. There is nothing conspiratorial in the decision of Canadians and Mexicans to exclude Americans from some aspects of the relationships unfolding in North America, to be sure. But it requires that Americans respect that, in the same way that they have matters with the Canadians that have nothing to do with the Mexicans, and vice versa, the same applies to Canada and Mexico. Corporate America must understand the nature of the nuances in the relationship between its neighbors, particularly after a decade of sustained Canadian investment in Mexico and the emergence of corporate Canada as a major player in the success of NAFTA.

## DISCUSSION

In the 1960s, it was not uncommon for Canadian bankers to make routine "pilgrimages" to Mexico. The business at hand was often to sign up privileged Mexicans into various "private banking" relationships, promote Canadian firms and Canadian exports, and explain the virtues of Canadian educational opportunities. That the two countries encountered familiar challenges in managing their relations with the United States, a nation that is often demanding and not always understanding, nurtured an understanding among Canadians and Mexicans. Canadians, in essence, were welcomed as a more calm English-speaking presence. This was further strengthened when Canadians and Mexicans realized that they shared similar ideas, and their philosophical worldviews dovetailed. Canadians and Mexicans continue to realize, at times to their own surprise, just how alike they are in many ways.

Americans, too, are surprised by the similarities between the Canadians and Mexicans. "I discovered some surprising aspects in which [Canadians] were not only different from Americans but similar to Mexicans," Anthony DePalma writes in *Here*. "Mexicans with sweaters, is how some Mexicans had described Canadians. As I found out, there was more than a little truth in that analogy."[1] Canada, in many ways, is a reality check for Mexicans perplexed by American intransigence. The idea that English-speaking nations (Protestants) are fundamentally at odds with Spanish-speaking nations (Catholics) is more attractive as an *idea*, but has little currency as a practical *reality*. The similarities between Canada and Mexico have resulted in convergence of interests, which are manifested in an understated bilateral approach favored by the two nations.

Consider how, in defiance of the United States, both Canada and Mexico maintain full diplomatic relations with Cuba, and reject categorically the U.S. trade embargo on that island nation.[2] Canada and Mexico, likewise, have long opposed American policy in Central America, with Canadians giving economic and moral support to Mexican initiatives to find peace, whether it was Mexican leadership of the Contadora Group or Mexico's hosting of peace talks among warring Salvadoran factions.[3] In turn, Mexico continues to support Canadian efforts to find creative solutions to the challenges Canada's indigenous peoples pose. Mexicans, too, have long sided with Canadian claims on their sovereignty over fishing waters off Nova Scotia.

Even in broad philosophical areas, there has been a charming reciprocity. Mexico has long championed Canada's continued involvement as a "Commonwealth" nation, which, in some ways, functions as a support group for Canadians frustrated by their American neighbors. Canada, in turn, has encouraged Mexico to nurture its relations with other nations in Latin America—and forge closer ties with Spain. Both Canada and Mexico, mindful of the fickleness of America's ethnocentrism and the American penchant for intruding into her neighbor's domestic affairs, recognize the importance of asserting their own identities. Canada, after all, has been the more supportive NAFTA nation in Mexican efforts to reach out beyond the limits of NAFTA by entering into trade agreements with the European Union, Brazil, and Central America, and through its expansion of "bilateralism" with Canada.[4]

This bilateral approach is evident in several areas besides a striking similarity in foreign policies and how the rights of indigenous peoples are expanded. It is evident in personal relations between Mexicans and Canadians. Since the 1960s, for instance, the two groups have "migrated" across North America, in synchronicity with migrating birds. Each winter, along with the arrival of mallard ducks and geese, tens of thousands of Canadians descend on Mexico, escaping the winter months to bask in Mexico's warmth. Each spring, when the ducks, geese, and Canadians return home, tens of thousands of Mexicans head to Canada, often on student visas, to matriculate at prep schools, colleges, and universities. (Middle-class Mexican families prefer to send their teenage daughters to Canada rather than the United States, thinking the former is a safer, less violent alternative to the latter.) Thousands of other Mexicans visit on cultural programs, or to enroll in English-as-a-second-language classes. Mexican businessmen, often at the invitation of their Canadian counterparts and Canadian bankers, travel for business, or simply to understand better the nation where their money is safely managed. Canada, furthermore, has a sensible guest-worker program that allows hundreds of thousands of Mexican laborers to work in Canada, where their civil, labor and human rights are protected.[5]

Other kinds of interactions, not immediately obvious, have been unfolding for decades. The migration of ducks and geese, for instance, strengthened the alliance between Mexico and Canada in a logical—if roundabout—way. Ducks Unlimited Mexico America Canada, known as Dumac®, for instance, embarked on programs to protect the wintering grounds of waterfowl across the continent. Conservation and environmentalism in Mexico, then, has a distinctly Canadian influence, one that dates back to the 1960s. Though Mexican environmentalism has grown fantastically under the able stewardship of talented and dedicated Mexicans, the conservation ethos in Mexico has its origins in Canadian intellectual thought and civic concern. In all fairness, a good number of dedicated Americans have been instrumental in this process, and organizations such as the Nature Conservancy, continue to provide material and management assistance. But it is the pioneering work of Canada that is most noticeable.[6]

In other areas, too, there is a convergence of interest between Canada and Mexico. Both nations are outraged at the failure of the United States to abide by the Vienna Convention on consular matters, and are horrified that, in violation of the Universal Declaration of Human Rights, to which the United States is a signatory nation, America still imposes a death penalty.[7] That Washington has frustrated efforts to work with Mexico City to resolve continuing immigration matters confounds Canadians, who support Mexican demands for U.S. immigration reform.

In areas more pressing to Americans than anyone else, Canadians and Mexicans are of like mind. In Mexico's dispute with the United States' failure to comply with terms granting Mexican trucks access to American highways, Canada sided with Mexico. At the time Canada announced it was prepared to "apply appropriate diplomatic pressure" on American officials on Mexico's behalf. What is striking is the matter-of-fact nature of the cooperation between Mexico and Canada. When the Nisga'a people of British Columbia demanded to establish their own "nation" in 1998, for instance, Mexico supported Canada's insistence that no indigenous people had a right to threaten either the territorial integrity of the nation or the federal nature of government.

Mexico similarly supported English-speaking Canadians who insisted that Quebec had no right to establish an independent state. Canada, in turn, has voiced its support for the idea that whatever claims the Maya nations within Mexico might have, any "autonomous" claims must not undermine the integrity of Mexico as a republic. And both nations have used their policy towards Cuba as a measure of what makes them independent of Washington—and closer to each other. The emerging Canada-Mexico consensus on the decriminalization of drugs, for instance, indicates that America's puritanical impulses may be undone this century, much as Prohibition was doomed to failure last century.

On an individual basis, also, there are unexpected currents linking Canadians and Mexicans in surprising ways. The Quebecois, for instance, display an unusual affinity for Mexicans.

French-speaking Canadians see themselves as oppressed by the majority of their English-speaking compatriots, of course. What is not widely known among Americans, however, is that there is a reciprocity of sympathy, by which I mean that the Quebecois are unusual defenders of Mexico, and Mexican interests, simply because they see Mexicans as being oppressed by the other English-speaking majority on the continent: the Americans. It is not uncommon to see cars and recreational vehicles with the "Je Me Souviens" ("I remember") license plates of Quebec all over Mexico during the winter months. For their part, English-speaking Canadians display an astounding sensitivity in dealing with Mexicans; it is a sensibility refined over decades of dealing with the Quebecois that now bear fruit in the age of NAFTA.

One result is that Mexicans hold Canadians in higher esteem than they hold Americans. As Anthony DePalma writes with surprise bordering on an epiphany:

> Mexicans . . . rated Canada the second most desirable place to live, after only the United States. However, in most other categories intended to measure respect or admiration, Mexicans picked Canada over every other nation, including the United States. They see Canada as a haven of civility, justice, and order, and in Canadians they find a whole group of people who may not speak their language but who understand the great advantage and heavy burden of living alongside the United States. Because they relate this way across the continent, Mexicans have come to expect a greater degree of respect and sincerity from Canadians.[8]

Since the 1970s, this mutual goodwill has manifested itself in how Mexicans and Canadians interact with each other. Well-intentioned, gentle jabs at the United States, for instance, offer a glimpse of the depth and intimacy of the friendships Mexicans and Canadians cultivate. Mexicans flatter Canadians by saying that Canada is as close to heaven as one can expect to find in this world. To get to a Canadian heaven, the punch line goes, one must first traverse the purgatory that is the United States. Canadians, in turn, remark that if only Mexico could find a way of exporting civility and manners to the United States, Canada would be eternally grateful. This, then, is the quiet banter between Mexicans and Canadians.

Mexicans also look to Canada with optimism, as representing what Mexico should expect of the English-speaking world. For Mexico, as Anthony DePalma observed, "Canada represents a notable exception in today's world, a country that possesses the desirable aspects of American society—a high standard of living, a dynamic economy, widespread concern for social condition—but without America's baggage of racism, excess, and violence."[9] Canadians, for their part, see Mexicans as a people trying to find their way in the world. Though Canadians' sensibilities are offended by the lack of democracy and the proliferation of corruption throughout Mexican society, they empathize with the broader social goals of Mexican Paternalism, particularly in its effort, however imperfect, to provide housing, food, and medical care to as many people is possible.[10]

In a defensive reaction, Americans dismiss these observations as valid only among Mexican and Canadian "elites." Perhaps an appreciation of Canada is more defined among more privileged Mexicans, the ones who can afford to send their sons and daughters to Canadian prep schools, or the entire family for summer holidays in Ontario and Quebec. This observation is mistaken. Millions of middle-class Mexican families routinely include Canada in their travel plans. "Visit the United States and Canada" is a ubiquitous sign in Mexican travel agencies; itineraries to New York or Chicago routinely include Toronto and Montréal. Trips to San Francisco and Seattle routinely offer Vancouver as part of the package.

Among working-class Mexicans, Canada's "guest worker" program, likewise, finds an orderly, sensible, and humanitarian approach to a common problem: a labor shortage in Canada and surplus labor in Mexico. "Mexicans," Anthony DePalma explains, "routinely tell survey takers that they like Canada's fairness and open society best—sentiments I heard repeated by the migrant farmworkers in Ontario who returned to Canada each year to work in the fields."[11] Unlike the United States, where American executives at Tyson® are indicted for hiring illegal aliens to work at their plants, and where poor Mexicans die crossing the desert, Mexico and Canada have a working program that successfully addresses the concerns and interests of their people.[12] Decades of success reinforce the observation that Canadians and Mexicans, philosophically, culturally, and politically, are very much alike—and that their alliance will continue to grow and strengthen as this century unfolds.

Canadians and Mexicans empathize with each other over the demands of living next to the United States. Canadians, for instance, famously roll their eyes when they are told that the problem with Canada is that it is *just* like America, but not *enough* like

America.[13] Mexicans understand that frustration, and this itself strengthens bonds across the continent. For corporate America, the intimate nature of Canada-Mexico relations represents a competitive disadvantage. Consider, for instance, how Americans often fail to see in themselves what other sees in them. "It has been two decades since Mexico committed itself to free-market reforms aimed at propelling this country into the developed world. The North American Free Trade Agreement, considered the centerpiece of the new Mexican philosophy, has generated a quarter trillion dollars in cross-border trade with the United States. The treaty helped turn a closed, inefficient economy dominated by state-owned companies into one that was flooded by foreign investment and driven by foreign competition," Ginger Thompson reported in 2002. "But government statistics show that economic liberalization has done little to close the huge divide between the privileged few and the poor, and left the middle class worse off than before. Battered by a series of severe recessions, teachers and engineers, nurses and small-business men, all find themselves swinging above and below the poverty line with the rise and fall of the peso, interest rates and the unemployment rate."[14]

It is true enough that since the crisis of August 5, 1982, Mexico has gone through various roller coaster rides, which explains why the economic and financial aspirations of reaching the middle-class have been frustrated. Time and again, families who work hard to achieve middle-class status have seen their dreams dashed, whether as a consequence of a currency devaluation, runaway inflation or crushing recessions. It is not without good reason that the 1980s are remembered as the "lost decade." But if democracy and market reforms do not lead to sound economies in which middle class life flourishes and allows families to prosper in Mexico, will this be considered an anomaly endemic to Mexico, or is it a problem that will burden market economies in the 21st century?[15]

Let us examine how middle-class American families fared during the same period in question. "What's really frightening is the effect of this trend on double-income families," Thane Peterson reported in *Business Week*, on the phenomenon of American workers having to work longer and longer hours to keep from losing economic ground. "According to *The State of Working America 2000-01*, a study made last year by the Economic Policy Institute, a Washington think tank, the average middle-class American husband and wife worked 3,885 hours in 1998, an increase since 1989 of 247 hours—the equivalent of an additional six 40-hour work-weeks."[16] For America's middle- and working-class families, the hours worked each week have increased, while inflation-adjusted real incomes have fallen over the past two decades.[17] Hardship is not relegated to American blue-collar workers, of course. "Years of progressively better jobs and higher salaries, for many solidly in the six figures, primed their expectations and shaped their lives," Anthony DePalma wrote of the displaced white-collar middle class. "Now many of these professionals—a broad range of college-educated managers, administrators and mid-level executives—have been out of work for a year or longer, especially in the hard-hit worlds of finance, communications and information technology that are concentrated in the New York area."[18] Like joggers on a treadmill who have to run faster and faster just to stay in place, Americans from all walks of life are working more and more to maintain the same standard of living. The same challenges affect Canadians—one reason why Canada, as a matter of policy, has aggressively pursued business opportunities in Mexico to increase the standard of living of the Canadian people.

Canadian workers, oddly enough, *also* saw an increase in their workweek in the 1980s, before the trend reversed itself in the mid-1990s. "In Canada, the average has fallen by a full week, to 1,732 hours per year," Thane Peterson reported, making the case that Americans learn to relax—and take time off from work to spend with their families.[19] What is clear, then, is that middle- and working-class families in the *three* NAFTA nations are under economic pressure. They have to work longer hours to maintain their current standard of living. The economic pressure is a *continental* problem.[20] Indeed, the most accurate characterization of the continent's middle class is this: By 2002, Americans had become the hardest-working people in the industrialized world, and Mexicans, despite the benefits ushered in during NAFTA's first decade, continue to have to struggle to remain in the middle class.

For policy makers in all three countries, furthermore, it is sobering to realize that working families are only a few paychecks from poverty; Americans' historic record number of personal bankruptcy filings underscore the vulnerability of the American family. Mexico's middle class, curiously enough, is going through a process that, in startling ways, resembles Canada's experience a decade before. "An increasing number of middle-class men and women have joined the exodus of Mexican immigrants to the United States," [Rodolfo] Tuiran, [a government demographer] said, "with one out of 17 professionals abandoning the country in the last two decades," Thompson reported in the same article.[21]

The exodus of *professionals,* or "brain drain," from Mexico is striking in its similarity to what occurred in Canada years back after the implementation of the U.S.-Canada free trade accord; the trend subsequently reversed.[22] But what concerns political leaders in all three countries is the sustained pressure on middle-class families throughout North America and on the quality of life issues that arise when families are neglected. One development that suggests the complicated issues at stake is seen in the role of women during a period of great turmoil and tensions among families, work, and family well-being. "Globalization and the extension of the market economy have changed [the role of women] in Mexico not only for the poor, but also for the middle class," Elena Poniatowska argued. "The demands of the market have forced many women out of their homes and into the workplace and allowed others to choose to go there. This has changed the role of women in our society and in our literature."[23]

One unexamined consequence of NAFTA, of course, is that the exodus of professionals—the "brain drain"—is often accompanied by a "care drain" as low-income caregivers leave Mexico to provide housekeeping and childcare services for America's professionals. That their work is now being recognized in the literature bodes well for addressing the needs of this class of workers.[24] Apart from this encouraging development in the socioeconomic empowerment of women, what are the factors on an international basis, leading to the general ruination of middle-class life?

This is important, particularly since not all Mexicans with American blood in their veins are finding everything smooth sailing: Fox is a case in point. "His promises are a national wish list for transforming Mexico: a rapid end to conflict in Chiapas; new trade alliances with Central America to help lift this nation's south out of poverty; new jobs to keep young men from migrating to the United States; a truthful accounting of hideous crimes in Mexico's past; better salaries, training and equipment for teachers and the police; an end to government corruption," Ginger Thompson reported. "With a salesman's hype, he raised expectations that he could offer same-day delivery for those hopes. The gaps between Mr. Fox's rhetoric and reality allow his critics to say that he acts as if he were the chairman of Mexico Inc., issuing policies and promises like business plans and projections. But Mr. Fox has realized—slowly, say allies and enemies alike—that he cannot govern Mexico the way he once ran Coca-Cola's operations here."[25]

In other words, Americans are quick to criticize shortcomings in their NAFTA partners, when the same phenomenon—longer workweeks, political agendas in disarray—are problems that affect the entire trading bloc. Decades of good will have given Canadians a competitive advantage in Mexico. Canada's Scotia Bank acquired control of Grupo Financiero Inverlat in March 2000, giving Canadian banks a major competitive advantage in Mexico—and through Mexico in Central America. Canadian agriculture enjoys a dominant presence, oftentimes at the expense of American Midwest farm products. The 55-story Torre Mayor, the highest office building in Latin America, was built by the Toronto real estate developer Paul Reichmann. Bombardier's Mexican plant manufactures subway trains for the Mexico City rapid transit system. In 1994, Canada ranked ninth in total foreign investment in Mexico; by 2004, it had catapulted to third, superseded only by the United States and the Netherlands. Corporate Canada invested an astonishing $3.8 billion during NAFTA's first decade, an enormous sum given that, at 32 million people, the United States has eight-and-one-half times as many residents.[26]

In the 2004–2014 time frame, the most significant business opportunities in Canada center on Canadian-Mexican investment and business. Canadian multinationals from across the business spectrum have, since 1998, accelerated their projects and presence in Mexico, fueling a sustained integration the likes of which few observers thought was possible prior to NAFTA's implementation. Corporate Canada's bottom lines have been fattened by their investments in Mexico, and the pace of Canadian investment is expected to accelerate in NAFTA's second decade.

## SUMMARY

1. Since the 1960s, Mexicans and Canadians have been forging close ties in economic, political, and foreign policy areas.
2. During NAFTA's first decade, corporate Canada exploited its historic ties to Mexico to gain significant market share, a considerable competitive advantage.
3. During NAFTA's second decade, corporate Canada has identified its major growth opportunities as being in the Mexican economy.
4. The Mexico-Canada economic "alliance" constitutes a major challenge to corporate America.

# ENDNOTES

1. *Here: A Biography of the New American Continent,* by Anthony DePalma, page 231.
2. Its criticism of the American embargo notwithstanding, Fox has signaled his government's commitment to reforms on the island. "Mr. Fox is the first Mexican head of state to meet in Havana with dissent leaders," Ginger Thompson reported. "The sensitivity of the 30-minute gathering at the Mexican Embassy seemed clear from Mr. Fox's behavior. He said he had told Mr. Castro ahead of time about this plan to meet with dissidents. But he did not announce the meeting to the press and did not issue a statement about it until he had left Cuba." See "On Cuba Visit, Mexico's Chief Meets Quietly with Dissidents," by Ginger Thompson, *New York Times,* February 5, 2002.
3. During the Summit of the Americas in Quebec, Canada's warm relations with so many Latin American nations surprised American officials. See "Canada Is Set to Display Its Links to Latin Lands," by Anthony DePalma, *New York Times,* April 18, 2001.
4. The economic impact on Mexico of American preoccupation with the "war" on terrorism and the crises in Argentina and Brazil are two reasons Fox has worked to forge closer ties to South America. When he traveled to Brazil and Argentina in July 2002, his emphasis on increasing trade was a signal that, when coupled with Mexican ties to the European Union, Mexico needs to insulate itself from the fallout of American domestic political concerns. Trade pacts, too, have been used to advance foreign policy objectives. When Fox was in Brazil in July 2002 to sign a bilateral trade pact, the purpose was to promote economic growth between Mexico and Brazil, which have a combined population of almost 300 million consumers. "I have little to add about the sense of disappointment we feel when rich countries insist on maintaining all sorts of barriers to free trade," Brazilian then-president Fernando Cardoso said at the time, expressing his frustration at the imposition of trade barriers by the Bush administration. See "Mexico and Brazil Sign Bilateral Trade Pact," by Tony Smith, *New York Times,* July 4, 2002.
5. Throughout 2002, strains between Fox and Bush grew, as American focus on the "War on Terror" derailed bilateral negotiations on immigration reform, drug interdiction, and developing a master "North American Security Perimeter." One backlash was Mexico's challenging the United States on human rights. "The government of Mexico, in a direct challenge to the Bush administration, asked the International Court of Justice today to block the executions of 51 Mexicans on death row in the United States," Tim Weiner reported from Mexico City. "Mexico contends that American officials, both state and local, have ignored the [1963 Vienna Convention] treaty. It seeks a ruling ordering new trials for the condemned Mexicans, most of whom are imprisoned in California and Texas. The case focuses attention on the widespread use of the death penalty in the United States, which, along with Japan, is the only industrialized nation to impose capital punishment." See "Mexico Asks World Court to Block the Executions of 51 in the U.S.," by Tim Weiner, *New York Times,* January 22, 2003.

6. The Nature Conservancy's "Last Great Places" program, for instance, stands as a defining moment in shaping Mexican public opinion in the area of conservation, almost as important as the founding of the Group of 100, an organization of intellectuals and artists who wanted to make the protection of the environment a government priority. Many Americans, too, continue to play important roles in Mexican environmental organizations, and their work constitutes important legacies.

7. Capital punishment in the United States continues to strain relations with other countries. See "An Execution in Texas Strains Ties with Mexico and Others," by Ginger Thompson, *New York Times*, August 16, 2002.

8. DePalma, *Here*, pages 235–236.

9. Ibid.

10. Americans, perhaps jealous of the admirable way Canada and Mexico can get along without the United States as the defining point of their relationship, have been less than charitable. Anthony DePalma, for instance, sums up a dim Canadian view of Mexico as "a tableau of evils and depredations like a canvas by Hieronymous Bosch." This could very well sum up Canadians' view of, say, America's criminal justice system, or how Wall Street firms plundered the savings of millions around the world through the shameless promotion of morally bankrupt firms like Enron and WorldCom that ended up financially bankrupt as well. For DePalma's comments, see *Here: A Biography of the New American Continent*, page 176.

11. DePalma, *Here*, page 256.

12. The Tyson executives were found not guilty in March 2003. "A federal jury acquitted Tyson Foods and three of its managers today of conspiring to bring illegal immigrants from Latin America to work in their poultry plants," Sherry Day reported. "The case was closely watched by immigration lawyers and labor leaders because it focused on the recruitment, employment and treatment of illegal immigrants, practices in which many large food processing companies are said to engage to meet staffing needs in low-wage jobs." See "Jury Clears Tyson Foods in Use of Illegal Immigrants," by Sherry Day, *New York Times*, March 27, 2003.

13. In a less direct way, Americans have longed to say the same of Mexico. "People from the United States have had a hard time seeing Mexico straight," Tim Weiner wrote. "Millions come here and never see it at all, spending their days in tourist enclaves speaking English and spending dollars." See "America's Dream: A Mexico Like Itself," by Tim Weiner, *New York Times*, February 18, 2001.

14. "Free-Market Upheaval Grinds Mexico's Middle Class," by Ginger Thompson, *New York Times*, September 4, 2002.

15. Linking democracy and economic prosperity is an American mantra. "Democratic freedoms cannot flourish unless our hemisphere also builds a prosperity whose benefits are widely shared. Open trade is an essential foundation for that prosperity and that possibility," George W. Bush argued. See "Bush Says He'll Press Effort for Hemisphere Trade Pact," by Christopher Marquis, *New York Times*, April 18, 2001.

16. "Take a Break, and the Rest Is Easy," by Thane Peterson, *Businessweek.com*, August 28, 2001. Peterson continues: "It's time for Americans to acknowledge that we've been buying productivity through overwork and

that the gains don't justify the psychic costs. According to the ILO [Geneva-based International Labour Organization] study, despite the long hours American workers are putting in, American productivity grew only by 22% between 1980 and 1996, vs. 30% or more in Europe and 43% in Japan. A lot of people were ecstatic when U.S. productivity growth reached 2.5% on an annualized basis in the second quarter of this year, but that still is no better than Europeans are achieving while working far fewer hours."

17.  "Since the [trucking] industry was deregulated in 1980, the wages and quality of life has spiraled downward for the trucker while the hours worked have doubled," Charlie LeDuff writes of American, not Mexican, truckers. "The new rules allowed free entry into the carrying market, eliminated indirect routes, to protect the carriers, and at the same time did away with collective rate-setting." As a consequence, as Michael Belzer, associate director of the Trucking Industry Program at the University of Michigan told LeDuff, "Typically these guys make about 31 cents a mile. By law they can only work 10 hours straight. Then they must rest 8, and then they can work 10 hours again. They have to cheat to make it." See "Seeing Hardship Through a Truck Windshield," by Charlie LeDuff, *New York Times,* January 26, 2001. One significant consequence is the economic disparity as fewer and fewer Americans are able to purchase their own homes. "In many places, people who did not join the ranks of homeowners in the last decade face greatly diminished financial prospects, having missed out on a home-price boom that added tens, if not hundreds, of thousands of dollars to other families' wealth, economists say," David Leonhardt reported. "Making matters worse, many renters invested in the stock market in recent years, to build up savings for a down payment or children's future college expenses, only to lose money or earn a meager return on their investment, while the homes they want to buy were soaring in value." See, "Earning More, But Struggling to Own a Home," by David Leonhardt, *New York Times,* November 4, 2002.

18.  "White-Collar Layoffs, Downsized Dreams," by Anthony DePalma, *New York Times,* December 5, 2002.

19.  "Take a Break, and the Rest Is Easy," by Thane Peterson, *Businessweek.com,* August 28, 2001.

20.  It may also be a worldwide problem for one reason: globalization has not delivered on the promises of its potential. "Globalization, or the fast-paced growth of trade and cross-border investment, has done far less to raise the incomes of the world's poorest people than the leaders had hoped, many officials here [in Monterrey] say. The vast majority of people living in Africa, Latin America, Central Asia and the Middle East are no better off today than they were in 1989, when the fall of the Berlin Wall allowed capitalism to spread worldwide at a rapid rate," Joseph Kahn reported. See "Losing Faith: Globalization Proves Disappointing," by Joseph Kahn, *New York Times,* March 21, 2002.

21.  "Free-Market Upheaval Grinds Mexico's Middle Class," by Ginger Thompson, *New York Times,* September 4, 2002.

22.  The flight of professionals from Mexico, it should be noted, is different from the experience of other Latin American nations, such as Argentina and Venezuela. "In Venezuela, which has long had an international

business class, leaving the country to get away from political and economic strife is not a new phenomenon," reported Simon Romero. "Over the last two decades many Venezuelans, particularly those with ample bank accounts and business contacts abroad, have periodically spent time outside the country in times of crisis." See "Descendants of Venezuelan Immigrants Flee to 'Old Country,'" by Simon Romero, *New York Times*, May 22, 2000.

23. "Literary Candor, Straight from Latin America," by Tim Rutten, *Los Angeles Times*, April 9, 2001. Poniatowska received Spain's prestigious Algauara Prize for her novel *Heaven's Skin* in March 2001. "My book is a vindication of science," she said, about the novel that tells the story of an astronomer against the backdrop of the blossoming of democracy in Mexico.

24. The feminization of immigrant labor, where maids, nannies, and adult caregivers arrive in the United States to work to provide for their own families back in Mexico and other developing countries, has only recently been addressed. Barbara Ehrenreich and Arlie Russell Hochschild edited a collection of essays examining this phenomenon in *Global Woman: Nannies, Maids and Sex Workers in the New Economy*.

25. "Great Expectations of Mexico's Leaders Sapped by Reality," by Ginger Thompson, *New York Times*, September 4, 2001.

26. Canadian investment in Mexico consists of manufacturing (61 percent), financial services (15 percent) and mining (11 percent), with the balance in the service sector.

# PART II

# MARKET OPPORTUNITIES IN NAFTA'S SECOND DECADE

4

# 4

# The Infrastructure of North America

## EXECUTIVE ABSTRACT

Enormous opportunities exist throughout North America in upgrading and building the continent's infrastructure. Decades of neglect, coupled with a failure to implement a comprehensive plan in this area, have resulted in historic opportunities. With an estimated $3 *trillion* in infrastructure projects among the three NAFTA nations and as provisions envisioned in NASP come online, an integral part of protecting North America must include comprehensive plans for expanding and upgrading the continent's infrastructure. In the United States, more than $1.3 trillion is required for this purpose.[1] In Canada and Mexico, experts estimate that an additional $1.5 trillion must be invested over the next decade in order to accommodate economic growth and the strategic defense requirements of North America. Whether it is expanding seaports, building electric power generation capacity, or expanding intercontinental highway and railroads, capital improvements are required the likes of which have not been seen since the United States embarked on the Eisenhower Interstate Highway System in the 1950s. That at present there is no continental strategy for upgrading and expanding the NAFTA nations' infrastructure is one reason why North America must look to the example of the European Union. The Blackout of 2003, when eight U.S. states and two Canadian provinces were convulsed in the largest electrical power failure in history, brought this continental failure to upgrade North America's infrastructure to the forefront. In addition to the importance of infrastructure to NASP, Mexico confronts a monumental housing shortage, one that will require an estimated $65 billion during 2004–2014. The accumulated housing deficits over the past two decades, however, offer Mexico the rare opportunity to avoid the mistakes that American communities have made since the 1960s, mistakes that have impoverished the quality of lives of Americans.

## DISCUSSION

American, Canadian, and Mexican officials have lacked the vision—and political wherewithal—to implement a continent-wide program for upgrading and expanding North America's infrastructure. (Though technically a part of a nation's infrastructure, a discussion of Mexico's wastewater management industry is provided in Chapter 8.) The belief that market forces alone will take care of comprehensive plans is misplaced, and misguided. This attitude fails to consider that, in previous generations, nation-building infrastructure expansions—the transcontinental railroad in the nineteenth century, the interstate highway system in the twentieth century—were the product of carefully laid plans and a clearly articulated vision. If Canadians have been mindful of this if not effective at it, and Mexicans have been cognizant but cash-strapped, it is Americans who have been slowest to respond. When almost one in three bridges in the United States is in disrepair, priorities should be scrutinized.[2] The crumbling American infrastructure is but one problem confronting the NAFTA nations. The American Society of Civil Engineers (ASCE) reports that the United States alone requires $1.3 trillion to repair *existing* infrastructure.

"For Mexico and Canada, it can conservatively be estimated that a similar investment is required," an official at Bechtel® in San Francisco offered. "If a coordinated 'master' plan for the whole of North America were developed, it could be higher."[3] A conservative figure put forth by Mexican officials put the cost of infrastructure investment requirements at $520 billion over the next decade. "The National Infrastructure Commission has begun work on coordinating, promoting and prioritizing long-term infrastructure development projects," the Lloyd Mexican Economic Report stated in April 2002. "The ten-member commission is headed by Eduardo Sojo, the federal government's coordinator of public policy, and includes both government representatives and leaders of private sector groups such as the National Chamber of the Construction Industry. The Chamber . . . estimates that 33 billion dollars is needed annually for investments in basic infrastructure (energy, water, environment, communications), together with a further 19 billion dollars a year for housing, health, education and tourist infrastructure. Highway improvement will be one of the Commission's priorities."[4] Financing is lacking, however. Though the North American Development Bank was established to lend to border states for water-related projects, hundreds of billions are needed—$30 billion along the U.S.-Mexico border for wastewater treatment plants and sewer systems alone—for the overall border region in the years ahead. By comparison, Texas lawmakers put the price of upgrading their state's wastewater treatment plants at $80 billion. Clearly, developing a comprehensive plan to rationally integrate Canada, the United States, and Mexico is an economic and political strategic imperative during NAFTA's second decade.

## The Infrastructure for Planes, Trains, and Automobiles

When George W. Bush flew to Mexico on February 16, 2001 for his first foreign trip as president, he expressed optimism about the opportunities. "Some look south and see problems. Not me, I look south and see opportunities and potential," he said in a speech to State Department officers prior to leaving on his trip. "These are exciting times in Mexico."[5]

The opportunities precipitated by these "exciting times," however, require significant investments. In the same way that the European Union provided funding and loans necessary to incorporate Spain and Portugal into the European community of modern nations, so, too, must the United States and Canada embark on a program to improve the infrastructure of North America.[6] If there are insufficient resources for these expenditures, then other mechanisms are in order. These range from privatization, as Mexico has done to airports and seaports, or the use of deficit financing, consistent with Keynesian economics, as has been favored in Canada. The Bush administration, following the precedent set by the Eisenhower administration, must embark on a comprehensive program to repair the nation's infrastructure. In the 1950s, the United States committed $50 billion to build the interstate highway system. In the 2000s, $500 billion must now be spent to repair those same highways. An equal amount must be spent to repair or replace bridges, and an additional $300 billion must be spent on upgrading the nation's airports and seaports.

The opportunities in Mexico are significant as well. Canadians are more cognizant than Americans of the need to evaluate and pursue these opportunities. "Mexico needs a lot of infrastructure investment—roads, airports, energy capacity, electricity grids—to support its future growth process," Stephen S. Poloz, Vice-President and Chief Economist of Export Development Canada, said. "The bottom line? Like all economies, Mexico's shortcomings appear more compelling the closer one looks. But, from a global perspective, Mexico's strengths clearly outweigh its weaknesses."[7] When asked to elaborate on the greatest obstacle, Poloz offers one word: funding. Without a continental initiative headed by Washington, Ottawa, and Mexico City, funding for the *trillions* required will not be forthcoming. An overview of the opportunities in the 2004–2014 period is discussed, with the caveat that the financing for these infrastructure projects must come from government, international development loans, and the private sector.

**Seaports and Airports.** During NAFTA's first decade almost all of Mexico's seaports were privatized. The port of Veracruz, for instance, was renowned around the world for its corruption. With the port run by ruthless labor leaders, the Zedillo administration had no other alternative than to privatize it, as much to end the stranglehold of corrupt union bosses as to affirm Mexico's commitment to market reforms. In the years that followed, the entire port was taken over by the private sector, the pre-existing union was disbanded, and, though labor activists denounced the "breaking" of labor, the reforms proved so successful that Veracruz became a model for other privatization efforts. "As a result, this is where we've seen the best results of all," Aaron Dychter, Transportation Undersecretary, explained. "We have created a virtuous circle of steadily increasing efficiency and lower costs. Ports like Veracruz on the Gulf of Mexico and Acapulco and Manzanillo on the Pacific, are completely competitive with any port you can name in the United States."[8]

These achievements, however, suggest that such transformations require revolutionary changes—in this case privatizing facilities that previously were state-run—and a medium-term time frame. It took almost a decade to achieve a turnaround in the way Mexican ports are operated. The sustained economic expansion, however, is straining these seaports' capacity. Mexican seaports require significant investment to accommodate the growing trade, particularly now that Mexico has concluded a free trade agreement with the European Union. "Our ports have now reached a level of efficiency comparable to what one finds in the developed world," Aaron Dychter explained. "The next challenge is to expand these facilities to make sure that they do not operate in an over-capacity level, which is what has happened to our airports."[9]

In confidential reports prepared by American construction management firms, U.S. engineers theorize that the total investment in Mexican seaports over the next ten years may exceed $30 billion. "If what we are talking about in a post-September 11 world is securing the integrity of North America, then it is in the national defense interests of the United States to ensure that Mexican ports are state-of-the-art and are part of a continental network," an official at the Pentagon explained.[10]

Significant investments are also in order at Mexican airports. Whether it is building a new terminal at Cancún's airport, or the multibillion-dollar program to give Mexico City a new, smart airport capable of accommodating 50 million passengers annually, air transportation is no longer a luxury in Mexico. It is a necessity for the Mexican economy in the age of NAFTA. Though it is not without controversy, given the geographic realities, Mexico City's proposed alternative new airport was a reasonable compromise, one that represented a superior societal outcome under difficult circumstances.[11] "Every care was taken to ensure the new airport's technical, sustainable and financial viability. The main thing is that it gives us the room to grow—eventually to handle 50 million passengers, more than double the current airport's capacity—and this will make Mexico City's airport comparable to other world-class hubs, such as Atlanta or Heathrow," Aaron Dychter explained. Perhaps, but the original proposed site for that airport had to be changed abruptly after opposition from affected residents, similar to the not-in-my-backyard, or NIMBY, syndrome common in the United States and Canada.[12]

It is a paradox, of course, that the critical need to expand civilian and military airport capacity in Mexico, which is estimated to require $15 billion over the next decade, stems from the turnaround in how Mexican airlines operate. Recall Alain Giberstein's comment that remarkable changes in how Mexicans conduct their daily business lives. When Miguel de la Madrid was president, for instance, Aeromexico operated as a state-run carrier, one in which bureaucrats managed and labor unions dispensed patronage to their members. Fares made even less economic sense than they generally do in the aviation industry worldwide, and service was erratic. Mexicans used to joke that Aeromexico would do well to change its name to "Aero-maybe." In one dramatic confrontation, however, the airline workers went on strike, directly challenging the president.

Enraged, de la Madrid shut down the airline and shortly thereafter it was declared bankrupt. Though Mexico's aviation industry suffered for several years after Aeromexico ceased operations, when it resumed it embarked on a steady program to build its business and credibility. Gerardo de Prevoisin spearheaded the purchase of Aeromexico's assets in 1989, and his corporate turnaround proved legendary, for several reasons.[13] New management built on the commercial successes beginning in 1994 while curbing alleged excesses, excesses that resulted from unseemly revelations concerning the relationship between the airline and the PRI. In the intervening eight years, Aeromexico, incredibly, has emerged as one of the best airlines in the world. "We're the most punctual airline in the world in certain areas. That's been widely recognized and it means a lot as it reflects our dedication to being a trustworthy carrier," Alfonso Pasquel, Aeromexico CEO, said in the summer of 2002.

This kind of corporate excellence, moreover, has been repeated at other regional airlines, form Aeroliteral® to Aviacsa®. This, in turn, has further fueled internal demand for air travel in Mexico to an unprecedented degree, straining existing facilities. The strategy of privatizing airport terminals has been successful, with one caveat. Failing to have a national master plan for how the entire air traffic should function has created problems. Consider, for instance, how failure to coordinate how the airports on the Yucatán peninsula—Cancún, Mérida, Cozumel, Campeche, Chetumal and Cozumel—operate creates inefficiencies. While Cancún's airport continues to struggle to accommodate demand, Campeche's languishes with over-capacity. At the same time, the absence of a master plan has resulted in improvised expansion of the airports at Mérida and Cozumel. Conversely, Chetumal lacks a medium-term development plan as "Maya World" ecotourism matures as a sustainable industry. Those quick to point out that airports—and air traffic controllers—should be privatized fail to consider that Mexicans are not convinced that all public services are run best by the private sector.[14]

As the decade-long debate about the future airport at Mexico City demonstrates, it is imperative that Mexico create a master plan that envisions the aviation needs of the nation. California's Silicon Valley industry, for instance, requires continuous air shipments to assembly plants in Guadalajara to manufacture and assemble circuit boards used by the computer industry. The airports serving Tijuana are straining as the maquiladora industries along the border continue. Monterrey's airport is under strain as that city emerges as the leading center of growth in NAFTA's second decade, as are the airports on Mexico's Caribbean.

**RAILROADS.** When NAFTA went into effect, Mexico's railroads were in such a state of disrepair that the Japanese balked at acquiring them. It was a sad commentary, and hard to believe, that when they were built under Porfirio Díaz at the end of the nineteenth century, Mexico's railroad system was hailed as one of the engineering marvels of the world. Not unlike their American counterparts, as trucks, cars, and airplanes supplanted railroads, it became impossible to operate railroads as a viable business. In the second half of the twentieth century, subsidies were required to keep the trains running, inefficiently at best, as a populist measure that proved politically expedient to elected officials.

It was the cumulative impact of this state of affairs that frustrated efforts to introduce "rationality," a political euphemism for market forces, into this equation. Ever since Mexico entered GATT in 1988, government officials quietly sought ways of introducing market reforms in the hopes of extricating the nation out of this quagmire. In more than a decade only three segments of Mexico's railroads have been privatized. Those segments that have been sold to investors—Mexican and foreign—have benefited from the capital improvements necessary to turn the industry around.

Of the three segments of Mexico's railroads that have been privatized, the one serving Monterrey has made the most significant gains towards sustainable profitability. The northeastern trunk, comprised of 2,660 miles, which links Mexico's major ports and urban centers with principal rail links to the United States Northeast, has benefited from greater investment. Transportación Ferroviaria Mexicana, or TFM, was created when GTMM and the Kansas City Southern Railroad acquired this railroad. With more than $900 million in capital improvements, TFM links the Mexican ports along of Veracruz, Lazaro Cardenas, and Tampico-Altamira to the two major points of entry for freight along the U.S.-Mexico border: Nuevo Laredo-Laredo and Matamoros-Brownsville.

Although these improvements represent a significant investment, and they constitute an impressive testament to the turnarounds possible through capable management, the total investments made by TFM represent only 5 percent of the total investment required in Mexican railroads over the next 15 years. If the United States, Canada, and Mexico are to integrate their railroad networks into a continental system that can move freight from the Valley of Mexico to Ontario through the Midwest, greater cooperation is required. Market forces alone are insufficient to ensure a logical, and strategic, integration of North America's railroad system.

**HIGHWAYS.** Mexico's highways are inadequate for the sustained economic growth currently underway. The National Chamber of the Construction Industry estimates that 27,000 miles of highways have to be constructed or repaired during NAFTA's second decade.[15] While significant improvements have been made in certain specific geographic areas, the privatization of highways has met with mixed results. The concessions granted have been predicated on the collection of tolls. These, however, have been so exorbitant that many bus and truck companies eschew using these "super-highways" to save on tolls. The result is that existing public roads are congested, while new highways remain underused. A balance has to be reached, simply because Mexico must find a way of allowing private capital to invest in upgrading the nation's highway system while ensuring that both users enjoy a cost-effective means of transportation and investors enjoy a fair return on their investments.

"Our major highway trunks need to be upgraded to a minimum of at least four lanes, particularly along the heavily transited axis stretching from Mexico City to Nuevo Laredo, Texas," Aaron Dychter, Transport Undersecretary, explains. "At the same time, our government needs to channel resources to maintain and expand the rural road system. At present we are looking at new ways to attract investment."[16]

In other words, if, as most experts agree, Mexico requires an investment of $100 billion over the next generation to duplicate what the United States accomplished with the Eisenhower Interstate System, new approaches must be introduced. Unless development loans or guarantees are forthcoming during NAFTA's second decade, Mexico's highway system will remain the weakest link in North America's infrastructure, and this will cost business and consumers in all three countries billions. Attracting investment is imperative, particularly given the billions of dollars required to carry out the highway expansion programs on the drawing board. In addition to improving the highway system radiating from Mexico City to Monterrey, Querétaro, Veracruz, and Puebla, there are other ambitious projects. The Puebla-Panama Plan, a 25-year plan to link the cities of Puebla and Panama with a multimodal transportation highway, is expected to cost as much as $5 billion.[17] This highway, however, is seen as the lifeline that will link all Central American nations, including Belize, into a single artery first to Mexico and then, by extension, to the United States and Canada.[18] An impediment to extending free trade throughout Central America is regional concerns about dismantling specific welfare benefits. Costa Rica, for example, created an exemplary welfare state under the administration of Rafael Calderon, Franklin Delano Roosevelt's contemporary. Costa Ricans, unsure about how opening their economy to regional integration and competitive market forces will impact their social safety net, are reluctant to embrace free trade, as have other Central Americans, specifically Salvadorans. These are the political challenges that confront economic expansion.

Grupo ICA®, Mexico's largest construction firm, is keenly aware of the need to involve foreign companies in the Mexican market as national, regional, and continental infrastructure projects emerge. "Joint ventures are very important to us [at Grupo ICA]. We have had many good partners in all the principal countries of the world and feel that it is to our advantage to always be open to joint ventures, where we can share our strengths and risks," Bernardo Quintana, of Grupo ICA CEO, argues.[19]

In recent years Grupo ICA has successfully engaged in joint ventures with American companies, such as Flour Daniel Corporation®, in a variety of construction companies. What is lacking, however, is an articulated vision of where Mexico's highway system should be headed, the market mechanism for realizing these goals, and the kind of cooperation with the United States and Canada needed to ensure that the roads across the continent are upgraded and expanded within a broader master plan. This is bound to encounter greater opposition from Americans than Canadians, but as Washington defines how "Homeland Security" and NASP complement and overlap, the importance of a highway system cannot be ignored. In fact, NASP gained currency during the conflict with Iraq. "Mexico is sending 18,000 soldiers to secure airports, seaports, border posts and bridges with direct links to the United States," Tim Weiner reported after hostilities between the U.S. and Iraq broke out. "At least half will be based within a few miles of the border, many serving as sentries in the desert. Others will serve in the interior, guarding tourist resorts and oil refineries, the two great sources of foreign revenue for Mexico. . . . These linkages and the coast-to-coast mobilization by both nations represents the birth of an international national-security network, American and Mexican officials said. . . . By collaborating against a foreign threat, both nations are crossing a line that they had never breached."[20] It is clear that protecting the whole of North America requires a united effort by the United States, Canada, and Mexico.

"If Mexico is to become a truly modern society, more of its citizens must become part of the middle class," Fernando Margain and Walter Russell Mead wrote in the *New York Times*.[21] To accomplish this, the interrelated nature of infrastructure development and a nation's standard of living are higher on the agenda of officials. At the "Border Summits," for instance, "high-ranking officials" convene with "representatives of major national foundations and corporate leaders" in order "to examine international trade, energy, telecommunications, utility infrastructure corridor development, border manufacturing opportunities, water, housing and health issues."[22]

To date, unfortunately, Mexico has been unable to find the right formula for attracting adequate private sector investment to build highways. The infrastructure of the entire continent is under greater scrutiny as economists and engineers document how North American facilities are falling behind those of the European Union. Though Mexican infrastructure remains the most underdeveloped, crumbling infrastructure in the United States and strained facilities in Canada impede sustained economic growth. "[W]eak infrastructure at both borders [has] raised the cost of doing business," Robert Pastor opined in the *Los Angeles Times*, taking the U.S. to task for failing to improve its infrastructure along the U.S.-Canada and U.S.-Mexico borders.[23] The weakest infrastructure, however, remains Mexico's, an assessment that frustrates efforts to move forward on the proposed superhighway for North America. "The Superhighway provides a 'seamless link' connecting major commercial centres of Mexico, the United States and Canada," the London (Canada) Economic Development Corporation argued. "Such a link allows for the efficient flow of people and goods between these three countries to capitalize upon the new trading patterns that are continuing to grow and develop."[24]

American officials are less forthcoming in recognizing the need for an approach similar to that taken by the European Union. "What about infrastructure investment in Mexico and other developing countries?" Federal Reserve Board Governor Edward M. Gramlich said at the Texas Trade Corridors New Economy Conference held in San Antonio, Texas in August 2001. "The

evidence from Mexico, as well as national and cross-country studies more generally, suggests that public capital formation in developing countries has had significant productivity and growth effects," he went on to say. But, backing away from the position that
an initiative modeled along the lines of the Eisenhower Interstate
Highway by the federal governments of the NAFTA nations is required, Gramlich concluded, "[g]overnment certainly should ensure that the existing public infrastructure is properly managed
and maintained. But, in general, government's role should be to
make industries as competitive as possible."[25]

Officials in Washington and Ottawa have not understood that
given the billions of dollars that have to be invested in Mexico's
infrastructure in the next decade, the United States and Canada
must work with Mexico, consistent with how Germany and France
worked with Spain toward similar goals. "Although the qualitative
links are clear, there is less consensus about the exact magnitude
of the effect, given that economic growth and infrastructure
spending are simultaneously determined variables, and it is difficult to isolate the direction of causation," according to Gramlich.
"Studies have also found that whereas non-infrastructure public
spending appears to crowd out private investment, public expenditures on infrastructure seem to encourage private investment."[26] Without a coordinated program by Washington, Ottawa,
and Mexico City to upgrade and expand the continent's infrastructure, the economic integrity and physical defense of North
America is undermined.

## A Housing Crisis, A Homebuilding Opportunity

Mexico's National Chamber of the Construction Industry estimates that in NAFTA's second decade, Mexico will require $65
billion in housing.[27] While highways and airports, like most other
large infrastructure projects, garner considerable interest from
politicians, economists, and the public, housing in Mexico remains an overlooked industry. Over the past two decades, however, a cumulative impact of annual shortfalls in meeting Mexico's
housing needs has precipitated a critical shortage of housing.
One reason, of course, is that housing is seldom seen as a national
asset. Another reason is found in how housing fell under the political sphere of Mexican Paternalism.

Through Infonavit, a federal agency of the Mexican government, housing was treated as a social good, designed to allow
workers to purchase their own homes. A worker, of course, was

someone gainfully employed within the formal economy; taxes paid by employers financed, in part, the agency that administered the sale of subsidized homes to working- and middle-class families. The intent is to give as many people as possible a stake in society. By helping Mexican families own their own homes, families are protected economically, and they are also given a stake in society. People who own their own home are involved in civic matters, and are more involved in what happens in society; a nation of homeowners is a nation of successful families.

Infonavit itself was inspired by the example set by the United States. At the conclusion of World War II, the United States embarked on a grand social and economic experiment about how people could own their own homes and live their lives. The traditional role of the city as an urban center where people both lived and worked was turned inside out. It began in the 1940s when developer William Levitt built 2,000 simple, identical homes, moderately priced, for returning GIs. The United States, in the throes of a nationwide housing shortage, embraced this form of mass housing, christened the community Levittown, and gave birth to suburbanism as a lifestyle. With the popularization of automobiles after World War II, people could live far from where they worked, and the nature of urban life itself changed.

"Suburbs" revolutionized the landscape of modern societies— and not for the better. Andres Duany, Elizabeth Plater-Zyberk, and Jeff Speck, authorities in city planning and community revitalization programs, describe the impact of suburbs by pointing out that:

> [i]n traditional neighborhoods, all streets except highways are "fronted" by salable lots on both sides; none of the infrastructure is wasted on transportation alone. . . . There is another way in which traditional neighborhoods offer savings over sprawl: they can be built in much smaller phases. Smart developers do their best to serve many different market segments at once—"starter," "move-up," "family," "retirement," and so on—but in suburbia they must build an independent pod for each market segment, since different incomes must never mix.[28]

The detrimental impact of "suburbanization" is summed up thusly:

> Suburban sprawl . . . ignores historical precedent and human experience. It is an invention, conceived by architects, engi-

neers, and planners, and promoted by developers in the great *sweeping aside of the old* that occurred after the Second World War. Unlike the traditional neighborhood model, which evolved organically as a response to human needs, suburban sprawl is an idealized artificial system . . . Unfortunately, this system is already showing itself to be unsustainable.[29]

The creation of suburbs—facilitated by the embrace of an automobile culture—also had its urban counterpart: a concentration of skyscrapers that discouraged pedestrian traffic on city streets. Indeed, with private automobiles on surface roads, urban planners sought to limit downtown pedestrian foot traffic. Office highrise buildings, connected by elevated walkways, effectively did this. "We know now that that's the wrong way to plan a city," John Kriskiewicz, an architectural historian from the Parsons School of Design in New York said. "In the 1960s and 1970s we thought that it was a good idea, but that wasn't the case. The more successful urban spaces have a vibrant street life and robust pedestrian traffic. We have to restore that in [American] cities."[30]

This, of course, is hardly a revelation. As early as 1961 architecture critic Vincent Scully, Jr. decried "the death of the street" in American urban design, where vibrant pedestrian life was being destroyed by misguided urban planning and design. "Modernity," in essence, turned inside out how humans had traditionally organized their communities. Historically, the central square is a place where citizens come together and encounter one another as they go about the business of their lives. Communities built after the widespread use of the automobile have decentralized spaces, hostile to pedestrians and neighborly interaction, and we decry the impact this "sprawl" has on the quality of our lives and the impersonal nature of our modern communities. This is how Paul Tillich explains the importance to the community of architecture in the history of Europe:

> Take a medieval town, the town of Chartres, for instance. Not only its cathedral is important—which you must look at to understand the Middle Ages—but also the very way in which it stands on the hill in the middle of a small town. It is a tremendous cathedral, overlooking the whole surrounding country. In it you find symbols of the daily life—the nobility, the craftsmen, the guilds, and the different supporters of the church. The whole daily life is within the walls of the cathedral in consecrated form. When people went into it, their daily life was represented in the sphere of the holy; when

they left it, they took with them the consecration they had received in the cathedral back into their daily lives.[31]

The cumulative impacts are several, and it is here that Mexico has an opportunity to avoid the mistakes the United States and Canada have made. Robert Putnam, author of *Bowling Alone,* decries the social impact of suburbanization in the lives of Americans:

> Suburbanization of the last thirty years has increased not only our financial investment in the automobile, but also our investment of time. Between 1969 and 1995 . . . the length of the average trip to work increased by 26 percent, while the average shopping trip increased by 29 percent. While the number of commuting trips per household rose 24 percent over this quarter century, the number of shopping trips per household almost doubled, and the number of other trips for personal or family business more than doubled. And each trip was much more likely to be made alone . . .
>
> One inevitable consequence of how we have come to organize our lives spatially is that we spend measurably more of every day shuttling alone in metal boxes among the vertices of our private triangles. American adults average seventy-two minutes every day behind the wheel . . . This is, according to time diary studies, more than we spend cooking or eating and more than twice as much as the average parent spends with the kids.[32]

The litany of complaints against suburbs and automobile-friendly cities continues. "Fifty years ago, America's cities provided a pedestrian environment that compared favorably with the world's best cities. What has happened in the intervening decades has been sheer lunacy: in an attempt to lure auto-dependent suburbanites downtown, consultants of every ilk turned our cities into freeways," Andres Duany, Elizabeth Plater-Zyberk, and Jeff Speck write.[33] Not to be upstaged, Robert Putnam chimes in with this damning assessment:

> Could [civic] disengagement perhaps be linked not to urbanization, but to suburbanization? . . . Suburbanization meant greater separation of workplace and residence and greater segregation by race and class. Such segregation was hardly new to American cities, but increasingly in the postwar period it took on a new character. In the classic American city neighborhoods tended to be homogeneous, but municipalities were heterogeneous . . . In a suburbanized

America municipalities were increasingly homogenous in ethnic and class terms. . . . At century's end some . . . suburbs were white, but others were black, Hispanic, or Asian . . . Many suburbs had come to resemble theme parks, with uniform architecture and coordinated amenities and boutiques.[34]

What is clear is that, as Mexico struggles to build 3,500,000 homes throughout NAFTA's second decade, Infonavit must work to nurture civic and community lives by modeling new developments on traditional town models. Infonavit's housing developments, while utilitarian and within the means of many Mexican families, have impoverished Mexican societies. The country has provided adequate housing for millions, but at high social and economic costs. It is ironic that, because Mexican consumers cannot afford as many cars as either Americans or Canadians, Mexico has been spared the social and economic costs imposed by suburbanization.

"Traffic jams in the United States are costing Americans $68 billion each year in wasted time and fuel, according to a new report. Based on the analysis of 75 U.S. cities, the annual Urban Mobility Report from the Texas Transportation Institute finds the average rush-hour driver—not just commuters, but all drivers—wastes about 62 hours in traffic each year," CNN published on June 20, 2002, confusing the obvious with news. "The study also found that rush hours are lasting longer. In 1982, the report found traffic was congested about 4.5 hours a day for the 75 cities studied. In 2000, traffic was congested an average of seven hours a day."[35] This grim report is consistent with Robert Putnam's observation made years earlier that, "[a]s the twentieth century ended, Americans gradually began to recognize that the sprawling pattern of metropolitan settlement that we had built for ourselves in the preceding five decades imposes heavy personal and economic costs—pollution, congestion, and lost time."[36]

Mexicans who live in Mexico City, Guadalajara, and Monterrey certainly lose a great deal of time in traffic. The ribbons of highways that ensnarl these communities were modeled on Mexican attempts to emulate American highways, first introduced in the late 1950s. Recall that however popular automobiles had become by the 1920s, it took another 30 years before the U.S. Congress passed the National Defense and Interstate Highway Act in 1956 that authorized the building of 42,000 miles of four-lane highways designed to link the nation in a network of roads.

Addressing Congress in 1956, President Eisenhower presented his vision of a grand network of highways linking the American landscape this way:

> Our unity as a nation is sustained by free communication and by easy transportation of people and goods. The ceaseless flow of information throughout the republic, matched by individual and commercial movement over a vast system of interconnected highways crisscrossing the country, joined our national borders to the north and south.
>
> Together, the united forces of our communication and transportation systems are dynamic elements in the very name we bear—United States. Without them, we would be a mere alliance of many separate parts.[37]

Before automobiles could play their role in promoting economic growth, in other words, highways that united the nation in a cost-effective grid were required. To achieve this goal, Eisenhower urged "adequate funding there must be, but contention over the method should not be permitted to deny our people these critically needed roads." To accomplish this national undertaking, more than $50 billion was invested in creating the concrete arteries required to transport the lifeblood of the American economy across the North American landscape, linking the whole of the United States internally and to the international border crossings with Canada and Mexico.[38]

Known as the Eisenhower Interstate Highway, this national network linked the entire continental United States. Aggressive lobbying by the automobile industry at the local level further encouraged reliance on the private automobile. Some negative consequences of this strategy, however, have been traffic congestion, social alienation, and the economic inefficiencies associated with longer commute times and expense. Each of these, in turn, creates challenges for urban planners and transportation officials, particularly given the tens of billions of dollars that are incurred in social costs associated with how American communities are structured. Again, as Robert Putnam says, the, "[s]uburbanization of the last thirty years has increased not only out of financial investment in the automobile, but also our investment of time. . . . The car and the commute, however, are demonstrably bad for community life. In round numbers the evidence suggests that *each additional ten minutes in daily commuting time cuts involvement in community affairs by 10 percent*—fewer public meetings attended, fewer committees chaired, fewer petitions signed, fewer church services attended, less volunteering, and so on." [Italics in the original.][39] The importance of having a master or regional transportation plan cannot be underestimated. "What's really impressive to me is the way that medium-size metropolitan areas, like Atlanta or Houston, have managed to mismanage their development so completely that they have worse traffic congestion than metropolitan New York, which has five times their population," Paul Krugman wrote with unwarranted delight in the *New York Times*.[40]

It is clear, then, that, absent a master plan, Mexicans run the risk of repeating America's mistakes. Indeed, consider how incorporating housing to make viable communities continues to be neglected. Commenting on the $460 million JVC Culture, Convention, and Business Center® under development by Jorge Vergara outside Guadalajara, a skeptical Clifford Pearson, an editor at *Architectural Record*, pondered, "For all the talk of creating a new kind of development, it is unclear if the JVC Center wants to be a real city, a satellite of downtown Guadalajara, or just a culturally savvy corporate park. Although it has an intriguing mix of uses, it does not now include any housing. Without people living there, can the JVC Center ever function as a real community?"[41]

## A Tale of Two Opportunities: Querétaro City and Ciudad Juárez

An analysis of the kinds of housing Mexico requires shows how Mexicans can avoid the kinds of problems that have affected most Americans and Canadians in this area. Mexico is right in being stubborn in its urban planning and how it approaches residential communities. If tens of billions of dollars are to be invested in housing over the next decade, it must be done in a way that does not result in tens of billions of dollars in social costs subsequently. To understand this, consider how the middle-class housing needs of Querétaro City contrasts with the working-class housing needs in Ciudad Juárez. Querétaro City is located 120 miles northwest of Mexico City. One consequence of the 1985 Mexico City earthquake was that some middle-class families began to leave the Valley of Mexico. Concerned about the quality of life, including air pollution, congestion, crime, and earthquakes, many professionals have steadily moved to other communities. Ciudad Juárez, in contrast, is a bustling border community to which hundreds of thousands of working-class Mexicans have flocked in search of jobs. Opposite El Paso, Texas, Ciudad Juárez has struggled to provide municipal and public services to the burgeoning communities that encircle it.

Communities like Querétaro are experiencing an influx of well-heeled, middle-class families. "The middle class is flowering here," Robert Flores, president of the real estate association in Querétaro, told a reporter from the *Los Angeles Times*.[42] The transformation of Querétaro into a bastion of middle-class respectability, however, risks pricing out the working class and the poor. "The growing numbers and comparative wealth of these migrants [from Mexico City] have transformed the town," Jill Leovy reported. "Apartment rentals and land costs have nearly doubled in two years . . . Food and transportation costs are higher here, government sources say, and federal figures show that inflation has exceeded the national average over the past three years."[43]

Querétaro stands to benefit from its urban planners, such as municipal city planner Mauricio Cobo, many of whom were trained in the United States, and who are cognizant of the class divisions that are part of the urban-suburban rivalry of American communities. Rolando Garc´a, Querétaro's mayor and a member of the opposition PAN, is aware of the challenges his administration faces in managing the development of Querétaro. "We have to manage our growth, particularly of residential areas. We have to find a way of growing in a family-friendly way, where the quality of life is protected," Mayor Rolando Garc´a said.[44] City officials in Querétaro would be wise to bear in mind the observations of Andres Duany, Elizabeth Plater-Zyberk, and Jeff Speck, who argue that in "a traditional neighborhood, every market segment can be served through the construction of a single mixed-use area, thus limiting infrastructure. Finally, there are the efficiencies that result from building at slightly higher densities, something that is viable within a traditional street network but is rarely achieved gracefully in sprawl."[45]

The importance of heterogeneous community life cannot be overstressed. "By creating communities of homogenous political interests, suburbanization reduces the local conflicts that engage and draw the citizenry into the public realm," political scientist Eric Oliver argues.[46] Officials in Querétaro instinctively recognize this challenge. "Querétaro is not viable without the poor. We must find a way to include them," Saul Ugalde, a spokesperson for Querétaro city government, is quoted as saying.[47] That city officials are aware of the need to nurture diverse communities is encouraging, for it demonstrates that Mexico is determined to avoid the kind of compartmentalization one sees in American communities, an unfortunate trait that is blamed for the sustained decline in community life.

The United States offers solutions for the problems Querétaro confronts. In the U.S., the "New Urbanism" movement advocates the return to more pedestrian-friendly communities. Seaside, Florida is hailed as a successful prototype for the revitalization of community life. "People fundamentally like small towns more than sprawl, and in many cases are moving back to older urban neighborhoods and even central cities," Peter Calthorpe, founder of the Congress for a New Urbanism, argues.[48] Mexico's Infonavit would do well to study and emulate the more sustainable approaches to community life advocated by this movement and others. Another example of a successful urban development worth study is the Embarcadero Center in San Francisco. How this downtown complex incorporates office buildings, hotels, retailers, and restaurants into a flourishing community is extraordinary, for it maintains a human perspective. The middle-class aspirations of a thriving community like Querétaro are not like the challenges confronting most of Mexico, of which Ciudad Juárez is representative. Managing wealth is only possible when that wealth trickles down into the hands of its residents. "You have a city that produces great wealth, but that sits in the eye of a storm," Gustavo Elizondo, mayor of Ciudad Juárez, told the *New York Times*. "In one way it is a place of opportunity for the international community. But we have no way to provide water, sewage and sanitation for all the people who come to work. Every year we get poorer and poorer even though we create more and more wealth."[49]

Future historians and social scientists will look back and marvel at the fact that NAFTA's first decade witnessed the largest internal migration of Mexicans since the Mexican Revolution of 1910–1917. "In the last five years more than one million Mexicans have moved to the border. Many come not to cross the border but to work in thousands of mostly foreign-owned manufacturing plants, known as maquiladoras," Ginger Thompson succinctly described. "The explosion has created one of the most dynamic industrial zones in the Americas—and all the problems associated with explosive growth. The overwhelmed Mexican border cities lack the means to provide the most basic services."[50]

This internal migration strains municipal resources throughout Mexico. Entire rural villages in states like Michoacan and Puebla have been emptied, far eclipsing fabled Mexican migration to the United States. When an American commentator like Richard Rodriguez argues that Mexican migration has "arrived" in America "silent as a Trojan horse, larger than a flotilla of scabrous boat people, more confounding in its innocence, in its power of proclamation," his words masterfully exploit American fears about Mexico, of course, but offers nothing for balance. He fails to consider the tens of millions of Mexicans who, in search of jobs, have been convulsed in a massive *internal* migration.[51]

Americans, similarly, fail to consider how globalization is also changing the face of American rural communities. "Since the last recession, in the early 1990s, China, Russia and the former Soviet republics have charged into the world's commodity markets," Peter Kilborn reported, on the plight of small American towns. "At the same time, new trade agreements have erased quotas and tariffs that long insulated United States industries from foreign competition. While freer trade benefits American consumers and industries that can now buy cheaper imported commodities, it has been rough on places whose livelihoods depend on raw goods. For these already-struggling communities, the first post-globalization recession may break the old sequence of boom-bust-boom, and erase any hopes of long-term survival."[52]

A "continental" problem precipitated by globalization is thus presented as a "Mexican" phenomenon. In one regard it is: the emptying of Mexico's countryside by the internal movement of people from destitute rural communities to bustling industrial parks that surround the border cities is a familiar process. Consider how economist John Kenneth Galbraith describes the similar process as it occurred in the United States decades before American reporters commented upon how the lure of jobs has far outstripped the ability of local governments to provide basic services:

> The poor in the United States, while none could doubt their degradation and misery, were once largely invisible—poor blacks were hidden away on the farms and plantations of the rural South with primitive food, clothing and shelter, little in the way of education and no civil rights. Many poor whites were unseen on the hills and in the hollows of Appalachia. Poverty was not a problem when distant, out of sight. Only as economic, political and social change brought the needy to the cities did welfare become a public concern, the poor now living next to and in deep contrast with the relatively affluent.[53]

The arresting success of NAFTA in creating jobs, however,

poses tremendous challenges to the Fox administration, and not just because the needs of the working poor are more in evidence.

Whereas Ernesto Zedillo struggled with the challenges of implementing NAFTA, Vicente Fox must now implement a program to develop urban planning assistance for the dozens of communities overwhelmed by job seekers. In Ciudad Juárez, hundreds of thousands of people resort to the shantytowns that circle the industrial parks and the outskirts of established towns. "None of the dwellings had running water," Ginger Thompson reported after visiting one of these communities outside Ciudad Juárez. "None were connected to city sewage lines. Hundreds of improvised electricity wires crisscrossed the dirt roads. The air was filled with the smells of human waste and burning garbage."[54]

Amid all this squalor, the fact that Ciudad Juárez is an economic engine is easy to overlook. "What the maquilas provide to Mexico are jobs. And that is good. It is very good. But it is not enough," Mayor Gustavo Elizondo says, reflecting the thinking that accompanies the transition from short- to medium-term development.[55] It is at this stage that urban planning, increasing wages, redistribution of taxes, and regional development plans are put into place. Ernesto Ruffo, the "Border Czar" appointed by Vicente Fox, is cognizant of the need. "Our people will have houses that are small but honorable," he explained. "And we are going to ask companies to collaborate on the costs of these houses because they have seen that Mexican workers are responsible, loyal and want to learn more. But they cannot learn and grow unless they have stable living conditions."[56]

If Mexico is to succeed in this area, Ruffo must avoid the low-income housing disasters that have plagued American cities. Indeed, he would do well to remember the conclusion that Andres Duany, Elizabeth Plater-Zyberk, and Jeff Speck reached: "Unlike the traditional neighborhood, sprawl is not healthy growth; it is essentially self-destructive. Even at relatively low population densities, sprawl tends not to pay for itself financially and consumes land at an alarming rate, while producing insurmountable traffic problems and exacerbating social inequity and isolation."[57]

That Mexico's border cities are in the throes of massive migration should not prove discouraging. "New York has always been the quintessential immigrant metropolis, a place of dreams and magic, opportunity and hardship," Kenneth Jackson, author of *Crabgrass Frontier: The Suburbanization of America*, argues. "And everywhere we look, newcomers are giving life to neighborhoods that otherwise would be in decline. Twenty years ago, the South

Bronx was full of abandoned buildings; today, it is thriving. Similarly, since 1975 the borough of Queens has become the most ethnically diverse place in the world."[58]

The Fox administration has a historic opportunity to move on solving Mexico's housing crisis in ways that improve the quality of community life, reaffirm social values, and strengthen democracy and civic participation by learning from the mistakes of the past half century committed by the United States and Canada. Corporate America, for its part, stands to profit handsomely by showing initiative and offering creative solutions for the Mexican market.[59] "With Mexico's baby boomers now coming of age, the housing shortage is estimated at some 6 million [houses as of 2001]," *Business Week* reported, with a price tag through 2006 estimated at $20 billion.[60] For the duration of NAFTA's second decade, however, the value of the entire housing market is significantly higher The border communities require $32 billion in housing and urban planning along the Mexican side of the U.S.-Mexico border, with an additional $33 billion required for the rest of the nation. This constitutes a significant market opportunity for American banks, mortgage companies and construction firms.

## SUMMARY

1.  The NAFTA nations have failed both to develop a master development plan to coordinate the upgrading and expansion of infrastructure, and to provide the hundreds of billions the North American Development Bank requires to finance the repair, upgrade, and expansion of the continent's infrastructure.

2.  Mexico is in the throes of a sustained economic expansion that requires hundreds of billions of dollars of investment over the next two decades. These investments in infrastructure range from airports to building residential communities, from water treatment facilities to integrating Mexican railroads to those of the United States and Canada.

3.  Tremendous opportunities exist in meeting Mexico's demand for working- and middle-class housing by developing communities that avoid the problems that the United States encountered in the second half of the twentieth century through a misguided embrace of suburban culture.

4.  The total market value of the opportunities in the various in-

frastructure projects among the three NAFTA nations approximates an astounding $3 *trillion* between 2004–2014.

## ENDNOTES

1. Addressing the infrastructure crisis in the United States has not been a priority for leaders in Washington. The only Congressional bill, for instance, to tackle this problem is the "Rebuild America: Financing Infrastructure Renewal and Security for Transportation (Rebuild America First) Act," which calls for a paltry $50 billion. This constitutes a mere 4 percent of what the American Society of Civil Engineers (ASCE) estimate is required over the next two decades.

2. Twenty-eight percent of all bridges in the United States are in a state of disrepair, according to NBC News report of May 6, 2002.

3. Personal communication, May 2000.

4. *Lloyd Mexican Economic Report,* April 2002.

5. "Bush Heads to Mexico for Talks," MSNBC Staff, February 16, 2001, *www.msnbc.com/news/531305.asp.*

6. Spain's economy has grown so fast since it joined the EU that it requires immigration to fill all the jobs. Indeed, when Spain introduced a tougher immigration law in January 2001, labor and business groups alike protested, since it was interpreted as an obstacle to continued economic growth. See "Protests in Spain as New Immigration Law Begins," Reuters.com, January 23, 2001.

7. Speech delivered April 10, 2002.

8. Interviews in April 2002.

9. Ibid.

10. Private communication, March 2002.

11. Environmentalists opposed the construction of the new airport, pointing out that wetlands would be endangered. All other alternatives, however, are unworkable. As it stands now, the airport in Toluca is used for cargo and freight air transportation; there is simply not enough space within the Valley of Mexico for infrastructure projects requiring significant acreage.

12. Interview April 2002. Despite "every care" being taken, farmers slated to be displaced by the $2.3 billion airport protested in July 2002, taking officials hostage, blocking roads, and underscoring the challenges of the resolving conflicting interests and rights as the nation develops. The government capitulated to NIMBY activism sweeping Mexico, as it does increasingly as it becomes more like the United States. While many civic groups praised the decision to relocate Mexico City's new airport as evidence of the Fox administration's sensitivity to local communities, others disagreed. Political analyst Denise Dresser dismissed such an interpretation. "What this demonstrates is that there is no one in this administration who is willing to risk political capital and jump into the fray for something that the country really needs. At the first sign of resistance the government steps back, saying that it's democratic when really it's just ineffectual," she said.

13. But in a measure of the entrenched corruption under the PRI, Gerardo de Prevoisin was forced to resign in 1994 after certain irregularities were alleged. Upon further scrutiny, tens of millions of dollars were found missing, a scandal that became more embarrassing when Mr. de Prevoisin revealed, from his native France to which he had fled, that he had been "coerced" by PRI party officials to contribute millions of dollars to the then-ruling party's coffers for campaign expenses.

14. "Commercialization is good for airlines; it's not good for air traffic controllers," Marc Baumgartner, president of the International Federation of Air Traffic Controllers, and a controller in Geneva, Switzerland, said, after that country's privatized air traffic control system was blamed for an accident that killed scores when a Russian passenger jetliner and a DHL® cargo plane crashed mid-air in the summer of 2002.

15. *Lloyd Mexican Economic Report,* April 2002.

16. Interviews in April 2002.

17. The first phase of the Puebla-Panama Plan, announced in March 2001, consists of a $433 million infrastructure program in the southern Mexican states of Puebla, Oaxaca, and Chiapas. See "Fox Plans Southern Mexico Boost," Associated Press, March 13, 2001.

18. In the development of Central American nations, Mexico continues to be a leader. Belize, for instance, is dependent on Mexico for electricity. During the conflicts that engulfed the region, Mexico led peace efforts, has provided subsidized oil as a form of foreign aid, and provided sanctuary to more than 250,000 Guatemalan Maya people during the decades-long civil conflicts. Indeed, even when development plans are threatened, Mexico remains steadfast in offering assistance. See "Upbeat Plan for a Dam in Belize Turns Nasty," by David González, *New York Times,* March 2, 2001.

19. Press conference, March 2002.

20. For more information, see "U.S. and Mexico Coordinate Efforts for Mutual Protection," by Tim Weiner, *New York Times,* March 23, 2003.

21. "A Fast Track for Mexico" by Fernando Margain and Walter Russell Mead, *New York Times,* June 24, 2001.

22. For more information on the Border Summits, see *Bordersummit.com.*

23. "Shine NAFTA's Light on the Darker Corners," by Robert A. Pastor, *Los Angeles Times,* February 15, 2001.

24. *http://www.edc.ca/docs/Country/Economics/Commentary/w04-10-2002_e.htm.*

25. See Remarks of the Federal Reserve Board, Texas Trade Corridors New Economy Conference, held on August 3, 2001 in San Antonio, Texas. In a measure of the denial that characterizes the thinking of American officials, Governor Edward M. Gramlich said, "The lesson to be learned by the United States, by Mexico, and indeed by all countries, is that the role of government in infrastructure investment may be more subtle than one might have thought. There may still be some industries in which government should actually invest physical capital."

26. Ibid. Gramlich concedes that what has proved historically successful for the United States may very well be what NAFTA requires: "Historically, it seems clear that infrastructure investment has been crucial to the process of economic development in America. In our nation's earliest days, construction of canals and turnpikes, followed by construction of railroads in the first half of the nineteenth century, greatly increased the

prospects for trade and development. Large-scale investment in electricity and telephone networks near the turn of the last century facilitated the development of a broad spectrum of innovations that, after a time, significantly improved the productivity of America's workers. From this overall picture, it seems that infrastructure is important to growth."

27. *Lloyd Mexican Economic Report,* April 2002.

28. Andres Duany, Elizabeth Plater-Zyberk, and Jeff Speck, *Suburban Nation: The Rise of Sprawl and the Decline of the American Dream,* North Point Press, pages 107-108.

29. Ibid.

30. Personal communication, May 2002.

31. Paul Tillich, *A History of Christian Thought: From its Judaic and Hellenistic Origins to Existentialism.* Simon & Shuster, 1967, page 211.

32. Robert Putnam, *Bowling Alone: The Collapse and Revival of American Community,* Touchstone, page 212.

33. Duany, et al., *Suburban Nation,* page 158.

34. Robert Putnam, *Bowling Alone: The Collapse and Revival of American Community,* pages 208–210.

35. "Report: More than Ever, Traffic Jams Waste Time," *Cnn.com,* June 20, 2002.

36. Putnam, *Bowling Alone,* page 407.

37. In his State of the Union address in 1956, Eisenhower stated his commitment to a national highway system by noting that, "Legislation to provide a modern, interstate highway system is even more urgent this year than last, for 12 months have now passed in which we have fallen further behind in road construction needed for the personal safety, the general prosperity, the national security of the American people. During the year, the number of motor vehicles has increased from 58 to 61 million. During the past year over 38,000 persons lost their lives in highway accidents, while the fearful toll of injuries and property damage has gone on unabated. In my message of February 22, 1955, I urged that measures be taken to complete the vital 40,000 mile interstate system over a period of 10 years at an estimated Federal cost of approximately 25 billion dollars. No program was adopted. If we are ever to solve our mounting traffic problem, the whole interstate system must be authorized as one project, to be completed approximately within the specified time. Only in this way can industry efficiently gear itself to the job ahead. Only in this way can the required planning and engineering be accomplished without the confusion and waste unavoidable in a piecemeal approach. Furthermore, as I pointed out last year, the pressing nature of this problem must not lead us to solutions outside the bounds of sound fiscal management. As in the case of other pressing problems, there must be an adequate plan of financing. To continue the drastically needed improvement in other national highway systems, I recommend the continuation of the Federal Aid Highway Program."

38. The lessons learned during the first half century of America's national interstate highway system must be applied as the United States, Canada, and Mexico embark on an international program to link their highway and railroad systems, a project with an estimated $60 billion price tag over the next quarter century.

39. Putnam, *Bowling Alone,* page 213.

40. "My Beautiful Mansionette," by Paul Krugman, *New York Times,* May 23, 2001.

41. "Making No Little Plans in Guadalajara" by Clifford Pearson, *Architectural Record,* February 20, 2001.

42. "A Mexican City's Middle-Class Transformation," by Jill Leovy, *Los Angeles Times,* February 18, 2001.

43. Ibid.

44. Personal communication, March 2001.

45. Duany, et al., *Suburban Nation,* pages 107–108.

46. As quoted by Putnam *Bowling Alone,* page 210.

47. "A Mexican City's Middle-Class Transformation," by Jill Leovy, *Los Angeles Times,* February 18, 2001.

48. "New Urbanism: Condensing the American Dream," by Peter Calthorpe, *www.cnn.com/specials/2000/democracy/sprawl/views/index.html.*

49. "Chasing Mexico's Dream into Squalor," by Ginger Thompson, *New York Times,* February 11, 2001.

50. Ibid.

51. "Across the Borders of History: Tijuana and San Diego Exchange Futures" by Richard Rodriguez, *Harper's,* March 1987.

52. "Changes in World Economy on Raw Materials May Doom Many Towns," by Peter Kilborn, *New York Times,* February 16, 2002.

53. *The Good Society,* John Kenneth Galbraith, page 11.

54. "Chasing Mexico's Dream into Squalor," by Ginger Thompson, *New York Times,* February 11, 2001.

55. Ibid.

56. Quoted in "Chasing Mexico's Dream into Squalor."

57. Duany, et al., *Suburban Nation,* page 4.

58. "Once Again, the City Beckons," by Kenneth T. Jackson, *New York Times,* March 30, 2001.

59. Here is one example. Given that job creation along the border has far outstripped the ability of Mexico's Infonavit to provide adequate housing to the newly-employed multitudes, this is a splendid opportunity for American manufacturers of mobile homes to enter the Mexican market. Mobile homes are economical housing that can be easily assembled into parks. Though by definition not permanent housing, officials at Infonavit have expressed "tremendous interest" in seeing if the temporary housing needs of thousands of Mexicans working at maquiladoras could be met through mobile homes.

60. "Can Fox Make Mexico a Nation of Homeowners?" by Elizabeth Malkin, *Business Week,* January 22, 2001. Malkin succinctly summed up the challenges: "A key goal of the reforms is to bolster Mexico's anemic mortgage market, which now revolves almost entirely around government-financed programs targeted at the lower classes. Members of the middle class, in contrast, have been unable to get bank mortgages since the December 1994 peso devaluation, which sparked a massive wave of debt defaults." Here, then, one sees how Mexican Paternalism's role in the lives of Mexicans decreases as their household income increases.

# 5

# The Integration of Financial Services

## EXECUTIVE ABSTRACT

The devaluation of the Mexican peso in December 1994 precipitated a banking crisis of historic proportions. To stave off a financial meltdown, Mexico was forced to implement a $100 billion rescue package and to accelerate the opening of its banking sector. The first measure preserved the country's financial liquidity, saving both the banks and the public's savings, an accomplishment in itself.[1] The second measure, more controversial, has resulted in foreign domination of Mexico's banking sector. Spanish, Canadian, and American banks have acquired all of Mexico's major banks. Citigroup's acquisition of Banamex in a $12.5 billion transaction in May 2001 is remarkable for both its size and the little controversy it sparked for Mexicans. The banking mergers and acquisitions during NAFTA's first decade, moreover, have strengthened the financial networks that link Mexico, the United States, and Canada. With more than $300 billion in annual trade taking place among the three NAFTA nations, and with the continuing challenge of detecting and controlling money laundering, estimated to exceed $100 billion, it is imperative that a more seamless integration of banking and financial services unfold. Newfound opportunities are emerging as Mexicans living and working in the United States become more affluent and seek greater banking services. With an estimated collective purchasing power exceeding $600 billion, it is expected that by 2005, more than $16 billion will be remitted to Mexico, a 50 percent increase from the level recorded at the end of 2002. Within Mexico there are significant opportunities. The market for individual savings and investments among Mexican consumers is estimated to be $65 billion. A tantalizing opportunity for capital formation is found in the $315 billion that the Institute for Liberty and Democracy (ILD) estimates can be created by bringing the extralegal economy into the formal economy, a process that entails simply titling hitherto untitled assets.[2]

## DISCUSSION

Mexico's banking and financial services sector is poised for sustained growth and continued integration. A stable exchange rate and low inflation under the leadership of Guillermo Ortiz, Mexico's central banker (whose calm reaction to the crisis precipitated by the December 1994 devaluation astounded many), have given the Mexican peso new credibility, despite reversals throughout 2002 in Argentina and Brazil. Sustained economic growth and the infusion of billions of dollars from foreign investment have, furthermore, raised reserves to record levels as Mexico's middle class continues to strengthen. The stability of the Mexican economy has made Mexican bonds—government and that of certain companies—investment grade.

Three other factors bode well for Mexico's finances. The country's free-trade agreement with the European Union is nurturing closer economic and financial ties with European nations, particularly Spain and France. Of equal importance is the economic and political ascendance of Mexicans living in the United States.[3] "The Anglo hegemony was only an intermittent phase in California's arc of identity, extending from the arrival of the Spanish," Kevin Starr, state librarian and author of cultural histories of California, said. "The Hispanic nature of California has been there all along, and it was temporarily swamped between the 1880's and the 1960's. But that was an aberration. This [Census 2000 report] is a reassertion of the intrinsic demographic DNA of the longer pattern, which is part of a California-Mexico continuum."[4] At home, if the Fox administration implements an aggressive program to title hitherto untitled assets possessed by Mexico's poor, capital formation can be accelerated, ensuring that hundreds of billions of dollars benefit the economic growth of the most disenfranchised.[5] Each of these developments offers opportunities that were inconceivable a decade ago. Let us now turn to them.

## Expanding Banking and Financial Services

While critics have called the aggressive takeover of Mexico's financial sector by Spanish banks "the reconquest of Mexico," the economic ascendance of Spain's BBVA® (Banco Bilbao Vizcaya) and Santander® is more than profiteering by acquiring distressed properties. When José Sevilla, the financial director for Latin America at BBVA, boasted that the "market has rewarded our investment in Latin America," some Mexicans were not amused. "Since 1995, the shares of BBVA have increased sevenfold," a contributor to the left-of-center news weekly *Proceso* noted. "Is this due to BBVA's business savvy—or a measure of how cheaply Latin Americans have been sold out?"[6]

Perhaps, but as any investor understands too well, in business there are no guarantees, as BBVA found out when its Argentine banks came under pressure in 2002.[7] But Mexico is not Argentina, as far as Spanish banks are concerned.[8] Mexico's free-trade agreements with both the European Union and its North American neighbors are a unique advantage. This European view was substantiated when London-based HSBC Holdings® acquired Bital®, Mexico's fifth-largest bank, in August 2002 in a deal valued at $1.14 billion. Coming just over two years after Canada's Scotia Bank purchased Inverlat, this deal gave the English a significant stake in NAFTA's future.[9] Nonetheless, it was Spain's BBVA's takeover of Bancomer®, the most prestigious of Mexico's banks, that gave this Spanish bank an entrée into the United States market by recognizing that AMAs, or Americans of Mexican ancestry, normally referred to as "Hispanics" or "Latinos," represent an enormous market.

"Mexicans in the United States now sending money transfers will be seeking credit cards, insurance or a house next year, or the next. We have analyzed all this and we are now at the stage of drawing up a business project for this market. I cannot tell how much of this market we will capture, but Hispanics in the United States are demanding greater banking services," Vitalino Nafria, BBVA Bancomer CEO, said. "To this end, BBVA is taking its time on coming up with an adequate strategy to gain market share in California, Illinois and Texas. We have to make sure we choose the right strategies for serving the financial needs of Hispanics in these markets. We are still deciding whether it would better to have a bank that serves certain ethnic markets, in this case U.S. Hispanics, or whether it is better to serve everyone in a given community. It certainly is an exhilarating opportunity for Bancomer and BBVA. Bancomer is a valuable brand for Mexicans in the United States, and that brand recognition would be a tremendous advantage for BBVA Bancomer expansion in the United States. For us, the border between Mexico and the United States is linguistic: if you live anywhere in North America and you speak Spanish, then you are our potential customer because you are part of the market we serve."[10]

This is not lost on corporate America, however late it may have been to identify opportunities in the Mexican market. "Today's announcement represents Citigroup's commitment to Mexico and to the belief in the potential of this country, to the belief in the further integration of Mexico and the U.S. economy, and to the grander vision of the North American economy," Robert E. Rubin, Citigroup Vice Chairman, said at a news conference when the purchase of Banamex was announced on May 17, 2001. "Mexico will have a world-class banking system which, for all practical purposes, is invulnerable to shocks. . . . In my view, the vision of NAFTA—the vision of these two countries being inextricably linked together economically—is a vision that is now well advanced."[11]

Wall Street hailed the move, noting that Citigroup was purposefully moving to expand banking services south of the border. As "NAFTA helps transform Mexico into an export economy attracting escalating levels of fixed investment in factories and equipment, economists say a strong peso is more a sign of Mexico's underlying economic health than a speculative boom. And the peso might well be stronger still if the central bank hadn't added to its foreign-exchange reserves by buying up many of the dollars streaming in from skittish investors fleeing other Latin American markets," Peter Fritsch reported in the *Wall Street Journal*.[12]

The acquisition of Banamex represented a strategic competitive advantage for Citigroup south of the border. With the acquisition of Banamex, Citigroup suddenly became the leading corporate bank, consumer bank, and issuer of credit cards in Mexico. It would be incomplete, however, to neglect certain market opportunities north of the border that provided certain incentives. "There is a large Hispanic economy in the U.S., which we can reach out to through Banamex. The G.D.P. of that population may be as much as 80 percent of Mexico's G.D.P," or about $500 billion, Robert Rubin elaborated when Citigroup's acquisition of Banamex was announced. "American Hispanics familiar with the Banamex brand are now our potential customers as well."[13] The market is the more tantalizing when one considers that, by 2010, Hispanic-Americans in the U.S. are expected to control almost $1 trillion in purchasing power.[14]

Banamex's management experience in the U.S. market—the company owns California Commerce Bank®, long favored by Mexico's elite for business and commercial financial services in the United States—stands to benefit the integration of consumer marketing plans. Wall Street analysts saw this as a win-win situation. "Citigroup was able to acquire the best banking franchise in Mexico. Banamex gains the Citigroup's funding advantage and wide product mix, and Citigroup gains a dominant position in a fertile banking market," Brent Erensel (at Deutsche Banc Alex Brown) told reporters.[15]

Indeed, Citigroup's acquisition of Banamex underscores how large Spanish banks loom over the horizon—and over the border. "This is not just about growth of the Mexican market but the fast growth of the Hispanic population in the U.S.," Citigroup Chairman Sanford I. Weill said. "Together I think we can go after that market."[16] The true competition emerging in Mexico in NAFTA's second decade is thus defined. Domestically, Spanish, American, and Canadian banks will compete for the growing middle class. As we shall discuss below, the significant part of this strategy consists in competing for Mexicans' savings and in providing investment opportunities as capital formation increases the economy's total resources. A more intriguing possibility emerges as NAFTA enters its second decade.

It would be wrong for Americans to discount the marketing prowess of the Spaniards. When BBVA acquired Bancomer in July 2000, the latter had a market capitalization of a mere $4.5 billion. Less than two years after the masterful management, however, Bancomer's market capitalization surpassed the $11 billion mark. Citigroup management will have to deliver superior results if it can approximate a similar turnaround in Banamex's finances in such an abbreviated time frame. A competitive struggle for the Mexican consumer is sure to occur on both sides of the border as Spain's BBVA, through the Bancomer brand, and America's Citigroup, through the Banamex brand, seek to establish both these brands throughout the United States, particularly in the Texas, California, and Midwest markets.

Legal reforms making it easier for banks to repossess collateral on defaults must be made stronger; banks' continued reluctance to lend remains an impediment to economic growth. "In December 2000, according to Moody's Investors Service®, the level of lending by banks in Mexico to the private sector was 19.7

percent of gross domestic product, way behind that in the United States (71.5 percent), Chile (64.4 percent) and Brazil (34.2 percent), though it did beat Venezuela (13.4 percent)," Elisabeth Malkin reported. "And the comparison has changed little since then."[17] Banks need to expand their financial services—and start lending—if small and medium-sized businesses are to thrive. And banks must become a proactive part of economic growth if Mexico's middle class is to prosper.

## Opportunities in Mexicans' Private Savings and Investments

The Retirement Savings System, or SAR, was reformed under the Zedillo administration as a way of giving Mexicans—rank-and-file union workers, government employees, and middle-class professionals—greater investment options. During the second half of the 1990s, Mexicans—astounded at the record-breaking pace of record highs on Wall Street during a period of "irrational exuberance" and outrageous bamboozling of the world's investors during the Internet mania—wanted to change the kinds of investments permitted under Mexican law for retirement accounts. Not unlike the ongoing debate in Washington about granting individuals the right to determine how their contributions to the Social Security system are invested, Mexican officials looked for successful models around the world for increasing the savings rate of Mexican consumers—and their investment options.[18]

Mindful of the obstacles other nations have suffered, Mexican officials have been cautious, so much so that impatient Mexicans have been critical. Prudence is in order, of course, particularly in emerging markets. Mexican officials point to Argentina's disastrous experiment in privatizing its pension funds as a cautionary tale of why privatized pensions should not be allowed to invest in stock markets, or in high-risk instruments. Every dollar Argentines invested through the Retired and Pension Fund Administrators, known as AFJPs, since the mid-1990s has been reduced to a few pennies. Apart from the collapse of the Argentine economy beginning in December 2001, analysts point to the exorbitant management fees charged by the administering institutions. "They were used first as a way for banks to make enormous profits," Christopher Ecclestone, an analyst for the Buenos Aires Trust®, reported. "It was totally outrageous. These high fees reduced the capital-formation of the funds, and when the crisis emerged, they collapsed."[19]

Argentina's experience stands in contrast to successes in

neighboring Chile. Through a program of prudent investment during a period of sustained growth, privatized funds in Chile have delivered almost a 10 percent annual return for more than a decade. Chile, in fact, constitutes a role model for Mexico to emulate, particularly now that American, Spanish, and Canadian capital continues to strengthen the nation's financial system. "Perhaps Chile's most remarkable achievement has been to create a vibrant, domestic pension fund industry," Tarun Khanna and Krishna Palepu report in the *Harvard Business Review.* "In 1981, the government formed 12 institutional investors, or Administradoras de Fondos de Pensiones (AFP), and passed a law requiring all taxpayers to invest a certain percentage of their monthly earnings in a fund of their choice. The AFPs proved such a success that the government created more funds in 1986 and in 1992."[20]

Chile's example intrigues because not only was it the first privatized national pension program since the Great Depression, but also it remains among the most successful. "This is something novel and very interesting, in the sense that this is a system based primarily on individual savings," Jürgen Weller, an economist at the headquarters of the United Nations' Economic Commission for Latin America and the Caribbean, told an interviewer. "Its success obviously depends on the performance of the Chilean economy, but there is no denying that they have come up with a creative approach that is going to be of interest to others."[21] The nature of Mexico's banking—where millions of the poor and working poor are excluded—poses its own set of challenges. The expansion of banking and financial services must include strategies designed to bring banking services to millions of Mexican households that have never had access to formal financial institutions. This process of enfranchising the poor and working poor is not glamorous; most bankers would rather wine and dine billionaires than participate in community outreach programs to teach adults how a checking account works.

The cumulative purchasing power of the poor, however, is not insignificant. As Hernando de Soto reported in his analysis of the assets controlled by Mexico's poor, this sum exceeds $300 billion. It may not be glamorous, but it is enormous. It is, however, imperative that Mexico launch a campaign to enfranchise millions of Mexicans currently excluded from formal banking services if this unproductive "capital" is to be put to sound economic use. "This system is something that could work even better and more efficiently in a country like Brazil or Mexico," German Azevedo, the director of the government commission setting up the plan to further privatize Chile's pension funds, argued. "The bigger the labor market and the capital market, the better."[22]

If Mexico can look to Chile to see how a national pension and savings program is successfully privatized, then it can look to the United States to see how community outreach programs successfully bring banking services to disadvantaged communities. Indeed, how Mexican banks develop this market and pursue opportunities in this decade could very well be modeled on successful strategies pursued by American banks in reaching out to inner-city communities. Comparing the swank neighborhood of Pacific Palisades in Los Angeles with the impoverished South Central a few miles away, Larry Fondation, Peter Tufano, and Patricia Walker write in the *Harvard Business Review* that "[t]he banks, mutual fund vendors, insurance agents, and securities dealers taken for granted in Pacific Palisades are notably absent in South Central. There, the financial service sector is made up of check-cashing outlets, rent-to-own stores, pawn shops, and auto title shops." The authors continue:[23]

> By definition, the resources of any one household or family are meager in poor neighborhoods. Both income and savings lack scale. That's why financial institutions do not find it cost-effective to market or service small customers. But pooling makes the collective investments of low income families attractive to financial service firms. A single investor with $500 does not warrant much attention; 20,000 such investors collectively wield $10 million.
>
> Many basic financial services in South Central could be made available or improved by combining small transactions. Consider the thousands of residents who wire money to relatives in Central America each month. The costs of these wire transfers are steep: one person pays $15 to wire just $200. . . .
>
> Yet, suppose a church—or better still, a network of churches—approached a fund management company or a bank's fund group with 10,000 potential investors willing to invest an aggregate $5 million. At this scale, serving those investors becomes an economic possibility. For a start, the company avoids the cost of obtaining all those new accounts—not a trivial savings when you consider that the costs of distribution typically consume half the fees charged by providers. In our plan, churches could also help to further reduce costs by taking on administrative chores such as en-

tering data and collecting money—perhaps after services on Sunday. We see churches as instigating the move toward adopting electronic account handling. Finally, by providing ongoing financial education to their parishioners, churches could motivate their congregations to save more.[24]

Though enormous discrepancies between the services available to the middle class and to the working poor are starkly clear, they are not insurmountable obstacles to building successful banking relationships. If Mexico is to increase its savings rate, and if pension plans are to be privatized in a successful manner, expanding banking and financial services and enfranchising millions of Mexican households represent clear opportunities.

## Titling Hitherto Untitled Assets and Capital Formation

"In Mexico alone, according to our research," Hernando de Soto, author of *The Mystery of Capital,* reported, "the poor today own assets worth $315 billion, seven times the value of Pemex, the nation's oil monopoly."[25] This analysis confirms the observation that the poor remain poor simply because they do not have clear and free titles to the assets that they do possess. "They are not as poor as you think," the London *Economist* concurred. "People in poor countries have assets—lots of them. But because they rarely have formal title, they cannot use these assets as collateral to raise cash."[26] That Mexico's underclass lacks access to render creditworthy in a market economy what they possess denies the Mexican economy an astounding amount of capital; if a person had title to the land on which he lives, however humble it may be, it nonetheless constitutes "real" property, and an asset.

"To explain these [developing] countries' underground economies, in which typically 50 to 80 percent of the people operate, in terms of tax evasion is partially incorrect at best. Most people do not resort to the extralegal sector because it is a tax haven but because existing law, however elegantly written, does not address their needs or aspirations," Hernando de Soto explains. "Extralegal businesses [therefore] are taxed by the lack of good property law and continually having to hide their operations from the authorities. Because they are not incorporated, extralegal entrepreneurs cannot lure investors by selling shares; they cannot secure low-interest formal credit because they do not even have legal addresses. They cannot reduce risks by declaring limited liability or obtaining insurance coverage. The only 'insurance' available to them is that provided by their neighbors and the protection that local bullies or mafias are willing to sell them. Moreover, because these extralegal entrepreneurs live in constant fear of government detection and extortion from corrupt officials, they are forced to split and compartmentalize their production between many locations, thereby rarely achieving important economies of scale."[27]

The Mexican National Statistics Institute, or Inegi, estimated that when NAFTA first went into effect in 1994, there were 2.65 million extralegal businesses; 150,000 of these businesses were street vendors in Mexico City. These millions of "mom and pop" operations constitute billions of dollars in assets that are excluded from the nation's formal capital markets. By being excluded from loans, titles to their assets, and a stake in society, millions of small businesses in the Mexican economy are being denied billions in resources that can be realized through the multiplier effect. Impediments to development are not limited to street vendors, of course. Consider the problems in redeveloping Alameda Park, located a few blocks from Mexico's presidential palace. Once a fashionable square in the mid-twentieth century, by the 1990s it had fallen into disrepair, was somewhat seedy and dangerous, its buildings collapsing, derelicts lingering in the corners. Plans by Canada's Paul Reichmann and the Zedillo administration to renew the square, building a state-of-the-art office and hotel complex, were complicated by the disarray in which the deeds to the properties, some centuries old, were found. Slanders of title, deeds in names of people who had long since died, liens, and incomplete records were the least of their problems. The tumultuous nature of human affairs has resulted in millions of people being unable to leverage their property for the lack of clear and free titles to it.

What this suggests is that this is an opportune moment for the Fox administration to establish a national program to expand property rights by giving people titles to what they already own. The "regularization" of real estate, homes, and businesses is the most efficient—and rational—way of ushering into the "formal" economy the multitudes that are disenfranchised. "If we could title what people presently owned we could triple the number of taxpayers," an official at Hacienda, Mexico's Treasury Department, said. Indeed, in what could best be called the "De Soto Program," the Mexican economy could benefit handsomely from the multiplier effect that arises when people are given deeds and titles that then give them access to credit. The institutional mechanisms are already in place; Inegi and Hacienda would launch a nationwide program to enfranchise millions of business and families throughout the country.

The United States increased its wealth during its nation building through homesteads by bringing tracts of wilderness into the realm of private property within the framework of codified laws. Mexico's Fox should use his term in office as a historic opportunity to standardize property rights, rectify slanders of title, and deed all real property through the implementation of the program proposed by Hernando de Soto. The total cost of a nationwide campaign to title hitherto untitled assets would be $38 million and would bring hundreds of billions of dollars to Mexico's financial system. This would, in effect, bring millions into the formal economy, increase the creditworthy assets of the nation, and help lift millions out of poverty.

## Opportunities in the Remittance Market

It is not unexpected that the Mexicans who migrate illegally to the United States are poor people who, without means or a college education, can only hope to sell their labor. It is also not surprising that of the millions of Mexican laborers working in the United States few have bank accounts, or are knowledgeable about international financial transactions. It is to be expected, therefore, that predatory pricing is the norm in the services provided to these unsophisticated consumers. But while Mexican laborers send only a few hundred dollars to their families at any given time, the entire remittance market approximates $11 billion in 2003. [28] "Remittances are Mexico's third-largest source of income, after oil exports and tourism. In much of rural Mexico remittances exceed local and state budgets," Ginger Thompson reported from Chicago.[29]

The nature of remittances is changing, however. As Mexican workers in the U.S. become more sophisticated and politically active, they have begun to fund economic development projects in their hometowns. "In addition to individuals sending money to their families, Salvadorans and Mexicans are increasingly coming together in American cities to send back funds for public infrastructure works, usually through a hometown association," the *New York Times* observed in an editorial. "President Vicente Fox of Mexico has started some innovative matching programs for such funds, and the Inter-American Development Bank is looking to do the same elsewhere in the region. Other experimental programs are aimed at helping migrants finance businesses they could return to, in an attempt to address the absence of economic opportunity that drives emigration in the first place."[30]

Of course, financial institutions have identified this market—and some have worked dishonestly to exploit the most vulnerable consumers, particularly where international transactions are concerned. "For many years until now, whenever customers charged something overseas using cards such as Visa and MasterCard, included in their purchase was a 1% foreign currency conversion fee, no matter who the issuing bank was behind the card," Christopher Reynolds warned Californians in the *Los Angeles Times'* Travel section. "These new fees, however, come on top of that 1% and are charged by the issuing bank, rather than the card company. . . . The move has been denounced by consumer advocates, from the editors of the Consumer Reports Travel Letter to travel guru Arthur Frommer."[31]

Mexican migrants don't have consumer advocates on their side. As a consequence, predatory pricing, exorbitant fee charges, and usurious interest rates have diminished their purchasing power; fees reaching 15 percent of what they send to their families are not unheard of, shocking considering that consumer advocates denounce a 2 percent surcharge for most American consumers. The abuses have been so egregious that many Mexican migrants have resorted to informal systems, similar to the *hawala* commonly used in the Middle East and Southeast Asia, to move funds from the U.S. to their families in Mexico.[32]

At the same time, the Mexican government has been forced to intervene to protect the consumer rights of their nationals. "Without admitting liability, [Western Union® and MoneyGram®] two industry leaders recently settled suits over the cost of sending money to Mexico by giving discount coupons to customers and making big contributions to Mexican-American community groups in the United States," Tim Weiner reported.[33] In the United States, greater scrutiny is also forcing changes. "A flurry of class-action consumer lawsuits alleging the companies charged steep hidden fees to customers wiring money to Mexico [has forced changes at MoneyGram]," Lee Romney wrote in the *Los Angeles Times.* "The majority of the lawsuits were settled . . . but they nevertheless damaged public relations."[34]

To its credit, the Fox administration is also moving forward with proactive measures to protect the purchasing power of Mexican migrants. "Mexican officials have also negotiated with banks and wire transfer agencies in the United States to make it easier and cheaper for immigrants to send money home. Beginning in

December [2002] some 15 banking institutions with branches from Los Angeles to Delaware agreed to allow immigrants from Mexico, whether in this country legally or not, to use identification cards they receive from Mexican consulates to open bank accounts," Ginger Thompson reports. "The accounts will allow immigrants to send ATM cards to relatives back home, so rather than spending $25 to send $200 at a typical money transfer counter, immigrants can give their families access to funds in the United States for about $3 per transaction"[35]

These exorbitant profits generated by exploiting Mexicans in the United States is one reason why BBVA's Bancomer and Citigroup's Banamex are gearing to enter the market. A measure of the potential of this market is seen when a concerted program of education and outreach is carried out. At the initiative of Mexican consular personnel in Oxnard, California, an agricultural community near the upscale community of Santa Barbara, Bank of America® was invited to help migrants open bank accounts. In recent years, as Mexican migrants have prospered, many have been subjected to robberies. Some hide their money in their bedrooms, under their mattresses, or in boxes, and burglaries while they are working in the fields are not uncommon. The average savings range from $3,000 to $4,000, a considerable sum. "Mexican officials said that during three weeks in December [2001] in Oxnard, Calif. some 12,000 new accounts were opened, averaging about $3,500 each. Officials at Bank of America estimated that new accounts had generated $50 million for financial institutions across California."[36] Consider how these simple initiatives challenge perceptions and popular views: a Mexican migrant has about seven times the savings of an American resident living in an inner-urban neighborhood. Bank of America officials were, of course, delighted to have these new account holders.

These small initiatives to defend the "consumer rights" of otherwise disenfranchised Mexican workers in the United States are all nice, and these stories are endearing. Remittances, however, are a multibillion-dollar industry, and they should be treated accordingly. It must be organized in a more efficient manner, one that does not rely on the kindness of community credit unions, church groups, human rights organizations, and low-level diplomats scattered around the country in an ad hoc manner. (A more sophisticated approach was taken recently by Nacional Financiera, Nafin, which, in cooperation with the U.S. Small Business Administration, established a "bi-national risk capital investment fund" to allow Hispanic business investors living in the U.S.

to invest in Mexico.[37]) If BBVA's Bancomer and Citigroup's Banamex are to make inroads, however, they must understand this consumer.

Since Mexican migrants in the U.S. are the same Mexicans who are denied banking services in Mexico, it is not a given that officials at either Bancomer or Banamex "understand" this client. To understand the remittance market, one has to understand the client's history and his or her aspirations. Consider Rose del Castillo Guilbault's experience growing up in the United States. Born in California to Mexican immigrants, she has built a distinguished career for herself, rising to the position of Editorial Director for the local ABC-affiliate television station in San Francisco, and currently the Vice President of Corporate Communications and Public Affairs for the California State Automobile Association.

She describes the mixed messages that characterize her family history in this manner:

> I watched my own father struggle with these cultural ambiguities. He worked on a farm for 20 years. He laid down miles of irrigation pipe, carefully plowed long, neat rows in fields, hacked away at recalcitrant weeds and drove tractors through whirlpools of dust. He stoically worked 20 hour days during harvest season, accepting the long hours as part of agricultural work. When the boss complained or upbraided him for minor mistakes, he kept quiet, even when it was obvious the boss had erred.
>
> He handled the most menial tasks with pride. At home he was a good provider, helped my mother's family in Mexico without complaint, and was indulgent with me. Arguments between my mother and him generally had to do with money, or his stubborn reluctance to share his troubles. He tried to work them out in his own silence. He didn't want to trouble my mother—a course that backfired, because the imagined is always worse than the reality.
>
> Americans regarded my father as decidedly [weak]. His character was interpreted as non-assertive, his loyalty as non-ambition, and his quietness as ignorance. I once overheard the boss's son blame him for plowing crooked rows in a field. My father merely smiled at the lie, knowing the boy had done it, but didn't refute it, confident his good work was well-known. But the boss instead ridiculed him for being "stupid" letting a kid get away with a lie. Seeing my embar-

rassment, my father dismissed the incident, saying, "They're the dumb ones. Imagine, me fighting with a kid."

I tried not to look at him with American eyes because sometimes the reflection hurt.[38]

Rose del Castillo Guilbault remembers her father's experience, which was of an honest way making an honest living and raising his family with pride and dignity in the United States during the 1950s and 1960s, when the *bracero* program was in place and Mexicans were taken for granted. The Mexican migrant of the 2000s has similar experiences, aspirations—and banking needs.

In a sign that American financial institutions now understand the opportunities available in a single "Mexican" market that is not defined by international borders, Bank of America spent $1.6 billion in cash to acquire 24.9 percent of Grupo Financiero Santander Serfin® in December 2002. "Bank of America says it will compete with Citigroup for Mexican and Mexican-American customers in the United States," Tim Weiner reported, signaling the emergence of a single North American Hispanic market.[39] That Spain's Santander Central Hispano® sold a portion of its stake is intriguing, for it heralds the entrance of European financial institutions into the U.S. market by way of Mexico. Acknowledging that Bank of America sought to—in the phrase of chairman and CEO Kenneth Lewis—"dramatically increase our market share" of the remittance market between the United States and Mexico, this development validates the quiet determination of an older generation of Mexican immigrants to the United States, best exemplified by Rose del Castillo Guilbault's father.[40] The purchase also underscores how the industry dynamics for Western Union and American Express MoneyGram have changed in fundamental ways after the Mexican government negotiated a reduction in the fees charged consumers for remittance services.[41]

In addition to the established banks, a new, Mexican-owned financial institution entered the consumer banking market. Banco Azteca®, a joint venture between Grupo Elektra®, the consumers goods and electronics retailer, and TV Azteca, Mexico's second-largest network, joined forces to bring banking services to millions of working-class Mexican families that have long been excluded from the financial system. Banco Azteca, the first Mexican-owned franchise licensed by the Finance Ministry since 1994, is evidence of the economic ascendance of Mexico's working-class families. "A major impediment to the growth of the Mexican middle class has been the lack of access to credit, one of the main vehicles for personal financial improvement," Ricardo Salinas Pliego, Grupo Elektra's chairman, told reporters in October 2002.[42]

With branches in Elektra stores, Banco Azteca opened for business in the fall of 2002 with 815 branch offices. Working similarly to the way consumer credit unions do in the United States, Banco Azteca required a minimum of 50 pesos, or about $5 U.S., to open an account, thus enfranchising millions who otherwise would never have qualified for opening a checking account at a major bank. Within the first six months of operation, Banco Azteca opened 1.2 million accounts, and began to make consumer loans for as much as $500 U.S. Banco Azteca, then, is developing a consumer credit model for lower-income families, a necessary step that traditional banks are reluctant to pursue. Though, with a total market capitalization of $73 million, Banco Azteca is a small bank, it nonetheless is serving a disenfranchised market, one that, armed with bank accounts, cannot only have access to consumer credit but also avoid the exorbitant fees charged on remittances. When a family in the United States deposit money into their own account, recipients in Mexico can withdraw pesos from an ATM, now that they are part of the formal banking system.

## The Unbearable Burden of Money Laundering

The Money Laundering Act of 1999 in the U.S. broadened the authority to prosecute money laundering, arms trafficking, and other "public corruption" acts. "Since NAFTA opened the doors of commerce in North America, U.S. and Mexican leaders have reveled in the growth it has spawned—fairly shouting that cross-border trade topped $200 billion [in 1999]. But NAFTA carries with it another, murkier, stream of dollars: the money from the drug trade. Dealing with tainted cash is such a profitable enterprise that U.S. banks have gotten happily in on the action," Julia Reynolds reported in the 2000, when Citibank had come under fire for its role in laundering hundreds of millions of dollars from Mexican and American citizens accused of corruption.[43]

It is estimated that as much as $100 billion was laundered through the U.S. and Mexican banking system in 2003. The magnitude of the problem is worrisome because Citibank has played a major role in allowing money laundering.[44] "[Citibank's then-CEO John] Reed failed to take decisive action after internal bank warnings for several years in the mid-1990s showed the bank was ignoring its own safeguards against money laundering, Senate investigators said yesterday," Kathleen Day reported in the *Washington Post* in November 1999. "The revelations about Reed's handling of the money-laundering issue illustrate a broader problem faced by U.S. commercial banks as they try to balance aggressive pursuit of new business against the possibility that some clients may be using the bank to hide ill-gotten gains." Indeed, Citibank private bankers, such as Amy Elliott, have been disgraced; others, such as Antonio Giraldi, were jailed. "No one seriously attempted to determine the actual origin of a client's money. Our world was all about playing the 'new deposits' game the way our management 'coaches' insisted we play it, about being rewarded by them when we 'succeeded,' and about being too naïve to realize how dangerous a game we were playing," he said in testimony before the U.S. Congress. "The money launderer has shed his or her conventional image and now wears a chameleon cloak, provided courtesy of the international private banking industry."[45] PBS's "Frontline," in fact, did an in-depth report titled, "Money, Murder & Mexico." That Reed is long gone now that Citibank is part of Citigroup should not bring automatic comfort. Sanford Weill has not addressed Citibank's complicity in money laundering directly. Citigroup Vice Chairman Robert Rubin, while at the Treasury Department, failed to consider how to correct the natural market imperfections that lead to market failures when demanding market reforms in emerging nations, with detrimental effects.[46]

Canadians have been much concerned about this problem. "In May 1998, the U.S. Customs Service linked 12 of the 19 largest Mexican banks and 112 individuals on charges of laundering millions of dollars for Latin American drug cartels. In lightning raids across the United States, dozens of suspects were arrested, including 15 Mexican bank employees and 16 members of Colombian and Mexican drug cartels. Over $100 million was forfeited, 1,754 [kilos] of cocaine and 8,000 [pounds] of marijuana were seized, and there were numerous spin-off investigations by police," Jim Lyon reported in *Canadian Banker*. "Operation Casablanca was three years in the making. Working out of a storefront in Santa Fe Springs, south of Los Angeles, undercover agents passed themselves off as experts in money laundering, advising all comers about how drug money could be channelled through companies and accounts to emerge sanitized. Ultimately, three of Mexico's largest banks were accused of knowingly aiding drug traffickers to launder hundred of millions of dollars."[47]

Citibank's euphemistic "ethical lapses," in John Reed's

favored phrase, evocatively connotes immoderation and abandon. Be that as it may, consider the aggressive marketing by other enterprising New York financial institutions in this matter. "The man accused of being a drug lord, Mario Villanueva, was governor of the state of Quintana Roo on Mexico's Caribbean coast from 1993 to 1999. During that time, prosecutors say, one of Mexico's most powerful cocaine organizations, which they called the Southeast Cartel, paid him $30 million. In return, they say, he offered the cartel the cooperation and protection of the police, and an airplane owned by the governor's office to store and transport cocaine," Benjamin Weiser reported in the *New York Times*. This was a few days after federal prosecutors in New York unsealed an indictment charging Mario Villanueva with helping to smuggle more than 200 tons of cocaine into the United States. "In March 1999, just before Mr. Villanueva was to leave office, losing immunity from prosecution in Mexico, he disappeared. It was around then, the indictment says, that the broker, Consuelo Márquez, began moving Mr. Villanueva's payoff money from Lehman Brothers' accounts to accounts harder to trace."[48] The indictment sought Mario Villanueva's extradition to the U.S. to stand trial.

Concern among the American business community was also evident. Money laundering had become a global problem, the *Wall Street Journal* opined, in an editorial titled "Money Laundering Alert." "Some of the biggest crimes of the 21st century, as we have noted in our observations on the BCCI case, will be global financial crimes. While money moves across national frontiers at the speed of light, methods of policing corruption and money laundering across borders remain back in the Stone Age."[49] Commentators have speculated that Mexico (and Canada) should adopt the U.S. dollar as the official currency. Though there are examples of Latin American nations—Panama almost a century ago, and more recently Ecuador and El Salvador—successfully adopting the U.S. dollar as their national currency, it is not likely that Mexico will replace the peso during NAFTA's second decade.[50] This is a concern, if for no other reason than that foreign exchange transactions can disguise the movement of illicit funds, though foreign exchange operations and cash transactions are not the exclusive instruments for money laundering.[51] Indeed, money laundering, now facilitated by computer-savvy criminals and criminal private bankers, is the greatest challenge to the healthy expansion of banking and financial services across the North America.

## SUMMARY

1.  From a devastating devaluation in December 1994 and a banking meltdown, under the leadership of Central Banker Guillermo Ortiz Mexico's financial sector and currency have enjoyed tremendous stability and a newfound respect.
2.  Since 1995, Spanish, American, and Canadian banks have acquired the major Mexican banks, effectively rendering Mexico's financial system on the cutting edge of globalization.
3.  Domestically, Mexico must expand banking and financial services to the middle class, particularly as pension plans are privatized. A concerted campaign to title hitherto untitled assets estimated at $315 billion—and in the process bring in millions of Mexican families and small businesses into the formal economy—is a political and economic challenge of capital formation in NAFTA's second decade.
4.  The Mexican banking brands of Banamex and Bancomer are poised to expand aggressively in the United States, hoping to tap into the estimated $1 trillion in purchasing power that will be controlled by Americans of Mexican Ancestry and other Hispanics, or AMAs, by 2010.

## A TIMELINE OF THE GLOBALIZATION OF MEXICAN BANKS

| | |
|---|---|
| May 1995 | Banco Bilbao Vizcaya (BBVA) of Spain acquires control of Banco Mercantil Probursa. |
| August 1996 | BBVA acquires the branch networks of Banca Cremi and Banco Oriente. |
| May 1997 | Santander of Spain acquires control of Inver-Mexico and Banco Mexicano. |
| August 1997 | Citibank acquires control of Banca Confia. |
| March 2000 | Scotia Bank of Canada acquires control of Grupo Financiero Inverlat. BBVA acquires 30% stake and management control of Bancomer. |
| May 2000 | Santander acquires control of Serfin, purchasing 30% equity from Britain's HSBC Holdings. |
| June 2000 | BBVA acquires control of Bancomer with a $2.4 billion capital infusion. |
| May 2001 | Citigroup acquires 100% control of Banamex for $12.5 billion, in its largest overseas acquisition to date. |

| August 2002 | London-based HSBC acquires Grupo Financiero Bital in a $1.14 billion transaction. |
| October 2002 | Banorte® remains the largest Mexican bank likely to be a takeover target by foreign banks. Banco Azteca is founded, aimed at providing banking and financial services to Mexico's working-class families. |
| December 2002 | Bank of America acquires 24.9 percent of Santander Serfin in a $1.6 billion cash deal. |

## ENDNOTES

1. Other nations have failed during similar crises. Argentina, for instance, has been unable to protect consumers' savings. The United States, too, it must remembered, failed to protect the life savings of hundreds of thousands of American investors who were victimized by the Savings and Loan scandals of the 1980s.

2. The Institute for Liberty and Democracy (IDL), founded by Hernando de Soto, has demonstrated that the process of titling hitherto untitled assets promotes capital formation and encourages economic development in all areas of economic life. For more information, see *The Mystery of Capital: Why Capitalism Triumphs in the West and Fails Everywhere Else.*

3. Indeed, consider how California became "Hispanic" in 2000. "A survey released last week of birth certificates statewide showed that for the first time since the late 1850's, just a decade after California was seized from Mexico in the Mexican-American War, a majority of newborns are Hispanic. More than two-thirds of the Hispanic babies are being born here in Los Angeles County and surrounding Southern California," Dean Murphy reported in early 2003. "The milestone, though long anticipated, carries great significance in symbolic and real terms, as Hispanics increasingly define what it means to be Californian, and American-born Hispanics assert numerical and cultural dominance over their immigrant counterparts." See "New California Identity Predicted by Researchers," by Dean Murphy, *New York Times,* February 17, 2003.

4. Kevin Starr is quoted in "California Census Confirms Whites Are a Minority," by Todd Purdum, *New York Times,* March 30, 2001.

5. This predicament is more grave in other parts of Latin America. In Brazil, for instance, communities known as *quilombos,* comprise descendants of African slaves who have few legal claims to their assets. "Since the runaway slaves were illiterate, there are no documents that would verify claims that their communities date to colonial times, and because they were fugitives, they rarely registered the births of their children," Larry Rohter reported. "The government ordered the destruction of all official records of slavery in 1890, further complicating the titling process now underway." See "Brazil's Former Slave Havens Slowly Pressing for Rights," by Larry Rohter, *New York Times,* January 23, 2001.

6. Private interview, December 2001.

7. BBVA-owned banks in Argentina, Banco Rio de la Plata® and BBVA

Banco Frances®, faced exposures in dollar-denominated loans totaling more than $6 billion.

8. Spain was affected terribly when Argentina collapsed in December 2001. "In all, Spanish companies have some $39 billion invested in Argentina, more than those of any other country," Emma Daly reported. "According to a report by Santander Central Hispano, Spain's largest banking group, they stand to lose nearly $3 billion because of the [Argentine] devaluation." See "Argentina Devalues, and the Spanish Feel the Loss," by Emma Daly, *New York Times,* January 8, 2002.

9. In London, HSBC Group Chief Executive Sir Keith Whitson commented that "The acquisition is in line with our strategy of increasing our presence in North America and will enable us to become one of the few banks that can facilitate trade seamlessly amongst the NAFTA countries." See "HSBC Agrees to Acquire Grupo Financiero Bital," press release posted at *Hsbc.com,* August 21, 2002.

10. Personal communication, May 2002.

11. Robert Rubin's remarks were made at the news conference in Mexico City, May 17, 2001.

12. "A Steely Central Banker Lends New Credibility to Mexico's Economy," by Peter Fritsch, *Wall Street Journal,* May 21, 2001.

13. Robert Rubin's remarks were made at the news conference in Mexico City, May 17, 2001.

14. "Promoting Hispanic TV, Language and Culture," by Mireya Navarro, *New York Times,* December 30, 2002.

15. Brent Erensel is quoted in "Citigroup to Buy Mexican Bank in a Deal Valued at $12.5 Billion," by Riva D. Atlas and Tim Weiner, *New York Times,* May 18, 2001

16. "Citigroup Agrees to Buy Mexico's Banacci," by Paul Beckett and David Luhnow, *Wall Street Journal,* May 18, 2001.

17. "A bank isn't supposed to just take deposits and buy government paper and charge high fees," Philip Guarco, senior credit officer at Moody's in New York, is quoted as saying. "Banks are really providers of dynamism to the economy. We would say that it is just not a successful banking system for the country." See "In Mexico, Banks Are Hesitant to Lend," by Elisabeth Malkin, *New York Times,* September 26, 2002.

18. Mexican officials fear privatizing the SAR in an irresponsible manner. The last thing anyone wants in Mexico is to end up in a situation in which millions of middle-class Mexicans lose their retirement savings. After the U.S. equities market began their sustained decline from their highs of March 2000, for instance, the Labor Department reported that the number of people over 55 in the labor force increased by 8.4 percent between June 2001 and June 2002. "What do you do if you find yourself at retirement age without enough to retire on?" John Rother, policy director of the American Association of Retired Persons (AARP), rhetorically asked. "You keep working." Statistics provided by the AARP, June 2002.

19. Private communication, March 2002.

20. "A Model for Reform: The Development of Chile's Capital Markets," by Tarun Khanna and Krishna Palepu, *Harvard Business Review,* July-August 1999, page 128.

21. "Chile Will Privatize a New Span of Its Noted Social Safety Net," by Larry Rohter, *New York Times,* June 24, 2002.

22. Ibid.
23. "Collaborating with Congregations: Opportunities for Financial Services in the Inner City," by Larry Fondation, Peter Tufano, and Patricia Walker, *Harvard Business Review,* July-August 1999, pages 57–58.
24. Ibid, page 60.
25. "The Constituency of Terror," by Hernando de Soto, *New York Times,* October 15, 2001.
26. "The reason extra-legal businesses and landowners in poor countries do not become legal is that their path is usually blocked by officialdom," the London *Economist* explains. "To illustrate: Mr de Soto's researchers set up a one-man clothing workshop on the outskirts of Lima, and tried to register it. The team worked for six hours a day, filling in forms, traveling by bus into central Lima and queuing before the relevant official desks. It took them 289 days to make their micro-enterprise legal, and cost $1,231—31 times the monthly minimum wage in Peru." See "No Title," the London *Economist,* March 31, 2001.
27. *The Mystery of Capital,* Hernando de Soto, pages 154–155.
28. While much is written on the estimated $11 billion that Mexicans in the U.S. were expected to send home to their families in Mexico in 2003, it is widely ignored that Mexicans and Americans send more than $3 billion from Mexico to their families in the U.S.
29. "Big Mexican Breadwinner: The Migrant Worker," by Ginger Thompson, *New York Times,* March 25, 2002.
30. "Contributing to the Old County," *New York Times* Editorial, June 1, 2002.
31. "Currency-Exchange Fees Taking Bite Out of Dollars," by Christopher Reynolds, *Los Angeles Times,* May 9, 1999.
32. In the *hawala,* sums of money are delivered in one place and paid out in another with a handshake and a code word, usually for a modest fee.
33. "Mexico Seeks Lower Fees on Funds Sent from U.S.," by Tim Weiner, *New York Times,* March 3, 2001.
34. "MoneyGram Revamps Money-Wiring Service," by Lee Romney, *Los Angeles Times,* January 31, 2001.
35. "Big Mexican Breadwinner: The Migrant Worker," by Ginger Thompson, *New York Times,* March 25, 2002.
36. Ibid.
37. In a statement issued January 21, 2001, the Nafin said, "Nacional Financiera will strengthen its relationship with the U.S. Hispanic market with the aim of bettering business ties and facilitating co-investment projects that contribute to creating jobs in Mexico."
38. "The Meaning of 'Macho'," by Rose del Castillo Guilbault, Pacific News Service, June 1986, *www.Pacificnews.org.*
39. "Bank Calls Purchase Way to Woo Hispanics," by Tim Weiner, *New York Times,* December 12, 2002.
40. Kenneth Lewis is quoted in "Bank Calls Purchase Way to Woo Hispanics," by Tim Weiner, *New York Times,* December 12, 2002.
41. The Mexican government succeeded in lowering fees across the board without having to file suit against the firms charging them with collusion and predatory market practices.
42. Ricardo Salinas Pliego is quoted in "A Bank for Mexico's Working Families," by Lucy Conger, *New York Times,* December 31, 2002.

43.  "The Cleanup Crew," by Julia Reynolds, *El Andar,* Spring 2000.

44.  Citibank, of course, does not have a monopoly when it comes to being accused of malfeasance. In her five-year investigation, playwright Barbara Garson told *Salon* the following of Chase: "Oh boy, everybody in New York who was into Latin American loans was a real hot shot, but I couldn't find an actual Mexican businessman who had borrowed money to build something constructive—or even something destructive, like a shrimp farm or a golf course. They complained to me that they couldn't get that money. When Mexico collapsed, it became apparent why. I had an old-fashioned idea: Loans had to be used to build something, or else how could you pay it back? But in Mexico, it was a collusion between my bank, Chase, and Mexican businessmen: The money would go straight there and then bounce back to Chase in the form of bank accounts. . . . I knew people were out for profit and out for money, but I thought it was all subtle. I thought it worked by the invisible hand. I didn't know it worked like a fist in the face." See "Follow the Money," by Andrew Leonard, *Salon.com,* April 16, 2001, or *Money Makes the World Go Round,* by Barbara Garson, New York: Viking, 2001.

45.  To understand the magnitude of this problem, suggested reading includes: "Transnational Narco-Corruption and Narco-Investment: A Focus on Mexico" by Peter Lupsha, *Transnational Organized Crime,* Spring 1955; *Bordering on Chaos: Guerrillas, Stockbrokers, Politicians, and Mexico's Road to Prosperity* by Andres Oppenheimer, Boston: Little, Brown and Company, 1996; "Mexico's Corruption, Washington's Indifference" by Susan E. Reed, *The New Republic,* March 17, 1997; and "Mexico as a Narco-Democracy," by Silvana Paternostro, *This World Policy Journal,* (Spring 1995). All these articles and books highlight Mexico as the PRI's hegemony ended.

46.  For an analysis of how blind faith in market forces leads to problems unless measures are taken to correct natural market imperfections, see *Globalization and Its Discontents,* by Joseph E. Stiglitz, New York: W. W. Norton, 2002.

47.  "Cleaning Up the Money Launderers," by Jim Lyon, *Canadian Banker,* Vol. 107, Number 4, Fourth Quarter 2000.

48.  "Ex-Broker Helped to Launder Drug Money, Prosecutors Say" by Benjamin Weiser, *New York Times,* June 2002. An unwelcome spotlight fell on Lehman Brothers, where Consuelo Márquez worked. "The money laundering scheme began to unravel in 1999, when Ms. Márquez began what prosecutors described as a blizzard of checks and wire transfers intended to liquidate millions in drug proceeds," Bill Berkeley reported. "They say she did so even as her client, a former Mexican state governor named Mario Villanueva Madrid, fled into hiding in Mexico after he became the target of a drug and racketeering investigation. A year later, Lehman fired her. Finally, last June, she was indicted." For more on this messy affair, see, "A Glimpse into a Recess of International Finance," by Bill Berkeley, *New York Times,* November 12, 2002.

49.  *Wall Street Journal,* Editorial, February 21, 1997.

50.  Costa Rica, Guatemala, Honduras, and Nicaragua are studying El Salvador's example. Many economists have urged Argentina to do likewise, one remedy for ending its cycle of economic crises. In Mexico, Francisco Gil Díaz, the Finance Minister in the Fox government, favors

"dollarization." "Adopting the dollar is a discussion that we will entertain for the rest of this decade [the 2000s]," he said.

51. "Law enforcement officials said today that Colombian cocaine traffickers seeking to launder tens of millions in drug profits from the United States and Mexico have begun exploiting an unlikely haven—life insurance policies," Eric Lichtblau reported. "Officials at the Treasury Department said they were so worried about the trend that they were pushing for tougher regulation of the insurance industry as a way of identifying suspicious insurance policies. A central concern for the authorities is that terrorist financiers, too, may seek to exploit vulnerabilities in the insurance industry to launder money for their operations." See "New Hiding Place for Drug Profits: Insurance Policies," by Eric Lichtblau, *New York Times,* December 6, 2002.

# 6

# The Energy to Power
# a Continent

## EXECUTIVE ABSTRACT

Mexico requires $325 billion in capital investments in its oil and electric power generation facility during NAFTA's second decade. This will, in all probability, remain an unrealized market. The politicized nature of oil in the Mexican imagination and unfortunate Constitutional restraints continue to impede the natural and healthy development of these two industries, to the detriment of the Mexican nation. While billions will be invested there, it is unrealistic to expect the Fox administration to succeed in privatizing, presuming they should so want, either Petróleos Mexicanos or Pemex; or opening the electric power generation industry completely. There is no doubt, however that there are tremendous opportunities, particularly as Pemex modernizes within certain political parameters allowed, and as new power plants are built around the nation. If American and Canadian companies are to participate in integrating Mexico more completely, creative approaches to the development of the oil and electric power sectors must be developed. While Mexicans must accept that Pemex must become more "professional" and businesslike, Americans must also accept that this can be done *without* the complete privatization of Mexico's oil industry. Private capital can play an important, and socially responsible, role in the growth of both Mexico's oil and electric power generation industries. Indeed, the rational management of its oil wealth and electric power generation resources are national security issues for the Mexican nation—and the other two NAFTA nations. Rational management, however, remains a Sisyphean task, one in which discredited nineteenth-century ideas come crashing down at the end of the day, rendering useless efforts to prepare Mexico for the economic, political and social opportunities of the twenty-first century.

## DISCUSSION

When President Lázaro Cardenas nationalized Mexico's oil industry in 1938, he did more than seize the assets of foreign investors, mostly British and American petroleum companies, and their Mexican partners. The nationalization of oil became an act of sovereignty, elevating oil to a symbol of nationalism and love of country. Not unlike the power of American myths, such as George Washington cutting down the cherry tree, in Mexico the act of the state reclaiming oil was a way for Mexicans to reclaim their independence.[1] The resulting mandate to manage, develop and exploit these resources as state monopolies were codified in law—and written as amendments into Mexico's Constitution, where only the state is authorized to develop the nation's oil resources. For national security reasons as well, Mexico rendered electric power generation a state monopoly, not unlike the way the United States established a state monopoly on the delivery of the mail, with all the accompanying ambivalence.

While private investors have bemoaned the fact that they are excluded from the oil industry in Mexico, it is more than a question of the "socialist" aspect of Mexico's oil industry that is concerned. For more than 50 years Americans have demanded that Pemex be privatized, pointing an accusing finger at the Mexican government for unjustly interfering in an area of economic life that would be better developed by an unfettered market system.

This is not to say that a state-owned monopoly is necessarily inferior. What should concern Mexicans is how Pemex has been—and continues to be—run. Having studied Mexico's oil and electric power generation industries since 1991 while first consulting for a report prepared on behalf of the U.S. Agency for International Development, it is clear that Pemex is inefficient, corrupt and highly politicized.

Critics point to this state of affairs and demand Constitutional changes to allow for the privatization of Pemex. Perhaps Mexico should completely sell off Pemex to private investors, some argue. (Impatient Mexican, American, and Canadian investors are not content with Fox's plan that "Pemex function now like any other business," simply because they believe that this is impossible as long as it is owned by the state.[2]) This is no guarantee, however, that the Mexican nation would be better served, particularly given how American and European oil companies have conducted themselves in other countries, including their own. It would also be wrong to point to Pemex and condemn all state-owned companies. If Pemex is inefficient, corrupt, and politicized, this might be a reflection of how Mexico has gone about developing its oil industry since the 1930s. One measure of these shortcomings is found by comparing Mexico's Pemex with Venezuela's state-owned oil company, Petroleos de Venezuela, known as PDVSA®.

When PDVSA was founded, a conscientious decision was made to create a world-class oil company. The Venezuelan government invested enormous sums in education and training to ensure that their managers and engineers were competent, efficient, and second to none. Thousands of PDVSA professionals studied in the United States and Canada, worked for foreign oil companies, and then returned to continue their professional careers at PDVSA. Venezuela, furthermore, sought to preserve the independence of PDVSA by appointing directors and management comprised of businesspersons experienced in running large companies. As a result, PDVSA ranks among the most efficient and profitable oil companies in the world, where the profits it generates benefit the whole of Venezuelan society while providing generations of Venezuelan professionals with enviable middle-class lives. Though no company is perfect, PDVSA generates 85 percent of Venezuela's export earnings, and the only difficulties encountered have arisen from the expansionary spending policies implemented in the 1990s that created fiscal difficulties as world oil prices weakened at the beginning of the 2000s. One measure of PDVSA's efficiency is evident in its wholly-owned subsidiary in the United States, operating gasoline stations under the brand name Citgo.® Millions of Americans fill up at Citgo gasoline stations, oblivious that this enterprise is an example of how a professional Latin American company can compete in the United States.

Pemex is PDVSA's mirror image. An organization where management and directors are appointed because of politics and not ability, it has seldom been managed consistent with the industry norms. Encumbered by an oil workers' union closely linked with the PRI, corruption and extortion have suffused the history of labor relations between the union and Pemex management. In what can best be described as systematic looting by officials, Pemex has failed to make the necessary investments to operate properly as a company, and its coffers have been routinely plundered by management to the tune of hundreds of millions of dollars.[3] It has not been able to build installations that meet world standards. The Pemex oil spill—the Ixtoc well in Campeche Bay Sound—remains the world's second-worst oil-related accident, surpassed only by the deliberate destruction of Kuwait's oil fields by the Iraqis during the occupation of Kuwait.

Indeed, were it not for extraordinary oil deposits, Pemex would not be able to provide much revenue to the Mexican government. Antiquated facilities, inadequate technology, and underdevelopment are painfully evident. Unable to capture the natural gas released when drilling for oil, its installations burn billions of cubic feet of natural gas worth billions of dollars.[4] Incapable of processing crude oil into unleaded gasoline to meet Mexico's demands, it is forced to sell oil to the United States, only to buy it back in the form of unleaded gasoline. In classical economics one measure of underdevelopment is examining if a nation exports primary goods (crude oil) and imports finished products (unleaded gas).[5] By this measure, Pemex contributes to Mexico's *under*development, a fact that its most ardent supporters cannot refute.

The arresting contrast between Pemex and PDVSA was in evidence in 2002. When Fox proposed to replace Pemex directors with individuals who had distinguished business careers, there was an outcry. Denouncing this act as a "prelude" to privatizing Pemex, political leaders denounced Fox's plan to *depoliticize* Pemex by replacing political appointees with business professionals. In Venezuela, on the other hand, when President Hugo Chávez sought to replace career managers with political appointees, there was a rebellion: PDVSA resisted any action that would *politicize* their operations.[6] It is an exquisite irony that, if Pemex and PDVSA were to trade places, both Chávez and Fox would be thrilled.[7] That's not likely to happen, and Pemex, in the final analysis, has failed to serve Mexico well.

It is important to understand, however, that Pemex is not an aberration. It was the natural state of affairs under Mexican Paternalism, with all its wretched excess and incompetence. Consider the situation at Aeromexico prior to its being privatized. Run by political appointees who had little experience in the aviation industry, and weighed down by a conflictive labor union, President Miguel de la Madrid grew so frustrated he simply shut the airline down after the union defied him and went on strike. Arguing that the nation's interests would be better served if Aeromexico ceased to operate, he applied a draconian solution to the mess. (In fairness, it should be pointed out that the current Aeromexico, privatized in 1989, has become an efficient, profitable airline that consistently exceeds world standards in the industry.) Pemex's critics point to Aeromexico as an example of the kind of bold decisions necessary if Mexico's oil industry is to experience a similar turnaround. That is a goal, not an assured outcome of privatization.

This is not to say that American and Canadian companies cannot participate in Mexico's multibillion-dollar oil and electric power generation industries. Despite the legendary corruption and inefficiency, Pemex remains the world's fifth-largest oil company, a testament to the vast oil wealth Mexico possesses. Indeed, after Venezuela, Mexico has the largest proven oil reserves in the Western Hemisphere, standing at 29.5 billion barrels. Under Zedillo, Mexico began a process of privatizing the "secondary" petroleum markets, allowing for greater fluidity in how the Mexican government interprets its Constitutional mandate. This flexibility, facilitated by Pemex being divided into four areas—exploration and production, refinery, gas and basic petrochemicals, and petrochemicals—is inadequate for addressing the challenges Mexico confronts. It will therefore be a test of Fox's political skills to see how far he can go to carry out his vision for Pemex. If Mexico's nationalism precludes privatizing Pemex, or granting rights to foreign companies to operate in Mexico, then Fox would be well advised to implement reforms at Pemex, using PDVSA as a model. If Fox's best possible world—substantial privatization—is not a realistic goal, there is no reason why Mexico still cannot achieve a superior societal outcome.

To be sure, the continued integration of the Mexican economy will exert pressure for reforms, and for the opening of Mexico's oil industry. The same holds true for the electric power generation industry. Constitutional requirements mandate a state monopoly on electric power generation through the Federal Electricity Commission, known as the CFE, and the Central Light & Power, known as the LFC. The Zedillo administration also recognized the severe constraints on the nation's ability to generate electricity, estimating that Mexico would need $50 billion invested between 2000–2010.[8] Private estimates now put the investment requirements at closer to $75 billion during NAFTA's second decade to meet with new demand generated by economic growth, and the pent-up demand, particularly in rural areas. These figures do not include the costs of *subsidizing* electricity, costs that in 2001 surpassed $3.5 billion.[9] The Fox administration is cognizant of these shortcomings. Mexican officials, in fact, have argued in the media in order to persuade public opinion, that:

> Mexico will be the victim of a crippling power crisis perhaps as soon as 2004. Number crunchers at the Energy Ministry figure generating capacity must double by 2008 to keep pace with demand, now growing at 8% a year. Officials estimate that the upgrade will cost Mexico $50 billion, money Fox thinks would be better spent improving education and on programs to combat widespread poverty. So the President's center-right National Action Party (PAN) has drafted legislation that would allow private investors to foot part of the bill. That would mean private companies could compete head-on with Mexico's state-run utilities, the Federal Electricity Commission and Central Light & Power. "Energy reform is the most controversial, complex issue facing the country right now," says PAN Senator Juan José Rodr´guez Prats, one of the legislation's sponsors. "An energy crisis would mean a real loss of economic opportunities for Mexico."[10]

An energy crisis, regrettably, is inevitable; upon taking the directorship of Pemex, Rafael Muñoz warned that if Mexico did not invest $3 billion in 2002, it would confront a crisis of "historic" proportions. "We have reached a dangerous point where we need to strengthen our competitive advantages," he said. "It's vital that Pemex grow and there is no time to waste."[11] Indeed, Pemex's importing of more than $5 billion in unleaded gasoline during the second half of NAFTA's first decade constitutes a catastrophic failure of Mexico's energy sector to provide the nation.

The shortcomings of Pemex and the CFE became more flagrant in light of Mexico's sustained economic growth under NAFTA and—ironically—after California experienced an energy crisis in the 2000. "We cannot do it, we cannot provide more electricity to California," Vicente Fox said at the World Economic Forum in Davos, Switzerland on January 26, 2001. "We wish we could but we don't have enough electricity for our own consumption. Those are the facts . . . What we need to do is develop a long-term energy policy with the United States and Canada."[12]

Two weeks later, President Bush arrived in Mexico City intent on "opening the border" to energy cooperation, which consisted of allowing for the freer flow of oil, electricity, and investment. "Only three obstacles stand in [this plan's] way: the laws of physics, the laws of supply and demand, and the laws of Mexico," Tim Weiner wryly reported from Mexico City.[13] American officials, acknowledging that Mexico required more than $200 billion in infrastructure upgrade and expansion to meet its demand, conceded that an addition $100 billion investment was needed before Mexico was able to export electric power. On top of this, an additional $50 billion investment was required before Mexico could produce and export natural gas for both domestic consumption and the U.S. market. (American officials also acknowledged that the United States itself, as the crisis in California demonstrated, had to invest $125 billion in new electric power generating capacity—and rethink how "deregulation" could work in the future, particularly in light of the stunning fraud at Enron.)

It is not clear if Mexico City, Washington, and Ottawa have the political wherewithal to forge an energy policy to power a continent. To be sure, Mexico's policies remain the most contentious—and frustrating—factor in North America's energy equation. This unfortunate state of affairs, of course, is a legacy of Mexican Paternalism. Prominent Mexicans recognize this, in Mexico—and in the U.S. press. Fox's attempt to reform Pemex by replacing its advisory boards with accomplished executives is a small step, but one that could set the stage for making Pemex more professional. Fox "may be hoping to get the best of both worlds—continued public ownership which is so important to Mexico's politicians, and private sector management," Peter Katel, *Time* magazine's Latin American bureau chief, said.[14]

Fox has articulated his position clearly enough. "We must, within the framework of an integrated fiscal reform, give Pemex the capacity it requires financially and operationally, but simultaneously make it accountable in how it operates on behalf of its only legitimate and sole owners: the people of Mexico," he said when George Bush was in Mexico for a meeting in March 2001. "Pemex must become one lean entrepreneurial machine. But for this to happen, we must find creative ways to ensure that Pemex has the resources it needs in order to move the nation forward."[15] There is no doubt that Fox would like to open the oil sector to foreign investment while making Pemex into a professional, efficient enterprise, similar to how PDVSA operates in Venezuela. That his plans are frustrated by Congressional opposition is an obstacle, of course, but it is not insurmountable.

Two factors work in Fox's favor. Foremost is the public outcry over revelations of ongoing corruption at Pemex. Within weeks of becoming director, Rafael Muñoz was confronted with the revelations about former Pemex officials. With a former accountant accused of stealing $1.5 million and under arrest, two other former officials were accused of embezzling more than $630,000. This continues a horrendous legacy in which managers—political appointees—had systematically plundered Pemex since the 1970s, and with a corrupt oil workers' union that extorted millions from Pemex.[16] As is the case with money laundering, many of these schemes to defraud are carried out with the assistance of corporate America. In the same way that the American public have grown disillusioned by the shocking revelations of corruption and malfeasance at firms throughout corporate America, Mexicans, cognizant of what it is like to live in a country that struggles to rein in excesses of the state-owned enterprises, are wary of how corporate America would conduct itself in Mexico's energy sector. If current Pemex management aggressively pursues those responsible for corruption, support for Fox's proposed "opening" would be better received.

The expectations of the Mexican public are now a factor, particularly the higher standards demanded of corporate citizens.[17] In fact, demanding responsibility of state-owned enterprises is part of what Mexicans increasingly expect from responsible corporate citizens. After a decade of seeing the opportunities available under NAFTA, there is also the growing consensus among Mexicans that, as Stephen Goldsmith, chairman of the Manhattan Institute Center on Civic Innovation and former mayor of Indianapolis, argues, "bureaucratic monopolies are bad for taxpayers and bad for public employees. When government insists that competition is off limits, it communicates to public workers that they are inferior. Competition creates the conditions for increased productivity and new partnerships in which the private sector provides some functions while public employees concentrate on what they do best—and where they are most needed."[18]

The stunning turnarounds in the airline and banking industries—both which were privatized—are encouraging. There is also the element of the personas of the U.S. and Mexican leaders, and the sincerity of their friendship.[19] Mexicans find Bush an affable man sincere in his desire to strengthen the political, economic, and human bonds between the United States and Mexico. Bush's "vision" of a hemispheric energy policy, one in which the U.S., Canada, and Mexico approach oil and power as a team, resonates with Mexicans. Misgivings about corporate America are eased by knowing that Canada—which like Mexico prefers a bilateral approach to problem solving—gives Mexicans tremendous encouragement. Indeed, they would prefer to allow Canadian companies into the energy sector over American companies if they had a choice—and they know they do. Political commentator Ernesto Teissier succinctly describes the nation's predicament, which is really an embarrassment of choices: "In Mexico we have time and we can choose whom we want as partners to come and earn money, but neither control nor exert political power."[20]

That this kind of civic debate is taking place in Mexico represents a sea change. Rather than seeing themselves as "trapped"— forced to capitulate to American demands and a destiny not of their own making—Mexicans are realizing they have options. They also have tremendous opportunities. While Pemex may have been an appropriate model under Mexican Paternalism, the demands of a more dynamic economy require changes. So do Mexican aspirations as their country takes a more important role on the world stage. In recent years, for instance, though not a member of the OPEC, Mexican cooperation with the oil cartel has been instrumental. Mexico has also taken a greater profile at the United Nations, where it sits on the Security Council.[21] The importance of oil, traditionally used in foreign policy—Mexico and Venezuela have subsidized oil to Cuba and Central American countries; Mexico has supplied Israel as a matter of principle— can now play an even greater role. For this to happen, of course, Mexican oil production and electric power generation must be integrated into North America.

### Integrating the Oil Industry

Where Mexico and oil are concerned, there are so many opportunities, but so few possibilities. "No one can really work in Mexico," said James J. Byerlotzer, CEO of Key Energy®, a Texas company that attended a conference in Mexico City to be debriefed concerning the Request for Proposals (RFP) issued by Pemex. "We can easily go across the border. Mexico really makes sense in terms of transportation costs, but American companies have been kept out because of the laws. It's a very frustrating situation, because everyone loses."[22]

That Pemex issued RFPs for long-term multiservice contracts, ranging from technical advice to the services to drill gas wells, is an encouraging first step, an admission that Pemex needs foreign technology, equipment, services, and capital to meet Mexico's energy needs. What would otherwise be seen as a "natural" step in the process of identifying project managers, construction managers, equipment suppliers, and construction management services providers became, in Mexico's Congress, a matter of "sovereignty." Witnessing the debates—their tone, their content—it would not be an understatement to compare Mexico's unhealthy relationship with oil with America's conflicted emotions about slavery. The coarseness of the debate, and the superficial nature of the rhetoric, were astounding in their shrill presentations. The circumstances under which Mexico nationalized its oil industry clearly constituted a trauma. All societies suffer traumas. In the same that, for instance, Americans remain conflicted over slavery's legacy—the United States has not yet apologized for slavery—Mexicans, for their part, remain conflicted over energy. They need to understand that oil, gas, and electricity are mere commodities, not a measure of their independence, patriotism, or sovereignty.

"Tens of billions would flow into Mexico from all kinds of American natural gas companies if the Mexicans put out the welcome mat," James J. Byerlotzer said.[23] Pemex officials estimate that Mexico will require $120 billion during NAFTA's second decade in order to upgrade and expand facilities for gas exploration and development. To understand the contentious nature of Mexico's energy sector, opposition congressional leaders have demanded public hearings to examine the terms of Pemex's RFPs and the terms under which it signs any contracts with a foreign company. At a time when Mexico is attempting to make Pemex into a modern corporation, it is revealing to see politicians attempt to micromanage and second-guess new, professional management. That Mexicans are now debating the merits of how their energy sector has operated for more than six decades is not a luxury but a necessity, one with national security implications.

Pemex director Rafael Muñoz understands the imperative of finding "creative" solutions. There is pressure from the United States, especially after the California power crisis in 2000. But within Mexico, too, there is pressure. That Pemex burns off a third of the natural gas that is released from the oil wells means that the domestic price of natural gas continues to increase. Hylsamex®, Mexico's largest steel manufacturer, was forced to lay off 1,350 workers when it closed four plants in the last quarter of 2000 as a direct result of high energy costs. "We need to establish a pricing system that works in the best interest of the country as a whole," Alejandro Barragán, president of Hylsamex, said. "What we're doing now is killing Mexico's industry and killing its workers."[24]

The frustrating fact, however, is that American and Canadian companies are prepared to invest billions—if only they could. Of the $250 billion that must be invested during NAFTA's second decade in the natural gas and oil refinery industries, a significant portion of that investment would come from companies in these two countries, with significant investment from Spain, France, and Japan. Added pressure, of course, is mounting from corporate Mexico. "[Pemex director Muñoz] says that by bringing in private capital and technology that Mexico lacks, the contracts, called multiple service contracts, will help Pemex develop the Burgos field and deliver one billion cubic feet of gas a day by 2005," Tim Weiner reported. "Mexico has 64 trillion cubic feet of proven gas reserves, or about a 50-year supply at present rates of domestic consumption, but it has been able to expand output only slowly, while demand for gas, especially to fire power plants, is growing rapidly."[25]

As Pemex continues to fall further behind in meeting Mexico's energy needs, corporate Mexico is suffering—and so are Mexican workers. Almost as if Pemex were operating behind the veil of Mexican Paternalism, changes in management notwithstanding, the rank-and-file bureaucrats at Pemex have been slow to conduct themselves as important actors in a global economy, to the detriment of efforts to "professionalize" Pemex's corporate culture. This is of great urgency, simply because Mexico's oil industry is confronting a crisis. Not unlike other developing nations, Mexico has been burdened by the failure to use its oil resources wisely. When the price of oil fell in the early 1980s, Mexico was unable to meet its financial obligations. A financial crisis ensued, which culminated in the devaluation of the peso in August 1982 and the nationalization of Mexican banks the following month by an enraged, and outgoing, president López Portillo.[26]

It would be wrong to blame this unfortunate crisis on Mexican mismanagement or corruption. It would be equally misguided to point an accusing finger at greedy foreign bankers. What Mexico experienced is what other societies, from Nigeria to Brunei to Saudi Arabia, also experience when there is an irrational—and speculative—belief that wealth is sustainable without education or work. "Saudi Arabia faces problems more typical of any other developing country, and young Saudis are confronting the fact that they will have to work at real jobs—if they can find them," Neil MacFarquhar explained to amused Americans in the summer of 2001. "It is a rocky transition for a country where the generation that came of age in the 1980's lived as if they had won the lottery. They garnered monthly stipends from the government for enrolling in college, and upon graduation were guaranteed a spot on the public payroll with hefty wages and a 10 a.m. to 2 p.m.

workday—basically a license to sit at home and do nothing. 'There is an Arabic word, itikali, when you always want someone else to do something for you,' said Prince Abdullah bin Faisal, 51, a nephew of the king and chairman of the Saudi Arabian General Investment Authority. 'Like now, some Saudis don't want to take work. They became lazy, spoiled.' "[27]

The Saudis weren't alone, of course. From Nigeria to Brunei, the medium-term wealth generated by oil profits was not enough for the growing demands of growing populations. Oil wealth masked significant problems that undermined the sustainable growth of a middle class.[28] It is tempting to point out that in these nations the state controls the oil industry, thus bolstering arguments for the privatization of state-owned enterprises. Perhaps, but there are some state-owned oil companies, such as Venezuela's, that have stellar reputations for efficiency, and there are many private oil companies that depend on the intervention of politicians to curry favor in the marketplace. What is important, however, is that, unlike Venezuela, Mexico's Pemex was used by the PRI for political objectives. While Mexico did emerge into one of the more important non-OPEC exporters on the world stage, Pemex served strategic political objectives domestically. More than a sign of nationalism, the oil workers' union provided significant support to the PRI, and oil revenues made it possible for the PRI to delay its day of reckoning—undermining the healthy growth of democratic institutions by decades.

Unlike other nations, such as Saudi Arabia, where large oil reservoirs were coupled with small populations, Mexico's significant oil reserves were taxed by the demands of a large—and growing—population. The challenge that Mexican leaders confronted during the 1990s was paradoxical: Pemex could not meet the energy demands of the growing Mexican economy in the age of NAFTA. Not only were the investments made during the 1990s inadequate, structural problems emerged. Neil MacFarquhar wrote of the Saudis: " 'The economy can't grow enough anymore just by dumping all the oil revenue into it,' said Mr. Bourland of the Saudi American Bank. 'It is not enough money to fuel growth for an economy of more than 20 million people,' Ibrahim A. al-Assaf, the finance minister, says that Saudi Arabia needs to spend $100 billion in the next 15 years to keep up with electricity demand, and that water treatment needs $27 billion in the next few years." This could very well describe the needs of Mexico in NAFTA's second decade.

Mexican government officials scoff at the suggestion that Pemex is keeping Mexico back. Their position is that Pemex is at the forefront of fueling Mexican development, pointing to the fact that oil exports account for about a third of the government's budget. These figures, however, mask hidden costs of Pemex. What is one to make of the bloated bureaucracy and corruption? Is it possible that entire layers of middle management are a drain on Pemex revenues? Is it possible that if the oil workers' union weren't run as a corrupt, private fiefdom, its labor practices might conform more closely to world standards for the industry? Isn't it in Mexico's national interest to have a well-run national oil company?

And the boast that Pemex is the second most important source of foreign currency is a hollow one, for it ignores certain social and economic costs. The Ixtoc oil platform in Campeche Bay Sound leaked crude oil into the Gulf of Mexico for years, but Pemex stubbornly refused the assistance of other oil companies to cap that well. On dry land, environmental despoliation is evident; driving near the installations around Minantitlán and Coatzacoalcos is a horrific reminder of the high price generations of Mexicans will pay for this folly.[29] And, of course, Mexico City's notorious air pollution is a byproduct of Pemex's leaded gasoline that, from the late 1950s through the mid-1990s, poisoned the Valley of Mexico in its entirety.[30]

Of more immediate economic concern, consider one simple analysis. Mexico exports oil to the United States only to buy it back, primarily, in the form of unleaded gasoline. In classic economics, exporting raw material (crude oil) and buying finished goods (unleaded gasoline) is consistent with underdevelopment. I know intimately how the energy market in Mexico works, having been a consultant for several U.S. Agency for International Development (USAID) reports prepared in anticipation of the passage of NAFTA. What alarms, however, is that few of the considerable investments first identified in 1992 were made in the intervening decade. In a series of comprehensive studies, structural problems and opportunities were identified. Constitutional barriers to reform, however, made it impossible for Ernesto Zedillo to modernize Pemex. The current administration of Vicente Fox, too, has encountered political resistance to preliminary reforms such as curbing the oil worker's union's use of the payroll to dispense patronage, or even appointing businessmen to Pemex's board of directors. A relic from a failed nationalistic past,

Pemex, quite simply, is the most important stronghold of Mexican Paternalism, and, as currently structured, represents a major obstacle in Mexico's development. If it isn't ironic enough that Saudi Arabia, a desert kingdom sitting atop an ocean of oil, suffers from rolling blackouts because it can't meet its own power needs, then the sublime touch is that this may very well be Mexico's fate by 2010.

## Integrating the Electric Power Generation Industry

A parallel predicament confronts Mexico's electric power generating industry. Electricity, however, is clearly less emotionally charged than oil, but not by much. After nationalizing the electric power generation facilities built by Canadians and the British in the 1960s, Mexico has struggled to meet the demand of a growing economy, and population. During the Zedillo administration, and without public outcry, Mexico quietly began to allow American companies to build generating plants in northern Mexico. Inter-Gen Corporation®, based in Boston, is constructing a 765-megawatt facility near Mexicali, but six miles from the California border. Two other, smaller plants will soon be online. "Now these twenty-first century plants—call them energy maquiladoras—represent a new way to generate wealth and power by capitalizing on the economic and legal differences dividing Mexico and the United States," Tim Weiner wrote. "Mexico's environmental law enforcement is weaker, its government less transparent, its desire for foreign capital bottomless. California's energy demand is enormous—as big as its citizens' resistance to huge power plants."[31] What has made these investments possible is an opportune loophole in current Mexican law that exempts power *exporters* from the ban on private companies competing with the state's monopoly on energy distribution.

These plants, then, could open Mexico's northern border to billions in investment—provided they are constructed for the sole purpose of selling their power to the United States. American companies, particularly California's Pacific Gas & Electric® and Sempra Energy International®, have expressed interest in building power plants on the Mexican side of the U.S.-Mexico border to supply California and the American Southwest. Several Mexican officials have pointed out that Mexico could very well model the development of the "power exporter" industry along the lines of how Canadians have approached the same situation.

"Ontario sits snugly at the center of the Northeast and Midwest. It's a natural place for electricity trade to take place," Graham Brown, the chief operating officer of Ontario Power Generation®, said when Canada opened its electricity market in May 2002.[32] The "deregulation" of Canadian power generation is consistent with integration fostered first by the U.S.-Canada free trade agreement and subsequently accelerated by NAFTA. The process by which these changes were made reflect the growing confidence nurtured by trade—and set a precedent for Mexico to follow, members of Fox's administration argue.

Anticipating stable growth, the provincial government in Ontario embarked on a program to let market forces play a greater role in electric power generation. In 1999, it broke up Ontario Hydro®, a regulated monopoly. Ontario Hydro's plants were transferred to Ontario Power Generation, then newly created. The transmission network was transferred to Hydro One®, which was also created as part of these reforms. More than half of Ontario Hydro's $24 billion debt was absorbed by the government, one strategy for giving these new companies a firm financial footing—and the ability to attract investment capital. Though Canadian critics have feared a U.S.-style electrical crisis, Ontario officials are confident that Ontario Power Generation, by 2012, will control no more than 35 percent of Ontario's electrical market.

These strategies are consistent with thinking in the United States. The U.S. Federal Energy Regulatory Commission (FERC) has approved Ontario Power Generation's plan to build an underwater cable across Lake Erie linking U.S. and Canadian power grids. Of equal consequence, the FERC has authorized Ontario Power Generation to sell electricity in the American market.[33] Officials in Ontario anticipate that they will make money by selling electricity to various American communities, allowing Ontario Power Generation to operate more efficiently—and increasing Canadian exports to the U.S.

If, when one turns on the lights, it makes no difference whether the electricity has a maple leaf or the Stars and Stripes, why should it matter if it has an Aztec eagle?

Perhaps, but two factors have undermined progress in opening Mexico's electric power generation market. The first is the country's Constitution, which mandates a state-owned monopoly. Of greater importance are the emotional politics that surround energy—electricity and oil—in the Mexican mind. Politicians across the political spectrum are reluctant to do anything that would weaken the state's role in producing either electricity or oil. The Fox administration therefore continues to move gingerly as it presses for more private sector involvement in the electric power generation industry. "We are also seeing greater investment in energy with the possibility of opening up the sector. In both natural gas and electric power generation there exists a substantial area for foreign investment," then-Economy Minister Luis Ernesto Derbez points out.[34]

On the surface it appears that this exemption could be used to begin to open Mexico's domestic electric power generation as an industry. Nothing, however, is as straightforward as it appears. In the one area where a convenient loophole stands to encourage the development of a "strategic continental energy policy"—in the words of Vicente Fox—it is American consumer advocates who are criticizing the construction of these plants. "What we are witnessing is Mexico being used by corporate America to pollute," Alejandro Calvillo, director of Greenpeace Mexico, said. "American companies that operate maquiladoras along the border have polluted, because in Mexico the environmental standards are lower than in the U.S.—and the companies violate even these lowered standards. These plants are being built in Mexico to evade emission standards. Corporate America flocks to Mexico because the environmental standards are lower, because the labor laws are weaker, because they have more power to do what they want with impunity."[35]

That American companies are accused of exporting their dirtier operations to Mexico, indifferent to the negative environmental impact, is a powerful argument that finds resonance in Mexican public opinion, particularly now that Mexicans are more sensitized to these issues. As will be examined in Chapter 8, environmentalism as an industry is poised for phenomenal growth in NAFTA's second decade. So as Mexico's energy sector is integrated more completely into the U.S. (and Canadian) power grid system, care must be taken that the same standards, and technology, are employed. If this does not occur and older, dirtier technologies are used in Mexico, American consumers stand to reject the importation of Mexican power, even if it is more cost effective.

For the nations of North America to achieve a communal societal outcome, Mexico must be the recipient of technological know-how as well as investment capital. Consider that when Pemex announced a new round of long-term multiple-service contracts for June 2002, more than 75 foreign companies expressed interest in competing for those contracts. In the electric power generation, more than 60 power producers from the United States, Canada, France, Germany, Italy, Spain, and Japan have expressed interest in these opportunities. Several European companies have speculated that "more than $120 billion" could be invested over 15 years building power plants that straddle the Mexican side of the U.S.-Mexico border. American executives, though less ambitious, recognize the dormant opportunities on their doorsteps. "Mexico is an untapped market, with tremendous potential," said Tom McKinney, Bechtel vice president said. "We have always had tremendous faith in Mexico and its future and we are excited being a part of Mexico's growth."

It is imperative, then, that as Mexico gingerly opens its electric power generation industry, measures be taken to assuage concerns that Mexico will be "exploited" by American companies intent on skirting environmental regulations with which they would otherwise have to comply. The ideological conflict is best personified by President Vicente Fox and Manuel Bartlett, a lifelong member of the PRI who is a senator in the Mexican Congress. Fox argues that the considerable investments required in expanding electric power generation are best done by the private sector; he would rather spend the money on education. Bartlett, on the other hand, scoffs at predictions of a looming energy crisis in Mexico, and mocks the idea that corporate America offers a better model. "Look at the energy chaos in California. Do they want to sell the American failure to us?" he told *Business Week* in 2002.[36]

That, of course, is inadvisable. But it does not detract from the enormous electricity power crisis that Mexico confronts: economic growth has far outstripped the ability of the CFE to meet demand. "Mexico, starved for electricity, is reviving plans to dam its biggest river, the Usumacinta," Tim Weiner reported, alluding to the cultural and environmental costs desperate scenarios envision. "The dam could provide power to millions, but at a cost: the destruction of precious Mayan ruins. . . . 'This is a disaster,' said Stephen D. Houston, an archaeologist at Brigham Young University. 'And if Piedras Negras is flooded, it would be the worst disaster ever to be visited on a classic Mayan site.' "[37] Destroying the environment and Mexico's cultural patrimony to humanity would be an equally failed model, to be sure. It is also one that must be avoided.

One approach to finding a superior societal outcome is to encourage partnerships that include Canadian companies, given the high esteem Mexicans have for corporate Canada, particularly given the Canadian government's historic concern with ensuring that the environment be protected. The credibility Canada enjoys cannot be underestimated; trust of Canada generates tremendous goodwill. As will be discussed later, Mexican ambivalence about the true intentions of corporate America distort how American overtures are received.[38] Whether rational or irrational, perceptions affect how Mexico rethinks its energy sector. This is all the more urgent given the Blackout of 2003, when the failure of the NAFTA nations to implement a continent-wide investment in upgrading our electrical grid became evident.

## Rethinking Public Ownership of Pemex

"However much Mexico's loony leftists might find the truth unpleasant, Mexico faces a clear choice," an official in the Fox administration said. "Mexico can open its energy sector to private investment as we integrate into North America, or we can start stockpiling candles and kerosene lamps."

Characterized in such a stark and unforgiving manner, it opens up possibilities. As Mexico has opened its economy and political system, it is increasingly receptive to considering how other countries address their problems. If Mexico is content on keeping Pemex an enterprise owned by the public, I have suggested that it look to Venezuela's PDVSA as a model of a successful, efficient state-owned enterprise that serves its nation in an apolitical manner. Another approach would be to consider how Pemex can truly "belong" to the people. This would allow Mexico to solve various problems at once. If, for instance, shares in Pemex were given to every Mexican citizen, they could be registered in bank accounts. Thus millions of Mexicans who are not part of the formal banking system would be brought into the formal economy by way of claiming their "birthright." Instead of Pemex turning over its net proceeds to the federal government, "dividends" could be paid out to the Mexican citizen. This would give every citizen a stake in society, provide the additional capital for the SAR private pension systems, provide forced savings for minors, amply fund "microlending" antipoverty programs, and keep billions out of politicians' squandering reach.[39] "A dividend payment from the government to the people is not unprecedented," Richard Freeman and Eileen Appelbaum opined in the *New York Times*. "Alaska has a fund through which the state distributes the economic rewards of its ownership of land and mineral resources. In 2000, Alaska sent a check for nearly $2,000 to every man, woman and child who was a permanent resident and had lived in the state for all of 1999."[40]

To be sure, $80 for every man, woman and child in Mexico is

not a great deal of money, but it is a considerable investment in a nation where 60 percent of the population is excluded from banking services. That Mexico's federal government would be pressed to find alternate source of income, however, is not an insurmountable obstacle, particularly if other reforms are implemented that encourage domestic capital formation and foreign investment. When one considers the opportunity costs—and the costs of having to import unleaded gas, the price of corruption— Pemex contributes far less to Mexico than it is widely believed.

Significant reforms are in order—and are inevitable. Years back, one of my great aunts confronted a peculiar problem. Though she owned three large estates, her cash flow was strained; the upkeep on three properties was burdensome. Reluctant to sell a single property, even the one that was unoccupied and simply languished, she was too proud to hear of selling her "patrimony." On several occasions I reminded her that she was like a mule carrying barrels of water across the desert. "There's the poor mule," I told her, "dying of thirst and burdened by the weight of those barrels of water."[41] And there is Mexico, confronting an energy crisis, while floating on one of the world's greatest oil and gas reserves, paralyzed by hubris, unwilling to let others with the capital and know-how participate in developing resources that it cannot develop on its own.

Mexico's future simply cannot afford the price Mexico's past exacts.

## SUMMARY

1. Political considerations continue to hamper the healthy, normal development of the oil production and electric power generation industries in Mexico, which remain state-owned and highly politicized.

2. Continued and sustained economic growth, however, requires Mexico to double its production of oil, natural gas, and gasoline from current levels by 2014. These economic realities are forcing political changes whereby foreign investment and participation will play a significant role.

3. Significant changes are beginning to take place as Mexico confronts the harsh reality that its nationalist development model for its energy sector is unable to meet the nation's demand. Anticipating an energy crisis, however reluctantly, Mexican politicians are moving toward opening its oil, natural gas, and electric power generation industries.

4. The potential market opportunities in Mexico's oil and electric power generation industries approximate $325 billion during 2004–2014.

## ENDNOTES

1. The act of claiming subsoil deposits for the state dates back to Roman law, where it was the state that owned everything beneath the surface. In pre-Columbian societies, too, the state owned subterranean deposits. Here, then, is one example where Mexican law, based on the Napoleonic Code and Roman law, coincides with the legal system, centuries before the arrival of the Europeans.

2. Vicente Fox's statements were made when he named leading businessmen, including Carlos Slim of Telmex and Lorenzo Zambrano of Cemex, to Pemex's board in February 2001—to tremendous controversy.

3. In a stunning example of the corrupt collusion between Pemex management and the oil workers' union, fugitive Pemex director Rogelio Montemayor surrendered to officials in Houston in July 2002. Charges that he authorized more than $200 million in illegal payments to the oil workers' union, to be funneled to the PRI, best illustrate how Pemex may have served the PRI but not the Mexican nation. The arrest of Mr. Montemayor proved embarrassing, particularly since it revealed how the failed presidential bid of Francisco Labastida was presumed to have been financed: through extortion and corruption, signature characteristics of how the PRI misruled Mexico.

4. Energy analysts estimate that fully one-third of Mexico's natural gas is burned off by Pemex, simply because it lacks the infrastructure and resources necessary to capture and move it to market, domestic and foreign alike.

5. The numbers are startling: Mexico imports 130,000 bbl/d of refined oil from the United States.

6. President Hugo Chávez went on television to denounce PDVSA managers who denounced his decision to replace 12 PDVSA executives with political appointees. "These people have become saboteurs of a company that belongs to all Venezuelans," President Chávez declared, vilifying the nonpartisan managers who had made the PVDSA a world-class company. This conflict, in fact, resulted in a failed coup that stunned the world and temporarily removed President Chávez from office in April 2002. Upon returning to the presidential palace, in a gesture of reconciliation, President Chávez vowed to keep PDVSA "apolitical." See "Tenuous Truce in Venezuela for the State of Its Oil Company," by Simon Romero, *New York Times,* April 24, 2002.

7. In fact, Chávez sought to "Pemex-ize" his nation's oil company by changing it into a political, not business, organization. "Energy Minister Rafael Ram´rez said today that the government planned to take the state-owned oil company, the world's fifth largest, and break it in two, hoping to snap the back of a devastating six-week strike aimed at driving President Hugo Chávez from power," Ginger Thompson reported from Caracas in January 2003. "He said the government would 'decentralize' the company by dividing it into Pdvsa East and Pdvsa West and hollowing

out the Caracas-based management. Such a move would effectively gut the company of middle- and upper-level executives who have joined a coalition of business and labor leaders in opposing Mr. Chávez, whose left-leaning policies they say are destroying the country." It was a brazen plan to transform an efficient, apolitical company into an agency that answered not to the Venezuelan nation, but to Mr. Chávez. "The plan, analysts said, appeared to be far less an economic strategy than a political one, aimed at purging the company of Chávez opponents once and for all and wrestling more political control over the industry, even if it means enduring sharp declines in production," Thompson reported. See "Venezuela, Seeking to End Strike, Plans to Split State Oil Company," by Ginger Thompson with Neela Banerjee, *New York Times,* January 7, 2003.

8. These figures used in this section are provided by the U.S. Department of Energy. For more information, see *www.eia.doe.gov/emeu/cabs/mexico.html.*

9. See "Roadblocks Right and Left for Mexican President," by Tim Weiner, *New York Times,* January 22, 2001.

10. "Mexico's Electric Power Struggle," by Geri Smith, *Business Week,* March 25, 2002.

11. Press conference held in Mexico City, February 2001.

12. Press conference remarks at Davos, Switzerland on January 26, 2001.

13. "Bush Is Due to Visit Mexico in Search of Oil and Power," by Tim Weiner, *New York Times,* February 13, 2001. Mexicans are wary of American intentions. When William Safire argues that the "best way to stop illegal border-crossing is to help Mexico become prosperous. The best way for Mexico to raise its standard of living is to open its vast energy potential to foreign investment," Mexicans wince. How would Americans feel if Mexicans opined that the best way for the United States to become civilized would be to abolish the death penalty? Or to "reform" its judicial system, which routinely sends the innocent to death row? (See "Fox, Bush & Helms" by William Safire, *New York Times,* April 2, 2001.)

14. "Despite Points of Contention, Mexico Is Bullish on Bush," by Tony Karon, *Time.com,* February 15, 2001.

15. "Bush Insists Mexico Open Energy Sector, As Mexico's Oil Company Announces Major New Oil Reserves," Notimex, March 19, 2001, *www.ncmonline.com/content/ncm/2001/mar/insists.html.*

16. In the early 1980s, while an intern in New York, a curious incident occurred where I worked. It appeared that two sets of invoices were being prepared for Pemex, one that went to one manager and the other that went to Pemex. It was clear that this duplicate billing—with a sizeable discrepancy—was being used to defraud Pemex for this particular manager's benefit. That this scheme was being carried out with the cooperation of an American firm is one reason why Mexicans are skeptical that corporate America would conduct themselves as socially responsible corporate citizens in Mexico's oil and energy sector.

17. For more information on corporate responsibility, see Business for Social Responsibility *(Bsr.org),* Social Venture Network *(Svn.org),* and Environics International *(Environicsinternational.com).*

18. "Competing for Better Government," by Stephen Goldsmith, *New York Times,* December 7, 2001.

19. The terrorist attacks of September 11th created first tensions and then distancing between Fox and Bush. "President Bush is somewhat a

different person than he was," according to a person who was present when both presidents attended an economic summit in the fall of 2002 in the Mexican resort of Cabo San Lucas. "He's less relaxed, he's much more intense. And that intensity sometimes makes relations a little more complicated. There's very little small talk or banter. Bush was remarkable at making people like Fox feel very, very comfortable. Now he is driven by a single issue. But the fact is, Fox doesn't lose sleep every night over what Saddam Hussein is going to do." Quoted in "Two Presidential Pals, Until 9/11 Intervened," by Elisabeth Bumiller, *New York Times*, March 3, 2003.

20. "Pemex y la CFE," by Ernesto Julio Teissier, *Proceso*, July 2001.

21. In the conflict with Iraq, for instance, Mexico held one of the swing votes on the Iraq resolution presented in October 2002. "Seldom have we been courted," Adolfo Aguilar Zinser, Mexican ambassador to the United Nations, dryly noted in November 2002.

22. Private communication, June 2002.

23. Ibid.

24. Press conference, January 2001.

25. "Mexican Energy Giant Lumbers into Hazy Future," by Tim Weiner, *New York Times*, February 1, 2003.

26. By contrast, in the United States, the government usually nationalizes not assets but obligations. Shortly after the LTV Corporation went bankrupt, the federal government took over the obligations of the pension plans affecting 82,000 workers, and valued at $4.4 billion. The federal program, the Pension Benefit Guaranty Corporation, in essence, administers one of the more socialist programs masquerading as an "insurance" operation.

27. "In Saudi Arabia, Ruling Class to Working Class," by Neil MacFarquhar, *New York Times*, August 26, 2001.

28. Consider the drama detailed in "From Oil Rich to Garage Sales," by Seth Mydans, *New York Times*, August 17, 2001. The article was summarized thusly: "Oil-rich tiny nation of Brunei is in state of financial collapse, hit hard by Asian economic crisis in 1997, drop in oil prices and by Prince Jefri Bolkiah's $15 billion spending spree; saga of profligate prince is latest cautionary tale about dangers of economic windfall; Nigeria, like Brunei, has been all but ruined by corruption spawned by discovery of oil; Brunei holds six-day auction of depleted assets of prince's construction and supply company, which went bankrupt in 1998; Prince Jefri, favorite brother of Sultan Hassanal Bolkiah, held dual positions of finance minister and head of Brunei Investment Agency, which invested huge oil wealth; his profligate spending has caused sultan's personal fortune to shrink by as much as three-fourths; last year sultan sued his brother and forced him to give back all his assets; Prince Jefri now lives abroad on monthly allowance of $300,000 as country he left behind tries to put itself back together in new form."

29. In 1993, on a guided tour of these installations, the smoke billowing from them was such—and the roads were in such disrepair—that the tour abruptly ended when the official crashed the car into a ditch. The smoke blinded him and we drove into what had, the previous rainy season, been a pothole, but by now had grown into a crater that occupied two lanes and the shoulder.

30. Indeed, the first study identifying acid precipitation in a tropical environment pointed an accusing finger at Pemex facilities as the source.

Thus in one stroke, Pemex was threatening not only tropical forests but also the ceremonial centers of the ancient Maya.

31. "U.S. Will Get Power, and Pollution, from Mexico," by Tim Weiner, *New York Times*, September 17, 2002.

32. Private communication, May 2002.

33. Consumer advocates in Ontario point out, quite reasonably, that if Ontario Power Generation will "control" only 35 percent of the market in Ontario, then fully 65 percent of Ontario's electric power needs will be met by companies outside Ontario. This increases the risks, they argue, of disruption of service or unexpected changes in prices.

34. Interview April 28, 2002.

35. Private communication, March 2001.

36. "Mexico's Electric Power Struggle," by Geri Smith, *Business Week*, March 25, 2002. Paul Krugman agreed with Manuel Bartlett's skepticism. "One indication of how badly [electric power] deregulation has misfired," he wrote in his column, "is this: while the error of the tech sector—overestimating demand for its services—was severely punished, the error of the California power companies—underestimating the demand for their product—has been richly rewarded. You don't have to be a raving populist to think that there is something wrong with that, and you don't have to be a conspiracy theorist to wonder whether there are some perverse incentives when an industry dominated by a few large players finds it hugely profitable not to invest." See "Real Reality's Revenge," by Paul Krugman, *New York Times*, December 31, 2000.

37. "Mexico Weighs Electricity Against History," by Tim Weiner, *New York Times*, September 22, 2002.

38. The American public at large, which has seen its net worth fall as scandal after scandal rocked Wall Street in 2001 and 2002, also has misgivings about the real intentions of corporate leaders.

39. There is concern among younger economists about precisely how to combat poverty. "A cadre of young economists who study development, including some of the most sought-after professors in the nation, are dissatisfied with supposed panaceas like balanced budgets, new infrastructure and financial stability," Daniel Altman reported. "These economists are using basic insights about people's motivation to guide policy in emerging economies, one piece and one country at a time." Such a sensible approach must be adopted in tailoring these programs to the specific needs of various constituencies in Mexico. See "Small-Picture Approach to a Big Problem: Poverty," by Daniel Altman, *New York Times*, August 20, 2002.

40. "Instead of a Tax Cut, Send Out Dividends," by Richard Freeman and Eileen Appelbaum, *New York Times*, February 1, 2001

41. In due course, she was convinced to sell one property—to a distant relative, allowing her to save face by pretending that the property remained "in the family."

# 7

# An Opportunity to Educate a Continent

## EXECUTIVE ABSTRACT

After decades of neglect, Mexico's educational system has emerged as a market with tremendous potential. With the fast-track development of the "e-Mexico" program, with the participation of Microsoft, to wire Mexico by 2006, the largest public works initiative of the Fox administration is underway. Along with a renewed effort to expand microlending programs designed to lift people from poverty, the linking of education with antipoverty campaigns constitutes a multibillion-dollar market in NAFTA's second decade.[1] Moreover, the political decision to bridge the "digital divide," coupled with outreach programs aimed at helping the children of migrant workers pursue their education, has given Mexico a historic opportunity to enact significant reforms aimed at making higher education an industry. Canada's Nortel Networks' aggressive establishment of a formidable presence in Mexico's wireless telephony technology gives impetus to expand education and to integrate further the NAFTA nations' future in the area of education. Finally, after NAFTA's first decade, the worldview of Mexico's indigenous peoples—who comprise the most disenfranchised of the Mexicans—is changing in ways that are amenable to sustained growth of education as a market. The total spending on education during NAFTA's second is expected to be as high as $370 billion.

## DISCUSSION

One of the achievements of the Mexican Revolution was to provide free public education. This commitment was extended to higher learning; Mexico's National Autonomous University, for instance, charged an annual tuition of $3, meaning that, provided he or she satisfies the academic requirements, any Mexican student is assured an education. In theory this is ideal; millions of American families would be grateful if their children's college tuition vanished so effortlessly. In practice, however, there are real-world limitations. If public universities are open to anyone meeting the entrance requirements, classes are crowded and there are long waiting lists. If universities cannot defray their expenses by charging tuition, they have to acquiesce to politicians who authorize budgets. If professors are overwhelmed by the number of students in their class and by the constant struggle with school administrators over department budgets and union leaders about their paychecks, it becomes demoralizing.

Not unlike free public health, many choose to opt out of the system entirely. Middle-class Mexicans send their children to private schools; competent professors are wooed away by private universities. Through scholarships and financial sacrifices, millions of Mexican students study in foreign countries, usually the United States, Spain, Canada, France, Italy, and England. The vast majority of Mexicans who do not enjoy such privileged circumstances depend on the national public education system, where their professional aspirations are developed. As is the unfortunate case the world over, political leaders are reluctant to make difficult decisions if the results will take decades to become evident. Deciding to invest a billion dollars to make sure that today's kindergarten students will be able to become doctors, architects, and engineers in two decades' time is seldom in the self-interest of a politician concerned with how his or her party will fare in the next election.

In Mexico's case, the integrity of public education has been compromised by other factors. Throughout much of the twentieth century, Mexico's population grew fantastically. In 1900, the population was 20 million. In 2000, it stood at 100 million. This growth strained the public education system, particularly as efforts were made to reach out to rural communities, areas where the local residents didn't even speak Spanish very well. The task of finding educators who were proficient in one of dozens of Native American languages proved to be another impediment to bringing education to the most disenfranchised of Mexico's peoples. Another complication emerged by the frustrating cycle of falling behind. "Standing still while everyone takes a step forward is like moving backwards," economist Robert Frank is fond of saying.[2] If Mexico is struggling to make sure that it can provide pencils and paper, blackboards and chalk to every classroom, and then suddenly other countries introduce computers, the relative standing of Mexican schools, consistently, worsens comparatively. Constrained by the inability to finance modernization through tuition and subjected to the political realities, Mexico's public education system has fallen further and further behind, particularly since the 1970s when technology first became part of the education systems in other countries. (Recall what happened with the introduction of calculators in American public schools in the early 1970s, a subject so controversial that *60 Minutes* devoted a segment to it.)

That Mexico's middle-class supported the private schools to which it sent its children and that other privileged Mexican families were loyal to the foreign universities where they sent their children did not improve matters. Private universities in Mexico have computers and state-of-the-art facilities; Mexican alumni generously give to their alma matters, from Harvard University to the London School of Economics. This has aggravated the plight of Mexico's public universities. While private institutions of higher learning in Mexico have prospered from the generosity of their alumni, large public universities languish. Donating millions to foreign universities has become a status symbol for the Mexican elite, resulting in the frustrating paradox that Mexican philanthropists are more eager to help rich institutions abroad than show concern for the dire circumstances confronting Mexican students. That well-to-do Mexicans have no vested interest in improving the nation's public education system constitutes yet another obstacle that must be addressed.

The disdain wealthy Mexicans display towards the nation's public education system is the result of yet another layer in this story, one that speaks as much of class difference as it does of political disaffection. That Mexican schools depend on public funding means that they are expected to serve an ideological role in the life of the nation. From the 1930s through 2000, Mexico's public education system was an important achievement of the PRI. The ruling party could, with self-satisfaction, cite the nation's public schools and universities as a triumph of its egalitarian aspirations, providing education regardless of race, creed, or economic circumstance.

In a nation in which Native Americans are the poorest and least educated, Mexican schools attempted to rescue indigenous peoples from the undeserved oblivion of modern life. The intellectual architect of this was the writer José Vasconcelos. In the first half of the twentieth century, the population was uncomfortable with the issue of race. Most Mexicans are "mixed race," meaning that they have Native American (Mongoloid) and European (Caucasian) blood. Miscegenation was a disturbing subject, not because of racism per se, but because it was part of the process of "Hispanization" under colonialism.[3] A simple way of understanding what this means is through an analogy. Most Americans are Christians of European descent. That means that at some point their ancestors converted to Christianity from one or other of the pagan belief systems of the ancient Europeans. It would, however, be futile if Americans brooded about the fact that, while they are Christian, at some point their ancestors participated in one kind of pagan fertility rite or other that they now found reprehensible.

Miscegenation, for Americans, is the breaking of unspoken rules of racial ideals.[4] Miscegenation, for Mexicans, too often results in feelings of ungenerous consequences of supposed racial inferiority. José Vasconcelos sought to do away with all of that. The present should be embraced, and Mexicans, he declared, were the product two great civilizations. As such, they were a "cosmic race." José Vasconcelos did not make this declaration as a demagogue; he meant it as a bold affirmation of identity. Indeed, the idea of a "cosmic race" occurred to him as he wrote down his impressions while traveling throughout Latin America. His writings were literary love letters of sorts. While in Buenos Aires, for example, he compared how different Argentines were from Brazilians. Argentines, mostly of "pure" Spanish and Italian descent, stood in stark contrast to the racial blending of the Brazilians. He grew excited at the vitality of Brazil, and, in profound admiration, he contemplated a future in which the nations of the Americas would lead the way in inventing a seemingly effortless society of European, Native American, and African peoples. His writings were wishful thinking of what the future of the Americas could very well become.[5]

Years later the Mexican government, enamored with the José Vasconcelos' generous philosophical construction, appropriated his arguments through the Mexican public school system. Consequently, social engineering became a greater imperative of the public education system, to no one's benefit. The result has been unfortunate; while Mexico's private schools continue to advance and provide world-class education to its students, the public schools and universities have descended into ineffectual debating clubs. Students chain-smoke their way through endless debates about "social justice" toward the Zapatistas or decry the "corrupt materialism" of the market economy, but offer no reasonable alternative. "Mr. Marcos, a former Marxist university professor who is not an Indian, probably has more followers in Europe and Northern California—where his Internet postings have made him fashionable—than in the poor southern state of Chiapas," the *Washington Post* editorialized in the spring of 2001, speaking of the revolutionary Subcomandante Marcos.[6] This view summed up the sentiment that foreign support for Marcos is a Maya attempt to retaliate against the continued Aztec (Mexican) "plunder" of Maya natural resources.

To wit, when the Zapatista delegation entered Mexico City in March 2001, it was led by a Maya woman whose *nom de guerre* is Commander Esther. In other words, foreign support for Marcos bolsters Maya claims against Aztec (Mexican) ownership of Maya subterranean natural resources—hundreds of billions of dollars of oil in Campeche Bay Sound, as if seizing natural resources would solve a humanitarian crisis in many ways created by politics. "Humanitarianism is, at its core, about war, and war casts its compromising shadow over humanitarianism's good intentions," Ian Fisher argues. "Aid, it turns out, works much better in natural disasters, earthquakes or floods. When politics provokes the crisis— when, for example, hunger is deliberately induced as an aim of war—things get much murkier."[7] "Justice," the more militant Zapatistas maintain, in other words, entails the dismemberment of the Mexican nation.

On more practical matters, the Zapatistas and their supporters are equally problematic. None of the striking university students interviewed, for instance, offered any answer to a basic question: How could the government correct the societal problems that arise when "traditional" lifestyles make it impossible to enjoy "modern" comforts. (The Innu, an indigenous people in the Canadian provinces of Quebec and Newfoundland, for instance, complain that "they have been scarred by substance abuse since the government forced them to give up their nomadic way of life in the 1950s and 1960s and subsequent hydroelectric developments flooded their hunting grounds," Elena Cherney reported in the *Wall Street Journal.* "The Innu say their children sniff to escape the harsh realities of their young lives: widespread alcoholism among parents, dilapidated homes with no running water, and a suicide rate 13 times the national average."[8]) Alas, despite the fact that this market system provides free public education for the Zapatistas, they plan boycotts that shut down universities, to the chagrin of their classmates who want to earn their degree and not be swept away by the political flavor of the month.[9]

It is clear that the more reasonable approach is to enfranchise indigenous people through education. "These are the poorest of the poor who have always been discriminated against and repressed," Fox said in an interview with the *Wall Street Journal*. "I think it's time to solve this problem and pay them back what we owe."[10] Thus Mexicans, whether they are politicians, businesspeople, or social critics, have grown more vocal in wanting to reform the nation's public education.

Increasing trade is one way of expanding educational opportunities. During NAFTA's first decade thousands of American companies opened for business in Mexico, often training the local workers. Whether it was a training team sent to teach the employees of a local Dairy Queen®, or seminars for managers at a Wal-Mart, or setting up an engineering design office to design General Motors™ vehicles, Mexicans have gained a new confidence, a confidence born of recognizing that they can be as competent as anybody else. Once trained, a manager at Dairy Queen can run that operation, whether it is in downtown Mexico City or downtown Chicago. General Motors vehicles are designed by Mexican engineers, and their work is second to none in the global automotive industry, which is a source of tremendous professional pride. The realization that, once trained and educated, Mexicans can compete on a global level continues to prove empowering, and expectations have been raised.

This newfound confidence instilled by NAFTA has changed public debate in Mexico. What holds true of other nations that fell behind in relative terms, also holds true for Mexico. Consider how Bernard Lewis describes how, "for the first time, [in the eighteenth century, Muslim thinkers] make comparisons between the Islamic Ottoman Empire and its Christian enemies to the advantage of the latter. In other words, the question now was not only 'what are we doing wrong?' but also 'what are they doing right?' And of course, the essential question: 'How do we catch up with them, and resume our rightful primacy?' "[11]

Now Mexicans are asking how they can "catch up" and modernize their public education system. The agenda emerging is one of major reforms, reforms that require $370 billion in direct spending and investment over the next decade. The avuncular parsimony under the PRI is giving way. Mexicans expect the public universities to educate without indoctrinating. Mexicans want education to make the nation computer literate. They want the public education sector to spearhead the improvement of the lives of millions left behind by linking education with antipoverty campaigns. They demand that billions be invested to build schools to reduce class sizes; that computers to be made available at schools, universities, and libraries; and that education play a critical role in ameliorating the negative impacts of natural market failures.

This is a tall order as NAFTA enters its second decade, but it is one that Vicente Fox has demonstrated he considers important. One of his first actions upon becoming president was to establish the e-Mexico program. E-Mexico seeks to hook up the entire Mexican nation to the Internet, thereby giving millions of people access to the technology. "This is the first time a Mexican president has put in black-and-white a government program to do something regarding technological development to help his country become more productive and competitive," Leonardo Ortiz, Microsoft's spokesman in Mexico City, said when a $6 million donation was announced on April 25, 2002. This was less than nine months after Microsoft announced a $60 million investment to train 20,000 Mexican software programmers.

Fox's initiative is a sea change, but it is consistent with the commitment best articulated at the Summit of the Americas held in April 2001. "Free trade and freedom work together to make life better and our neighborhood safer," Colin Powell argued on the eve of that gathering in Quebec. "But to take advantage of this opportunity, people need skills and education. Thus, the leaders will reaffirm their commitment to improve education systems, increase access to quality education, improve teacher training and expand use of modern information technology."[12] That Mexico's educational system has languished for decades has meant that the business of education—whether it is selling computers or textbooks or building new facilities—has lagged behind. Fox's e-Mexico stands to accelerate the modernization of Mexico's public education system, and create exciting new markets as Mexico links education with antipoverty programs that have proved successful.

One aspect of NAFTA's success that has been overlooked is the demand being created for education. Mexicans have seen that with certain skills, whether it is as computer programmers or being well-versed in the fundamentals of retail management, a world of opportunities open up. That there are millions of Mexicans working in the United States also sends a powerful message; 40 percent ultimately return, and their life experience in the United States includes not only a new respect for the Protestant work ethic, but an understanding of the importance of gaining an education. Following are overviews of the market opportunities during the 2004–2014 period.

## Bridging Mexico's "Digital Divide"

In sharp contrast to its computer-savvy elite, most of Mexico's people were left behind during the Internet revolution that wired the world during the 1990s. Cognizant of the role that technology can play in leap-frogging ahead, Microsoft chief executive Steve Ballmer has been working with Mexican officials since the 1980s, when the company made its first investment in the country. "I'm very optimistic about what is happening here in Mexico with the economy and the potential for improving technology," Ballmer said in an interview on August 23, 2001. "We want to cooperate with the government to utilize and make good use of the infrastructure and capability."[13]

Not unlike other nations where the distribution of income is greatly skewed, Mexico suffers from an enormous "digital divide" in which the nation's privileged elite is computer literate while the majority of Mexicans remain excluded. Consistent with the sustained economic expansion since NAFTA, however, demand for information technology in Mexico has risen steadily. Computer sales tripled in Mexico between 1995 and 2001, skyrocketing from $1 billion in 1995 to more than $3.5 billion in 2001. Demand for software and computer-related services also tripled, rising from $869 million to $2.5 billion. Fox's six-year e-Mexico program is designed to end the exclusion of Mexico's less privileged citizens. With the stated goal of "hooking up" the entire nation by 2006, Mexico's alliance with Microsoft is a fast-track attempt to bridge that digital divide. "We hope to have Internet service in libraries and schools across the country, giving everyone access to the Internet," Leonardo Ortiz said.[14]

This effort has not been without its detractors, however. Arguing that Fox is, in essence, granting Microsoft a de facto monopoly to the Mexican market, opposition legislators strained credulity by claiming to be "outraged." In a measure of the legacy of the PRI's tenure running the nation's public universities, Congressional opponents charged that e-Mexico would drive millions of new Internet users to Microsoft products, giving a damning blow to competitors. "Microsoft says its donation will help Mexico foster its national software industry by training Mexican engineers. Critics reply that what the engineers will be trained to do is to use Microsoft's technology," Graham Gori reported.[15] There is no doubt, of course, that Mexicans will naturally gravitate to Microsoft's brands once they start to use their products, but that is inevitable. If Apple Computer is terribly worried, it could very well introduce a program in Mexico similar to its practice of donating, or selling at cost, its products to schools, nonprofit organizations, and other groups. It is also not clear how Microsoft's participation in e-Mexico would undermine the ability of any Mexican programmer to participate in the development of—or use of—open-source software, such as Linux®.

The other argument offered by critics of e-Mexico is that the Fox administration, by solely using Microsoft products, has granted the Microsoft Corporation a tremendous and unfair competitive advantage because its products will be used by government agencies and publicly funded universities.[16] This is not to discount the fact that Microsoft has engaged in predatory business practices, as the antitrust lawsuit filed against the company by the U.S. Justice Department in 2000 and 2001 underscores. But unless Congressional critics are prepared to allocate $60 million to train 20,000 Mexican programmers and then provide an additional $20 million to buy the computers required to link up the entire nation, delaying e-Mexico only hurts Mexicans. If their concerns are sincere, there are other steps that can be taken to ensure that the market remains competitive, or that the worst excesses in which Microsoft has engaged in the past are not repeated.[17] What cannot be discounted, as well, is recognizing that Microsoft's participation in e-Mexico is consistent with Bill Gates' concern with correcting "market failures," a subject he first broached when he addressed the World Economic Forum meeting in Davos, Switzerland on January 29, 2001.

What is clear is that e-Mexico is a coherent program underway that has garnered the support of Microsoft in a historic way. Mexico's digital divide is what separates the haves from the have-nots. It is clear that there are certain resentments among opposition parties, jealous of the seamless way Fox has enlisted the participation of Mexico's private institutions of higher learning, such as the Tecnológico de Monterrey, in this program. "In a town where one phone line serves 1,400 people, 18 computers and a satellite link are giving this community a vibrant connection to the world. Housed in the town's only high school, students use the computer center to pursue degrees from the Virtual University, a program of Tec de Monterrey University," the Associated Press reported in

June 2002. "Community members also use the computers to send e-mail, shop, and read news."

Since January 2001, Mexico's government has been working on the e-Mexico project that seeks to put federal government services online. The e-Mexico project has established 47 digital community centers with a goal of constructing 10,000 centers by 2006. The Virtual University project is available at 5 sites with 88 enrolled students. A major benefit of the rural university branches is how they enable many students to stay in their communities. Nestor Rojo, who hopes to build businesses in the area, said, "There is a lot of poverty, and there are a lot of needs . . . I probably would have been yet another migrant to the United States. But not now. Now I'm here."[18] The ease of this success is a repudiation of the PRI's seven decades of socialist mismanagement.

Fox is correct in placing an emphasis on "hooking up" Mexico for one other reason: in the United States, Hispanics are fast moving to narrow their own digital divide. "Considering the gap in income, the degree to which Hispanics are adopting technology is beyond expectations," Felipe Korzenny, principal author of *The Digital World of the U.S. Hispanic,* a 150-page report published by Cheskin Research in 2000, said. "[Hispanics have a] very strong motivation of not being left behind."[19] That fear is also the fear of falling behind economically as well. As we will examine next, in fact, linking education to antipoverty campaigns has met with unexpected success—and computers play a central role in that success.

## Education to Fight Poverty

By every economic measure, the most materially disadvantaged group of people in Mexico are her Native American citizens. The ten million indigenous people of Mexico remain excluded from the economic, social, and political mainstream of the nation's life. Critics have often accused the Mexican state of racism for this exclusion. Such accusations ignore the fact that, more often than not, the Spanish granted considerable autonomy to indigenous communities. "Náhuatl [the Aztec language] remained the language of the majority, including the bulk of the ruling group, even as more and more intrusive terminology was being adopted," Robert Haskett reports, writing of Spanish colonial rule in Cuernavaca. "Yet an ability to read, write, and to speak and understand Spanish were useful attributes since officers with such skills were much better equipped to deal with the colonial system than those who lacked them. This meant that education was one factor marking off the various sociopolitical strata within the jurisdiction's ruling group. . . . [I]t is no accident than [non-Europeans] unable to read or write dominated the jurisdiction's lower-level offices and had little chance for upward mobility."[20]

Vastly outnumbered by indigenous people, Spain ruled New Spain, but only because it allowed indigenous leaders to govern their local communities. The mosaic of alliances in which Native American peoples pledged loyalty in exchange for peace, was not unlike the political empire under which the Aztecs themselves had ruled. In granting indigenous rulers this kind of autonomy, parallel societies emerged over the centuries. As the twenty-first century unfolds, there are 56 ethnic groups speaking scores of languages throughout Mexico. In some rural communities, very few people speak Spanish, and are thus unable to participate in Mexico's modern life. Many Mexicans, well-intentioned and earnest, become frustrated when trying to come up with a workable solution for giving Native Americans greater opportunities.

This frustration is not uncommon, of course. Consider how the English writer D. H. Lawrence came down on the matter after an extended sojourn throughout the American Southwest and Mexico. In the short story "The Mozo," he wrote:

> To the Indians, there is near and far, and very near and very far. There is two days or one day. But two miles are as good as twenty to him, for he goes entirely by his feeling. If a certain two miles feels far to him, then it is far, it is muy lejos! But if a certain twenty miles feels near and familiar, then it is not far. Oh, no, it is just a little distance. And he will let you set off in the evening, for night to overtake you in the wilderness, without a qualm. It is not far.[21]

Written in the first half of the 20th century, D. H. Lawrence mocks the worldview of Mexico's indigenous people. Other, more sympathetic observers, report similar conclusions when assessing how many non-Western people view the world and their place in it.[22] Referring to the Bajau, a people who live in the Philippines, James Hamilton-Paterson describes his own spin on these attitudes:

> They are mostly unconvinced by the idea of education, so are often unwilling to send their children to school. Nor do they seem keen to learn new skills. And as for taking part in any social or political activity, it has proved almost impossible

to interest them. They suffer, in short, from an admirable lack of ambition.[23]

Under what circumstances is a "lack of ambition" ever "admirable"?

The answer is never—if one wants to get ahead in the modern world. Not unlike American educators frustrated by students who insist they can get ahead in the world without getting an education, Mexicans have mixed feelings about the peculiar ideas of the indigenous people. The perception is that these are communities of people who have disdain for modernity, but feel entitled to enjoy the material wealth market economies can generate. This ambivalence distorts how the process of Hispanization continues to unfold in one fundamental aspect. Native Americans are rightfully proud of who they are and their heritage, but reluctantly accept that they must adopt Western ways if they are to prosper, though they do this to varying degrees.

The ability to resist the temptation of the goodies in a shopping mall is not unique. At times, repudiation of American consumer culture more than perplexes American commentators: it has monumental consequences. Indeed, it is difficult to believe that millions of Mexicans come to the United States, work very hard to save a few thousand dollars, and then want nothing more than to return home. "The terrorists don't want our stuff—they lived among us and resisted being seduced by it," Maureen Dowd wrote in the *New York Times* of the September 11th hijackers, but she could very well have been referring to other cultures that embrace their spiritual lives more than their material ones. "America is still stunned that our sophisticated stuff could not protect us, that our trillion dollars' worth of weapons, radars and satellites all fell flat against a few brutes with box cutters."[24]

In the same way that Native Americans who, in the eighteenth century, had to learn Spanish and learn to deal with the colonial authorities to get ahead, in the Mexico emerging a decade into NAFTA, the power of "demonstration effects," which economists define as socioeconomic changes in demand as a result of one group of consumers' contact with another, is changing the minds of Mexicans. "I used to think the whole world was like my village," Antonio Ek, a Maya handyman, described. "But when I went to Cancún I saw things I had never seen before. I saw airplanes and high-rise hotels. There were so many kinds of different people, so many wealthy people from all over the world. The stores were like dreams, selling everything you could imagine. It made me realize just how much there is in the world, and I understood how many different kinds of people there are in different countries. It also made me feel good that they would make the effort to come and visit my homeland, and that they liked it here."[25]

Education programs that reach out to indigenous communities have been successful around the world. In Guatemala, where the eBay Foundation has spearheaded efforts to help the indigenous Maya people of San Pedro La Laguna, similar results are forthcoming. "Our kids are getting three years of computer training. It's excellent," Emilio Battz, who runs the Colegio Bethel (Bethel School), said of eBay's® efforts to help connect this rural community to the information superhighway. "I'm a [Maya], and we're typically very timid and think we're less important than those people with blue eyes and blond hair. Now that the children are learning new skills, they are seeing their own value."[26]

The importance of bridging the "digital divide" is important, for it allows greater numbers of children to be educated faster than it would take to recruit, train, and equip teachers for life in rural communities where most families are not fluent in Spanish. "We can't let the technological gap go on, but you have to devise a way to make it economically self-sustaining," Mauricio Valdés, the Central America coordinator for the United Nations Development Program, said. "In poor, rural, isolated areas, you can't just have computer access at a school. It has to become an information center for the community, because otherwise it's too expensive. There are local merchants and professionals who can benefit from a connection and, with time, be able to pay something for it. But these issues have to be discussed at the local level, in the villages, and not by people in New York."[27]

Perhaps, but people in New York can't be left out of the process, particularly if they are expected to provide the financing. The same holds true for people in Microsoft's offices in Seattle who have decided to assist the e-Mexico program. What is clear, however, is that lifting people out of poverty does not, at the local level, necessarily require vast amounts of money. At the Microcredit Summit Campaign held in Mexico City on October 7, 2001, for instance, 600 experts gathered to discuss how loans to the world's poor was empowering people by giving them credit to start their own small businesses. "Microcredit programs make loans for as little as $40 to help poor people with no credit history start businesses," Ginger Thompson reported. "The programs are aimed mostly at lifting up impoverished areas of the third world.

A total of 13.8 million people have been granted loans in Africa, Asia, Eastern Europe and Latin America."[28]

The Grameen Bank® in Bangladesh launched the microlending programs a generation ago. This bank's approach has been duplicated around the world. "A year and a half ago the women of the impoverished Wapishana and Macushi tribes of Guayana were introduced to the Internet in a project sponsored by Bill Humphries, who headed Guyana Telephone and Telegraph at the time and was optimistic about technology's money-making potential," Simon Romero reported. "The tribal power structures were shaken. The women began making money by marketing their intricate hand-woven hammocks over the Web at $1,000 each. Feeling threatened, the traditional regional leadership took control of the organization, alienating and finally driving out the young woman who ran the Web site. The weaving group fell into disarray."[29]

Rather than being discouraged, however, failures such as these underscore the importance of linking antipoverty campaigns with education programs. That women are the primary beneficiaries of microlending programs should constitute one component as education and technology are brought to the disenfranchised. Mexico has a tremendous opportunity to reform its Public Education Secretariat, or SEP, building on the fast-track development of e-Mexico and the momentum generated by the United Nations conference held in Monterrey in March 2002. "Two weeks ago no one was even thinking about an increase [in aid to poor countries]," World Bank president James D. Wolfenson said. As a result of the conference, however, the United States and the European Union were "prepared to write checks," he told reporters. "That's not a Hollywood step, that's a real step."[30]

Mexico's Fox is also writing checks. Having promised to double his government's expenditures on education—and galvanized by the success of Progresa, a program that pays poor families to keep their children in school—Fox expects to spend $35 billion annually on education. Education throughout Latin America has increased, though the quality of that education still needs to catch up. "Two-thirds of Latin American children now get at least some secondary education, whereas only half did in the mid-1980s. Young Mexicans now receive, on average, 7.7 years of schooling, up from just 1.7 years in 1940," the London *Economist* reported. "Progresa, the Mexican scheme, has been so successful that some economists now urge it on the United States."[31]

The closed minds of a closed economy have given way to an

open economy that requires open minds. It is imperative, then, that educators be educated, particularly now that the needs of an open economy require changes in how Mexicans are educated. Decrying that disorganized "schools and poorly trained teachers mean that much education spending in Latin America is wasted," the London *Economist* pointed out that fundamental changes are in order. Lamenting that "[t]eachers often receive only the barest guidance on what to teach, and little or no training in how to teach it. . . . Many [teachers] falsely imagined that their pupils were doing well, the study found, and thus did not push them to achieve better," the London *Economist* suggests that there is a considerable opportunity in training Mexican teachers and providing lesson plans, textbooks, and materials. These problems have been perpetuated by an almost complete lack of accountability in education.[32] The market opportunity in teaching teachers is estimated at 20 percent of what Fox expects to spend on education, which amounts to $7 billion annually, or $70 billion over the next decade.[33]

As Fox moves to double the nation's investments in education, it is imperative that, as Progresa has demonstrated is possible, antipoverty programs be linked as an integral part of reaching out to the neediest. Indeed, that e-Mexico focuses on training 20,000 Mexicans in computer programming, which continues to be a profession dominated by men, could very well balance the gender issues that arise from the continuing expansion of microlending programs. The market opportunities found in providing complementary education and microlending programs are enormous. "More than 53 million Latin Americans are malnourished, with Haitians, Nicaraguans, Bolivians and Hondurans experiencing the highest rates," the World Food Program, known as the WFP, reported at the end of 2000, a reminder of the fact that Latin Americans are looking to Mexico.[34] That is not lost on officials at the World Bank. "If Mexico approached this as a market, it could launch a major campaign in which $750 million were used to bring education to the poor, and $250 million in microloans to the poor," an official at the World Bank argued. "Spreading this over ten years would close the digital divide—and you would see a significant closing in the income distribution inequalities, particularly when the role of remittances increase[s] Mexicans' savings."[35]

The importance of improving Mexico's educational system is of great economic importance. The loss of factory jobs along the border is consistent with several factors, each of which underscores the role of education in moving from an unskilled to a skilled labor force.[36] Mexico is promoting the establishment of in-bond operations away from the border, bringing jobs to where people are located being preferable to the social disruptions caused by massive internal migration. Maytag's expansion of its operations in Reynosa, for instance, creates jobs away from the border region, alleviating pressure on the social and economic infrastructure there. At the same time, as Mexico moves to second-stage operations, the emphasis is less on un- or semi-skilled labor and more on skilled labor; the jobs moving from Mexico to China consist of four 45-hour weeks paying between \$216–\$286 per month. Clothing manufacturers are less desirable than high-tech jobs.[37] One way of protecting Mexican employment, however, is to produce for the domestic market. "Efforts also are underway to reclaim a 100-million-strong domestic consumer market that has been almost entirely lost to competition from illegal imports," Lee Romney reported in the *Los Angeles Times.* "Fox—an avid free-trader who aims to increase the number of Mexico's global partners while developing higher-wage jobs at home—has pledged his help in that battle."[38]

These strategies—bringing jobs to towns in Mexico's interior; making sure that these are more skilled, higher-paying jobs; and producing for the domestic market—have repercussions along the border. The short-term effect is that the reconfiguration of the maquiladora industry in Ciudad Juárez, where the number of jobs declined from 220,000 to 160,000 between the end of 2001 and the summer of 2002, has repercussions for El Paso, Texas, where business depends on trade across the border.[39]

With the loss of more than 280,000 maquiladora jobs since the beginning of the economic downturn precipitated by the Internet bubble burst in 2000 and the heightened pressures associated with globalization, Mexico has been forced to embark on rethinking the role of its in-bond strategy. "Cheap as Mexico's labor is, it is not as cheap as that in Asia or Eastern Europe. They now attract the kind of manufacturing that sprang up here, first along the border with the United States and then farther south, in places like this balmy part of the Yucatán peninsula," Ginger Thompson reported. "Now, this area displays flickering signs of an industrial evolution in which Mexico's maquiladora industry moves to multimillion-dollar high-tech factories that offer skills, and even decent salaries, to workers."[40]

"We are not interested any more in these types of companies," Patricio Patrón, governor of the Yucatán state, told the *New York Times.* "They are part of an era we are trying to overcome. We want to give opportunities to higher level factories—and some are beginning to come." In these efforts, however, the legacy of Mexican Paternalism is evident. "Nonbelievers say such sentiments are wishful thinking. They note that the number of high-tech factories that have opened is relatively small, and say Mexico's poor education system cannot fill a labor pool large enough for highly skilled jobs."[41] Patrón anticipates the direction of Mexico during NAFTA's second decade, which is consistent with observations about salariat economies.[42] The concern here, then, is that the time when Mexico had to trade living standards for jobs is coming to an end.[43] "Mexico and its people came to accept these [draconian] conditions in return for steady jobs," Sam Dillon reported. "But now everyone from Mexican tax officials to environmental experts in both countries are debating the rules, written and unwritten, under which the mostly American corporations have operated on the border. There is rising concern that as factories making everything from sneakers to televisions have spread throughout the developing world, labor rights and environmental standards have often been overlooked."[44]

"I think there's this traditional archetype that technology is cold and it forms less whole people," Po Bronson, who chronicled the dot-com boom in Silicon Valley, said in an interview. "[Karl] Marx was watching the assembly line. You'd have one guy shape the nail, one guy sharpen the point, one guy place the head on, and so on. Now, I think, we've shifted to a more Japanese concept of teams and people working together to achieve quality. And under that model, I think things have changed. Many people now have wildly expansive jobs that are not well defined. . . . Yes, it is still capitalism, and it is still about profit, and who controls things still matters."[45] To manage effectively, however, requires an educated and experienced workforce. Finding qualified managers has long frustrated efforts to expand the number of more skilled factories. "A lot of times, when [companies] go down there, they can't find skilled managers, so they have to send . . . expatriates, and that's extremely expensive," Susan Kirchner, president of Kirchner International Marketing Group, told *Marketing News.*[46] Fox's emphasis on education as a national priority reflects the need to educate Mexican laborers, crucial if Mexico is to bridge the digital and educational divides that still exist.

### Education for Enriching Lives

The silver lining in having fallen behind is that when one decides to catch up, one can do so by getting the latest model, rather than by trading in to upgrade. "Countries like Mexico enjoy something of an advantage when it comes to such advanced technology," Anthony DePalma wrote of Mexico's introduction of wireless telephony technology. "Existing systems are so primitive that little is worth saving. Everything old can be replaced with the newest technology. 'We have a lot of customers who take pride in leapfrogging over existing technologies and bragging, "I have the same technology that MCI WorldCom has,"' [Martha Helena] Bejar, said."[47]

Bejar, the general manager of Canada's Nortel Networks Latin America, exemplifies the seamless ability of corporate Canada to become integrated into Latin America. "We were able to get in with our wireless products in Brazil, Chile, Colombia and Central America, and to capitalize on the liberalization of the markets," she told Anthony DePalma.[48]

Wireless communications has enormous potential for changing the lives of Mexico's poor, linking them to education and new opportunities. "Cellular operators in Southeast Asia witnessed long ago how rural populations can benefit from being connected. In Thailand, one operator found shrimp farmers calling Bangkok to get prices—and the upper hand on middlemen. Similarly, Smart Communications, a Philippine cellular operator, learned that vegetable farmers who had never had regular fixed-line phone service were using mobile phones to market their produce in Manila," Wayne Arnold reports.[49] That it has to be done by government, even if it requires Keynesian deficit spending, is not in doubt. "If it had been left to the private sector, the Interstates would never have been built," in the United States, Ken Gibson at McKinsey & Company's offices in Indonesia, said, underscoring the proper role of government in creating the conditions for markets.[50]

The role of education, apart from allowing an individual to earn a better living, is to provide him or her with a more rewarding life. The failures of the Mexican public education system in this regard are seen in the Mexicans migrants in the United States. The Census Bureau's analysis of the 2000 census indicated that, among Hispanics, Mexicans lag in education. One in 4 Cuban-Americans, for instance, has a college degree. One in 8 Puerto Ricans graduated from college. One in 15 Mexican-Americans, on the other hand, has completed a college education. Among the general population, one in 4 Americans has at least a college degree. As in Mexico, the ability of American Hispanics to pursue higher education is a question of costs. "Latino high school graduates enroll in college at a higher rate than non-Hispanic white students but are far less likely to earn a four-year degree—the single-most important key to higher earnings and leading jobs—a nonpartisan research group said here today," Diana Jean Schemo reported. "The report, issued by the Pew Hispanic Center, suggested that Latinos were held back by financial pressures, not a lack of interest in pursuing postsecondary education. Many enroll in two-year community colleges rather than four-year institutions, take partial course loads and must work to supplement their families' income."[51]

This is consistent with the reluctance of lower-income families to incur debt, even if it in the form of student loans; ample literature documents the risk-averse consumer behavior of the poor and working poor.[52] As a result, the educational disparities within Hispanics—with Cuban-Americans being on par with the national average and Mexican-Americans trailing horribly behind—are also a reflection of the educational systems in various countries.

This demonstrates the monumental failure of Mexico's public universities, where so many are excluded, and where, as in the United States, working-class families are reluctant to seek student loans in pursuit of higher education. Culturally, however, Mexico's poor are inclined to accept this philosophically (or fatalistically, depending on ones' degree of misanthropy). As a consequence, unlike the poor in other countries, Mexico's disenfranchised seldom feel helpless. "The depressed poor perceive themselves to be supremely helpless—so helpless that they neither seek nor embrace support," Andrew Solomon explains. "This means that most people who are poor and depressed stay poor and depressed. Poverty is depressing, and depression, leading as it does to dysfunction and isolation, is impoverishing."[53]

The challenges in expanding educational opportunities to the most disenfranchised Mexicans, for instance, are the same—on both sides of the border. Consider the problems encountered by the children of Mexican migrant workers in the United States. Following the harvest seasons in different parts of the country and for different crops makes it impossible for these children to participate in standard school years. "Students . . . almost inevitably lose time in the classroom when they shuttle between states with different school calendars," Pamela Mendels wrote in her report about a program to use the Internet to continue their studies. "The two-year-old project, known as Estrella ('star' in Spanish), is paid for with a $400,000 grant from the United States Department of Education. It seeks to use technology to alleviate a pressing problem among a group of high school students whose dropout rate is about 50 percent: lack of continuity in schooling."[54]

The living conditions of these children, of course, are another challenge they must overcome. "[M]any of the students do their lessons from their homes—often crowded, ramshackle housing that the program equips with phone service," Pamela Mendels reported. "Despite the obstacles, most of the 35 students who participated in the program's first year completed the classes, which are offered in subjects ranging from algebra to world history."[55]

Here, then, is an opportunity for Mexico's Education Secretariat, or SEP, to work with the U.S. Department of Education, since an estimated 2 million children move back and forth across the borders, and throughout the United States, on a seasonal basis. The success of the Estrella pilot program forms the basis of an international effort to provide education to the children of migrant workers. One source of funding are international agencies, including the World Bank, since officials contacted have expressed "tremendous interest in this proactive" pilot program that "could potentially benefit countless migrant children" whose education is "threatened by the circumstances of their parents' work."

The fluid nature of cross-border movement of the poor itself represents certain possibilities only now emerging. Not unlike the exponential growth of remittances as an industry, or the realization among American banks that the average migrant worker has $3,500 in savings, the worldview of Mexico's poor is changing rapidly. What Alain Giberstein reported as true among the Mexican business community also holds true for Mexico's working poor.[56] That more than three million Mexicans work in the United States seasonally and return to Mexico, is changing the aspirations of the working poor. Consider for a moment the challenges that poor people encounter when they are forced to learn rudimentary English, to use their wits to negotiate American society, and are able to gain employment, provide for themselves, save considerable amounts of money, return to their families, and repeat the cycle. This is not to say that Mexico should look to the United States for a public education model to emulate; Mexico would be better served by looking to the more sensible Canadians. That American public schools do a poor job is an understatement. Indeed, when social critic Camille Paglia decried the disparaging of trade schools and a bureaucracy that promotes the sustained "infantilization" of American youngsters in *Salon.com*, she generated more letters from the public than she had on any other subject.[57] Mexican executives, and to a lesser extent Canadian ones, remain perplexed why American parents encourage emotional dependence in their children. Anyone doubting this can watch episodes of MTV's *The Real World* as evidence of the infantilization of American youth.[58]

When Mexico's working poor arrive in the United States, there are certain changes that take place in how they see the world, and their place in it. Americans recognize this, and since the late 1980s a certain bias has emerged: American businessmen prefer to hire "Latino" immigrants over American-born job applicants. Only recently the subject of study by anthropologists, the idea that Catholic Latinos display a stronger Protestant work ethic than native Americans is absurd.[59] Indeed, the entire image of Latinos is being challenged within the Hispanic community in the United States. Hispanic cartoonist Lalo Alcaraz's nationally syndicated comic strip "La Cucaracha" spoofs the irony of the "Chicano" persona cultivated by certain segments of the Latino/Chicano/Mexican-American community.

'La Cucaracha' arrives with some big expectations," Natalie Hopkinson wrote in the *Washington Post*. "He'll rub them the wrong way sometimes," says Charles A. Ericksen, editor of the Washington-based news service Hispanic Link, which first published Alcaraz's editorial cartoons when he was in college. "But at the same time, they are going to have to recognize him as someone who truly stays in touch with the community and has developed a vehicle to educate the larger audience about what a Chicano is all about."[60]

This comic relief, however, underscores continuing social challenges Hispanics encounter. "In this all-black neighborhood [of Harlem], the likelihood of being rejected [for jobs] was greater for African Americans than it was for the Latinos who didn't live in the area. And this was in a black neighborhood with black customers, management and owners. This wasn't a racial divide, but a preference. Employers have a favorable impression of immigrant labor. Even though they themselves are black, they often have a jaundiced view of the urban, or African-American labor force. They had very fine-grain preferences when it came to immigrant labor," Katherine Newman, an anthropologist studying the working poor in America, told *Salon.com*. "I had managers say to me that what they really wanted were recent immigrants, people who grew up in really poor countries who would not think of this as a bad job, but instead as a king's ransom compared to what they might find in Haiti or the Dominican Republic. Latinos apply in smaller numbers than blacks but are much likelier to get hired."[61]

It is important to take notice of how NAFTA is changing long-held perceptions. The negative American view of Mexicans—as a sleepy workforce where everything could wait for mañana—has changed; Mexican immigrants are seen as harder workers than Americans. Managers, whether at meat-packing plants in North Carolina or at automotive engineering plants in Michigan, praise the work ethic of Hispanic factory workers and engineers alike. Here one sees yet another unintended consequence of NAFTA. The focus on education and educational opportunities also suggests how frustrated Mexicans are at their country's continued slide as first adopters. Mexicans, many Americans are surprised to learn, have historically been cutting edge in adopting technology; Mexico City boasted the first ATM network, among the first cordless phone technology, and Mexico was the first North American nation to introduce plastic currency.[62] These facts bode well for the success of creative educational reforms that recognize the newfound willingness of Mexico's uneducated and impoverished peoples to respond to new opportunities.

## SUMMARY

1.  After decades of languishing, Mexico's public education and public universities are poised to leap-frog ahead by linking education as an industry with antipoverty campaigns.

2.  The introduction of e-Mexico with the participation of America's Microsoft and the providing of wireless telephony services through Canada's Nortel Networks constitute a significant investment in the technological support required for a sustained expansion of education as an industry.

3.  International lending bodies have indicated support for Mexican efforts to assist both Mexico and the United States in meeting challenges the children of Mexico's working poor encounter on both sides of the border, offering funding for a heretofore neglected market.

4.  Mexico's investments in education, including the e-Mexico and microlending programs, are expected to reach $370 billion during 2004–2014.

# ENDNOTES

1. Fox has a stated goal of spending 7 percent of Mexico's GNP on education, which comes out to a minimum of $37 billion annually.
2. This is not to say that Frank is always right (though he is most of the time). A notorious misfire is his Op-Ed piece on the AOL Time Warner deal. See "A Merger's Message: Dominate or Die," by Robert Frank, *New York Times,* Jan 11, 2000.
3. The last American state to legalize black-white marriage was Alabama—in November 2000. "It's really interesting how much effort had to be undertaken by lawmakers in so many states in order to prohibit something that clearly was going on," Werner Sollors, author of *Interracialism: Black-White Intermarriage in American History, Literature, and Law,* said. "A whole apparatus of legislation arose to prohibit it, and in a way that runs against the grain of the democratic ethos. The free choice of the person you want to marry seems to be a pretty basic human right." Suzy Hansen's interview with Sollors is available at "Mixing It Up," *Salon.com,* March 8, 2001.
4. Consider what happened when a black female reporter was assigned to write a story on a white male teacher accused by students and their parents of racism. "I'm still trying to sort out what happened next, though admittedly, I'm not trying very hard," Erin Aubry Kaplan wrote in *Salon.com.* "The skeletal sequence of events goes something like this: [Alan] Kaplan and I talked some more [after the initial interview]; I interviewed more people, wrote a story in the span of about five days and published it. The story sympathized with racial inequities in public education, but disagreed with the black parents' indictment of Kaplan. . . . We did wonder aloud about the propriety of a reporter falling for a source, but we couldn't do anything about it except keep a low profile for a while." Miscegenation, then, is the process by which humans open their minds to new possibilities, including the exhilarating possibility of love. See "The Color of Love," by Erin Aubry Kaplan, *Salon.com,* February 14, 2001.
5. However well intentioned, José Vasconcelos' arguments are racist: arguing that one race is superior to or more desirable than another must be condemned in no uncertain terms.
6. "Mexico Meets the Zapatistas," Editorial, *Washington Post,* March 17, 2001.
7. "Can International Relief Do More Good Than Harm?" by Ian Fisher, *New York Times,* February 11, 2001.
8. "Native Canadian Children High on Fumes Fuel a Fight Over Who Should Help Them," by Elena Cherney, *Wall Street Journal,* January 10, 2001.
9. Capitalism is "disgusting," one student leader during the occupation of the Mexico City campus explained to me—before asking if I could donate a Palm Pilot. Without one, one presumes, anarchists have a hard time coordinating their protests in an orderly fashion.
10. "Mexico's Fox Moves Chiapas to Top of His List," by José de Cordoba and Peter Fritsch, *Wall Street Journal,* February 22, 2001.
11. *What Went Wrong?: Western Impact and Middle Eastern Response,* by Bernard Lewis, New York: Oxford University Press, 2001, page 25. Though an engaging discussion, it should be noted that Lewis presents certain ideas that are not as charitable toward Islam, particularly his argument that the

West has historically responded to Islamic provocations. On many occasions it is the West that has wronged Muslims; the expulsion of the Muslim people from the Iberian peninsula in 1492—and the subsequent sacking of Granada—is one flagrant example. Lewis' arguments, however, have gained currency, as more and more intellectuals have called for a Judeo-Christian "jihad" against Islam. "The terrorists chose their targets well when they struck on Sept. 11, 2001," David Rieff wrote, calling for war. "By destroying the symbolic center of international capitalism—the World Trade Center; what name could be more alluring if your aim was to bring globalization to its knees?—and the military command center of the most powerful nation in the world, the reality that no person, no place and no institution is beyond the terrorists' reach was driven. It will not be forgotten in the lifetime of anyone alive when the towers fell, whatever the outcome of the war against terrorism to which the United States has committed itself." See "There Is No Alternative to War," David Rieff, *Salon.com*, September 25, 2001.

12. "The Work of a Hemisphere," by Colin L. Powell, *New York Times*, April 19, 2001.

13. *LMT Business Journal*, August 23, 2001.

14. Press conference in Mexico City, April 25, 2002.

15. "Fears About Microsoft Return, in Mexico," by Graham Gori, *New York Times*, April 24, 2002.

16. For more information, see "Fears About Microsoft Return, in Mexico," by Graham Gori, *New York Times*, April 24, 2002. "The effort here is basically to create a cadre of trained professionals who are oriented to Microsoft products," Gary Chapman, director of the open-source initiative at the University of Texas, told Graham Gori. "It's a very good strategy because it comes across as being concerned about the developing world. But at the same time, these countries could be making themselves independent of Microsoft with free software." Then again, Mr. Chapman doesn't say where Mexicans can get computers on which to run the open-source software that's "free" for the downloading. Software may be "free"—but computers and Internet access are not.

17. There is also the real possibility that, having become the world's wealthiest man, Bill Gates is sincere in helping the world. "We're falling short for literally billions of children," Bill Gates told reporters covering the United Nations summit for children in New York on May 9, 2002. "And these micronutrients make a huge difference: if we have proper vitamin A support, it reduces mortality by over 30 percent, which means that alone is saving hundreds of thousands of lives." Announcing a $50 million gift from the Bill and Melinda Gates Foundation, this philanthropic gesture came with no strings attached. "It's really a virtuous cycle. . . . As children are more healthy, they're able to learn more . . . women choose to have fewer children, the ability to invest in education and having more economic opportunity goes up," Bill Gates reminded his audience.

18. "In a Remote Mexican Town, Internet Brings Higher Education to a New Class," Associated Press, June 11, 2001, *http://www.siliconvalley.com/mld/siliconvalley/news/editorial/3435611.htm*.

19. "Hispanics Are Narrowing the Digital Divide," by Kate Harner, *New York Times*, April 6, 2000.

20. Robert Haskett, *Indigenous Rulers: An Ethnohistory of Town Government in Colonial Cuernavaca,* Albuquerque: University of New Mexico Press, 1991, pages 144–145.

21. "The Mozo," by D. H. Lawrence in *Mornings in Mexico.*

22. D. H. Lawrence writes, of course, in a time when Europe looked down on the whole of the New World. The British thought of the United States as a primeval Arcadia, with Americans being a sturdy breed but totally lacking in sophistication. This national low self-esteem, after all, is what drove Americans like Henry James and T. S. Eliot to journey to Europe in search of tradition, history, and manners and to reinvent themselves. The same parent-child relationship between the British and the Americans one sees between the United States and Latin America. In the same way that after the conclusion of the Second World War this relationship shifted, the United States embodied the future vis-à-vis a ravaged Europe. It can now be argued that a parallel shift is unfolding, where the most compelling cultural forces are being nurtured in Latin America—and among Americans of Latin American descent.

23. James Hamilton-Paterson. *The Great Deep: The Sea and Its Thresholds,* New York: Random House, 1992, page 260.

24. "All That Glistens," by Maureen Dowd, *New York Times,* October 3, 2001.

25. Interviews with Antonio Ek, February 2001.

26. "High-Tech Philanthropy in a Low-Tech Guatemalan Village," by Abby Ellin, *New York Times,* June 4, 2000.

27. Ibid.

28. "Small Loans Help Millions of World's Poorest, Coalition Says," by Ginger Thompson, *New York Times,* October 8, 2001.

29. "How a Byte of Knowledge Can Be Dangerous, Too," by Simon Romero, *New York Times,* April 23, 2000. Gender tensions arise when women begin to earn money independently of men. "Redistributing income from men to women, sharing out the misery of a shrinking cake, is not going to solve other people's problems," Para Teare, a London-based social scientist, is quoted as saying in Simon Romero's article.

30. "More Entreaties in Monterrey for More Aid to the Poor," by Tim Weiner, *New York Times,* March 22, 2002.

31. "Cramming Them In," *The Economist,* May 9, 2002. The case for the United States adopting a program similar to Mexico's Progresa was bolstered when Manpower Research Demonstration Corp.® issued a report linking welfare reform and children's achievement in school. "Welfare-to-work programs that increase parents' income as well as hours on the job help children do better in school," Laura Meckler reported. "On one level, the report confirms what is almost a truism: Having more money is usually better than having less. But as policy makers work to improve the lives of the poor and to help kids do better in school, the study offers the first concrete data [in the United States] to suggest that spending tax dollars to increase family income translates into school improvement." See "Report: Welfare Reform, Achievement Linked," by Laura Meckler, *Salon.com,* January 23, 2001.

32. "Cramming Them In," *The Economist,* May 9, 2002.

33. There are critics of these efforts, however. "Hubert Kleinpeter, who recently completed his doctoral dissertation at Florida State University on street and working children in Mexico, said he is skeptical about what [a

program to help street children called] Ayúdame! can accomplish. Last
year, during his research, he drove along much of the Texas-Mexico
border. 'All across Mexico, they have these programs sponsored by local
state governments that want to sweep the streets of this nuisance called
children,' Dr. Kleinpeter said. 'Well, you've got to ask yourself, "Who's the
nuisance for?" ' " Brenda Rodr´guez reported. See "Young Workforce
Toils in Mexico," by Brenda Rodr´guez, *Dallas Morning News*, July 7, 2002."

34.   "U.N. Says 53 Million People Malnourished," *Los Angeles Times*, December
      13, 2000.

35.   Interview in March 2002.

36.   "The only companies that are operating successfully on the border are
      high-tech plants," John Christman at the Ciemex-WEFA consulting service
      was quoted as saying. "The low-skilled plants are either going to move
      inland or leave Mexico." See "Fallout of U.S. Recession Drifts South into
      Mexico," by Ginger Thompson, *New York Times*, December 26, 2001.

37.   Mexicans in California, in fact, are fast becoming a force in Silicon Valley.
      "Immigrant workers from Mexico are still struggling to make a living, but
      today they face exploitation not only in the fields, but on assembly lines
      of high-tech corporations in Silicon Valley such as Hewlett-Packard,"
      Elizabeth Gonzales reported. See "Mexican Workers Invisible Part of
      Silicon Valley Backbone," by Elizabeth Gonzales, *Pacificnews.org*, April 18,
      2001.

38.   "As U.S. Demand Shrinks, Mexico's Garment Makers Alter Strategies," by
      Lee Romney, *Los Angeles Times*, April 22, 2001.

39.   Royal Philips Electronics®, for instance, transferred its computer monitor
      production operations from Juárez to other plants in China in July 2002.
      See "Maquiladora Industry Suffers; Layoffs Continue," by Diana
      Washington Valdez, *El Paso Times*, July 10, 2002.

40.   "Mexico Is Attracting a Better Class of Factory in Its South," by Ginger
      Thompson, *New York Times*, June 29, 2002.

41.   "Mexico Is Attracting a Better Class of Factory in Its South," by Ginger
      Thompson, *New York Times*, June 29, 2002. "It's inevitable that countries
      that earn their money through relatively cheap labor, as their situation
      improves and the labor costs go up, they just have to move up on the
      technology scale," Sidney Weintraub, an economist at the Center for
      Strategic and International Studies, was quoted as saying.

42.   The well-publicized problems with garment factories are a concern for
      Mexican officials. The obstacles in standardizing labor practices are
      enormous, as I know from researching a previous book about the Gap®,
      Banana Republic® and Old Navy. Even when companies try to make
      right, it can be difficult. "The lesson from Gap's experience in
      El Salvador is that competing interests among factory owners,
      government officials, American managers and middle-class consumers—
      all with their eyes on the lowest possible cost—make it difficult to achieve
      even basic standards, and even harder to maintain them," Leslie Kaufman
      and David González reported. In that article, Kaufman and González
      report that to "duplicate these intensive efforts at each of the 4,000
      independent factories it contracts with would have taken about 4.5
      percent of [the Gap's] annual profit of $877 million last year." In other
      words, the cost to the Gap to bring some benefits to thousands of workers
      around the world would mean its profit would fall to $837 million from

$877 million in 2000; society expects better ethics from responsible corporate citizens. See "Labor Standards Clash with Global Reality," by Leslie Kaufman and David González, *New York Times*, April 24, 2001.

43. "Mexico has [historically] chosen to compete on labor costs, but because of that, it hasn't made the transition to more productivity-based industrial development," Richard Sinkin, managing director at the InterAmerican Holdings Company® in San Diego, commented on the exodus of maquiladora jobs from the U.S.-Mexico border to China. See "Manufacturing Jobs Are Exiting Mexico," by Elisabeth Malkin, *New York Times*, November 5, 2002.

44. "Profits Raise Pressures on U.S.-Owned Factories in Mexican Border Zone," by Sam Dillon, *New York Times*, February 15, 2001.

45. "5 Questions With . . . Po Bronson," by David Lawlor, *Business 2.0*, February 14, 2001.

46. Susan Kirchner is quoted in "Fox Plans Reforms," *Marketing News*, February 26, 2001.

47. The same technology, but not the same accounting practices, one would hope. See "Nortel Makes Inroads in Building Wireless World in Latin America," by Anthony DePalma, *New York Times*, June 19, 2000.

48. "Nortel Makes Inroads in Building Wireless World in Latin America," by Anthony DePalma, *New York Times*, June 19, 2000.

49. "Hook Up Rural Asia, Some Say, and Poverty Can Be Mitigated," by Wayne Arnold, *New York Times*, January 19, 2001.

50. Ibid. This point is not clearly apparent. Of any Keynesian approach to economic development, for instance, Mary Anastasia O'Grady of the *Wall Street Journal* offers no apologies: "It has failed repeatedly the world over, most recently in Japan, producing only more sophisticated methods of tax evasion and discouraging both consumption and investment. Mexico needs economic activity, something that is produced by minimizing taxation and regulation, thereby making the business environment more appealing to investors and entrepreneurs." See "Young Mexicans Thirst for Fox's Promised Prosperity," by Mary Anastasia O'Grady, *Wall Street Journal*, July 7, 2000.

51. "Finances Hold Back Hispanic College Students, Study Finds," by Diana Jean Schemo, *New York Times*, September 6, 2002.

52. Spectacular exceptions are seen in "get rich quick" schemes, whether in the form of pyramid schemes or the encouragement of gambling. What alarms is how the more vulnerable are deceived. "Intoxicated by the promise of easy money, thousands of Haitians here and abroad sold their cars, mortgaged their homes and emptied their savings account in recent months to invest in cooperatives that promised astonishing monthly returns of 10 percent," David González reported from Port-au-Prince in the summer of 2002. "More than $200 million has been lost in unsound or illegal cooperatives that took investors' money and bought luxurious properties, fleets of buses or just spirited it abroad." See "A Get-Rich Scheme Collapses, Leaving Haiti Even Poorer," by David González, *New York Times*, July 26, 2002.

53. "A Cure for Poverty," by Andrew Solomon, *New York Times*, May 6, 2001.

54. "Children of Migrant Workers Keep Up Studies on the Internet," by Pamela Mendels, *New York Times*, August 25, 1999.

55. Ibid. This is not to say that there aren't critics of the program. "It

promises to solve a problem without addressing the real nature of the problem involved—an exploitative labor system," Douglas M. Sloan, professor at Columbia University's Teachers College, told Pamela Mendels.

56.   Another measure of how Mexican attitudes are changing is seen in the healthy skepticism towards former leaders. When the disgraced Carlos Salinas wrote his 1,395-page book *Mexico: A Difficult Step to Modernity* in 2001, it was widely scorned. "Mr. Salinas conceded that he had very little credibility left among Mexicans and that many might regard the book as a self-serving attempt to rehabilitate his reputation," Anthony DePalma wrote in the *New York Times*. (See "Disgraced Mexican Is Back, with Accusations of His Own," by Anthony DePalma, *New York Times*, October 8, 2000.) "Salinas has the air of a once great man who cannot come to terms with his fall. . . . In the eyes of many Mexicans he remains a potent symbol of the hardships they faced after the economic crash [of December 1994]," Alan Zarembo wrote the following week in *Newsweek*. (See "A Man of His Words," by Alan Zarembo, *MSNBC.com*, October 16, 2000.)

57.   "Thanks for your great comments about how useless and destructive [American] high schools are," Judy Warner wrote, typical of the hundreds of letters sent via e-mail. See "Welcome to My World: Readers Respond to Camille Paglia's Recent Thoughts on Education," *Salon.com*, April 6, 2001.

58.   In *The Real World*, 21-year-olds behave at the maturity level of 12-year-olds; it documents how sheltered and shallow young American adults can be. Consider how Camille Paglia encapsulates the argument: "You say the young are far too immature to survive at 14? Well, that's proof positive that they've been infantilized by their parents in this unctuously caretaking yet flagrantly permissive culture that denies middle-class students adulthood until they are in their 20s and later—long after their bodies are ready to mate and reproduce. The Western career system is institutionalized neurosis, elevating professional training over spiritual development and forcing the young to put emotional and physical satisfaction on painful hold. The trades need to be revalorized. Young men and women should be encouraged to consider careers outside the effete, word-obsessed, office-bound professions. Construction, plumbing, electrical wiring, forestry, landscaping, horticulture: Such pursuits allow free movement and require a training of the body as well as the mind." See "Welcome to My World," by Camille Paglia, *Salon.com*, March 21, 2001.

59.   One unintended result of Mexican immigration to the United States is the importance of their support for the Catholic Church after the sex scandals rocked that institution. "If there is one group whose loyalty the Roman Catholic Church in the United States is counting on as it tries to repair the damage caused by revelations of sexual abuse by priests, it is the 21 million Hispanic-American Catholics who make up more than 30 percent of all Catholics in the nation," Anthony DePalma reported. "So far, that loyalty has remained steadfast." Relations between Mexicans and Catholic leaders are far different from what Graham Greene portrayed in his novel *The Power and the Glory*. See "Hispanics Still Backing Catholic Leaders, for Now," by Anthony DePalma, *New York Times*, May 1, 2002.

60.   "Stinging Insect: Lalo Alcaraz's 'La Cucaracha' Hits the Funnies" by Natalie Hopkinson, *Washington Post*, November 25, 2002.

61.  "Burger Barn Blues," by Daryl Lindsey, *Salon.com,* April 30, 1999. For more information on the urban working poor in the United States, see *No Shame in My Game* by Katherine Newman.

62.  The first ATM, operated by Banamex, went into use in the early 1980s in Mexico City. Following Australia's lead, Mexico announced in 2002 that it would start manufacturing plastic currency. (Australia introduced the plastic bank note in 1988 and about 20 countries around the world have followed suit, from New Zealand to Brazil to Thailand.)

# 8

# The Business of
# Environmentalism

## EXECUTIVE ABSTRACT

In response to the opposition to NAFTA by environmentalists, the North American Agreement on Environmental Cooperation, or NAAEC, was passed as a corollary to the NAFTA treaty. NAAEC's mandate to restore natural habitats remains largely unfulfilled. Critics point to the NAAEC's lack of authority and absence of enforcement mechanism as detrimental to any effort to safeguard the environment within the context of NAFTA.[1] But these shortcomings present rare opportunities. While Mexican officials too often fail to act—denying or granting a permit is a superior outcome to letting an application languish in a bureaucratic purgatory—there are signs that environmentalism is beginning to emerge as an industry as a consequence of two trends. First, erratic weather and changed climate patterns since the late 1990s associated with "global warming" theories have brought to the political foreground the need to manage resources among the NAFTA nations. Second, Mexico's "wastelands" problem is reaching a critical stage. While Mexican officials have been intimidated by the uncharted aspects of a state-of-the-art waste management industry, the effects of environmental despoliation make it impossible for Mexico to delay much longer issuing permits to American and Canadian companies that are leaders in this field and that hold the answers Mexico needs. The wastewater management crisis can no longer wait for officials who, as T. S. Eliot suggested in his masterful poem "The Waste Land," lack the strength to make decisions, or revisions.

## DISCUSSION

In the early 1990s, environmentalists opposed NAFTA fearing that under the guise of "free trade," corporate interests in the postindustrialized United States and Canada would pressure Mexico into commercial arrangements that exploited its weaker environmental laws. A more accurate assessment is slightly different. Foreign companies have, at times, taken advantage of Mexico's chronic shortage of qualified scientists, regulators, and knowledgeable public officials to circumvent expensive legal requirements in their home nations. Indeed, one argument against NAFTA raised by Ralph Nader was that this treaty would allow unscrupulous companies to shift operations to Mexico simply to avoid environmental protection regulation in the United States and Canada. The worst-case scenarios envisioned by alarmists prior to NAFTA—trucks filled with toxic materials, barges loaded with radioactive wastes entering Mexico and being dumped indiscriminately—have not come to pass.[2]

Of greater concern, however, is that Mexico has failed to protect its environment. The proper disposal of waste, whether produced by a growing economy or a flourishing population, lagged during NAFTA's first decade. The failure to develop environmentalism as an industry lies squarely in Mexico City. Though it can be argued that during NAFTA's first decade, it was premature for environmentalism to emerge as an industry, this excuse can only be offered for a certain time. It is also true that the Zedillo administration has been faulted for being overly cautious, particularly given a shortage of capable officials in Mexico familiar with the needs of waste management and environmentalism as an industry.

Criticisms that would have been harsh in the 1990s, however, are valid in the 2000s, particularly in light of the alarming stagnation during Fox's first two years in office in addressing environmental issues. Indeed, American and Canadian officials have expressed their frustration at the indecision of their Mexican counterparts with increasing resentment since 1999, one reason that the negotiations of a hemisphere-wide free-trade agreement includes the "greening" of NAFTA.[3] Expectations that the Fox administration would tackle these issues remain largely unfulfilled. The events of September 11, 2001, coupled with a hostile opposition in the Mexican Congress, have delayed Fox's agenda in critical areas. Complementary and overlapping interests—environmental management, air and water pollution control, and infrastructure improvements—could be best served in the metropolitan area by the creation of a comprehensive management plan that addresses the urgent needs of Mexico's maturing economy.

## An Unrealized Market

What emerges is the real threat that the Fox administration will further delay the creation of a modern waste management industry in Mexico and undermine the development of environmentalism as an industry. It is imperative for Mexico to seize unique opportunities during the 2003–2005 time frame. In the wastewater management industry alone, it is estimated that the market potential exceeds $40 billion.[4] When a fair assessment of the potential for environmentalism, as defined in the present discussion, is included, an additional $25 billion market emerges.

It is only fair to give NAFTA the benefit of the doubt, particularly since there is so much that is not known. When Richard Knight at Colorado State University, for instance, conducted the first-ever analysis of wildlife biology, comparing 93 sites in wildlife refuges, ranches, and subdivisions with one house per 40 acres in the American Southwest, the presumption that ranches encroach on native species was turned upside down. "He found that the ranches had at least as many species of birds, carnivores and plants as similar areas that are protected as wildlife refuges. Ranches also had fewer invasive weeds," Jon Christensen reported. "More important, the ranches provided a better habitat for wildlife than the ranchettes, which had fewer native species and more invasive species than ranches and refuges. Like many ecologists, Dr. Knight had assumed that grazing hurt wildlife. 'It finally dawned on me,' he said. 'We made a mistake.'"[5]

During the 1990s, the Mexican economy was not sufficiently developed for the emergence of waste management and environmentalism as an industry. The peso devaluation of December 1994 undermined the natural evolution of various industries. Mexican officials often lacked the experience to make sound decisions. But these circumstances have changed in the 2000s. The United States, Canada, and France are uniquely positioned to take advantage of establishing significant market shares as the market for waste management develops. In fact, as this industry unfolds, it is imperative to be mindful of the dispiriting antecedents that surround it. The lack of progress in NAFTA's first decade, however, is arguably a result of the lead time required for the proper development of this industry. Establishing fast food franchises or introducing expedited shipping services can be accomplished in a few years; complex environmental industries in which local, state, and federal jurisdictions overlap require a significantly longer lead time. American companies that attempted to secure "first mover" positions during NAFTA's first decade consequently have been disappointed.

Here are some suggestions for improvement and examples:

- *Heed the cautionary tales of the industry's "first movers" during NAFTA's first decade.* Waste management is perhaps the industry with the greatest unrealized potential, simply because it remains encumbered with the worst excesses of Mexican Paternalism. The story of Metalclad®, the Newport Beach, CA-based company that bought a landfill in Guadalcazar, San Luis Potos´ in 1993, is representative of the obstacles and frustrations encountered in the late 1990s. After spending millions of dollars, Metalclad found itself trapped in Mexican politics, in disputes with regulators and forced to file the first-ever complaint with NAFTA authorities.[6] Another tale of woe is found in the experience of Grupo Tec-Med®, the environmental services subsidiary of Spain's AVC® construction firm, in Sonora. The 52-acre landfill, built by the Ford® plant in the state and transferred to Sonora state government, which then deeded it to Hermosillo City, was sold to the Spanish firm in 1996. The problem arose when opposition leaders attacked the terms under which the landfill was sold and how it operated. Citing "sociopolitical problems," the National Ecological Institute, or INE, cancelled the operating permit and Grupo Tec-Med filed suit under an investor-protection treaty between Mexico and Spain—with free-trade negotiators of the European Union following developments closely.[7]

- *Proposals must reflect projects with sound track records.* When Gabriel Quadri headed the INE, he appointed Jorge Sánchez to head its Waste and Hazardous Activities department.[8] "We got rid of this idea that we've always viewed the businessman as the enemy. It had always been that way. We looked [instead] for an alliance with businessmen."[9] An arresting example of a success story under Jorge Sánchez's leadership was the creation of Mexico's domestic industry for handling hazardous hospital wastes. Whereas in 1994 Mexico had no capacity to do so, it can now process almost all of its hazardous hospital wastes.[10]

- *Allay Mexican concerns that U.S. companies seeking permits to operate landfills will smuggle U.S. toxic waste into Mexico.* When Servicios Ambientales de Mexico®, a partnership between Mexican investors and Laidlaw®, for instance, sought a permit to operate a landfill in Coahuila State, Mexican officials were stunned to find that the project proposal was written in English and listed as "clients" American concerns as varied as Chevron® and the Port Authority of New York and New Jersey. The implication was that the landfill to be operated in their state would, at some point, become the final resting place for toxic waste produced by American companies and municipalities.[11]

- *Include technology transfer as a part of a proposal.* The reality of a NAFTA "partnership" is best realized when Mexican officials understand that the development of a waste management industry in Mexico will offer opportunities to Mexicans. This has occurred with breathtaking speed in other industries. When American companies were hard pressed to find qualified software programmers in anticipation of the Y2K concerns, a few began to recruit at the Instituto de Tecnologia y Estudios Superiores de Monterrey (ITESM). Within three years, Mexico catapulted to the sixth out of more than 160 nations that sent skilled workers to the United States, behind only other English-speaking nations.[12] The proposal of creating a "school of waste management" in cooperation with a university or institution of higher learning in the host state would give a certain gravitas to a proposal for hazardous-waste treatment and disposal project.

- *Understand the learning curve that Mexican officials face.* Despite the imminent arrival of NAFTA's second decade, the waste management industry intimidates Mexican officials simply because it is a new industry. "In the U.S., you apply for something and you either get it or you don't. Personally, I think the people are scared to make a decision. But they keep making me think that it's just any time now I'm going to get approval," said Jack Menzie, a developer in Baton Rouge who proposed the 1,700 acre waste-treatment center in Méndez, Tamaulipas.[13]

Armed with the benefit of hindsight, these challenges can be met as a modern waste management industry develops.

The creation of environmentalism as an industry likewise requires vision. This can best be accomplished through the creation of environmental management areas. Indeed, as this second decade approaches, the United States, Canada, and Mexico would be prudent to establish "continental" strategies for managing their natural resources. It is not enough to say that America's demand for energy (from Mexico) and water (from Canada) will determine the timing and scope of how the region's resources are managed. Indeed, if Mexico's ambivalence frustrated its NAFTA partners for most of the 1990s, looming environmental crises reduce the government's room for maneuverability. Managing the environmental resources along the U.S.-Mexico border is creating conflicts, with mutual accusations and acrimonious relations undermining the cooperative spirit that NAFTA envisions. Within Mexico, millions of tons of hazardous wastes dissipate into the environment; more than three-quarters of the Mexican people live within five polluted river basins, representing a continued and sustained threat to their health.[14]

For the Fox administration, whose economic program has been hampered by a recession and the aftermath of the September 11, 2001 terrorist attack, it is imperative to realize that the waste management industry is a tremendous opportunity for foreign investment and job creation.[15] Standardizing the rules—leveling the playing field nationally—and mustering the political determination to open this market to domestic and foreign investment are necessary. A strong case can be made that the Fox administration could be successful in attracting significant foreign investment—and creating tens of thousands of jobs—in a comprehensive program to modernize Mexico's waste management industry.

NAFTA, however, envisions the creation of new markets. Some of these markets are characterized by a sense of urgency precipitated by unexplained climatic changes across the whole of North America. Other markets address the growing consensus that our planet's ecosystems are as interrelated as they are fragile and that it will take a partnership between government, academic, business, and civic organizations to protect and manage threatened habitats.

Following are five Environmental Management Areas (EMA) that represent the kinds of opportunities emerging in the new industry of environmentalism:

### 1. U.S.-MEXICO BORDER ENVIRONMENTAL MANAGEMENT (BEM).
A sustained drought that lasted almost half a decade precipitated a crisis along the Rĭo Grande by the spring of 2002. "That the Rĭo Grande is no longer strong enough to reach the sea is just another example of the crisis that threatens the river and the international region that depends on it," Jim Yardley reported in the *New York Times*.[16] The resulting "water war" among farmers on

both sides of the border, where the population is "exploding," highlighted not only increased tensions along the "faltering" river, but also how woefully inadequate American and Mexican officials were in the ecological management of the border region.

Depending on a treaty negotiated in 1944, American farmers decried Mexico's failure to release 350,000 acre-feet of water into the Río Grande from the Río Conchos reservoir.[17] The U.S., for its part, is committed to releasing 1.5 million acre-feet from the Colorado River, which has not, as we shall discuss later, been sufficient to prevent a crisis on the Baja peninsula. "This isn't water policy," Judge Gilberto Hinojosa, the highest elected official in Cameron County, where Brownsville is located, complained to members of the media.[18] American farmers claim that Mexico is hoarding the water. In their defense, Mexican officials argue that the Río Conchos's reservoirs are critically low. Texas farmers demand to have infrared satellite imagery used to determine if indeed there is a water crisis on the Mexican side. Mexican officials respond by citing the work of Mary Kelly, an American environmentalist at the Texas Center for Policy Studies, who reports that one of the Río Conchos reservoirs is only 25 percent full—and the other stands at a mere 10 percent of capacity.[19]

The recriminations across the border reveal a fundamental frustration that arises when a commodity is scarce. In addition to the drought, a population explosion along the border is to blame for the crisis: when the treaty was signed in 1944, 200,000 people lived in the border area; more than 20 million live there as of 2002. The crisis is as much about politics as it is about the weather. Had the Río Grande area been subjected to extraordinary levels of rainfall, for instance, farmers on both sides of the border would be pointing an accusing finger at each other for not being able to better manage the runoffs that would presumably threaten to flood farmlands and ranches. "What started as a local dispute along the Río Grande has turned into an international imbroglio, a question of national security for Mexico and a matter of survival for several million Texans and Mexicans," Tim Weiner reported from Mexico City. "The crisis is shocking people on both sides of the border into seeing that there may be limits to growth."[20] It is in the interest of all NAFTA nations for sustainable management of the Río Grande ecosystem to be implemented. It is self-evident that a treaty that was half a century old when NAFTA went into effect—and will be 60 years old next year—is inadequate.[21]

Considering the needs of more than half a century's sustained population growth and what appear to be climatic changes associated with erratic weather patterns widely believed to be part of global warming, Mexican and American officials need to establish a comprehensive Environmental Management Area within the framework envisioned by NAAEC.[22] Mexico's commitment to pay back its almost 500 billion gallon debt under the 1944 treaty is limited by depriving Mexican farmers of enough water to avoid ruin—and the cooperation of the weather. "The harsh truth is that the drought is a fact of life in northern Mexico and the southwestern United States," Patricio Mart'nez, governor of Chihuahua, told the *New York Times*.[23] Water has been used for political power—subsidized water has benefited farmers on both sides of the border—but now a different approach to the sustained challenges thrust upon the scene by nature is mandated. "It's unrealistic to expect Fox to repay a water debt accumulated after decades of PRI corruption, environmental degradation and improper planning on both sides of the border," Sergio Aguayo, a political analyst and human rights activist in Mexico, said. "It's an impossible request."[24]

Indeed, Mexico missed its deadline for beginning to repay its water debt a few weeks before summer 2002, underscoring the urgent need to establish an international management plan to protect the integrity of the border region.[25] The "water war" is a stunning example of the limits of growth, and how market forces alone are inadequate for the proper management of natural resources, particularly now that effects attributed to global warming are being felt. George W. Bush and Vicente Fox could use their personal friendship with border issues to make the management of the R'o Grande as an ecosystem, a model for the proper management of a sustainable habitat that satisfies society's wants and private needs.

**2. BAJA CALIFORNIA MANAGEMENT AREA (BCMA).** As the growing dispute among farmers and ranchers along the U.S.-Mexico border has begun to make headlines, another environmental crisis, perhaps of greater consequence, looms large. The depletion of nature's bounty on the Baja peninsula and in the Gulf of California, also known as the Sea of Cortéz, has reached a critical point. Not unlike the R'o Grande, the Gulf of California confronts a crisis precipitated by antiquated treaties that have not kept up with the growth of the American Southwest and Mexico's northwest border region; and by the absence of an overall management plan that treats the entire region as a sustainable ecosystem.

When the United States first dammed and diverted the Colorado River in the 1930s, the river, which flows into the Gulf of California, slowed to a trickle. The 1944 treaty requiring the United States to release 1.5 million acre-feet of water to nourish the river, forming the largest estuary where the river runs into the gulf, was insufficient. The cumulative impact of decades of a water shortfall transformed the estuary into a dry delta, one that, by failing to deliver nutrients into the gulf waters, undermined the ecosystem's health. For its part, the Mexican government neglected the Baja peninsula. Sparsely populated, the whole of Mexico's northwest was an empty space on the map, far away from Mexico City politicians, many presuming that a land hardly touched by humanity could not possibly be threatened. With limitless bounty, Mexican officials were not concerned when the American and Japanese fleets of trawlers arrived.[26] Through a series of concessions and permits issued by indifferent officials in distant Mexico City, the American and Japanese fishing fleets plundered the gulf—hunting sea lions for pet food was a typical outrage—with impunity for four decades.[27]

It was not until the late 1980s that the Mexican government became concerned about the emerging crises. In 1992, as part of his campaign to secure support for NAFTA, Mexican president Carlos Salinas deregulated Mexico's commercial fleet. Thinking that the laws of supply and demand would suffice, Mexican officials ignored the need to create and maintain a level playing field through licensing and permits. As Milton Friedman argued decades ago, the proper role of government regulation must be narrowly defined. "A government which maintained law and order, defined property rights, served as a means whereby we could modify property rights and other rules of the economic game, adjudicated disputes about the interpretation of the rules, enforced contracts, promoted competition," Friedman argued, "is a government that governs well."[28]

"It's the law of the jungle out there," marine biologist Luis Bourillon has complained. "You can do anything you want."[29] Mexican government officials agree that it's fair to say that a third of the gulf's catch is unlicensed—and illegal. The threats are considerable for the plundering is indiscriminate. "Gill nets trap everything: endangered sea turtles, sea lions, even the vaquita, a rare porpoise on the edge of extinction," Tim Weiner reported in a front-page report in the *New York Times*. "They take so many sailfish, tuna and marlins that the rich American sports fishermen who considered the gulf a paradise are staying home—another drain on the local economy."[30]

Not all news is bad news. "It's nice to see the [gray whale] species recovering," Gabriel Arturo Zaragoza, the census coordinator for the Vizcaino Biosphere Reserve, near Ojo de Liebre lagoon on the Baja peninsula is quoted as reported.[31] After almost a decade of decline in the gray whale population, scientists reported that the number of calves spotted off the Mexican coast has doubled. From its summer feeding areas off the coast of Alaska to its winter haven off Baja, the gray whales' 11,000-mile journey along the Pacific coast epitomizes the interrelated nature of ecology of the NAFTA nations. Mexico's unilateral decision to establish the world's largest national sanctuary for whales, comprised of 1.15 million square miles in the Atlantic and Pacific, in May 2002 won accolades from other nations.[32]

In previous years, the Zedillo administration's decision to cancel the construction of an industrial salt plant by Japan's Mitsubishi® is credited with the recovery of the gray whale population. The rebounding gray whale population underscores how further deterioration of the gulf's ecosystem can be reversed—and why it is necessary to have a comprehensive management plan for the entire peninsula.[33] The success with the gray whales, however, does not diminish the growing crisis in the Gulf of California. Consider the bitter experience in the United States. The Sustainable Fisheries Act of 1996 in the U.S. calls for the rebuilding of depleted fishing stocks. While noble in its aim, more than half a decade after it was enacted by the U.S. Congress, it has yet to be implemented. Mexican biologists fear that these failures will also plague any effort to restore the health of the Gulf of California if legislation is not accompanied by an enforcement mechanism to back it up. This frustration underscores the challenges faced in countries the world over.

To prevent the ecosystem in the Gulf of California from further degradation, it is imperative to rein in vessels operating in the gulf. There is an admirable example in how the salmon and halibut were restored in Alaska. In the 1970s, overfishing in Alaska precipitated a crisis of such proportions that the industry was declared a disaster by the federal government. A comprehensive management plan was implemented, strict permits were issued, and the quantities that could be caught were regulated. In the ensuing quarter century, the salmon and halibut of Alaska have been restored, and a sustainable fishing industry flourishes. Similarly, a disaster could very well be declared for the Gulf of California in

2003. Creating a comprehensive management plan can then be implemented, a crucial aspect of which must be a transparent program of licensing, concessions, and permits to vessels allowed access to the Gulf of California. The guidelines recommended by marine biologists should be used as the targets within which the total catch of the gulf should be maintained, consistent with norms refined in Alaska. Mexican officials furthermore need to engage the United States to renegotiate the water released from the Colorado River; the estuary's health needs to be restored.

One example of a successful strategy in which the environment is protected while economic development takes place is found in Puerto Escondido Bay, near Ensenada, where a thriving aquaculture industry is harvesting Pacific bluefin tuna raised in enclosures. At Maricultura®, which harvested more than 300 tons of bluefin tuna in 2002 (sending 95 percent of the catch to Japan), the pampered fish are fattened on a diet of sardines and harvested only as orders arrive from the buyers. Though the bluefin tuna is not, at present, farmed like tuna (raised in captivity from egg to adulthood), the industry Maricultura is pioneering is cutting edge. Only facilities in Australia use Maricultura's technique of fattening the bluefin tuna to prevent overfishing. It stands as a fine example of how the Gulf of California can be managed through intelligent aquaculture.

What many activists fail to realize is that environmental mismanagement happens on *both* sides of the border. A threat to Baja's ecosystem, for instance, increased when the United States changed the water distribution system of the Colorado River in February 2001. The changes increased the salinity of the discharge, affecting more than 200,000 hectares of agricultural lands near the city of Mexicali, and also threatened fish and wildlife that depend on the estuaries into which the Colorado River empties. Organizations working to protect the habitats for gray whales, sea lions, dolphins, sea turtles, and all manner of marine life can contribute positively to restoring the Gulf's health while working to provide for the people who depend on the Gulf, a significant number of whom are Mexican Native Americans.

This is the more urgent considering that the largest tourist development since Cancún is now underway on the Baja peninsula. Nautical Steps®, envisioned to comprise 2,500 miles of coast and designed to attract recreational boaters from the U.S., is a $240 million investment. "We are going from a passive mode to an active one," John McCarthy, director of Fonatur, the development agency of Mexico's Tourism Secretariat, told the *Washington Post*.[34]

(A sustainable ecotourist venture that has proved successful is La Ruta de Sonora, which conducts nature tours along the pre-Columbian trade routes of the Hohokam native people, bird-watching along the desert delta as they trace the steps of the early Spanish missionaries. On the other hand, La Concha Beach Resort in La Paz, which features dolphins as part of the "sustainable" tourism, has been criticized for overworking dolphins and keeping them in inhumane conditions.[35]) Mexico, which ranks eighth in the world for international tourists, hopes to make significant strides this decade and close in on the top four: France, the United States, Spain, and Italy.[36] "We've been unable to reach an environmental, social and economic equilibrium," Victor Lichtinger, Mexico's minister for environment and natural resources, said, vowing to encourage an "environmental conscience."[37] To accomplish this goal, the biological integrity of the Baja peninsula must be protected under an overall management plan.

**3. GULF OF MEXICO MANAGEMENT AREA (GMMA).** The Gulf of California's crisis portends a future for the Gulf of Mexico that must be avoided. Decades of oil spills, illegal fishing, and an inability to coordinate the use of the Gulf by the American and Mexican states that border this resource have undermined the sustainable development of the Gulf. The result is not only a natural resource that is does not meet its full economic potential, but also fails to be properly safeguarded. In NAFTA's second decade, it is imperative to develop a management plan for the Gulf, developed and administered by Mexico City and Washington, D.C.—with significant participation from the states of Alabama, Campeche, Florida, Louisiana, Mississippi, Tabasco, Tamaulipas, Texas, Veracruz, and Yucatán.

This management plan must focus on several fronts. Foremost is protecting the sustainable health of the Gulf as an ecosystem. The most efficient way to accomplish this is through a program of cost-benefit analysis that balances the environment's needs with the economic realities of the people who depend on the Gulf for their livelihood. Consider the misguided controversy that surrounded efforts to protect dolphins from drowning in nets used by tuna fishermen. Environmentalists denounced the use of unsafe nets by Mexican fishermen. American fishermen, in turn, complained that they were at a disadvantage because they were forced to purchase expensive dolphin-safe nets. U.S. and Mexican officials noted that different laws prevailed on the Gulf, simply because the United States and Mexico each had sovereign jurisdiction. This impasse resulted in American environmentalists calling for a boycott of Mexican tuna. The object was to draw attention to the plight of the dolphins, raise public awareness in the United States about fishing methods employed in the Gulf, and exert economic pressure on Mexican fishermen by shutting them out of the American market once the U.S. banned Mexican tuna.

The results were several. The consumer boycott of Mexican tuna forced the price of tuna up for American consumers. The income of Mexican fishermen was reduced by falling sales to the United States. Though a few switched to dolphin-safe nets, the process was slow; it was difficult for specific Mexican fishermen to exempt themselves from the boycott by demonstrating they employed dolphin-safe nets. The U.S. ban became a point of contention between Mexican and American officials. And perhaps most important of all, dolphins still drowned.

Had a simple cost-benefit mechanism been in place to adjudicate this dispute, however, a superior societal outcome would have prevailed for both nations. The total cost of the boycott is estimated to have been about $80 million per year, in terms of higher prices for American consumers and the lowered incomes for Mexican families. The costs of outfitting the Mexican fleet with dolphin-safe nets would have been around $30 million. Thus a $50 million a year "savings" could have been easily achieved if the nets had been made available to Mexican fishermen in the first place.[38] (The controversy over Mexico's fleet was finally resolved at the end of 2002 when the U.S. Commerce Department ruled that encircling dolphins with nets a mile wide affords the dolphins escape as tuna are caught.[39]) And the most important objective of all would have been met instantly: saving the lives of dolphins.[40]

Absent a mechanism for managing the overall resources, however, it is impossible to solve these problems in an equitable and timely manner. The same applies to other management issues. The Ixtoc oil spill—the largest accidental oil spill in history, which is discussed in the section that follows—is another example. How shipping lanes are used is another area that requires coordination, particularly given how vulnerable the Gulf is to being used by drug traffickers and potential terrorists. It is clear that the overall management of the Gulf has economic, law enforcement, and international security issues. To these one must add the specific interests of the various states that border the Gulf. The ports of Campeche, Galveston, New Orleans, Tampa, Tampico, and Veracruz have vested interests in cooperating with each other to manage their resources. Given the significant investments required to expand and upgrade the infrastructure of these ports, which will run in the tens of billions of dollars during NAFTA's second decade, it is imperative for these entities to coordinate their efforts. Such a strategy would facilitate the development of complementary functions and greater coordination among the various ports.

This approach to implementing an overall management strategy has more than economic and environmental aspects, of course. The scientific component is considerable. One example are the cumbersome bureaucratic obstacles that limit cooperation between, for instance, Mexican scientists and the Mineral Management Services, a U.S. federal agency with jurisdiction over the outer part of the continental shelf.[41] The proper management of the Gulf requires a bilateral approach, one that incorporates the needs of the individual Gulf states while adhering to a broader vision of the long-term needs of the Gulf. For instance, "coral cloning" in the Florida Keys is a bold attempt to restore damaged coral reefs. From Key West all along the gulf to Cabo Catoche at the tip of the Yucatán peninsula, imperiled habitats require a concerted program to protect, repair, and restore habitats through innovation.[42] The convergence of environmental, economic, and security needs during the first decade of the twenty-first century requires nothing less. This becomes the more urgent at a time when oil companies are increasing their investments in the Gulf. British Petroleum® (BP), for instance, announced plans to spend $15 billion from 2002–2010 on several large oil and gas fields in some of the more promising prospects, which happen to be in the Gulf of Mexico.[43] Industry leaders believe the known prospects have the potential to produce oil on the same scale as the North Sea or Alaska, indicating that throughout NAFTA's second decade, other companies will follow suit and make significant investments in the Gulf of Mexico. BP's ongoing investments in excess of $15 billion, for instance, are being made in six sizable fields and the construction of an undersea pipeline, developments with important implications for the health of the Gulf's ecosystem.[44]

Corporate America understands these challenges well. R. King Milling, president of the Whitney National Bank® in New Orleans, is spearheading efforts to protect the marshes now endangered deep in Cajun country. That the marshes of Louisiana are sinking into the Gulf of Mexico, threatening the installations that transport more than 1.5 million barrels of hydrocarbons daily—more than the Alaska pipeline—is a problem of the 2000s, not some distant, hypothetical future. Milling's vision, in fact, shows that the environment is an industry whose time has come, and that the proper management of the entire Gulf of Mexico as a single ecosystem is crucial to both the United States and Mexico. Given the interests of the oil and natural gas industry, the firms operating in Louisiana—and along the entire coast of the Gulf of Mexico—need to participate fully in restoring these habitats.

**4. MAYA AREA BIOSPHERE RESERVES (MABR).** Pemex operations in the Gulf of Mexico constitutes the greatest threat to the habitats of southern Mexico and the Yucatán peninsula. The link between Pemex's operations in Coatzacoalcos and Ciudad del Carmen and environmental despoliation were first brought to the world's attention more than a dozen years ago. Pemex has not lived up to its social responsibilities and corrected the ecological damage its installations continue to cause. Of greater concern is the company's failure to adopt state-of-the-art technological innovations widely used in the oil industry worldwide. Due to decades of Pemex's recklessness—best exemplified by the Ixtoc offshore drilling platform that leaked oil for years in the 1980s— the habitats along the southern shores of the Gulf of Mexico are faltering from the continued environmental stress.[45]

The true measure of Pemex's shortcomings remains Ixtoc. An exploratory well in the Bay of Campeche that blew on June 3, 1979, it took over a year to contain. By the time it was capped, it had spilled more than 140 million gallons of oil into the Gulf of Mexico, making it the worst oil spill in history.[46] Only the deliberate destruction of Kuwait's oil facilities by the Iraqis on January 26, 1991 has surpassed the Ixtoc catastrophe.[47] And even when their installations operate properly, Pemex still pollutes the tropical habitats south of Campeche Bay Sound. The release of nitrogen oxides and sulfur produced in the burning of petroleum products is the root cause of the acid rain falling across a wide path area inland. As *New York Times* science writer John Noble Wilford succinctly reported, "acid rain, which can blight forests and lakes as well as damage stone structures, is not confined to the world's northern industrial regions. It is a clear warning signal, environmental experts say, that this form of 'chemical weathering' is threatening the millions of acres of tropical rain forests in southern Mexican and Central America."[48] More than a decade after scientists documented the spread of acid rain, commercial interests deny the existence of the problem.[49]

Whereas Mexico's oil exports represented the single most important source of foreign revenues through the 1980s, the role of remittances from Mexicans living abroad and tourism have eclipsed oil exports, one indication of the faltering ability of Pemex to contribute to Mexico's economic development. (When one considers that Pemex is forced to buy back the oil it exports in the form of unleaded gasoline, its contributions to Mexico's economy are diminished further.) It is the emergence of ecotourism as a sustainable industry that is bringing Pemex's impact on southern Mexico and the Yucatán peninsula under greater scrutiny. The idea of protecting the habitats surrounding Maya ceremonial centers, creating, in essence, "biosphere reserves" that encourage the sustainable development of ecotourism, was first proposed by Joann Andrews and Barbara MacKinnon Montes in the early 1980s. Andrews, founder of Pronatura, and Montes, who spearheaded efforts to protect habitats south of the Cancún-Cozumel corridor, worked to secure feasibility studies by American, Canadian, and Mexican researchers to understand how these biosphere reserves could be realized. Mexico, furthermore, is now beginning to follow Brazil's lead and develop exports that nurture sustainability and marketability, which is no longer an oxymoron, since conventional wisdom has long held that "sustainable" enterprises would fail in the marketplace.[50]

Mexico, Guatemala, Belize, Honduras, and El Salvador subsequently embraced the idea of a regional sustainable tourism industry in the Maya Culture Area (MCA) known as "Mundo Maya," or "Maya World." In the 1990s, commercial interests rallied behind the idea of creating a network of interrelated biosphere reserves within a greater MCA. Tour operators, airlines, hotels, and regional governments worked to with national governments, international agencies and foreign investors to create a viable tourism industry. The Maya World's strategy lies in using Cancún as a gateway for bringing ecotourists. But the environmental integrity of the region must be protected. The emergence of Calakmul in Campeche State—which now boasts the first of a "soft adventure" luxury resorts—is a model for the kind of ecotourist vision for the region.[51] Indeed, with so many regional nations hoping to lift their constituents out of poverty through the creation of a sustainable ecotourism industry, pressure on Pemex is mounting.[52]

Whether it is Tikal in Guatemala, Copan in Honduras or Chichén Itzá in Mexico's Yucatán, it is clear that the establishment of Maya Area Biosphere Reserves (MABR) must form an integral part of the Maya World effort by participating nations. The creation of a Master Environmental Plan for the Maya World should include an international consortium of biologists, archaeologists, regional governments, tourism industry businesses, nongovernmental organizations, and international lending organizations. The protection of the Maya World's environmental patrimony, however, falls on Mexico, which must rein in Pemex's excesses. In the 1980s, Maya ruins in Guatemala were afforded protection by the forest canopy from the acid rain. Now that tourism is being encouraged throughout the Maya World, the ability of archaeological sites to escape similar damage by virtue of being less accessible to tourists is no longer the case.[53]

There are political reasons for Mexico to move forcefully into the ecotourism industry. Consider that while it is true that millions of Americans spend billions in Mexico on holiday, millions more Mexicans spend billions more in the United States. As a consequence, Mexico, in fact, runs a significant trade deficit in tourism vis-à-vis the United States for one simple reason: Mexicans spend more in the United States than Americans spend in Mexico. Every day, 30,000 Mexicans enter the United States legally, as tourists, students, or on business.[54] "We have a tremendous potential for ecotourism, we have colonial cities, and we have archaeological sites with ancient ruins," Leticia Navarro Ochoa, Mexico's Tourism Secretary, said. "Travelers go to France or Italy and they spend a lot of money on nice things. What we have to do is create a better product. Nice hotels, good shopping, cultural products and archaeological sites."[55]

**5. VALLEY OF MEXICO METROPOLITAN AREA (VMMA).** Mexico City has the unfortunate distinction of having among the world's worst air pollution.[56] Despite the introduction of catalytic converters on new vehicles, the widespread use of unleaded gas, tax incentives to relocate factories to areas outside the Valley of Mexico, and the phasing in of more stringent emission standards, Mexico City is only slowly beginning to improve the air quality of the largest metropolitan area on Earth.[57] Over the past quarter-century, the Mexican government has struggled to monitor and reduce pollutants released into the air. The geographic characteristics of the Valley of Mexico complicate efforts to combat pollution. A volcanic basin surrounded by mountains, the high altitude results in less efficient combustion of fossil fuels.

The deterioration of the air quality in the Valley of Mexico, where one in four Mexicans live, is reported daily on the news as part of the weather report.[58] The Metropolitan Air Quality Index, known as IMECA, is also reported on the weather page of the city's papers, next to the reminder of which license plate vehicles are banned from traffic on that day.[59] Mexico City residents plan their daily activities, from school outings to jogging, depending on the IMECA reading. The monitoring network, known as RAMA, consists of more than two dozen automatic stations that measure specific pollutants and meteorological readings.[60] For more than a decade progress has been steadfastly made in curbing, and reducing, pollution.

Not unlike Los Angeles, which required several decades to reverse the effects of air pollution, however, Mexico City is only now beginning to see the benefits of its concerted antipollution program. To be sure, there have been obstacles. Early efforts to address pollution were truncated; politics and lack of funding clashed with resistance from civil society.[61] Through the late 1980s, Mexicans were prepared to trade air quality for urban living; employment was a higher concern than improving the air and water quality.[62]

In the late 1990s, however, the Zedillo administration made significant progress in securing lines of credit earmarked for combating air pollution and increasing Mexico's capability to process municipal and industrial wastewater. Long tarred by allegations of corruption and backroom dealing, it was Ernesto Zedillo who began to adhere to the spirit of the 1988 General Ecology Law that governed industrial wastewater and effluent emissions. Alarmed by reports from the Interamerican Development Bank (IDB) that indicated that more than half of Mexico's population lacked access to "formal" sewerage systems and just under a third lacked access to potable water, the Mexican government made significant billion-dollar investments through the 1990s to rectify this situation. Throughout NAFTA's first decade these investments, however, were incomplete. And at times, when the investment was possible, there was no upkeep. In Chiapas, for instance, though there are 13 treatment plants, not one is operating.[63]

If Mexico is to provide wastewater treatment services and potable water to 90 percent of its population by the year 2010, National Water Commission (CNA) estimates that total outlays of $15 billion are required.[64] If history is any indication of how these investments will be made, half will come from Mexican governments (federal and state), one-fourth will be financed by international lending bodies (the World Bank and the Interamerican Development Bank), and the balance from private investors. If these projects are awarded consistent with historical patterns, just over half will go to American and Canadian firms.[65] Germany, Japan, and France will share the remaining 45 percent of the market, with a greater percentage going to the European Union nations.[66] These investments have gained greater currency in light of the success of cleaning up the air—commentators in *Slate.com* expressed disbelief that, upon arriving in Mexico City, the sky was blue and the days were sunny.

While it will take almost two more decades for the air quality in the Valley of Mexico to improve substantially, this initial success has, fortuitously, proved galvanizing. Government, environmentalists, business and civic leaders are speaking about the proper management of the Valley of Mexico as an ecosystem, linking air, water and land management. The acrimonious debates about where Mexico City's new international airport should be built, for instance, reflects the democratic debate emerging in Mexico.[67] This is discussed in greater detail in Chapter 4. Of greater consequence, however, is that the creation of a unified environmental management plan for the Valley of Mexico represents an enormous market opportunity. In the 1990s, the total air pollution control market in Mexico exceeded $600 million, with the market for monitoring and control, equipment exceeding an additional $275 million. Pemex investments in clean fuels production in the 1990s exceeded $900 million.[68] Significant expenditures are being made for steel industry dust collection, chemical industry air pollution reduction, power plant air pollution control and coal power plant electrostatic precipitators. By 2004, these figures are expected to triple.

Efforts to rein in air pollution are being matched by significant investments in wastewater management. These include pretreatment equipment, water pollution monitoring equipment, build-operate-transfer (BOT) service contracts with municipalities and consulting to federal, state, and industry. Though discussed in greater detail in Chapter 4, it is important to bear in mind that these significant market opportunities remained largely unrealized in the 1990s from a lack of political will on the part of the Mexican government. By not making the difficult decisions, Mexican officials have delayed critical projects.

Throughout the greater Valley of Mexico area, moreover, there are other problems of grave concern. Mexico's failure to license and regulate logging, for instance, threatens the habitats of the monarch butterfly in Michoacan State, a lightning rod that subjects Mexico to international scorn. "There has been a massive slaughter of the butterflies in two sanctuaries," Homero Arigjis, who heads the environmental organization Group of 100, told reporters in March 2001 after loggers deliberately sprayed pesticides, killing millions of wintering monarchs.[69] In 1986, the Mexican government established the Monarch Butterfly Special Biosphere Reserve consisting of five sanctuaries, comprising 140,000 acres, where the monarchs winter. "From the cornfields of Iowa to the suburbs of Boston, they come in by the millions, monarch butterflies flying the distance to spend the winter in fir trees in the mountains of Mexico," the *New York Times* posted on its website. "Logging is legal and thriving outside the sanctuaries protecting the butterflies, and experts say illegal logging is thinning the sanctuaries themselves."[70]

Within two weeks, Profeca, Mexico's environmental protection agency, announced tougher measures to protect those wintering grounds of the monarch butterfly. The fracas, however, underscored that the Fox administration is *reactive* to environmental issues throughout the Valley of Mexico, not *proactive*—and certainly lacking in a master plan for the entire area. Critics in Mexico further pointed out that Fox was more interested in foreign opinion—officials in Washington, editors in New York—than in that of the Mexican public. The international rebuke, while highlighting what appears as a failure of the Fox administration to live up to the expectations made by the world community on his administration, was not the complete story. Cognizant of the need to find creative solutions, in the same way that, through Progresa, poor families are paid to keep their children in school, the government is changing the economics that drive illegal logging, and the monarchs are being saved.

"It's the first time in the history of Mexican protected areas that we are providing compensation to make a logging ban achievable," Juan Berzaury, director of the World Wildlife Fund's Mexican office, explained. "People have legal permits to cut trees [in protected monarch butterfly sanctuaries]. We're buying the permits. People are seeing it's real."[71] The pioneering program is called the Monarch Butterfly Conservation Fund and it purchases logging rights for about $18 per cubic yard from many subsistence farmers—mostly indigenous peoples in adjacent communities—to protect and restore these forests.[72]

This is not to say that the Fox administration has not moved decisively at times. Mexico spearheaded a response to growing concerns that one unintended consequence of academic research in the age of globalization was "biopiracy," by which biological thievery by researchers would result in the patenting of genetic material. In February 2002, Mexico hosted a meeting in Cancún attended by, among other nations, representatives of Brazil, India, and China, which together represent more than 60 percent of the world's biological diversity. These nations formed the Group of Allied Mega-Biodiverse Nations, or GAMBN. One of the aims of this organization is to certify the legal possession of biological material such as one's DNA. This was a response to the peculiar fact that, nine years after the Convention on Biological Diversity was created, a series of meetings were convened at the Hague in response to complaints that, under the guise of scientific research, scientists were engaging in "bioprospecting."

Biologists, who championed the passage of the Convention in 1993, now complain about the cloud of suspicion it has cast over them, particularly given the daunting speed with which genetic engineering and genetic patents have exploded as a multibillion-dollar industry. "Academics have been kind of naïve to the question of ownership of genetic material," Eric Mathur, of Diversa®, a San Diego-based company working to find enzymes to make drugs, told interviewers. "They think that under the guise of academia they can do whatever they want. But if their work results in any kind of invention—and most come serendipitously—you can be sure their institution will want to own it and make money from it."[73]

Protecting the integrity of North America's habitats is an urgent task across the entire continent. Critics of NAFTA, for instance, predicted that a free-trade agreement with Mexico would result, in the words of Ralph Nader, in "an environmental catastrophe." But an analysis of the North American Commission for Environmental Cooperation released in the spring of 2002, found unexpected results:

> Looking across five years, the news has been decidedly mixed. We have made some real progress, particularly with air emissions. Yet we continue to send toxins into our environment—including the air—at an alarming rate. In 1999, the latest year for which matched datasets are available, almost 1 million tonnes of dangerous chemicals were pumped into the sky—more than were released on land, underground, or into water combined.
>
> The good news is that this figure represents a 25 percent drop over five years. The bad news is that pollutants dumped into lakes, rivers, and streams jumped by 26 percent in that same period. Our success in curbing air emissions must

continue, but we clearly need to extend it to water and land.[74]

Ralph Nader personified the American liberal complaint against NAFTA on the environment: that corporate America would exploit unsophisticated Mexican dupes and that Mexico would become America's dumping ground for toxic wastes. The opposite has happened: *Canada* is the nation that has emerged as the "dumping ground."

"Trade liberalization seemed to have had a paradoxical effect: while NAFTA might have inspired stricter regulations in Mexico—responding to fears about becoming the North American dumping ground—in Canada the treaty had apparently encouraged less regulation, as a way to gain an economic edge," John Whalen stated in the report "Borderline Hazards." "The researchers claimed that this was particularly true in Ontario, where the provincial government's 'Common Sense Revolution' ushered through a series of business-friendly reforms beginning in the mid-1990s. As Ontario's Ministry of the Environment put it in 1996, according to the report, 'a reformed system of environmental regulation will contribute to a competitive business climate.' "[75]

The problem was that these "reforms" weakened environmental regulations in Ontario. So while Mexico strengthened its regulations during NAFTA's first decade, an unintended consequence was that Canada weakened its laws protecting the environment. "Environment Canada had been reviewing its own statistics and had arrived at some of the same conclusions as the independent researchers—that strict US rules encouraged American industries to ship their toxic waste to the more accommodating provinces of Canada," John Whalen continues. "Among the unsettling facts the agency uncovered was this: almost a third of all hazardous waste shipped from the US in 1998 wound up in Sarnia, Ontario, to be dumped or incinerated at a single facility owned by the Safety-Kleen Corporation."[76]

It is important to realize that the challenge of creating these "management areas" to address the problems of specific geographical areas is an industry in itself. The water war along the border in no uncertain terms underscores the gravity of the crisis both the United States and Mexico confront. Through its leadership position at GAMBN, Mexico, however, now has demonstrated that it has put in place the mechanism necessary for turning environmentalism into a leading industry, one that can address the environmental issues that, in NAFTA's first decade, languished to the degradation of Mexico's biological legacy to humanity.

## SUMMARY

1. Waste management and environmentalism as an industry in Mexico is estimated to constitute a $65 billion market between 2004–2014.

2. Sustainable development of this market, undermined by politics in NAFTA's first decade, has reached a critical point; Mexico must open its waste management industry to avoid an environmental disaster.

3. A bilateral method of conducting cost-benefit analysis between the United States and Mexico is necessary to resolve disputes and achieve superior societal outcomes that are necessary for the sustainable development of environmentalism as a vibrant industry as the twenty-first century unfolds.

4. The establishment of Environmental Management Areas is the most prudent way of nurturing environmentalism as an industry. This approach allows the environmental, economic, and political needs to be included in an overall sustainable development plan. Environmental Management Areas are expected to constitute a $35 billion market in the 2004–2014 time frame.

## ENDNOTES

1. "While NAFTA is still in its infancy, the signs that these institutions will be moving in a direction of environmental concerns are not optimistic," a report issued by the Commission for Environmental Cooperation (CEC) released in 1999 stated. "The political will to ensure that NAFTA institutions fulfill their environmental obligations is lacking."

2. For an analysis of the opportunities in environmentalism as an industry, see *NAFTA and the Environment: Seven Years Later,* by Gary Clyde Hufbauer, Daniel C. Esty, and Diana Orejas, Editors, Institute for International Economics, 2000.

3. In one of the more comprehensive analyses of the environment under NAFTA, Gary Clyde Hufbauer and Jeffrey J. Schott concluded that NAFTA's environmental record was "imperfect." "In determining whether the NAFTA has improved or damaged the North American environment, it is critical to define the relevant counterfactual," they report. "Some environmentalists believe that tougher environmental clauses could have been built into the agreement. Most negotiators disagree: the side agreements crafted by the Clinton administration in 1993 stretched the

patience not only of Mexico and Canada, but also of Republicans in the U.S. Congress. In our view, the relevant counterfactual was not tougher provisions, but no NAFTA. Without the NAFTA, the Mexican government would have had less incentive to pass environmental legislation or to improve its enforcement efforts, and the achievements, modest though they are, of Commission on Environmental Cooperation, NADBank, and BECC would not exist." See "North American Environment Under NAFTA," Gary Clyde Hufbauer and Jeffrey J. Schott, Institute for International Economics, October 2002.

4. The figures for this market estimate are based on interviews with officials at the Inter-American Development Bank, the World Bank, private economists, executives, and industry leaders in Mexico, the United States, and Spain.

5. "Environmentalists Hail the Ranchers: Howdy, Pardners!" by Jon Christensen, *New York Times*, September 10, 2002.

6. Of the frustrations Metalclad experienced, CEO Grant Kesler told reporters, "I see zero future [in this industry] unless the government of Mexico applies the political will necessary to make these projects succeed. If they do that they'll attract more capital than their wildest imagination could conceive." See "Mexico's Wastelands," by Sam Quinones, *Mexico Business*, April 1999, pages 38–46.

7. It is ironic that pro-business PAN leaders attacked the PRI's privatization of the landfill. Foreign investors were stunned by the capricious nature of this about-face. "I buy a facility that's operating by government permit and after buying it they tell me that I'm violating the law for a series of things that had been permitted [when the government owned it]. Why didn't this happen before when the government owned it?" Enrique Diez-Canedo, director of Cytrar®, the operating name of Tec-Med's landfill, is quoted in "Mexico's Wastelands," by Sam Quinones, *Mexico Business*, April 1999, pages 38–46.

8. The INE is part of the Secretariat of the Environment, Natural Resources and Fisheries, known as the Semarnap.

9. "Mexico's Wastelands," by Sam Quinones, *Mexico Business*, April 1999, pages 38–46.

10. Prior to 1994, hazardous hospital wastes were simply sent to municipal dumps and disposed of in a haphazard fashion.

11. In March 1987, a barge named *Mobro* set sail from Islip, New York carrying 3,186 tons of solid waste. After six U.S. states refused to grant permission to have this vessel dock with its load of toxic waste, it continued south, wandering the waters off the coasts of Mexico, Belize, and the Bahamas, with each nation refusing to allow the U.S. vessel to dock. Finally, after a 6,000-mile, 162-day odyssey, the barge—with its toxic waste—returned to New York on September 1, 1987. This incident became a rallying cry for environmentalists who accused the U.S. of seeking to turn other countries into its dumping ground for toxic waste. For more information, see *www.greenpeace.org*.

12. "Programmers are such a mobile group now. Anyone with significant skills who becomes known in the U.S. industry might get offered a job," Scott Cooper, with the immigration law firm of Fragomen, Del Rey, Bernsen & Loewy, was quoted in "Networking Over Borders," by Christine MacDonald in *MB*, April 1999.

13. "Mexico's Wastelands," by Sam Quinones, *Mexico Business*, April 1999, pages 38–46.

14. The five most polluted river basins in Mexico are, in descending order, Panuco, Lerma-Santiago, San Juan, Balsas and Blanco. An alarming 80 percent of Mexico's populations live within these basins.

15. More than a year after the terrorist attacks, the Mexican peso came under pressure as military action against Iraq loomed. "Government officials and most private analysts say the trend must have little if anything to do with conditions in Mexico, because those conditions are positive at the moment," Elisabeth Malkin reported. "Foreign-exchange reserves are at a high of more than $48 billion, high world oil prices are pouring dollars into government coffers and the country is having no trouble financing its current account deficit. Guillermo Ortiz, governor of the Bank of Mexico, declared this week that much of the fall in the peso was speculative, driven by global uncertainty over a war against Iraq and the slow pace of the American economic recovery. 'The bank is only worried about the volatility in the financial markets and the exchange rate's depreciation in as far as they have an effect on inflation,' he said on Wednesday [January 29, 2003]." See "With Mexican Peso Falling, Officials Search for Answers," by Elisabeth Malkin, *New York Times*, January 31, 2003.

16. "Water Rights War Rages on Faltering Ro Grande," by Jim Yardley, *New York Times*, April 19, 2002.

17. One acre-foot consists of 326,000 gallons; Mexico's shortfall of 1.5 million acre-feet is the equivalent of billions of gallons.

18. "For the longest period of time, the Ro Grande has had a water policy in which we hope and pray for a moderate-sized hurricane every 8 to 10 years that would bypass the Valley, land in the watershed and dump in the reservoir," he is quoted in "Water Rights War Rages on Faltering Ro Grande," by Jim Yardley, *New York Times*, April 19, 2002.

19. "There is just no way that they are able to release 1.5 million acre-feet of water. The larger issue is that this drought has shown us that we do not have a plan to manage the river in times of drought," Mary Kelly is quoted in "Water Rights War Rages on Faltering Ro Grande," by Jim Yardley, *New York Times*, April 19, 2002.

20. "Water Crisis Grows into a Test of U.S.-Mexico Relations," by Tim Weiner, *New York Times*, May 24, 2002.

21. Indeed, even the partial water deal announced on July 4, 2002 is a stop-gap measure; a comprehensive environmental management plan for the entire U.S.-border region must be developed and implemented during the next decade to ensure economic and ecological sustainability.

22. The water crisis was portrayed as "The Water War" by left-of-center *Proceso*, the Mexico City weekly. The water crisis, they argued, was exacerbated by an outdated treaty that failed to consider the hundredfold increase in population of the border region, and the changed weather patterns, a combination that stood to undermine the economic and political relations between both nations.

23. "Water Crisis Grows into a Test of U.S.-Mexico Relations," by Tim Weiner, *New York Times*, May 24, 2002.

24. Personal communication, June 1, 2002.

25. "Not even draining all the reservoirs would satisfy that demand," Alberto

Szekely, Mexico's national water secretary, told reporters on May 29, 2002, explaining that Mexico would be unable to begin repaying the 456 billion gallons of water owed under the 1944 treaty. "Let's share the water that there is. The suffering has to be shared," Jeffrey Davidow, the U.S. ambassador in Mexico City, said.

26. It is curious to realize that some Americans, like writer John Steinbeck and environmentalist Joann Andrews, first raised concerns decades ago. John Steinbeck accused the Japanese—as far back as 1940—of "destroying the ecological balance" of the Gulf of California; Joann Andrews warned of "catastrophic harm to the region's ecosystem." See *Log of the Sea,* by John Steinbeck and Edward Nicketts, New York: Viking, 1941; Joann Andrews, personal communication with author, February 1998.

27. The decline of the sea population throughout the Sea of Cortéz has been startling. As fish populations collapse from overfishing, several organizations have established efforts to coordinate their activities. The Sea of Cortéz Fund, for one, "aims to strengthen the effectiveness of conservation organizations, which are collaborating with local communities." At present there are 26 Mexican nonprofits addressing programs to promote conservation. Decades of overfishing became evident during the administration of Mexican President Ernesto Zedillo (1994–2000). This is a worldwide problem. See "Has the Sea Given Up Its Bounty?" by William J. Broad and William C. Revkin, *New York Times,* July 29, 2003.

28. Milton Friedman, "The Role of Government in a Free Society," in *Private Wants and Public Needs,* Edmund Phelps, Editor, W. W. Norton, 1965, page 115. First published in *Capitalism and Freedom,* by Milton Friedman, University of Chicago Press, 1962.

29. "In Mexico, Greed Kills Fish by the Seaful," Tim Weiner, *New York Times,* April 10, 2002.

30. Ibid.

31. "Gray Whales Rebound for West Coast Ritual," Greg Winter, *New York Times,* March 17, 2002.

32. Only Japan and Russia expressed concern that Mexico's unilateral decision would harm the global whaling industry.

33. Japanese umbrage at being made the scapegoat for the plight of the whale populations was clearly evident in the spring of 2002. At the International Whaling Commission, for the first time in the 56-year history of the IWC, Japan voted against allowing aboriginal subsistence whaling quotas. "They talk about the Inuit needs. What about the needs of our whaling communities?" Masayuki Komatsu told reporters gathered at Shimonoseki, Japan. (Curiously, Japan's vote, which would protect whales at the expense of the Inuit's traditional culture, enraged environmental groups. "Using native Arctic nations as pawns in a political battle between superpowers is unconscionable. It has done enormous damage to Japan's reputation," Richard Mott, of the World Wildlife Fund, said. For more information on this situation, see "Japan Cuts Whaling Rights for Native Peoples of the Arctic" by James Brooke, *New York Times,* May 25, 2002. In their defense, it should be noted that all cultures are subject to change over time, including the Japanese tradition of eating whale meat. After World War II, whale meat comprised more than half of

all the animal protein consumed in Japan. By 1958, fully one-third of the Japanese consumed whale meat, where it remained through the 1970s. By contrast, fewer than 4 percent of Japanese adults routinely ate whale meat by 2001—and less than 1 percent ate whale meat regularly. The Japanese born after 1970 are conscious of the need to protect whales, and aware of the world's disapproval of consuming whale meat, simply do not eat it. Another consideration is that concentration of polychlorinated biphenyls, or PCBs, that accumulate in the whale blubber.)

34. There are critics, of course. "I would like to think that this is a low-impact project. But there are few examples of those in the world," said Wallace Nichols, a biologist at Wildcoast, a California environmental organization. See "Environmentalists Protest Mexican Plans for Baja California," by Mary Jordan, *Washington Post,* May 6, 2001.

35. "These dolphins are overworked and in horrible conditions," Homero Aridjis of the Group of 100, said, sounding at times more like labor organizer than an environmentalist.

36. Mexican officials remain concerned that, when it comes to tourism, Mexico incurs a deficit vis-à-vis the United States: Mexican tourists spend more money in the United States than American tourists spend in Mexico. Development of other resorts on the Yucatán peninsula, including a high-end ecotourist resort near the border with Belize, are scheduled to be completed in NAFTA's second decade.

37. "Mexico's Green Dream: No More Cancúns," by Tim Weiner, *New York Times,* January 12, 2001.

38. The costs could have been absorbed in the form of grants, or low-interest loans from the Mexican government, or the American government, or both. Another option would have been to secure loans from international lending bodies, or outright grants. Any creative combination would have sufficed.

39. "Dolphin-safe means that dolphins can be encircled or chased, but no dolphins can be killed or seriously injured in the net in which the tuna are harvested," William Hogarth, the assistant administrator for fisheries of the Commerce Department's National Marine Fisheries Service, said at the time of the ruling. See "U.S. Rules That Foreign Fleets' Use of Tuna Nets Is Safe for Dolphins," by Christopher Marquis, *New York Times,* January 1, 2003.

40. Relations across North America are complicated by a certain kind of bias that affects business, specifically, the penchant of American liberals to demonize Mexico. "Any time we can block trucks rolling in from Mexico with tuna caught by killing dolphins, we'll consider that a good day," David Phillips, director of the radical Earth Island Institute's International Marine Mammal Project, told reporters. Rather than advocating negotiations to conflicts, organizations like Earth Island Institute seek confrontation, expressing disappointment when conflicts are resolved. "This won't work and it will fail," Phillips said after an agreement was reached to protect Padre Island in Texas. What NAFTA has shown is that Mexico and the U.S. can be partners in the stewardship of natural resources. The resolution over tuna fishing in the Gulf of Mexico is one example. That natural gas production can take place in a nature sanctuary on Padre Island, evidence of a fluid give-and-take to ensure that the legitimate interests of all parties can be taken into

account, is another. See respectively, "Rule Weakening Definition of 'Dolphin Safe' Is Delayed," by Christopher Marquis, *New York Times,* January 10, 2003 and "They Brake for Turtles in Padre Island Park," by Blaine Harden, *New York Times,* December 1, 2002.

41. Another measure of the lack of cooperation is seen in the dearth of joint articles by Mexican and American researchers in *The International Journal of Nautical Archaeology,* alarming considering the hundreds of shipwrecks and artifacts that litter the ring of the Gulf of Mexico.

42. Coral cloning as a technique to repair damaged coral reefs is opportune, given the sustained damage to the coral reefs off the coast of Cozumel inflicted by cruise ships, particularly severe in the second half of the 1990s.

43. "BP is the largest single producer of oil and gas in the United States, and the deep water [of the Gulf of Mexico] will sustain that position as well as making a crucial contribution to America's energy needs," Lord John Browne said when the investments were announced at a news conference.

44. BP plans to increase its production to 700,000 barrels a day by 2007, overtaking Royal Dutch/Shell as the largest producer of oil and gas in the Gulf of Mexico where the U.S. has jurisdiction.

45. Indeed, the U.S. Coast Guard ranks the Ixtoc oil spill among the greatest maritime disasters to affect the Gulf of Mexico. See *http://www.uscg.mil/hq/g-cp/history/Disaster_I.html.*

46. For rankings of the world's worst oil spills, see *International Oil Spill Statistics,* 1997.

47. In Kuwait, the withdrawing Iraqi army set terminals and tankers afire, destroying the Sea Island Kuwaiti installation. A total of 240 million gallons of oil were spilled in Kuwait, off the coast in the Persian Gulf and in Saudi Arabia.

48. "New Threat to Maya Ruins: Acid Rain," by John Noble Wilford, *New York Times,* August 8, 1989.

49. Apart from Pemex's environmental despoliation, a considerable threat arises from poverty. "Seen in satellite images, the green land of the bioreserve [in Chiapas] shrinks every year, like a lake slowly going dry," Tim Weiner reported. "The trees are cut, the undergrowth is burned, the thin topsoil planted with corn until the crop fails, the land then grazed by cattle until the rains wash the earth away. Hundreds of settlements struggle in isolation, sharing little sense of community, rarely seeing eye to eye, often lacking a common language." Thus the menagerie of Mexico's impoverished Maya peoples struggle in Chiapas, destroying the cloud and rain forests as they struggle to survive. See "Growing Poverty Is Shrinking Mexico's Rain Forest," by Tim Weiner, *New York Times,* December 8, 2002.

50. Consider the successful launching of "Jungle Honey," made by Maya cooperatives from honey made by bees pollinating rainforest blossoms. The development of sustainable "eco-friendly" products first began in Brazil. "These days, guarana provides a clear example of the way many of the 20 million Brazilians living in the Amazon River Basin are seeking to harness the region's exotic flora and fauna to promote economic development," Simon Romero reported from Brazil. "What better product to represent the Amazon than a natural stimulant that is harvested without harming the environment?" Valmi Ferrari rhetorically

asked. See "Industry and Nature Meet Along the Amazon," by Simon Romero, *New York Times,* June 17, 2000.

51. Group Posadas®' Explorean Kohunlich is an upscale adventure resort. "The Explorean opens the doors to a unique kind of vacation that seeks to not only capture the beauty of nature and climate, but also allows visitors to take home something special from their unique experience," Gaston Azcarraga, president of Grupo Posadas, said.

52. For more information on domestic political pressure on Pemex, see "Are Mexicans Finally Going Green?" by Elisabeth Malkin, *BusinessWeek,* May 24, 1999.

53. "New Threat to Maya Ruins: Acid Rain," by John Noble Wilford, *New York Times,* August 8, 1989.

54. The distinctions between Mexicans with MICAs and those without are enormous. A measurement of this difference is seen in the statistics compiled by the U.S. Commerce Department. In 2001, just over 30,000 MICA-carrying Mexicans were admitted into the U.S. on average *every day*. More Mexicans were welcomed to the United States than from any other nation other than Canada. Of the more than 53 million foreigners who visited the United States in 2001, one out of every five was a Mexican national. Their impact is enormous, fueling the American economy.

55. Leticia Navarro Ochoa, the highest-ranking female executive at Gillette, returned to Mexico and was shortly thereafter recruited by the Fox administration, a position for which she took a significant pay cut. Her salary as Tourism Secretary is less than her annual bonus at Gillette, where she pioneered the way for other women. See "From Gillette to Mexico's Cabinet," by Graham Gori, *New York Times,* January 14, 2001.

56. One measure of concern for the air pollution is that the National Association of Physicians for the Environment (NAPE) conducts studies on the effects of the air quality on the health of residents of Mexico City. For more information, see "National Conference on Air Pollution Impacts on Body Organs and Systems" available at *http://www.easi.org/nape/aircon.html.*

57. "There are data that suggest that the air may be improving," Mario Molina told the *New York Times.* "Mexico City's air can improve as much as Los Angeles's did, and in a shorter time. That's a goal that can be achieved." See "Terrific News in Mexico City: Air Is Sometimes Breathable," by Tim Weiner, *New York Times,* January 5, 2001.

58. A blueprint for managing the Valley of Mexico is found in the United Nations' report *The Basin of Mexico: Critical Environmental Issues and Sustainability,* available at *Un.org.*

59. Power and industrial plants account for almost all the sulfur dioxide in the Valley of Mexico. Automobiles, buses and trucks account for almost all the carbon monoxide in the air. The pollutants most monitored by authorities are ozone, carbon monoxide, nitrogen dioxide, sulfur dioxide, lead, volatile organic compounds (VOC) and partially combusted hydrocarbons.

60. RAMA measures HCNM, O3, Nox, NO2, CO, HeS, and SO2; and wind speed, wind direction, humidity and current temperature.

61. Businesses, government agencies, and the public alike were loath to relocate from Mexico City; many protested that moving their factories,

businesses, or agencies to another city would deprive their employees and families of the choices a sophisticated urban center offered. For more information, see the United States-Mexico Chamber of Commerce at *www.usmcoc.org*.

62.  Mexicans fear that the aquifers beneath Mexico City will be poisoned the way other freshwater rivers have been ruined in the United States. The sediment of the Passaic in New Jersey, for instance, is "a poisonous bisque of heavy metals and noxious chemicals left over from the hundreds of smelters, tanneries and refineries that once nourished former industrial giants like Paterson, Passaic and Newark," as Andrew Jacobs reported. The cleanup bill, in the billions, is ominous for Mexican officials considering the requirements of the Valley of Mexico. "In a Herculean effort to bring back a semblance of the lower Passaic's ecosystem, the United States Army Corps of Engineers and the Environmental Protection Agency are planning to remove tons of toxic sludge, dismantle ecologically damaging bulkheads and restore long-vanished wetlands along the river's most damaged portion in and around Newark," he reported. See "Hoping Egrets Replace Pollutants as River Undergoes Intensive Care," by Andrew Jacobs, *New York Times,* July 22, 2002.

63.  "Water has been used as a political tool in Mexico for decades," Tim Weiner reported in the *New York Times.* "Under the Institutional Revolutionary Party, known as the PRI, which ran almost everything in Mexico from 1929 until Mr. Fox took office on Dec. 1 [2001], 'water was a key to getting votes,' [Environmental Minister Victor] Lichtinger said. 'Decisions about where to deliver water were linked to politics, political favors, political alliances. Promises were made "If you vote for us, you'll get water"—and that meant a lot.'" See "Mexico Grows Parched, With Pollution and Politics," by Tim Weiner, *New York Times,* April 14, 2001.

64.  For more information, *see http://bancomundial.org.mx/*.

65.  Ibid.

66.  These statistics are provided by the U.S. Agency for International Development's Office of Energy & Infrastructure.

67.  While critics decried the "importation" of the American "Not In My Backyard," or NIMBY, syndrome.

68.  For more information, see *http://www.pemex.com*.

69.  These developments came after a fierce winter storm decimated the monarchs. "After a severe winter storm in mid-January [2002], dead monarch butterflies lay in piles on the ground, in some places more than a foot high. Between 220 and 270 million frozen butterflies had rained down from roosts where they normally festooned towering trees, researchers estimated," Carol Kaesuk Yoon reported. Fortunately, nature rebounds splendidly. "It's more than surprising," Bill Calvert, an American biologist, told the *New York Times* the following winter. "It's amazing that they recovered so well." "This winter, researchers found that monarch roosts covered nearly 20 acres of forest in the mountains of Mexico, almost as much as the average over the past decade, around 24 acres of roosts," Carol Kaesuk Yoon reported on Valentine's Day 2003. See, respectively, "Storm in Mexico Devastates Monarch Butterfly Colonies," by Carol Kaesuk Yoon, *New York Times,* February 12, 2002 and "Monarch Butterflies Alive and Well in Mexico," by Carol Kaesuk Yoon, *New York Times,* February 14, 2003.

70.  See "Even in Their Winter Retreat, Monarchs Are Beset by Threats," *New York Times,* March 13, 2001, *www.nytimes.com/2001/03/13/13MONA.html.*

71.  "Protecting Monarchs by Trying to Protect Forests," by Carol Kaesuk Yoon, *New York Times,* July 9, 2002.

72.  This program is modeled after the Michoacan Reforestation Fund. Supported in part by the U.S. Fish and Wildlife Service, it plants two oyamel fir trees for every dollar donated in Michoacan. The same forest needs to be protected and restored in the monarch butterfly sanctuaries.

73.  Private communication, March 2002.

74.  "Measured Success," in *Trio,* Spring 2002, by the North American Commission for Environmental Cooperation, available at *Cec.org.*

75.  "Borderline Hazards," by John Whalen in *Trio,* Spring 2002, by the North American Commission for Environmental Cooperation, available at *Cec.org.*

76.  Ibid.

# PART III

# INTEGRATING THE POLITICAL ECONOMIES OF NORTH AMERICA

# 9

# The Persistent Appeal
# of Paternalism

## EXECUTIVE ABSTRACT

Price controls on consumer products; subsidies to industry, business, and consumers; and paternalistic social welfare institutions have been the signature characteristics of Mexican Paternalism. In political terms, patronage was dispensed not only to incur political support, but also to arrive at social compromises. The PRI's ability to use the nation's economic wealth, however, required limits on the role of money in the Mexican economy, first legislated in the 1930s. The result of this political decision is that a set of distortions continues to reverberate and affect Mexico's economy. The market "reforms" inherent in NAFTA, however, require limits on the role of money—limits that, for instance, disguise the total compensation workers receive—be phased out. As Mexican Paternalism changes consistent with the market requirements necessary under NAFTA, the Mexican political economy is undergoing significant changes regarding how Mexican workers are compensated. As market forces—direct monetary compensation to employees—become a more transparent part of the Mexican economy, health care, housing, consumer purchasing power, and how capital goods are purchased will continue to undergo significant changes. There are, moreover, social forces that resist increasing the role of money; Mexicans demand socialized health care, for example, and resist the introduction of market forces in other areas of their lives. Mexicans are in the throes of deciding how to balance the demands of a market economy and welfare economics, and in deciding how limits on the role of money will be modified to reflect these new realities.

## DISCUSSION

Not everything has a price in this world. Our sensibilities are offended when "markets" emerge in some areas of our lives. Few want to live in societies where, say, babies or sex are bought and sold. To reflect these human values, societies have long used ethics to limit the role of money in the economy. Economist Robert Frank has written extensively on how and why this should be so. "Why, for example, do we consider it unethical for a couple to have and sell a baby to some other couple who desperately want one of their own? Why, similarly, would it be considered unethical for a person to sell one of his kidneys to a person who will die unless he gets a kidney transplant? And why is prostitution so strongly frowned upon in many ethical systems?" he asks, in a discussion about the devices employed by many societies to manage how its members determine the distribution of status among themselves.[1]

Economists, including Frank, argue that many organizations display counterintuitive characteristics precisely because people care about their relative ranking in local hierarchies for status. "Recognition of the fact that people's status in local hierarchies is important to them, much more important perhaps than their status in the overall population, thus makes for a significant transformation in the nature of status. . . . If status in income hierarchies is like other things that yield satisfaction, people will differ substantially in the sacrifices they are willing to make to attain it. In particular, variations in earning power are likely to cause differences in demands for status," Frank writes.[2]

"Paternalism" as a development model entails substituting cash for benefits. When this happens, a market economy is undermined. Mexico's transition from a *benefits* economy to a *cash* economy has been a difficult process, but the phenomenon is not unique to Mexico. Whether it is weaning poor families off welfare or offsetting higher wages by reducing perks, every society confronts these challenges. For all its shortcomings, Mexico's PRI did take care of the people. "For better or for worse, [the PRI] has also been the people's principal provider, using a vast system of patronage to buy off the nation's political conscience," Ginger Thompson reported in July 2003, when the PRI made significant gains in the mid-term elections.[3]

Consider how the banking industry is characterized by elaborate rankings in titles; most banks have "vice presidents" of one kind of another for just about everything. Titles, as Frank notes, are free for the giving, and as a consequence, they are lavishly bestowed, free of charge, by banks to their employees. There is also a social aspect to why titles are given freely by bankers but raises in salaries are not. Limiting the salaries of those around one is an important component of reducing tensions and fine-tuning the distribution of status throughout an organization. As Frank ponders:

> Why are workers more tolerant of a co-worker's lofty title or costly fringe benefit than they would be of his higher salary? After all, titles are printed on one's door, visible for all to see, whereas salaries, even if known, come in sealed envelopes. A possible answer may be that the maintenance of a collegial environment involves interactions not only between co-workers themselves, but between their families as well. Tensions arise when some members of a group can afford to take frequent vacations and send their children to private schools while others cannot. Differentiation through the use of job titles and certain fringe benefits, rather than through salaries, would limit such tensions.[4]

Managers familiar with the workings of human resources know firsthand how *employee benefits,* whether one is speaking of organized labor or among executives, are subject to scrutiny and the cause of unhealthy competition among employees. Authorities on corporate compensation understand fully that just as union leaders insist that privileges be dispensed "by the book," senior executives are often reduced to childish pettiness when comparing their own corporate perks with those of their peers.

But consider the distortions: when an American company pays an employee's health insurance, rather than giving her a sufficient raise in salary that would allow her to purchase her own insurance on the open market, this limits the role of money in the economy. The same concern found in the corporate world about limiting the role of money to preserve the integrity of status in a company's hierarchy, one finds in society at large. Governments thus at times choose to limit the role of money in the economy. Whether this is done to create an equitable distribution of incomes or to regulate the distribution of status in local hierarchies, it has economic consequences. If throughout corporate America the dispensing of nonpecuniary compensation has become a corporate science, under Mexican Paternalism it was elevated to a social art form.

## Limits on the Role of Money and Labor Wages

In Mexico's case, paternalism took several forms, each designed to replace a market economy with one based on social benefits. Money in the form of wages, for instance, was kept artificially low under Mexican Paternalism for two reasons. First, it made Mexico competitive on world markets, encouraging foreign investment. Second, it allowed the PRI to create an extensive—critics charged, intrusive—welfare benefit system that allowed the ruling party to dispense patronage in exchange for political support. It has worked, perhaps too successfully at times. In a report on the urban "squalor" that accompanied the "undisciplined" growth of industry in Ciudad Juárez, Ginger Thompson alludes to the failure of Mexican technocrats to provide for the quality of life of a bustling community. "Juárez is . . . an economic powerhouse, the seventh largest city in Mexico with one of the strongest local economies," Thompson writes, pointing out the critical housing crises that have forced factory workers to live in "squalor." Indeed, despite the strength of the local economy, there is an insufficient tax base for providing basic services to the tens of thousands of residents.[5]

What is important to keep in mind, however, is that most of these people were previously *destitute,* so having *any* job is a move in the right direction. Indeed, having a bona fide job in Mexico ushers one into an extensive array of social welfare and entitlement benefits. Social benefits are the enticement for entering the "formal" economy, where the embrace of Mexican Paternalism reigns. In fairness, and for comparative purposes, it is necessary to point out that 6 of the 15 poorest metropolitan areas in the United States are also on the border—evidence of decades of neglect by both Washington, D.C. and Mexico City.[6]

Then there is the economic paradox that it is not uncommon for prospering communities to have the median income decline during precisely the period of sustained economic growth.[7] "You see how the arithmetic works?" Gary Burtless, an economist at the Brookings Institution, said of decline in New York City's median income during the 1990s, a time of sustained economic expansion. "When you have a lot of people entering from the rest of the world, and many of them enter at the lower rungs of the wage distribution, then you can have a situation where everyone is prospering and the median income is declining."[8]

What holds true north of the border also holds true south of the border. In Ciudad Juárez, amid sustained economic expansion, the median income is falling and Mexican Paternalism is unable to provide the social services that community requires. Mary Anastasia O'Grady of the *Wall Street Journal* has thought about the inability to local governments in Mexico to provide basic services to their communities. "Rationalizing the size and scope of the federal monstrosity, devolving power to the states, and increasing private property rights are all musts if the country is to improve incomes and living standards during the [current] administration of President Vicente Fox," she opined in January 2001. "It is also necessary if the government wants to lay the moral groundwork for a new culture of tax-law compliance and do more than pay lip service to helping the poor. Mr. Fox's cabinet has a heavy tilt toward classical liberal policy makers, but the politics of freeing the economy from stifling statism will be nasty."[9]

The result is, on the surface, paradoxical: If the *monetary* wages of Mexican workers were kept low artificially—to the horror of American labor activists and union officials—it is only fair to consider how Mexican Paternalism distributed *nonmonetary* social benefits (housing subsidies, price controls on food, medical insurance, etc.) to workers. One doesn't need to make that much in wages if rent is $50 a month, milk costs 25 cents a gallon, and medical care is a right of every bona fide employee, after all. It is therefore disingenuous of American activists who compare apples and oranges—accusing Mexico of mandating "slave" wages while ignoring the fact that while Mexican workers are cash poor, they are benefits rich. American and Canadian executives need to have a fundamental understanding of the institutional agencies the Mexican state set up to limit the role of money; this will demonstrate the far reaches of Mexican Paternalism. The replacing of social benefits with higher wages is already being felt, along with the side of globalization that champions labor rights "Hearing that Mexmode workers [in Atlixco, Mexico] were fired for their cafeteria boycott, leaders of an activist coalition supported by students and administrators from about 85 American colleges and universities rushed here to investigate," Ginger Thompson reported. "The group, the Workers Rights Consortium, heard complaints about low wages, verbal abuses and corruption among union officials, then began a high-profile campaign that threatened the image of the Nike swoosh."[10] Thus the dismantling of the darker side of Mexican Paternalism—lack of independence among labor unions—was quietly accelerated.[11] The purpose of these institutions is to ensure that the low wages Mexican workers receive are complemented by social welfare benefits to support an adequate standard of living.

Let us now consider how the role of money has been limited in the areas of health care, housing, and consumer foods.

In Mexico, every full-time worker is entitled to benefits from the Instituto Mexicano del Seguro Social, known as Imss, a national health-care program. Unlike America's Social Security, which is a retirement and disability program, Mexico's Imss is open to all full-time workers and their families. Everything from flu shots to chemotherapy is provided, free of charge. Workers are also encouraged to participate in a housing program run by the state agency known as Infonavit. Under these programs, contracts to build housing developments to be sold at "social" prices are awarded by the government and housing sales are managed through Infonavit. Not unlike Fannie Mae, whose mission is to make American families become homeowners, Infonavit allows workers to own their own homes. The homes, however modest they may be by American standards, constitute adequate housing.

Mexico, furthermore, has elaborate price controls on the "essential" basket of consumer goods that at one time consisted of thousands of items. Once managed through an arrangement of "voluntary" price controls negotiated by the government between producers and the private sector in an arrangement called Pacto, these controls are being lifted. During NAFTA's first decade, however, it was not uncommon to see consumer items bearing the "Precio de Pacto," meaning "Pacto Price" on the price sticker. Outright price controls continue to be mandated on hundreds of items, including the staple food products: milk, eggs, flour, bread, tortillas, beans, rice and on and on.[12]

To be sure, within the framework of Mexican Paternalism, for an array of political reasons, the role of money has been limited as a mechanism of subsidizing business, generating support for the government, and regulating the consumption patterns of Mexican workers.[13] Under Mexican Paternalism, wages were kept low, but workers' purchasing power was protected through price controls on basic foodstuffs, elaborate subsidized housing schemes, and free health care. Indeed, through a complex—and breathtaking—bureaucracy at these social welfare institutions, armies of technocrats managed the mathematical equations necessary to figure out how to make it all work.

For instance, if the minimum wage was "X," then the price of milk had to be "Y," which, in turn, meant that farmers had to be subsidized "Z." How much, then, did the stores selling the milk need? And what was the price for the diesel fuel needed to drive the milk to market? What about subsidies to make milk products? How much did electricity have to be subsidized to allow farmers to make cheese? And what proportion of the store-owner's electric bill should be credited to compensate for the electricity needed to run the refrigerators where the milk and cheese were kept? Bureaucrats wanted to know, in order to enhance social engineering.

For decades American labor activists focused on the wage component of Mexican workers' compensation to disparage the Mexican state and the quality of life of Mexican workers who were part of the formal economy. By noting that Mexico's *daily* minimum wage traditionally approximated the *hourly* minimum wage in the United States, for instance, a disingenuous argument was presented. This is how Richard Rodriguez described the matter in an anti-NAFTA tirade in *Harper's:* "There is complicity between businessmen, hands across the border, and shared optimism. . . . What American capitalism has in mind for [Mexico] depends on the availability of great numbers of the Mexican poor; on the willing acceptance of Third World wages by the Mexican poor; on the poor remaining poor."[14] There is no mention of Imss, Infonavit, Pacto, and so on.

It was *because* of a decade of hard work since NAFTA, however, that the economic reforms now benefit workers in concrete ways, including the growing independence and strength of the unions. "Each morning, as the sun rises over Tijuana, thousands of workers stream out of dusty barrios, up the hillsides, and into the industrial parks on the mesas above," reported David Bacon, a labor activist and journalist in San Francisco, on June 11, 1997, a few years after NAFTA went into effect. "They surge into the city's countless assembly plants, or maquiladoras. But on June 2, few workers entered the gates of Han Young de Mexico. When the plant's 120 employees arrived at the factory, most huddled in knots in the street outside instead of trooping into work, their calls to mobilize for a strike rising loudly in the morning air. For two days they demanded negotiations—first with their bosses, then with the National Conciliation and Arbitration Board (Mexico's equivalent of the National Labor Relations Board). By the end of the second day the company had agreed to negotiate all of the strikers' demands. That was a historic achievement in the maquiladora industry, which has a dark history of denying workers' rights."

This historic achievement, made possible through the careful and deliberate dismantling of Mexican Paternalism, would have been impossible if NAFTA did not exist. Throughout NAFTA's first decade, Mexican technocrats have been involved in social engineering: If we reduce housing subsidies and price controls on basic foodstuffs by this much, how far do wages have to increase? That they have been successful also shows how even anti-globalization activists are maturing in their own approach, in view of NAFTA's successes. "To a remarkable degree, the anti-globalization protestors have changed the international debate over trade since their emergence in Seattle in 1999," Daryl Lindsey reported. "Their public presentation is excellent," says Gary Hufbauer, a senior fellow at the Institute for International Economics and author of a book praising the economic growth that resulted after the implementation of NAFTA. "They're not saying they're against agreements, full stop. They're saying they will support the agreements, but that they want a lot of social values to be included—like increased democracy, women's rights, Native American rights and also provisions for the environment and better labor conditions. These are all values that Americans embrace, so the question is what's negotiable."[15]

## Losing a Safety Net

Mexican workers, then, may be cash poor, but they are benefits rich. How quickly limits on the role of money should be lifted is, however, a contentious issue. Mexicans recognize that the labor market needs to "rationalize," but they fear that the reckless dismantling of the social welfare benefits workers enjoy will be done prematurely, or incorrectly. The greatest fear Mexicans have is losing their health benefits, or access to programs that enable them to become homeowners. The loss of hundreds of thousands of unskilled maquiladora jobs between 2000 and 2002 demonstrates, however, that the "rationalization" of Mexico's labor market is resulting in three things. Foremost, unskilled jobs are being sent to other countries, such as China and the Philippines. Second, higher wages are being paid for factory jobs requiring semiskilled and skilled workers.[16] Third, workers are being unionized, often with the assistance of American labor organizers, in a bid to help equalize labor standards along the U.S.-Mexico border.[17]

For the business community, there is ambivalence. Higher wages, naturally, increase the costs of doing business in Mexico. When workers have more disposable income, on the other hand, they can consume more. Not unlike Henry Ford's rationale for paying his workers well—that he wanted each of his workers to be able to afford one of the cars they built—Mexican officials are committed to increasing the standard of living of Mexican workers by increasing their monetary compensation. When Fox announced that this could best be achieved by improving the training and education of Mexican workers, the response was enthusiastic.

"Marketers may get the most direct boost from the president's pledge to fight poverty by elevating Mexican workers' level of education and training. The promise of a developing middle class with confidence in the economy and disposable income is music to marketers' ears," *Marketing News* reported.[18] This was reinforced on a bilateral level. In his first meeting with Jorge Castañeda, Secretary of State Colin Powell endorsed this approach. "The thing that really has to be done to solve this problem [of illegal immigration] is to continue to help the Mexican economy grow, so that jobs are in the south, so that the great magnet is no longer just in the north, but it is also within Mexico," Powell, said.[19]

There is nonetheless great uncertainty as Mexico moves from unskilled to semiskilled and skilled labor markets. To be sure, the process by which this occurs is readily understood by economists but may not be evident to others. "I was dazzled by the sheer extravagance of it: an army of workers paid for doing a task that might have been possible to achieve by machines at the quarry," Anthony DePalma writes, visiting a construction site in Mexico. "But the salaries of the workers were so low—the minimum wage at the time was just over the equivalent of $4 a day—that it made sense to have them do it on-site."[20]

An economy that is labor rich but capital poor relies on *workers*. An economy that is capital rich but labor poor relies on *machines*. In the United States, machines do the work of laborers because machines are cheaper than workers. In Mexico, on the other hand, laborers do the work of machines because machines are expensive. In an economy undergoing structural changes, resources must be used efficiently during this transition. If this means using labor where labor is plentiful, and trying to limit the use of scarce capital except where necessary, then so be it. As an economy becomes wealthier, machines proliferate and do the work of people, whether it is a bulldozer on a Mexican construction site or a ticket vending machine at Grand Central Station in New York City. "Precisely because poor people (by definition) have little economic capital and face formidable obstacles in acquiring human capital (that is, education), *social* capital is disproportionately important to their welfare," Robert Putnam argues, underscoring that what holds true for social relations also holds true for business.[21]

Mexican misgivings about embracing U.S.-style capitalism outright, however, center on the social consequences of doing so. Mexicans fear the destruction of their social welfare system, replaced by the kind of system that Americans passively accept as the price of capitalism. Consider, for instance, the dilemma confronted by Tonya, one of the participants in MTV's *Real World: Chicago*. Throughout that season she faced the agonizing choice of seeking medical treatment for her chronic medical conditions, or pursuing higher education. At times she cried on the phone, her voice quivering as she discussed her dilemma before the camera.

This sad state of affairs was handled with nonchalance, however. That this fact of American life was never challenged by her, or by any of her roommates, or by the production crew filming the program, speaks volumes about American expectations. German colleagues who first alerted me about this were scandalized at such a failure in American society.[22] In any other developed nation, questions would have abounded. Is an economic system in which young adults are forced to choose between health care and pursuing an education acceptable? How can the wealthiest nation in the world have arrived at such an impoverished place? Is this kind of disenfranchisement what the rest of the world aspires to? Does America's brand of capitalism result in health care being a "luxury" beyond everyone's reach?[23]

Such absurdities are not uncommon in American life, however. Responding to a woman who wondered if a "Medicaid divorce"—one in name only so her husband could get long-term medical care—Randy Cohen, who writes "The Ethicist" column for the *New York Times,* reflected the passive acceptance of such extreme situations.

> So it is through divorce, paradoxical as it sounds, that you can best honor your marriage vow to cleave to your husband for better or worse. Preserving your small savings will be enormously beneficial to you both. I can understand his fear that divorce could be the prelude to your abandoning him, but you can help him most by offering tenderness and reassurance, not by joining him in penury. If you become loving but unmarried companions, your ethical obligations to one another will not be transformed. It is a grim irony that while

the president touts marriage as the road to financial security, your staying married would mean a descent into poverty.

Then he continued, alluding to the inherent injustice of a situation that politicians are loath to rectify: "Yours is a situation in which an individual moral goal—to behave honorably toward both your spouse and the law—is best facilitated through political action. Both major parties must make changes, embracing measures to protect the assets of middle-class seniors and taxing the assets of the rich (including through the estate tax) to provide all Americans with catastrophic medical care."[24]

Recommending complying with martial vows—for better or for worse—by dissolving one's marriage defies comprehension. That Americans passively accept this state of affairs troubles Mexican policy makers charged with "rationalizing" Mexico's social welfare system. Similar social impoverishment of Mexican society weighs heavily as market reforms continue to be introduced: not everything about America is worth emulating.

Mexicans are confronted with increasing their physical capital while protecting their social capital. Robert Putnam explains it this way:

> Whereas physical capital refers to physical objects and human capital refers to properties of individuals, social capital refers to connections among individuals—social networks and the norms of reciprocity and trustworthiness that arise from them. In that sense social capital is closely related to what some have called "civic virtue." The difference is that "social capital" calls attention to the fact that civic virtue is most powerful when embedded in a dense network of reciprocal social relations. A society of many virtuous but isolated individuals is not necessarily rich in social capital.[25]

There is, nonetheless, the consensus that Mexico must change without adopting American failures, social or economic.

Recall Bartlett's objections to opening up Mexico's electric power industry to deregulation: Why would Mexico want to create a situation in which it could be subjected to a California-style power crisis, or be visited by the unprecedented corruption of an Enron? Consider Fox's concern that "market reforms" result in a situation where national health coverage to working- and middle-class families is in any way diminished.

Nevertheless, for decades, critics have charged that the PRI strove to duplicate the parental relationship between the government and the people.[26] Indeed, it is evident that the PRI found inspiration throughout the twentieth century in the arguments of Max Weber. "[R]ational calculation is manifested at every stage [of bureaucratic organization]," Max Weber argued. "By it, the performance of each individual worker is mathematically measured, each man becomes a little cog in the machine and aware of this, his one preoccupation is whether he can become a bigger cog . . . it is horrible to think that the world could one day be filled with these little cogs, little men clinging to little jobs, and striving towards bigger ones . . . this passion for bureaucracy is enough to drive one to despair.[27]

If driven not to despair, then at least to lifetime employment at some ministry or other, of course.

## Persistence of Paternalism in Mexican Thought

Mexico's "culture" of paternalism, moreover, creates certain expectations—but it also imposes limitations. Recall how Fox's efforts to reform Mexico's value-added tax system ran up against the paternalistic protections extended to the poor. Fox argued that "the impact on the poor will be softened by targeted subsidies and better welfare benefits," underscoring how imperative it is to recalibrate reforms and changes in the logarithms of Mexican bureaucratic life.[28]

Corporate Mexico championed tax reforms, evidence of how the intellectual tide shifted during NAFTA's first decade towards a sustained reexamination of all aspects of Mexican Paternalism. "The Mexican tax system is fraught with inequity, complexity and disincentives, and is incapable of providing the revenues necessary to run the government," Manuel Sánchez, chief economist at BBVA Bancomer argued in the *Wall Street Journal*. "Among the more high-profile problems is the drain on resources caused by government-owned oil, petrochemicals, power generation, natural gas and a host of other services. In addition, more than 80% of educational and health-care services are provided by the state. If private investment were encouraged in these areas, the government would have more available resources for the provision of law enforcement and basic public infrastructure."[29] Despite his initial skills in negotiating with opposition members in the Mexican Congress, Fox was only able to pass limited reforms, which do not fully meet the requirements of Mexico's economic needs for NAFTA's second decade.[30]

This difficult balancing act contributed to the sustained support for the PRI, precisely because the "social capital" of Mexican

Paternalism is its social legacy. In a nation where the majority of people live with material deprivation, the importance of social relations cannot be understated. As Robert Putnam argues:

> Countless studies document the link between society and psyche: people who have close friends and confidants, friendly neighbors, and supportive coworkers are less likely to experience sadness, loneliness, low self-esteem, and problems with eating and sleeping. Married people are consistently happier than people who are unattached, all else being equal. . . . The single most common finding from a half century's research on the correlates of life satisfaction, not only in the United States but around the world, is that happiness is best predicted by the breadth and depth of one's social connections.[31]

There is security in the "social connections" nurtured by Mexican Paternalism. This is why reports of the death of the PRI are greatly exaggerated in the American media. In much the same way that American critics of Mexican wages fail to mention the extensive social entitlements workers enjoy, the importance of social capital is likewise discounted.

In a curious example of how alliances shift, although the PRI enacted the most draconian laws to limit the influence of the Catholic Church, now that Mexico has emerged as a bona fide democracy, it is the PRI and the Catholic Church who caution against dismantling Mexican Paternalism. The leadership "of the Catholic Church, which paved the way for a Fox victory by teaching voting as a Christian responsibility, are delighted that Fox won a truly democratic election," Roderic Ai Camp, author of *Politics in Mexico: The Decline of Authoritarianism,* opined in the *Los Angeles Times.* "But they are also the most vocal critics of [the unchecked market imperfections] of the North American Free Trade Agreement, the support of which was a cornerstone of Fox's economic agenda. The church might well become an intense critic of Fox's macroeconomic policies if they fail to produce positive benefits for working-class families."[32] That the PRI and the Catholic Church defend patronage does not surprise, but that the latter is sympathetic to the political agenda of its historic nemesis intrigues, for it strengthens the legitimacy of the PRI's claim to the Mexican imagination.[33]

American commentators, nevertheless, too often fail to understand the intricate sensibilities of balancing the desire for change with the need for the comfort of stability, and the competing impulses these contradictory desires foster, which too often results in a superficial analysis of developments in Mexico. Andrew Reding, an analyst at the World Policy Institute, offered a common, albeit premature obituary of the PRI. "The Cactus Wall that has separated Mexico from the rest of North America is beginning to rot away," Reding wrote, referring to democratic elections in Mexico. "Contrary to conventional wisdom, the Institutional Revolutionary Party (PRI) will not long endure as a major force in national politics. Though it won a third of the seats in Congress [in the July 2000 elections], it will begin to disintegrate. Unlike the communist parties that governed behind the old Iron Curtain, the PRI has no real ideology to hold it together. . . . Its glue has been patronage, not the force of ideas or ideology. Take away that glue, and there is little to hold it together."[34]

Nothing to hold it together? What about the gratitude of millions of Mexicans who have health care, own their own homes, and survived the hyperinflation of several crises by strict price controls on basic commodities that the PRI managed? Reports of the end of communist parties throughout the republics of the former Soviet Union and throughout Eastern Europe, after all, have not come to pass. After more than a decade of capitalist reforms, Moldova voted the communists back into power in a landslide in February 2001, to the bafflement of (some) Western analysts. In the elections held since July 2000, Mexicans have rallied behind the PRI, mindful that despite all its flaws, in a democracy it's important to have a viable opposition to balance whomever is in power.[35]

"Cactus Wall" or no "Cactus Wall," in the 1980s, Mexico's public debate centered on the wisdom of NAFTA. In the 1990s, public debate focused on the socioeconomic implications of its integration into North America. In the 2000s, that debate reflects how the social contract changed when the nation became a democracy with a competitive market economy, and has, as a consequence, made Mexico subject to the fortunes of the American economy. "Probably the most important U.S. official for Latin America is the chairman of the Federal Reserve Board, for U.S. interest rates are a crucial determinant of Latin America's economic prospects," Abraham Lowenthal wrote in the *Los Angeles Times*. "How the U.S. economy does, more generally, is the single biggest factor in shaping the economic performance of our closest neighbors."[36]

In the same way that American public debate obsesses about "soft money," Social Security "insolvency," and gun violence, Mexican public debate is riveted by the pros and cons of how to go about the complex task of dismantling Mexican Paternalism. There is, however, a curious paradox; whereas American public debate offers problems without remedies, Mexican politicians are formulating achievable advances, one small reform after another.

## SUMMARY

1. Mexican wages will increase as limits on the role of money in the Mexican economy are lifted, and benefits-rich compensation schemes give way to cash-rich worker salaries.

2. The process of "rationalizing" the Mexican economy, consistent with a capitalist market system, requires fundamental reforms in Mexican social welfare institutions.

3. Though Mexicans remain apprehensive about becoming disenfranchised if their social welfare system is dismantled inappropriately, or if a misguided Mexico emulates failed U.S. models, this debate is defining the parameters within which socially responsible companies will operate in Mexico.

4. For industries involved in the health care and housing industries, a period of transition should be expected, one in which private and public funds will be available to provide the social welfare needs of Mexican workers without infringing on the private sector opportunities meeting the needs of either the middle class or the wealthy.

## ENDNOTES

1. Robert Frank, *Choosing the Right Pond: Human Behavior and the Quest for Status,* page 181.
2. Ibid, pages 42–43.
3. Of the PRI, Thompson writes: "Its teachers' unions gave home loans to loyal members. Peasant farmers' associations distributed land. Its legislators passed laws that protected national industries from foreign competition. Its free health-care system for workers was the envy of Latin America." Ah, the benefits of paternalism, all bankrolled by Mexico's oil. See "Why Mexico's Political Machine Keeps Chugging," by Ginger Thompson, *New York Times,* July 9, 2003.
4. Frank, *Choosing the Right Pond,* page 93.
5. "Chasing Mexico's Dream into Squalor," by Ginger Thompson, *New York Times,* February 11, 2001.
6. For further information on demographic statistics, consult *http://www.census.gov/.*
7. During the economic expansion of the 1990s, for instance, the median household income in New York City declined. The explanation for this counterintuitive observation is that so many poor foreigners arrived in

New York that, while their absolute incomes rose compared to what they made in their own homelands, their median income declined relative to other residents in that same community. Along the border, when the rural unemployed move to cities and start working, their absolute income increases, of course. This doesn't mean, however, that whatever that income happens to be bolsters the entire *community's* median income. This paradox is one reason why a "living wage," which would link more closely absolute and relative incomes, doesn't make much sense, since relative standards are difficult to determine and would be arbitrary to impose. In the United States, El Paso, McAllen, Laredo, and Brownsville in Texas; Las Cruces, New Mexico; and Yuma, Arizona are among the fifteen poorest metropolitan areas, again reflecting the distortions that occur when poor people migrate to urban areas in search of jobs.

8. "Census Finds Rising Tide, and Many Who Missed Boat," by Janny Scott, *New York Times,* June 17, 2001.

9. "Federal Gluttons Starve Mexico's Towns," by Mary Anastasia O'Grady, *Wall Street Journal,* January 12, 2001.

10. "Mexican Labor Protest Gets Results," by Ginger Thompson, *New York Times,* October 8, 2001.

11. This is part of a global trend. "This week the National Labor Committee and several unions, religious groups and community organizations are starting a push to persuade Congress to enact legislation that would bar imports from sweatshops," Steven Greenhouse reported of an effort to improve conditions at a shirt factory in Bangladesh. See "A Push to Improve Labor's Lot Overseas," by Steven Greenhouse, *New York Times,* September 27, 2002.

12. It is not a great leap of the imagination to see where opportunities for corruption lie in these schemes. Under the administration of Carlos Salinas, for instance, Conasupo, a program designed to provide foodstuffs to rural dwellers and the urban poor at below-market prices, was plundered by the president's brother, Raúl Salinas, who was subsequently arrested. Conasupo was a fantastic bureaucratic maze, to be sure. Designed to subsidize inefficient rural farmers, Conasupo paid a farmer $2 for something it then sold to the public for $1, the loss being absorbed by the state. (In the United States, a similar transfer of purchasing power from taxpayers to farmers is administered through farm subsidies.) This corruption has been widely documented, from newspaper reports in the United States (see "Hard Times Finds the Salinas Brothers," by John Ward Anderson, *Washington Post,* March 13, 1966) to official reports by the Mexican government (see "Special Commission Says 1.45 Billion Pesos Illegally Diverted from the Now-Defunct Foodstuffs Agency CONASUPO" available at *http://www.ssdc.ucsd.edu/news/smex/h99/smex.19991027.html#a1*).

13. An element of bureaucratic contempt is seen in all paternalistic schemes: Mexican bureaucrats thought it best to limit the cash workers received in part because of the belief that the poor were too ill prepared to be entrusted with handling money. The consumption patterns of the poor in the United States—where a disproportionate percentage is spent on alcohol, cigarettes, gambling, and junk food lacking in nutrition—is seen as evidence that the working poor are not responsible consumers.

14.  "Across the Borders of History: Tijuana and San Diego Exchange Futures" by Richard Rodriguez, *Harper's,* March 1987.

15.  "Free Trade, Closed Talks," by Daryl Lindsey, *Salon.com,* April 20, 2001.

16.  The availability of Mexico's skilled labor is, at times, leading edge on a global scale. "The fundamental motive for the shift in North America vehicle production to Mexico remains the same as with transnational production, the lure of low wage labor," Carl Dassbach wrote. "But the recent shift to northern Mexico differs from transnational production insofar as it incorporates the organizational logic of lean production." See "Future of the North American Automobile Production," by Carl Dassbach, available at *www.sociology.org/content/vol001.001/dassbach.html.*

17.  For decades, American labor unions kept their distance from their Mexican counterparts. The reason was that Mexican labor functioned as an extension of the PRI. Indeed, imagine if, for instance, when the leaders of the United Auto Workers sat down with representatives of the Ford Motor Company, they were accompanied by officials from Washington. These officials were not there to *mediate,* but to *negotiate.* Imagine if wage concessions by Ford management were to be balanced with concessions for housing benefits from HUD and medical benefits from Medicare. That is how Mexican labor functioned under Mexican Paternalism. American labor unions scoffed at the lack of independence of Mexican labor unions. In addition, through the North American Agreement on Labor Cooperation, or NAALC, the NAFTA nations are working to improve labor rights, working conditions, and living standards across Canada, the United States, and Mexico. Though NAALC needs to have its authority augmented, it is one mechanism through which meaningful improvements can be realized during NAFTA's second decade.

18.  "Fox Plans Reforms," *Marketing News,* February 26, 2001.

19.  Press conference, State Department, Washington, D.C., January 30, 2001.

20.  Anthony DePalma, *Here: A Biography of the New American Continent,* page 41.

21.  Robert Putnam, *Bowling Alone: The Collapse and Revival of American Community,* page 318.

22.  The absence of a national health-care program creates all kinds of problems, even when federal programs try to provide basic care to children. "For the last year, an ambitious campaign by this border city focused on a critical if not particularly glamorous goal: enrolling poor children for federal health benefits. Television and radio advertisements urged parents to apply, while volunteers handed out applications at schools and shopping malls. There was even a telethon," Jim Yardley reported. "And here in the fifth-poorest metropolitan area in America, where some people still live without indoor toilets or running water and about 38 percent have no health insurance, something unlikely happened: It worked. The number of children enrolled in the federal Children's Health Insurance Program has jumped to roughly 23,000, from 867. Yet if the enrollment drive has been an unexpected success, it has also revealed an unexpected problem: El Paso is not ready for the torrent of new patients, and may never be. There are, by one count, 46 pediatricians in a city needing 100. There is no children's hospital, making El Paso and its surrounding county, with nearly 700,000 people,

one of the largest areas without one. There is not a single pediatric surgeon." El Paso is a glimpse into America's future this century if the crisis in health care is not addressed promptly. See "A City Struggles to Provide Care Ensured by U.S.," by Jim Yardley, *New York Times*, August 7, 2001.

23. An equally appalling situation is the fact that American children often go hungry. In New York City, there is a "Summer Food Service Program for Children." Conceding that for instance, many children only eat balanced meals at school, this program seeks to provide at least one healthy meal per day to children in New York when school is out for the summer. For more information, see *www.opt-osfns.org*.

24. "Get a Divorce," by Randy Cohen, *New York Times*, July 28, 2002.

25. Putnam, *Bowling Alone*, page 19.

26. In fact, many critics accused the government of promoting atheism by seeking to supplant the role of religion in the lives of the citizenry.

27. *Max Weber and German Politics, A Study in Political Sociology*, J. P. Mayer, London: Faber and Faber, 1956 page 127.

28. "Vicente Fox May Be Setting Himself Up for a Fall," by Geri Smith and Elisabeth Malkin, *Business Week*, December 4, 2000.

29. "Two Cheers for Mexico's Tax Reform," by Manuel Sánchez, *Wall Street Journal*, March 30, 2001.

30. "Fox may not have realized the change he was setting in motion. In the democratic transition of Mexico, Congress has been remade from an institution that rubber-stamps presidential initiatives to one that holds the cards," Ginger Thompson explained. "But no single party or coalition is in control, and because of term limits, many members are neither experienced nor close to their voters. In that situation, the 128 senators and 500 members of the lower chamber of deputies have diluted and even dismissed Mr. Fox's initiatives, alternately seizing and ignoring responsibility for Mexico's agenda, domestic and international." See "Congress Shifts Mexico's Balance of Power," *New York Times*, January 21, 2002.

31. Putnam, *Bowling Alone*, page 332.

32. "Vicente Fox's Election is Just the Tip of the Iceberg," by Roderic Ai Camp, *Los Angeles Times*, January 14, 2001.

33. In a measure of the need to court the Catholic Church, Fox has been accused of acting improperly. When Fox kissed the Pope's hand upon the pontiff's arrival in Mexico City for his fifth visit to Mexico on July 31, 2002, he committed an error, critics charge. It's important to remember how the pontiff was welcomed by then-president José López Portillo on January 26, 1979. "Sir, you are welcomed to Mexico," he said. "May your mission of peace and harmony, and that your efforts for justice that you carry out meet with success in the coming days. I take leave of you in the hands of leaders and faithful of your Church, and may everything be for the good of humanity." By "taking leave" of the Pope, López Portillo reaffirmed the separation of Church and state.

34. "Spain at Our Border? Fox's Vision for Mexico," by Andrew Reding, *Pacificnews.org*, July 3, 2000.

35. American commentators do not have a monopoly on misreading Mexico under NAFTA. Carlos Fuentes, whose career was based on being an apologist for the PRI, is backpedaling as fast as he can. Speaking of the

PRI after Fox came to office, for example, he notes that he sees "all these reptilians . . . these fugitives from Jurassic Park who are still around." Mexicans' resentment of Fuentes' complicity in defending the PRI's hegemony is such that the death of his son, a young photographer who aspired to write, at the age of 25 elicited little sympathy. "It is tragic that his son paid for the sins of his father," one official with the Fox administration said, "but the loss of his son is, perhaps, divine punishment for the harm Fuentes did to Mexico's democratic aspirations" for so many years. For his part, Fuentes is reduced to keeping the unfulfilled promise of his son. "Now it is my turn to keep alive the promise of my son; I have been a keeper of his flame, and that keeps him very close to me," he argues, like a broken and pitiful old man. Both Fuentes quotations are found in his interview "Fuentes Finds His Powers Have a Will of Their Own," by Ginger Thompson, *New York Times,* January 31, 2001.

36. "Be Aware of Our Shadow on Latin America," by Abraham Lowenthal, *Los Angeles Times,* January 3, 2001.

# 10

# Dispute Resolution Strategies for Greater Economic Efficiencies

## EXECUTIVE ABSTRACT

The NAFTA nations elected to surrender certain aspects of their sovereignty in economic matters to encourage economic development. The dispute resolution mechanisms created by NAFTA have their origins in the American and Canadian mistrust of the Mexican judicial system to settle disputes fairly.[1] The purpose was to ensure the expeditious resolution of disputes that could interfere with trade and commerce. The business communities of the three nations, however, have not been served well by how disputes among the NAFTA partners are addressed. Because the dispute resolution mechanisms have functioned in an inconsistent and slow manner, the NAFTA nations also availed themselves of provisions within the World Trade Organization, with limited success. Whether telecommunications, tuna, trucking, or sugar, what is clear is that an expedited manner for fast-track resolution is the better alternative, one that arrives at a superior continental outcome in a more efficient manner. Corporate managers need to be informed and cognizant of the political turmoil that frustrates the expeditious resolution of trade disputes. Policy makers need to understand how superfluous political issues complicate and delay equitable resolutions. As NAFTA enters its second decade, the business community must demand that political considerations not impede superior collective outcomes for all three nations; without a fair and expeditious dispute resolution, NAFTA's efficacy is diminished and all three nations are worse off.

## DISCUSSION

The failure of the United States, Mexico, and Canada to establish an efficient mechanism for resolving disputes threatens economic growth. As was discussed in Chapter 8, the failure, inability, or unwillingness of the United States and Mexico to conduct simple cost-benefit analysis resulted in problems for all involved. Indeed, in the dolphin controversy discussed earlier, American consumers paid higher prices for tuna, Mexican fishermen were excluded from selling their catch in the U.S. market, and dolphins drowned. "Our common border is no longer a line that divides us, but a region that unites our nations, reflecting our common aspirations, values and cultures," Secretary of State Colin Powell said.[2] If this is the case, then it is imperative that Mexico, the United States, and Canada establish the mechanism for resolving disputes that reflects our common economic aspirations.

It is not unusual for business executives to decry the detrimental effect of meddlesome politicians and misguided bureaucrats at regulatory agencies. At the root of this complaint is the observation that the political and bureaucratic processes nurture an unhealthy distrust of the market economy and the private sector. Consider how Robert Putnam describes the effects of diminishing trustworthiness in society:

> A society characterized by generalized reciprocity is more efficient than a distrustful society, for the same reason that money is more efficient than barter. If we don't have to balance every exchange instantly, we can get a lot more accomplished. Trustworthiness lubricates social life. Frequent interaction among a diverse set of people tends to produce a norm of generalized reciprocity. Civic engagement and social capital entail mutual obligation and responsibility for action.[3]

In fact, what Putnam argues about social capital, many business executives agree also holds true of economic capital. The absence of a mechanism for expediting disputes continues to undermine economic growth, and this was one of the shortcomings of the NAFTA accord. "NAFTA's failure has come from what it omitted. . . . The three North American countries should learn from the Continent's experiment on integration. The European Union's mistake was to over-bureaucratize. NAFTA's was the opposite—it has no serious institutions," Robert Pastor, a political scientist from Emory University, opined in the *Los Angeles Times*.[4] To see how these shortcomings frustrate economic growth, let us now consider how the failure to comply with the provisions of NAFTA has adversely affected the trucking, telecommunications, and sugar industries.

## Trucking

NAFTA's progress is impeded by the absence of expeditious dispute-resolution, which is a different way of saying that it's bad for business when politicians improperly interfere with business. The drama surrounding the implementation of NAFTA provisions allowing Mexican trucks to enter the United States is a case in point. When the Bush administration announced its intention to reverse the Clinton administration decision to delay allowing Mexican trucks access to U.S. highways on February 7, 2001, there were familiar protests. "Union officials voice fears that Mexican truckers, who often earn one-fourth as much as unionized American truckers, will take American jobs. And consumer groups, noting that 41 percent of Mexican trucks failed American inspections at the border, argue that the trucks will endanger Americans," Steven Greenhouse reported.[5]

When it comes to the awkward manner in which the NAFTA nations resolve their trade disputes, one knows the familiar drill. First, Americans are shocked, shocked that Mexican trucks would have unfettered access to U.S. highways. Then Mexicans decry American refusal to implement NAFTA accords as scheduled. Washington politicians then follow, in an attempt to use this controversy to grandstand for their constituencies. Then corporate America quietly points out that business is being hurt by this dispute. Finally, arriving on this scene, cable television cameras in tow, are extremists—of the left and the right—who use any dispute as an opportunity to feed the shoutfests that characterize public discourse on American television to strengthen their political agenda.[6] This process is as irrational as it is inappropriate.

In the case of trucking, the fact that the border is open to Mexican truckers doesn't mean that a Mexican manager in Mexico City is going to allow his trucker to deliver a shipment to an address in Manhattan. "Most people are under the impression that if they open it tomorrow, we are going to be bombarded by Mexican carriers on United States highways," said Francisco Benavides, the manager of the Laredo, Texas office for M. S. Carriers®, one of the largest American trucking concerns. He explained that practical problems, such as language difficulties, unfamiliarity with the American interstate highway system, and lack of emergency repair crews, posed the same challenges for Mexican trucking companies that American trucking companies faced entering Mexico. "It's going to be gradual."[7]

At present, most Mexican trucking company executives feel comfortable allowing their drivers to make deliveries 25 miles north of the border. For most of the 12,000 other trucks moving through Laredo, where fully 60 percent of the trade between the U.S. and Mexico travels, there is the hand-off point, where hundreds of billions of dollars worth of international cargo clears customs, through a chain of brokers, warehouses, and transfer trucks, in both directions. How this industry evolves during NAFTA's second decade represents tremendous opportunities, for it constitutes the systemwide modernization of transportation across the continent. The politicization of this process is disheartening, as it illustrates the obstacles that impede sound business decisions and economic growth.

Let us examine how this controversy emerged. When the Clinton administration first refused to implement the trucking provision in NAFTA in 1995, Mexico filed a complaint with a five-member arbitration board. The dispute, which took *six years* to be finally settled in Mexico's favor, resulted in the U.S. being ordered to grant Mexican trucks access to U.S. highways. The *Los Angeles Times* ran an editorial urging the Bush administration to "honor the NAFTA panel's decision." The editorial noted that during "the debate nearly a decade ago on the free trade agreement, Washington successfully insisted on allowing free travel of trucks on both sides of the border as long as they met mutual safety standards. Subsequently, then-President Bill Clinton, influenced by the powerful Teamsters Union, declared all Mexican trucks unsafe and countermanded the NAFTA ruling."[8]

"The first time one of these dangerous trucks kills somebody, that crash will become the face of NAFTA," alarmist Lori Wallach, of Public Citizen's Global Trade Watch, told the *Wall Street Journal*, failing to note that the fleet of trucks operated by Mexican trucking companies engaged in *international* trade are as modern as their American counterparts. "Think about it—Bush wants to expand NAFTA. Well, our big leverage is that if this administration allows those big dangerous trucks, once someone gets killed— and they will—it ruins the whole trade agenda."[9]

Wallach's deceptive arguments ignore the dozens of mutually beneficial joint ventures between U.S. and Mexican trucking firms that, since NAFTA's first decade, already allow freight delivery to each nation's interior to avoid long international runs. In 1999, for instance, 63,000 Mexican trucks made more than 4.5 million crossings, without any higher rate of traffic accidents than their American counterparts.[10] One wonders if the first year's passage without one American being killed in an accident involving a Mexican truck on an American highway subsequent to the implementation of this order proved disappointing to Ms. Wallach.

She, of course, was not alone in hoping for the worst in order to make her political case. "We believe these [Mexican] trucks, particularly the older trucks, which represent a substantial part of the Mexican fleet, represent a serious threat to the environment," Al Meyerhoff, the attorney for the coalition that sued to stop the implementation of the NAFTA provision, was quoted as saying, even though during NAFTA's first decade, the one NAFTA nation that has suffered *environmental* degradation was *Canada*.[11]

Such nonsense aside, when the *Los Angeles Times* is forced to run an editorial about trucks, and when misguided leftists long for a pedestrian to be run down by a truck to score a political point, the dispute resolution mechanism in place is not working in an optimal manner.

## Telecommunications

Despite the neat and tidy resolution of the dispute over tuna, or the discredited concerns about cross-border trucking, there are continuing conflicts in many areas of economic life. "Mexico's market remains dominated by a single company with a government mandate to set high wholesale prices," U.S. trade representative Robert Zoellick complained in the first half of 2002.[12] At stake in the $12 billion Mexican telecommunications market was a legacy of Mexico's paternalism; Teléfonos de Mexico, known as Telmex®, was once a state-owned monopoly that was privatized to a group of politically well-connected investors led by Carlos Slim.

Telmex's socialist circumstances—a culture of paternalism, political maneuvers by well-connected insiders, competitive advantages monopolies inherently enjoy—continue to inhibit the development of a competitive marketplace. For American and Canadian officials, in fact, the pace at which Mexico's telecommunications have opened up has proved frustrating, for it undermines their own nations' ability to enter a lucrative market. For consumers in all three nations, artificially high prices for telecommunications services inhibit growth, making everything from cell phones to Internet access fees higher than they would be otherwise. Seven decades of paternalism, however, are difficult to undo in a single stroke. Within the context of NAFTA, Robert Zoellick's complaint that through Telmex's unfair market share, Mexico maintains, in effect, "an anticompetitive cross-border telecommunications regime"[13] succinctly describes the business community's sentiment.[14]

The failure of Mexico to open its telecommunications market mirrors the failure of the United States to open its highways to Mexican trucks. This is not to excuse Mexican recalcitrance, but rather to demonstrate how the absence of an expedited dispute resolution mechanism negatively impacts economic development. It also underscores the kinds of issues and concerns that will arise throughout the 2000s. Robert Zoellick's complaint about anticompetitive regimes will resonate as discussions about Mexico's electric power and oil industries surface. The same paternalistic sentiment that continues to inhibit the development of a fully competitive telecommunications market will create maelstroms as the electric power and oil industries—with a combined market value of $110 billion—become highly contested.

Tuna and trucks, however, offer guidelines on how these disputes can best be approached. It is impossible for an industry to prosper if it is based on a technology that drowns dolphins. It is detrimental to continental relations if acrimonious arguments are employed to disparage the cross-border transportation industry. Of equal concern, then, is how in the 2000s, rather than offering a gentle understanding of the complexities involved in first privatizing telecommunications and then transforming the business and bureaucratic cultures as Mexico has made the transition to a market economy, American officials too often have lost patience.

That Telmex acts like a bully in the marketplace is not at issue; that is easy to document. That it has used its economic power to unfairly defend its market share has also been amply documented. What has been absent, however, is an understanding that how Mexico goes about making its telecommunications into a more perfect market will set the stage for how the electric power and oil industries are modernized. Of course, it should be noted that Telmex is not alone in engaging in unfair market practices. Netscape®'s complaint against Microsoft's Internet Explorer led the Clinton Justice Department famously to file suit against Microsoft. Of equal concern is the curious reference to the paradox of "improving" upon "perfect" competition.[15] As executives in the telecommunications industry seek to pressure Mexico to move forward in its compliance with NAFTA provisions, policy makers on both sides of the border must address the peculiar problems associated with divorcing elements of paternalism that slow modernization.

"Although the Mexican market has been open to competition for four years, the company is still a quasi-monopoly. Telmex boasts 58% of the market for international calls originating in Mexico, 68% of the domestic long-distance market, and 97% of the local market," *Business Week* reported in 2001, echoing American frustrations.[16] When threatened with regulatory effort to foster more competition, Telmex chairman Carlos Slim is masterful at undermining such efforts. When Fox took office, for instance, he reached an agreement with Avantel® and Alestra® (whose American partners are, respectively, MCI® and AT&T®) aimed at lowering fees these long-distance rivals pay to complete calls on Telmex's local network.

These "good faith" efforts to "foster healthy competition," as Carlos Slim characterized the move, however, are consistent with the piecemeal attempt to foster fair competition.[17] Avantel and Alestra, for instance, petitioned Mexico's telecom regulatory agency, known as Cofetel, for two years before the agency moved on their complaints. Apparently fearful of taking on Telmex's political and economic clout, it was only in March 2000 that Cofetel imposed new regulations on the prices Telmex could charge, and requirements on its service.[18] The continuing complaint leveled by Avantel, Alestra, MCI, and AT&T is about the interconnection fees Telmex charges long-distance competitors to complete long-distance calls on its local network. In complaints filed with regulators—in Mexico City and Washington, D.C.—Telmex is accused of impeding fair competition by charging interconnection fees that are two to three times higher than prevailing international benchmarks.

In its defense, Telmex counters that it has lost more than 30 percent of the market to competitors since its monopoly ended, and that its high interconnection rates are needed to expand local telephone service and invest in equipment to connect. Mexico has far fewer telephones per capita than either Canada or the United States.

Perhaps, but a report from the Organization for Economic Cooperation & Development issued in 2000 found that Mexican phone charges were the highest among member countries, save for Japan. Telmex's corporate culture's anticompetitive tendency has also caught the attention of American regulators; in 2000, the

Federal Communications Commission (FCC) fined Telmex's U.S. subsidiary $100,000 for refusing to provide telephone lines and circuits to competitors in Mexico. AT&T and MCI argued at the time that this was precisely the kind of unfair business practices in which Telmex engages in the Mexican market.

Unending rankling, a weak regulatory agency incapable of nurturing healthy competition, and an industry giant with enormous market power all work to undermine any attempt to resolve disputes expeditiously. In fairness to Telmex, when it was privatized, the government granted a seven-year continuation of its monopoly to recoup the $7 billion investors made for buying out the company; higher interconnection rates were also authorized to upgrade and expand Mexico's telecommunications infrastructure. Telmex officials argue that they have been "in open competition" only "since 1997" and that they have "made tremendous strides" in five years in opening the market to new competitors.

Mexican and American critics ignore these real issues. Rather, officials chose instead to file complaints and impose trade sanctions; this works, of course, but not without costs. Perhaps their arguments are not without merit, but from a public relations point of view, one measure of how poorly Telmex has made its case to the Mexican public is its lost credibility. Indeed, Telmex, which was privatized in December 1990, remains one of the most vilified companies in Mexico, a fact that stands to undermine its ability to compete as the telecommunications market becomes more highly competitive.

## Sugar

The disputes over sugar are firmly based on the interference by domestic politics with the international economics of this industry. The United States continues to subsidize inefficient American sugars for political, not economic, reasons. The powerful sugar lobby in Florida, in fact, has benefited greatly from federal subsidies and import restrictions that keep the price Americans pay for sugar artificially high.[19] Subsidizing domestic sugar growers is not an American monopoly, of course. "For most of the PRI's seven-decade reign . . . the system fostered political peace in Mexico's vast countryside," Peter Fritsch explains. "What it didn't do was bring Mexico's antiquated sugar refineries, some nearing 100 years old, any closer to financial viability. In fact, the system seemed to draw its economic inspiration from the playbooks of communist central planners. Today, for example, it costs more to buy a ton of sugar cane in Mexico than to buy a ton of refined sugar on world markets."[20]

It would appear that Mexican Paternalism has influenced American policy, were it not for the long history of government intervention in the market for political purposes. That both the United States and Mexico subsidize their respective agricultural producers to the tune of billions of dollars creates distortions in each nation's economies, of course. When these domestic priorities conflict with international commerce, however, domestic prerogatives become trade disputes. "Under the terms of the original draft of the North American Free Trade Agreement," Peter Fritsch reported in the *Wall Street Journal,* "Mexico was to be able to export its entire sugar surplus to the U.S. beginning [in 2000]. But an 11th-hour side agreement negotiated in late 1993 under pressure from the U.S.'s powerful sugar lobby severely limits that access. Mexico says that side agreement was never a done deal. Indeed, the side letters accompanying NAFTA's enabling legislation say different things in their Spanish and English versions."[21]

American subsidies, Mexican oversupply, and interference in the free markets by powerful political interests create a situation in which disputes are inevitable. It could be argued that the simple fact that both Mexico and the United States subsidize their farmers creates an even playing field of sorts. Consider the bemused manner in which Robert Frank makes this observation:

> In Ithaca, New York, where I live, the cable TV system carries most New York Yankee baseball games. One August night, sportscasters Phil Rizzuto and Bobby Murcer were calling a slow game between the Yankees and the Milwaukee Brewers. Between pitches, Rizzuto was looking over his record sheets and remarked that the Brewers had done much better in day games than in games at night. Murcer checked his own records and found that the Yankees, too, had a much higher winning percentage during the day. With characteristic enthusiasm, Rizzuto then conjectured that *all* teams have better records for day games. . . . But the "fact" that Rizzuto and Murcer were trying to explain was of course not a fact at all. Without consulting any baseball records, we know that it is mathematically impossible for all teams to have better records during the day than at night. For every team that loses a night game, some other team must win one. Lighting conditions at night may indeed be poor, but they are poor for both sides.[22]

The problem, of course, is that it is inadvisable to argue that if one runner in a relay race shoots herself in the foot, the others should do likewise for the sake of maintaining an even playing field. The dispute over Mexican and American sugar, however, suggests the entrenched and institutional nature of the emerging disputes. The controversies over tuna, trucks, and telecommunications are rather straightforward compared with sugar—and with the environmental disputes arising, not just over how sugar is grown, in the 2000s.

The one mechanism for dispute resolution that is in place and working centers on controversies that arise between investors and host governments. Noting that "corporations—American, Canadian and Mexican alike—that directly invest in neighboring countries are thrilled that NAFTA provides some protection," Anthony DePalma reports that the way these disputes are settled has prompted "foes of the trade pact [to] say some of their worst fears about anonymous government have become reality."[23] Though well intentioned, there are problems with how the disputes are addressed, with the absence of transparency for the citizens of all three nation, and with how appropriate such a dispute resolution mechanism can be for democratic nations. "The lack of traditional appeal process, transparency and legally binding precedent, along with the wide scope of what can be challenged under the free-trade investment rules, have made many people wary in all three nations, including government officials," Anthony DePalma reported. "Pierre Pettigrew, Canada's minister of international trade, has written to his counterparts in the United States and Mexico to begin a process of what he calls 'clarifying' the limits of NAFTA's investment protections and perhaps amending the agreement before negotiations begin in earnest on the Free Trade Area of the Americas."[24]

Not unlike most "tribunals" convened by government, it is unfortunate that the one expeditious dispute resolution NAFTA has in place is unsatisfying for everyone involved. That this needs to be remedied is an urgent task, simply because of the nature of other disputes now becoming evident.

In fact, though the water dispute along the U.S.-Mexico border was discussed at length in Chapter 8, what is now emerging are more complicated problems that, absent a mechanism for dispute resolution, stand to create acrimonious debate in all three NAFTA nations. Consider two environmental disputes that first emerged during NAFTA's first decade: "bioprospecting" and water security. Bioprospecting refers to the commercialization of biological products without proper compensation for intellectual rights. Water security disputes refers to the economic distortions that arise when water is subsidized to one community, or party, without properly compensating another community. In response to bioprospecting, for instance, the Rural Advancement Foundation International, or RAFI, maintains that "without impugning the goodwill or honourable intentions of anyone, RAFI regards all bioprospecting agreements to be biopiracy," though acknowledging "the right of indigenous and local communities and nations to reach their own conclusions" on the matter.[25]

As far as the failure to properly compensate communities where water is plentiful to benefit water-scarce human populations, consider the comparative analysis of the American Southwest and the Middle East. "[D]eeply ingrained attitudes and vested interests still represent formidable obstacles to changing water use and management practices. Continuing down the current path of inefficient and highly subsidized agricultural water use; escalating urban demands; and neglecting ecosystems, is a recipe for conflict and decline."[26] This is of special concern for Canada, the one NAFTA nation that will, in the decades to come, be expected to supply water to the United States, and perhaps even to Mexico.

In addition, one must now consider the volatile nature of other areas of dispute—corruption and illegal drugs—that will be discussed in later chapters. The absence of an expedited mechanism for a cost-benefit analysis dooms the United States, Mexico, and Canada to *years* of inefficiencies, as the crises over tuna, trucks, and telecommunications demonstrate. What is clear is that cost-benefit analysis can ensure superior *continental* outcomes. Indeed, as NAFTA's second decade unfolds, American, Mexican, and Canadian policy makers should be mindful of the Vietnamese saying, "Argue with a smart man, can't win. Argue with a stupid man, can't stop."[27] The NAFTA nations, availing themselves of cost-benefit analysis in a timely manner, should not be arguing at all.

## SUMMARY

1. Absent an expedited dispute resolution mechanism in place that incorporates cost-benefit analysis, as the tuna, trucking and telecommunications disagreements during NAFTA's first decade illustrate, problems for all three countries result.

2. Energy, water, and immigration issues present the greatest challenges as NAFTA moves into its second decade in order to achieve superior economic efficiencies.

3. These disputes interfere with the goals of NASP, so it is imperative that the governments of the three nations work to level the playing field in these markets and implement legislation that will encourage market capitalization and sustainable development of these resources consistent with the interests of the private sectors and the public's expectation of responsible corporate citizens.

4. The interests of states, whether the American and Mexican states that share the Gulf of Mexico or the states on both sides of the U.S.-Canada and U.S.-Mexico border, must be represented as the master development plans require greater economies of scale on regional bases.

## ENDNOTES

1. "I remember my father regularly remarking . . . how in Mexico a person is guilty until proven innocent; whereas in the United States, the opposite faith prevails," Richard Rodriguez writes, repeating a popular American slander of Mexico's legal system. The truth is that in Mexico the guilty party is presumed to have been charged; all that is required, however, is to establish doubt. In the United States, on the other hand, a trial by jury does not necessarily benefit society—or result in justice. The presumption of innocent until proven guilty is a polite fiction; hundreds of innocent people have been sent to death row in the United States. And while Americans express shock that Mexico's legal system does not employ a jury, Americans express no such discomfort with other, similar, legal systems that also do without juries, including the one that convicted the men accused of blowing up Pam Am Flight 103. "After months of testimony, judges . . . began deliberations on the fate of two Libyans accused of blowing up Pan Am Flight 103 in 1988 over Lockerbie, Scotland," the Associated Press reported, to Americans' collective satisfaction. In fact, most international systems, even those empowered to supersede local laws, do not include juries at all. "Section 8 of the United Nations Regulation 2001/4—which supersedes pre-existing local laws— declares that providing evidence of trafficking protects the woman against charges of prostitution," Sebastian Junger reports. "Major criminal trials in Kosovo have two international judges sit on the panel with three local, or 'lay,' judges. This panel hears all evidence and then comes to a verdict." The paradox, then, is that in Mexico a good number of guilty people are free walking the streets, but in the United States, there are a lot of innocent people behind bars—and on death row. See, respectively, *Brown: The Last Discovery of America*, Richard Rodriguez, page 222; *Actual Innocence: When Justice Goes Wrong and How to Make It Right*, by Barry Scheck, Peter Neufeld, and Jim Dwyer; "Judges Deliberate Lockerbie

Verdict," Associated Press, January 18, 2001; and "Kosovo's Sex Slave Trade," by Sebastian Junger, *Vanity Fair,* July 2002.

2. Press conference, State Department, Washington, D.C., held on January 30, 2001.

3. Robert Putnam, *Bowling Alone: The Collapse and Revival of American Community,* page 21.

4. "Shine NAFTA's Light on the Darker Corners," by Robert A. Pastor, *Los Angeles Times,* February 15, 2001.

5. "Bush to Open Country to Mexican Truckers," by Steven Greenhouse, *New York Times,* February 7, 2001.

6. Cable television programs such as *Crossfire* and *Hardball* speak volumes about the state of public discourse in the United States. American "public affairs" programs are, increasingly, spectacles of the peculiarly American secular worship of things trivial. "One of the true dangers of endless blather on talk television is that pundits can, and too often do, say anything they want—whether it's true or not," Alicia C. Shepard wrote. "In the writing process, most journalists are forced to stop and think: Can I really back that up? Is the person who said this qualified to make this claim? And if they don't ask those questions, their editors often will. But on the shout show circuit, a rumor is often given the same weight as a fact." See "White Noise," by Alicia C. Shepard, *American Journalism Review,* January/February 1999, available at *Ajr.org.*

7. Quoted in "Truck-Choked Border City Fears Being Bypassed," by Jim Yardley, *New York Times,* March 15, 2001.

8. "Release the Brakes on NAFTA," Editorial, *Los Angeles Times,* February 22, 2001.

9. "U.S. Is Told to Let Mexican Trucks Enter," by Helene Cooper and Kathy Chen, *Wall Street Journal,* February 7, 2001.

10. "Feds: 63,000 Mexican Trucks Crossed," Associated Press, April 17, 2001.

11. "Suit Seeks to Halt Bush Plan on Entry of Mexican Trucks," by Steven Greenhouse, *New York Times,* May 2, 2002.

12. As quoted by Bloomberg News in "Telmex's Dominance Draws Complaint from U.S.," February 14, 2002.

13. Ibid.

14. This is also the concern of consumer rights advocacy groups that express their frustration that individual households pay exorbitant fees for international phone calls to and from Mexico. Accusations against Telmex engaging in monopolistic behavior are legendary. "American trade officials have gone so far as to threaten to drag Mexico before the World Trade Organization to force Mexican regulators to level the playing field for competitors," Anthony DePalma reported back in 2000. See "Once a Monopoly and Still a Threat," by Anthony DePalma, *New York Times,* October 26, 2000.

15. America's Founding Fathers, by seeking to create a "more" perfect union, suggested that perfection was something that could be improved upon, thus undermining the very idea of what makes anything "perfect" in the first place. Even perfect competition, I argue here, can therefore benefit by being improved upon.

16. "Telmex: Mexico's 800-Pound Gorilla," by Elisabeth Malkin, *Business Week,* June 18, 2001.

17. Personal communication, May 2001.

18. Cofetel derives its oversight authority from the 1997 ruling by Mexico's Federal Competition Commission (CFC) which found that Telmex enjoyed a "dominant power" in local, national and international telephony services. Critics, however, accuse Cofetel of being intimidated by Carlos Slim, Mexico's wealthiest man, and reluctant to enforce conditions that would foster competition.

19. In Florida, furthermore, it is astounding that sugar growers receive federal help to grow sugar that entails despoiling the Everglades—the tangled web that's woven when infectious private greed, unprincipled political ambitions, and a fragile ecosystem collide.

20. "Looming Sugar Crisis May Sour Honeymoon of Mexico's President," by Peter Fritsch, *Wall Street Journal,* November 30, 2000.

21. Ibid.

22. *Choosing the Right Pond: Human Behavior and the Quest for Status,* Robert Frank, page 3.

23. "NAFTA's Powerful Little Secret," by Anthony DePalma, *New York Times,* March 11, 2001.

24. Ibid.

25. "Messages from the Chiapas 'Bioprospecting' Dispute," in *Rafi.org,* December 19, 1999.

26. "Environmental Water Security: Lessons from the Southwestern U.S., Northwestern Mexico, and the Middle East," by Jason Morrison and Aaron T. Wolf, presented at the United States Global Change Research Program Seminar, November 23, 1998.

27. Vietnamese saying translated by Linh Dinh. And there, in one sentence, one can summarize the misguided political career of Robert McNamara, who cowrote a book titled, with unintended irony, *Argument Without End.*

# 11

# Understanding the Origins and Role of Corruption

## EXECUTIVE ABSTRACT

One American perception about Mexico is that corruption permeates all aspects of life, personal and business, in that country. American executives are apprehensive about how to conduct business in an environment in which everyone—from the humblest cop walking his beat to some of the most powerful political leaders—routinely engage in corruption. These perceptions, however, are distorted by a peculiar set of circumstances that are unique to the economic development model Mexico has chosen and to specific cultural distinctions between the United States and Mexico. Although the level of *low corruption*—the cop on the beat—has few counterparts vis-à-vis the United States, *high corruption*—institutionalized wrongdoing by each nation's elite—is comparable in both nations. Furthermore, there is in Mexico a strong tradition of exaggerating claims of corruption, or *exaggerated corruption,* as a way of voicing political dissent while in the United States there are cultural forces that dismiss American corruption through the use of euphemism and denial. As the NAFTA economy unfolds, moreover, there are forces that threaten the continued viability of low corruption in Mexico. On the other hand, there is no mechanism in place that stands to rein in high corruption. In fact, evidence suggests that the level of high corruption in both nations has risen, since both nations are failing to confront adequately the corruption associated with the money laundering of the drug trade, or *drug corruption.* What is clear, however, is that low corruption is exacerbated when the role of money is limited in an economy and high corruption is a characteristic of authoritarian economies. Accusations of corruption, as we shall examine, are also a form of political protest and social unrest. Exaggerated corruption is thus politically in decline as Mexican democracy strengthens and becomes more responsive to the public's needs. As for drug corruption, it is a malady for which there is no immediate remedy.

## DISCUSSION

The business and economic life of Mexico is undermined by the distortions that arise from corruption. There are four fundamental forms of corruption. Low corruption affects most people in their daily lives. High corruption challenges business executives because, by virtue of involving powerful business leaders and well-connected politicians, it constitutes an unfair business practice and oftentimes has considerable macroeconomic consequences.[1] Exaggerated corruption is the false accusation of corruption that in Mexico became a form of political speech, a phenomenon that stood in stark contrast from the denial favored by Americans when discussing corruption in the U.S. A final form, drug corruption, arises from money laundering associated with drug trafficking.[2] Each of these forms of corruption operates under its own set of rules and has distinct dynamics. Taken together, however, they create certain distortions that challenge the healthy and sustainable development of the economies of Mexico, the United States, and Canada. To understand how and why this is so, it is necessary to examine more closely each form of corruption. Let us now consider each in turn.

### Low Corruption

An economy that limits the role of money makes cash that much more coveted. To a bureaucrat who is salary poor but benefits rich, being offered cash constitutes a disproportionate temptation to what it would be under other circumstances. A police officer who is similarly cash poor, when offered cash—a *mordida,* literally a "bite" out of your wallet—to look the other way, is more likely to rationalize doing just that. Any attempt to limit the role of money in an economy, clearly, engenders low corruption. Whether it is an official at the department of motor vehicles who expects a "gratuity" to issue a license, or an inspector who insinuates that the process can be expedited through a "tip," the proliferation of low corruption increases as the role of money is limited.

Low corruption, of course, occurs wherever money is restricted in an economy, often through artificially low salaries. As a result, cash becomes disproportionately important—causing low-salaried officials, from neighborhood police officers to clerks at city offices, to seek "tips" for routine functions. Consider one American example of how limiting the role of money through salary reductions produces low corruption. Unintended corruption is evident in something as innocuous as attempting to provide a fringe benefit to employees at one of America's largest companies, headquartered in New York. This titan of corporate America manufactures cigarettes. Rather than giving employees a salary increase to allow them, after taxes, to buy a carton of cigarettes each week, for instance, management had decided instead to *give* a carton of cigarettes in lieu of money. This "perk," by virtue of being non-cash, presents several problems. What if an employee doesn't smoke? What if an employee would rather have the cash and not a weekly supply of cigarettes? What if this "benefit" favors those employees who smoke relative to non-smokers?

These problems could be easily solved if the company simply gave their employees the cash to go out and buy a carton of cigarettes in a store—or pocket the money if they didn't smoke. With the distribution of cartons of cigarettes, however, corruption ensues. The firm's headquarters have become, in fact, a bastion of low corruption. Employees who do not smoke themselves have created a network where these cartons are exchanged for cash on a black market. Cartons of cigarettes are stolen and sold on the streets of New York. Other cartons are illegally sold to convenience stores. The government is deprived of tax revenues, petty theft proliferates throughout the company, and black market cigarettes find their way into the hands of youngsters. The corruption that follows limiting the role of money is such that the firm's security personnel resort to hidden cameras to tape employees, plant decoy cartons of cigarettes in internal sting operations, and hire private detectives to follow the trail of bootleg cigarettes.[3]

Policing costs money, is a terrible distraction for the firm, and corruption ripples through the local economy. Through a misguided attempt to provide a benefit to employees, an opportunity for crime emerges. But this is human nature—and the inevitable result of limiting the role of money. It is difficult to believe that institutional low corruption suffuses life in the headquarters of one of the largest companies in corporate America.[4]

Now consider not *one* office building of one misguided company in the United States, but an *entire* government policy constructed along these lines. Given the havoc created in one office building in New York, what is one to make of the cumulative impact on a society where benefits replace cash in a society? Robert Frank explains that the "use of nonpecuniary devices to reduce compensation costs is an art perhaps nowhere more finely developed than in the bureaucracies of various governments. As anyone who has ever served in the federal government knows, there exists an extremely broad range of ability and dedication among the ranks of upper-level civil servants. Some routinely put in 70-hour work weeks, while others accomplish little more each day than a careful reading of the *Washington Post*. Yet the presence of salary ceilings has all but completely eliminated any differences in the monetary compensation these bureaucrats receive."[5]

The annoying low corruption that one encounters in Mexico—from giving a police officer a couple of bucks not to write a ticket to giving a "tip" to an official to expedite the issuance of a permit—is a measure of the extent to which paternalism suffused the whole of the Mexican economy. That Mexican civil servants are salary poor but benefits rich limits the role of money in their lives. The absolute power of this limitation in fostering low corruption cannot be underestimated. "The problem of corruption [in Mexico's civil service], and the lack of information rights that helps cause it, is seen . . . dramatically from the perspective of the people," Alejandro Junco opined in the *Wall Street Journal,* where he called for Fox to model reforms based on the Freedom of Information Act in the United States. "If a body receives a single dollar in public funds, the citizens have a right to follow its trail and learn how it was spent. No one can question the request for information; no one can refuse to provide it."[6]

It is precisely the frustrating, petty nature of low corruption that infuriates with its absurdity—and not just where civil servants are concerned. "Every employee I ever worked with in my old cubicle-dwelling days was pillaging the company on a regular basis," Scott Adams confessed in the *New York Times,* by way of making light of the corporate scandals of the early 2000s. "The C.E.O.'s and C.F.O.'s aren't less ethical than employees and stockholders; they're just more effective. They're getting a higher quality of loot than the rank and file, and for that they must be punished."[7]

Low corruption remains corruption nonetheless. It can be easily remedied, however, by increasing salaries (while modifying how social welfare benefits are construed) and rendering more professional how business is conducted. Corporate America, from GM managers who instill professionalism in their Mexican plants to the McDonald's trainers who instill a sense of pride in doing a job well done, has contributed significantly to changing the business climate in Mexico throughout the last decade. During NAFTA's first decade, in fact, a sense of pride and optimism about integrity was evident. This is one reason low corruption has become so stigmatized—and why Mexicans now tell tales about challenging what had been the status quo and *not* paying a bribe.

## High Corruption

The nature of Mexican Paternalism, where the ruling party was indistinguishable from the government, and where state-owned enterprises were used to advance the interests of the ruling party, engendered high corruption. As we saw in Chapter 6, Pemex, though one of the world's largest oil companies, is perhaps the most corrupt and inefficient enterprise in Mexico. The revelations during the summer of 2002, when more than $100 million was believed to have been funneled from Pemex to the PRI in connection with the presidential elections of 2000, are consistent with how the PRI used Pemex for its own ends.[8] In one preliminary study I saw, it was estimated that, since 1975, more than $18 billion had been siphoned from Pemex by the PRI.[9]

If the PRI thus encompassed a "revolutionary family"—as the descendants and associates of the leaders of the Mexican Revolution of 1917 are called—its members looked after each other and themselves, thereby forming an elite class that governed the nation throughout much of the twentieth century. Carlos Hank González, for instance, rose from a schoolteacher's salary to become one of Mexico's richest men. "A politician who's poor is a poor politician," became his signature aphorism and the disgusting mantra of his followers.[10] An imposing, towering man—"Hank" is a German surname, and not, as American reporters often assumed, an Americanized nickname—he engendered a political dynasty in which his sons have created a far-flung empire.[11]

To understand the beguiling charm of the PRI's most sophisticated miscreants, consider the following anecdote. When Carlos Hank González served as Secretary of Tourism in the mid-1980s under the administration of Miguel de la Madrid, he spoke before the San Francisco Chamber of Commerce, which threw a lavish dinner and reception for him. Hank González was only too happy to deal with his distinguished hosts and their guests whom he considered his peers. It was certainly a peculiar sight, however.[12] There were two or three Americans of Mexican ancestry, or

AMAs, present—guests among the more than 100 Anglo businessmen and public officials attending the dinner.

It was clear that these may have been guests of the well-intentioned (but undeniably misguided, from the Secretariat of Tourism's perspective) members of the Chamber of Commerce, but it went without saying that no Mexican official considered any of them to be their equals. Indeed, during a question-and-answer session following a speech about investment opportunities in Mexican resorts, particularly Cancún, the historic snub of Mexicans who reside outside Mexico was evident. Carlos Hank González refused to answer a question posed by an American reporter who identified herself as "a Chicana." He pretended not to hear the question, then made a witty comment about the Diego Rivera murals that grace the Chamber of Commerce building in San Francisco, bringing the question and answer portion to an abrupt close. Mexican officials, in fact, brushed all other motions aside with a condescension that was palpable—and embarrassing to those of us cognizant of what was going on.[13]

It is this kind of arrogance—and impunity—that characterizes how high corruption flourished in Mexico. That it has continued for as long as it has, however, is not a reflection of the Mexican character—passive in the face of injustice, resigned to fatalism, or unwilling to stand up for his or her rights. Rather, the nature of high corruption in Mexico is not fundamentally different from what one finds in other countries.

High corruption is not the accumulation of wealth for the wealth's sake. Its purpose is, in a perverted sense, altruistic: it is the *accumulation* of wealth in order to *dispense* patronage. To understand this counterintuitive construction, it is necessary to consider, first, an anthropologist's research on the subject, and, second, the fundamental nature of Mexican Paternalism under the PRI. In his cross-cultural examination of the idea of "manhood," anthropologist David Gilmore explains that:

I was prepared to rediscover the old saw that conventional femininity is nurturing and passive and that masculinity is self-serving, egotistical, and uncaring. But I did not find this. One of my findings here is that manhood ideologies always include a criterion of selfless generosity, even to the point of sacrifice. Again and again we find that "real" men are those who give more than they take; they serve others. Real men are generous, even to a fault . . . Non-men are often those stigmatized as stingy and unproductive. Manhood therefore is also a nurturing concept, if we define that term as giving, subventing, or other-directed. It is true that this male giving is different from, and less demonstrative and more obscure than, the female. It is less direct, less immediate, more involved with externals; the "other" involved may be society in general rather than specific persons. . . . To be generous, he must be selfish enough to amass goods, often by defeating other men; to be gentle, he must first be strong, even ruthless in confronting enemies; to love he must be aggressive enough to court, seduce, and "win" a wife.[14]

Carlos Hank González, to be sure, took very good care of all those who were loyal to him, and through his malfeasance he was able to provide for their well-being. The ability of politicians to dispense patronage to their loyal followers is crucial to their success. In the United States, consider the way politicians, from Chicago Mayor Richard J. Daley to Tammany Hall's William Marcy "Boss" Tweed, all took care of their own by redistributing corruptly accumulated wealth through the dispensing of patronage.

The continuing appeal of Mexican Paternalism, in fact, while seemingly benign in its nature, encourages high corruption to continue. "Unlike most long-standing regimes . . . the PRI rarely used repression: it was not so much a strict father as a rich, if whimsical, uncle," the London *Economist* succinctly summed up seven decades of rule. "It co-opted trade unions and their block votes by lavishing money and power on their leaders. It bought the peasants' eternal gratitude by breaking up huge plantations and handing out millions of small tracts of land. Instead of censoring the press, it kept newspapers afloat—and loyal—with cheap newsprint, floods of government advertising, and generous gifts to journalists. It was the greatest patron of the arts. Sometimes it even funded opposition political parties, both to give its critics a little space to vent their feelings, and to make sure they stayed divided. Its rule was based on collaboration, not coercion. Only when all else failed did it resort to electoral fraud."[15]

This kind of high corruption, of course, is facilitated by the absence of democratic institutions. What are now called "lobbyists" in the United States, after all, were originally defined as "a term applied collectively to men that make a business of corruptly influencing legislators."[16] *To lobby* is the modern way *to corrupt* in America.

In other words, where accountability is weakened, the balance of power shifts from the governed to those who govern.

The success of the Fox administration in making strides toward ending high corruption depends on its ability to depoliticize the process by which the affairs of the nation are carried out, and to encourage the development of strong civic organizations that can become watchdogs and hold public officials accountable. It is also important to note that Max Weber suggested that the greater a nation's bureaucracy, the higher the probability for corruption. "If organizations are the form of our modern condition," he wrote, "one cannot help but note that this is frequently represented less as an opportune or benevolent phenomenon but more as something which is constraining and repressive."[17] The problems Fox has encountered in pushing forth his reforms— whether of how Pemex is managed or how requests for bids for public works are reviewed—are a measure of how entrenched high corruption remains.

What is often overlooked, however, is that high corruption has a private sector component. While Americans raise their eyebrows when told that the PRI plundered $18 billion from Pemex over a quarter century, consider how dispiriting it is for Mexicans to learn that private sector corruption in the United States far eclipses these figures. "[I]nsurance fraud costs property and casualty insurers—and their policy holders—approximately $30 billion each year," Julia Dubner reported in "Insurance Fraud: The Costly Crime with Millions of Victims," published in an industry newsletter. "Those $30 billion translate into $200 to $300 in higher insurance premiums for the average household, according to the National Insurance Crime Bureau (NICB), a non-profit organization that partners with insurers and law-enforcement agencies to help detect, prevent and deter fraud and theft."[18]

Companies, in turn, act corruptly towards their clients. In the late 1980s, for instance, the State of California sued Pacific Bell® for "over-billing"—a gracious euphemism for theft. The company defended itself by saying that "aggressive marketing" was the reason customers were signed up for services—call waiting, call forwarding, regional discount plans, and so on—without their knowledge. The state ordered the company to reimburse customers who had been billed for services not requested. Shortly thereafter Pacific Bell sent me a letter stating that the company owed me "more than an apology."

Two decades later, corruption remains a fact of corporate life in the United States. "Corporate corruption cases are inevitable during the trough of the boom-bust economic cycle . . . [b]ut this wave is different," Stephen Labaton reported. "Some statistics indicated that these fraud cases were actually on the rise during the boom cycle. . . . 'What we are seeing in a variety of areas is fraud on the rise at the same time other crimes are going down,' said Joseph T. Wells, a former F.B.I. agent and the founder of the Association of Certified Fraud Examiners, which trains members of government, corporations, and accounting firms in ferreting out fraud. 'There are at least two reasons. Crime is largely a factor of age, and fraud is the crime of choice of the older perpetrator, so as the society ages, you have, and should continue to see, an increase in fraud cases. A second reason is that the education level of society has come up in the last 20 years, and the message is clear in the mind of the better-educated public that if you want to commit a crime, fraud is the way to go . . . The take is better, and the punishment generally is less.' "[19]

It's hard to reconcile the image of the United States with this reality. Which is worse? Having to pay hundreds of dollars a year because of private sector corruption, or having to do without public services because of public sector corruption?

It is clear that Mexicans, burdened by public inefficiency due to the excesses of the PRI's brand of paternalism, want to put an end to the impunity with which public affairs have been managed. This is not only because it's the right thing to do, but also because it's the right time to do it. In his influential book *Political Order in Changing Societies,* published in 1968, Samuel P. Huntington argued that high corruption was endemic in societies undergoing rapid economic development. Bureaucracies were made more responsive, if not more accountable, through bribes, and patronage diffused power in otherwise authoritarian regimes. As things "get done," however, the economy matures, and there is a rapid decline in the marginal utility of continuing corruption. The corruption that once facilitated things "getting done" now interferes with getting things done correctly.

Mistrust of the state has likewise long fostered a disregard for the law; where money allows someone to flaunt the rules, there's little incentive for those less privileged to comply with the law. Ameliorating corruption among the police, exacerbated by a shortage of law enforcement officials, is a high priority. Ensuring the independence of the judiciary, where the legal system can hold the corrupt accountable, is equally important. Taken together these priorities constitute instilling the "rule of law" as a mechanism for combating high corruption.[20] "A . . . problem for Mexico is that much of the current legislation on the books contradicts the rule of law necessary for development. In centrally planned economies, as the late Austrian economist Friedrich von Hayek argued convincingly, there was no rule of law even when the law was respected," Luis Rubio, director of the Center of Research for Development in Mexico City, opined in the *Wall Street Journal.* "This was due to the fact that legislation granted arbitrary powers to the authorities, leaving it to them to decide whether the law should be enforced in a particular case by reference to what is considered 'fair' or according to 'the common good.' When legislation is written in this way, it undermines the principle of formal equality before the law and implies that government may, with greater ease, grant legal privilege to its constituencies."[21]

For all its problems, however, Mexico's legal system, arguably, is more benevolent that America's. While Mexicans become exasperated at the impunity with which the rich and powerful can maneuver in Mexico, there is also much to criticize in the American legal system in this respect. However many times I explain to Mexicans that the United States is a nation of laws, not a nation of justice, they remain incredulous. The American legal system, in fact, is primarily concerned with enforcing laws, while the Mexican legal system strives to dispense justice. In the United States, laws are often enforced without regard to justice: the guilty wealthy may be set free, and the innocent poor sent to death row.[22] It is a measure of Mexicans' unhealthy belief in the United States that they resist these ideas, insisting that they would foolishly place their fate in the hands of an American court. Where would you rather live: where a few of the guilty go unpunished, or where the innocent are put to death?

## Exaggerated Corruption

If low corruption is the stuff of daily annoyances and disclosures of high corruption are what fills tabloids and television news programs, the cumulative impact is one of discouragement. Coupled with the resentment felt towards the authoritarianism of Mexican Paternalism, one then finds that accusations of corruption become a form of political protest. That intellectuals enjoy greater influence and respect in Mexican society than their counterparts do in the United States creates public debate that is of a more polemical nature. In addition, Mexican middle-class professionals foster a lingering resentment and anger about American complicity in the student massacre of 1968 and the American bailouts of the PRI's corruption and mismanagement in 1982 and 1995. One manifestation of Mexicans' anger for this state of affairs is uniquely, exquisitely perverse: false accusations of public corruption as a form of political protest.

It is worth noting that false accusations of corruption have characterized other nations. "The political state of Russia may be defined in one sentence: it is a country in which the government says what it pleases, because it alone has the right to speak," the Marquis de Custine observed of Czarist Russia in the nineteenth century.[23] What was true of Czarist Russia was true of Mexico under the PRI. Oftentimes these false accusations—tales of corruption as a form of urban legend—center on the perceived complicity of American officials in enabling the PRI's corruption. This complicity usually includes accusations that the United States actively participates by either bailing out the PRI or colluding in the cover-up of corruption among Mexican public officials. This can be done by refusing to prosecute American companies, such as Citibank, that participate in laundering the ill-gotten gains of the privileged Mexicans affiliated with the PRI, most notoriously Raúl Salinas, brother of disgraced former president Carlos Salinas, who languishes in jail.

The belief has been that, to United States policy makers, the PRI's corruption was a small price to pay for political stability at America's southern border. Anthony DePalma describes the phenomenon this way:

> Mexican intellectuals resented the U.S. aid [to Mexico under the PRI]. To them, Washington's repeated bailouts of Mexico showed how America propped up the corrupt ruling party and, by extension, the forces preventing Mexico from achieving true democracy. Sergio Aguayo, a security analyst at the Colegio de Mexico and one of the country's most outspoken democracy activists, argued that without this kind of American support, the PRI would have crumbled once and for all, clearing the way for the democratic transition that had eluded Mexico for so long. America was widely perceived as the PRI's bodyguard, and when groups of campesinos came to Mexico City to protest anything from farm subsidies to land distribution policies, they marched in front of the American embassy.[24]

In the minds of many Mexicans, Washington's support for the PRI was itself a form of corruption, for it undermined the democratic values Americans espoused—and encouraged others to emulate. Thus to protest the PRI's monopoly on power—a monopoly made possible in part by American bailouts—and falsely accuse the government of corruption was one form of political protest.

Not unlike those Americans who dismiss all politicians as crooks, some Mexicans dismiss anything that goes wrong as the result of corruption. Indeed, when Miguel de la Madrid was president in the early 1980s, cynicism became so endemic that the government was forced to launch a national public relations campaign. "If we want to be better, let us also speak about the good things," was the slogan that appeared on television, radio, and print media.[25]

To be sure, this tendency for Mexicans to be harsh in their criticism of things Mexican is historically linked to the idea of "malinchismo."[26] But what is at work in exaggerated corruption is more complex. Consider how it finds its way into post-NAFTA Mexican culture. In the critically acclaimed film by Alfonso Cuarón, *Y Tu Mamá También,* the protagonist is named Tenoch, an abbreviation for the Aztec name for Mexico City. His father is a corrupt millionaire politician, an *arriviste* whose surname is Iturbide, the name of the nineteenth-century leader who declared himself emperor of Mexico in 1821 and who ruled for less than a year before republican rivals ousted him. It is through political corruption, then, that Mexico's current generation of pampered middle-class youth, known as "Generation Mex" by savvy marketers, is born. "Behind every great fortune is a great crime," Balzac famously said. Mexicans have a penchant for invoking this aphorism when making accusations of corruption.

What is clear, however, is that "institutionalized" government corruption, as Alexis de Tocqueville observed, is incompatible with democracy over time. "In the United States those who are entrusted with the direction of public affairs are often inferior both in capacity and in morality to those whom an aristocracy might bring to power; but their interest is mingled and identified with that of the majority of their fellow citizens," he observed. "Hence they may often prove untrustworthy and make great mistakes, but they will never systematically follow a tendency hostile to the majority; they will never turn the government into something exclusive and dangerous. . . . Corruption and incapacity are not common interests capable of linking men in any permanent fashion."[27] In truth, widespread corruption in Mexico was inevitable under Mexican Paternalism, but will be more difficult to sustain in a market-oriented, democratic nation. Continued false accusations of corruption, more and more, are now used not to register a political protest against the government, but to sustain all manner of rationalization: to cheat on taxes, to remain uninvolved in civic matters, to look upon public service with cynicism.

## Drug Corruption

To paraphrase Lord Acton's 1887 observation of the Catholic Church's power, "Prohibition tends to corrupt and absolute prohibitions corrupt absolutely."[28] Thus one can understand the quagmire NAFTA now finds itself in with the War on Drugs, since it is, in fact, a "war without end."[29] Indeed, consider the following statement, and the futility it reveals: "There is no match for a united America, a determined America, an angry America . . . If we fight this war as a divided nation, then the war is lost," the first president Bush said on September 5, 1989, announcing the "war" on drugs. "Victory, victory over drugs is our cause, a just cause."

More than a decade later, not much has changed. "Drug traffickers as well as terrorists are well-financed, sophisticated, very mobile, and very global," Donnie Marshall, the former chief of the Drug Enforcement Administration, is quoted as saying. "Both prey on weak and vulnerable people, prey on unsuspecting, innocent civilians."[30] If Colombia is representative of how a country can be torn asunder by the War on Drugs, it is imperative that the United States, Mexico, and Canada learn from the experience of others.[31] Mexicans have become concerned that they could be drawn into a "war" that is spreading across borders.

"These are not silly concerns. These are the concerns of very reasonable people and the United States should listen to these things," then-Mexican Foreign Minister Jorge Castañeda warned in 2001.[32] Indeed, to see how insidiously drugs and corruption are intertwined, consider the curious case of Col. James Hiett, the former commander of the U.S. anti-drug efforts in Colombia who was sentenced for his part in a drug-running operation masterminded by his wife. Writing in *Salon.com,* Bruce Shapiro notes:

> The Hiett scandal is already an international embarrassment to the United States . . . In the mid-1990s, while Hiett was still stationed in the United States, his wife Laurie Ann Hiett was treated in an Army hospital for drug addiction. Later Hiett was named by the Army to head the 200-strong battalion of military advisors in Bogota. The couple went— even though Laurie had lapsed into addiction, snorting cocaine in front of her husband.

Soon she was buying cocaine through her Army-employed Colombian driver. By 1998 she was under investigation by the Army, not only for using drugs, but for shipping $700,000 worth of coke, wrapped in brown paper, to the United States in diplomatic mail.[33]

To make matters worse, while the Army was investigating Mrs. Hiett, it worked to protect the Colonel. "Army investigators tipped him off about their investigation, in particular their pursuit of a $25,000 roll of cash Laurie had handed him," Bruce Shapiro reports. "Then after his wife was arrested, those same Army investigators quickly cleared Hiett of any wrongdoing. It was only U.S. Customs Service director Ray Kelly who insisted on pushing the investigation further after his agents became convinced of the officer's complicity in his wife's actions."[34]

It appears that the U.S. Army, in its denial, became an accomplice and an enabler. The corrupting influence of drugs on militaries is more familiar to Americans when it concerns foreign militaries. When Brig. General Ricardo Mart´nez and his aides, Capt. Pedro Maya and Lt. Javier Quevedo, were arrested by the administration of Vicente Fox, it was shocking news to Americans.[35] But American military personnel itself is not immune to corruption. "There's always been a fear of this [kind of corruption] by sensible people in the Pentagon," former U.S. Ambassador to El Salvador and Paraguay Robert White said of the affair. "The legend is that the United States military is incorruptible, but that has proven not to be the case. There are quite a few instances of this corruption."[36]

The culture of corruption that suffuses the drug economy knows no borders. "The annual [marijuana] crop comes in at an estimated $4-billion-plus yield of high-grade produce that flows illicitly to markets of the Northeast willing to pay some of the nation's highest street prices," Francis Clines reported in the *New York Times*.[37] Marijuana, which was heralded as "bigger than tobacco" by Roy E. Sturgill, the director of the Appalachia High Intensity Drug Trafficking Area, thus became Kentucky's top cash crop as the 1990s ended. "It's kind of like the old moonshine days with neighbors making a living at it," Sgt. Ronnie Ray is quoted in the report. "Everybody seems to know somebody who grows it, sells it, smokes it. . . . It's the dirty little secret of Kentucky."[38]

It's one thing to send the U.S. Army into Colombia, but how does one wage the War on Drugs against Kentucky?

One answer lies in how Mexico, under Fox, continues to demonstrate the importance of political resolve. The arrest of

Jesús Quintero, who inherited the Juárez cartel after the death of Amado Carillo in 1997, demonstrated that the impunity with which drug traffickers had been allowed to operate had come to an end. "The chiefs of the Tijuana and Sonora cartels are under arrest, as is the second-in-command of the Gulf cartel," Tim Weiner reported. These arrests, in addition to the arrests of corrupt local and federal law enforcement officers, signaled a sea change. "Taken together, the arrests are a remarkable reversal from the 1990's, when the gangs clearly had the upper hand over authorities."[39] Two reasons offered for this about-face are familiar. First, Mexico, fearing that it would be torn asunder like Colombia has been, realized it had no option. Second, Mexico, freed from the corrupt PRI, is enjoying a strengthening of its democratic institutions, including the rule of law. The success against corruption under Fox can, in fact, be empirically measured. "Since President Vicente Fox took office in December 2000, no federal agency has undergone as thorough a house-cleaning as the customs service," Elisabeth Malkin reported from Manzanillo.

> Some 80 percent of the professional customs service employees have been replaced, including almost all of the 48 port directors, sometimes several times. Screening of top officials and inspectors now include lie-detector tests. The agency's annual budget has grown tenfold, to almost $150 million. That has permitted José Guzmán Montalvo, general administrator of Mexico's customs service since January 2001, to double or triple salaries and buy up-to-date gamma ray scanners to view the contents of containers.[40]

There are other factors as well. Foremost, Mexico realizes that as domestic drug consumption increases, unless it acts now, it will experience a catastrophic drug epidemic similar to what has occurred in the United States. Another reason is Mexico's determination not to have its sovereignty as a state undermined by drug cartels that, with the cartels' ability to spend money on public works projects, bought complicity from the poor, undermining the authority of the Mexican state.

Finally is the economist's admiration for the superior societal outcome that is possible when government and law enforcement institutions are run honestly. As discussed, when the role of money is limited, petty corruption suffuses society. What Tocqueville observed of the United States also applies to Mexico. "I have never heard it said in the United States that a man used his wealth to bribe the governed, but I have often heard the integrity of public officials put in doubt," he wrote. "So while the rulers of aristocracies sometimes seek to corrupt, those of democracies prove corruptible."[41] This corruption is exacerbated when paternalism drives a nation's economic development. Thus where money replaces subsidy schemes, not only are market distortions eliminated, but also the opportunities for bribery are limited. Furthermore, Mexicans' infatuation with their strengthening democracy is curbing corruption in all forms; it is seen as unpatriotic.

To understand the attitude about the drug war, consider the Mexican public's admiration for the professionalism of American law enforcement officials, something that Americans themselves often don't realize. When Charles Bowden writes, "in Mexico a D.E.A. agent is despised by every man, woman, and child as a foreign police agent operating on their soil," he could not be more mistaken.[42] What Bowden alludes to is an American fear first identified by Tocqueville, who observed that "[t]he Americans are obviously preoccupied by one great fear. They see that in most nations of the world the exercise of the rights of sovereignty tends to be concentrated in few hands, and they are frightened by the thought that it may be so with them in the end."[43] What Mexicans see is that, provided they are not allowed to carry firearms, American law enforcement officials conduct themselves admirably.

Mexicans are less fearful of such an end per se. Thus the sight of American D.E.A. agents is, in some ways, reassuring. In fact, there's an abiding respect for these agents in some social circles that is at times embarrassing.[44] That these sentiments are not openly expressed has more to do with implications: the *idea* of D.E.A. and F.B.I. agents operating in Mexico startles on *principle*, though it is reassuring in *practice*.[45] One reason for this feeling is the fact that drug corruption continues to suffuse American society in frightening ways. "The smugglers moved with ease through Miami International Airport and even made their way onto American Airlines planes parked at the gates, stashing heroin in coffee containers in the planes' galleys and hiding cocaine and marijuana in suitcases," began a typical report by Rick Bragg about the ability of drug traffickers to corrupt Americans.[46] A month later, the story went on, "Undercover agents working to bring down a widespread drug-smuggling operation at Miami International Airport thought that the arrests last month of more than 40 baggage handlers and food service workers on drug charges might force other suspects," Rick Bragg reported.[47] "The three wooden cargo crates dropped off by a courier at the international airport in San Juan, P.R., for a Delta Air Lines flight to New York City looked harmless," Mireya Navarro reported. "But when the courier's nervousness raised suspicions about their contents," the story continues to its familiar tale of corruption and woe.[48]

And this is influencing drug corruption in Mexico. "For a year the Clinton Administration has presented the stunning arrest of Mexico's drug-enforcement chief as proof of that government's strong will to fight corruption," Tim Golden reported. "But now United States analysts have concluded that the case shows much wider" involvement by the Mexican military.[49] The considerable challenge Mexican authorities combating corruption face in providing simple law enforcement exacerbates the problem. If the perception is that Mexican police are corrupt, the fact is more sobering: public safety is undermined not by unscrupulous police officers, but by a shortage of law enforcement officials. The need to render Mexico's police more professional resulted in a curious development: Mexico City contracted former New York City Mayor Rudolph Giuliani as a consultant.[50] Of the 2,395 municipalities in Mexico, for instance, 335 of the smallest communities have no police officers. Of equal concern, moreover, is that 69 percent of all police officers are concentrated in the largest 87 communities.[51] This shortage in law enforcement professional represents a unique opportunity for Canada. Mexicans, cognizant of the racism and violence that pervade American police departments, favor the more civil reputation of Canadian law enforcement.

Drug corruption, in the final analysis, is a problem without a solution as long as consumers want to consume products that governments want to prohibit. Thus, rather than making a blanket statement about corruption in Mexico, it is now possible to think through the challenges confronting Mexico during NAFTA's second decade.

By limiting the role of money, low corruption proliferates throughout the whole of society. By the inherent nature of authoritarianism, human evolution encourages the accumulation of wealth (through political corruption) for the subsequent redistribution of wealth (through dispensing patronage), a process that creates inefficiencies and distortions throughout the economy. By creating a monopoly on political power, members of society become resentful, resorting to accusations of corruption as a form of political protest. By rendering criminal commodities that people want to consume, whole segments are criminalized, weakening the state's monopoly on violence. When one limits the role of money in an economy, one finds corruption without limit. Mexico thus *appears* to be more corrupt than it is in fact.[52] This, however, does not diminish the impact of corruption, real and perceived, on diminishing trust, or what economists call "positive reciprocity," which is crucial for economic growth and development. Ending the appearance of corruption is as important as ending actual corruption. Three forms of corruption—high, low, and exaggerated—are declining as NAFTA enters its second decade. Drug corruption, unfortunately, is on the rise, and in all three NAFTA nations

## SUMMARY

1.  Mexico is not as corrupt as Mexicans claim; accusations of corruption have, since the 1960s, been a form of political protest against the PRI.
2.  Low corruption, the day-to-day petty annoyances, has its origins in the premium on cash that arises in an economic development model where the role of money is limited; this form of corruption is diminishing as market reforms are introduced.
3.  High corruption is the natural outgrowth of a paternalistic political economy in which an elite enjoys disproportionate access to government access and business opportunities; it is more prevalent in Mexico than in the United States, but not by as much as Americans are willing to admit.
4.  The strengthening of democratic institutions, economic growth through NAFTA and the development of pride in serving the nation honorably and honestly are changing how public servants perform their duties, from postal workers to custom agents, contributing to a mindset where there is less tolerance and acceptance of corruption.

## ENDNOTES

1.  American business executives, of course, are prevented from engaging in corruption overseas by the Foreign Corrupt Practices Act.
2.  Increasingly, the illegal pursuits of drugs and smuggling migrants go hand in hand, and not even Homeland Security can do anything about it. "More recently, though, federal and local law enforcement officials say the same pipeline of immigration and trade has been exploited by Mexican drug traffickers, who have helped turn this corner of northwestern Georgia into a busy distribution center for methamphetamine and other drugs," Tim Golden reports. "In Dalton

[, Georgia] and surrounding areas, drug arrests have steadily risen since the late 1990's, police officials said. Gang-related violence has become common. Outside the police headquarters, a fenced-in lot is perpetually filled with cars, most of them impounded from people suspected of being in the drug trade." See "A Georgia Pipeline for Drugs and Immigrants," by Tim Golden, *New York Times,* November 16, 2002.

3. The most draconian limits on the role of money, of course, are when bank accounts are frozen. During the Argentine crisis of 2002, for instance, Argentines resorted to "barter" clubs—exchanging goods and services through rough valuations. See "Hard Times Squeeze Millions of Argentines Out of the Middle Class," by Pamela Druckerman, *Wall Street Journal,* February 1, 2001.

4. The absurdity of having private detectives plant decoy cartons of cigarettes in executives' offices is too sublime to contemplate, illustrating the dangers of any economy where the role of money is limited.

5. Robert Frank, *Choosing the Right Pond: Human Behavior and the Quest for Status,* page 93.

6. "Mexico Can be Cleaned Up—By Mexicans," by Alejandro Junco, *Wall Street Journal,* December 4, 2002. The problem, however, is that officials often attempt to frustrate efforts to release information, especially in law enforcement and intelligence agencies. Files released with most of the text blocked out are not an uncommon frustration among those seeking to exercise their rights. There are, however, instances where the civil service is so corrupt that massive firings are in order. Fox's Customs director José Guzmán, for instance, took over in December 2000 and after a two-month review of his agency, chose the most draconian course of action. "In Mexico's latest salvo against decades of widespread government corruption," the Associated Press published on February 1, 2001, Customs director Guzmán "fired nearly all of the agency's upper management in a top-to-bottom overhaul." "We found personnel who were totally disconnected from the agency, administrators who felt that they were independent. They didn't take orders from anyone, they weren't meeting the requirements of the law, and they weren't properly supervised," Guzmán told the Associated Press. "I am trying to clean up this place," Jorge Pasaret, appointed head of Customs in Ciudad Juárez, told the *Washington Post.* "But every time you pull a curtain back you find something else. It is really, really messy." See "Mexico Rids Corruption with Firings," by the Associated Press, February 1, 2001 and "Mexico Fights Broad Customs Corruption," by Mary Jordan, *Washington Post,* April 22, 2001.

7. "Cubicle Crimes," by Scott Adams, *New York Times,* July 11, 2002. "Apparently, without anyone's noticing, our entire universe collapsed into a black hole and emerged in another dimension where everything is backward: Bill Gates (who used to be evil) is spending billions to vaccinate children in third-world countries, while the Catholic Church (which used to be good) is defending priests accused of molesting children." Though intended as humor, Adams' statement suggests that low corruption suffuses American society.

8. "The Pemex investigation could reach the highest echelons of the previous government, possibly involving Francisco Labastida, the former presidential candidate who continues to wield influence within the party,

and the former president, Ernesto Zedillo," Ginger Thompson reported in early 2002. See "Politics Fuels Graft Inquiry, Ex-Leaders of Mexico Say," by Ginger Thompson, *New York Times,* January 27, 2002.

9.  This estimate did not include money believed to have been plundered by Pemex officers, many of whom became "inexplicably enriched," as Mexicans euphemistically phrase it when public officials become filthy rich after their stint in public office.

10. Hank González's saying in Spanish, which succinctly summed up how Mexico was mismanaged under the PRI, was "un pol´tico pobre es un pobre pol´tico." At the time of his death, political analyst Homero Aridijis summed up Hank González's role in Mexican life this way: "He personified Mexico's political businessman. He was the most powerful fixture in Mexican politics for 30 years because his influence extended beyond the length of any one presidential term."

11. His son Hank Rohn became notorious for using Citibank to launder and funnel hundreds of millions of dollars. Classified as "Confidential Client Number One," Hank Rohn introduced a menagerie of rogue clients to Citibank's private banking, from Raúl Salinas (currently serving time for the murder of his former brother-in-law and political rival) to Gerardo de Prevoisin (who fled to France after his theft of millions from Aeromexico was exposed). In a separate fracas, published in the *New York Times,* Tim Weiner reported on June 1, 2001: "Carlos Hank Rhon, one of the richest and most politically connected businessmen in Mexico, will pay a $40 million fine to settle charges that he violated banking laws when he bought Laredo National Bancshares in Texas, the Federal Reserve Board said today." More information on the audacious Hank family is found in *Ojos Vendados: Estados Unidos y el Negocio de la Corrupción en America Latina* by Andres Oppenheimer, the Pulitzer-Prize winning correspondent for *The Miami Herald.*

12. The only other Mexicans from Mexico who were not part of his entourage in the banquet hall were those working for the caterers. The Mexican delegation acted as if their fellow countrymen were invisible, ignoring them the way one pays no attention to servants going about the business of being servile.

13. When a Chicano reporter asked if Mr. Hank González would have time to meet with leaders of the Chicano community in San Francisco before continuing on to Japan, Press Officer Javier Treviño responded, in Spanish, "Are there such creatures as *leaders* among Chicanos?" He smiled at the notion.

14. *Manhood in the Making: Cultural Concepts of Masculinity,* by David Gilmore, page 229.

15. "Revolution Ends, Change Begins," the London *Economist,* October 26, 2000.

16. This is the entry in the 1888 *Dictionary of American Politics.* See Richard C. Sachs, "Lobbying," in *The Encyclopedia of the United States,* Donald C. Bacon, Roger H. Davidson, and Morton Keller, editors, New York: Simon & Schuster, 1995, Vol. 3, p. 1303.

17. *Max Weber and German Politics, A Study in Political Sociology,* J. P. Mayer, London: Faber and Faber, 1956, page 125.

18. Julia Dubner, "Insurance Fraud: The Costly Crime with Millions of Victims," *Geico Direct,* Spring 2001. It is curious to note that while

Mexicans are scandalized by the theft of $18 billion in its oil industry over a *quarter century,* Americans are nonchalant about the theft of almost twice that in their insurance industry in *one year.*

19. "Downturn and Shift in Population Feed Boom in White-Collar Crime," by Stephen Labaton, *New York Times,* June 2, 2002.

20. "Strengthening the rule of law is the most daunting challenge and greatest opportunity facing the Fox administration," read the first sentence of the second paragraph in a *New York Times* editorial heralding the inauguration of Vicente Fox. See "A Historic Transition in Mexico," *New York Times,* December 1, 2000.

21. "A Rule of Law Emerges in Mexico, Slowly," by Luis Rubio, *Wall Street Journal,* April 27, 2001. In establishing the principle of the rule of law, however, Mexico is making enormous strides. Consider how the country affirmed the principle of universal jurisdiction when Judge Jesús Guadalupe Luna ruled that Ricardo Miguel Cavallo, an Argentine navy lieutenant accused in Spain of terrorism and genocide during Argentina's "dirty war," could be extradited. Not only did human rights organizations around the world applaud the decision, but it also placed Mexico at the forefront of affirming universal human rights. Much remains to be done, however, particularly where women's rights are concerned. A complete overhaul of how women are treated under the law is in order. Consider, for instance, the obstacles placed in the way of women who are raped. In her book *The Crime of Being a Woman,* Elena Azaloa enumerated the ways in which Mexican laws are biased against women, and how the "rule of law" has to be changed in order to offer women equal protection, particularly when they are the victims of violence.

22. See *Actual Innocence: When Justice Goes Wrong and How to Make It Right,* by Barry Scheck, Peter Neufeld, and Jim Dwyer.

23. Custine, The Marquis de, *Empire of the Czar: A Journey Through Eternal Russia.* New York: Doubleday, 1989, page 531.

24. Anthony DePalma, *Here: A Biography of the New American Continent,* page 89.

25. In Spanish, the slogan was: "Si queremos ser mejores, contemos también lo bueno. Gobierno de la República."

26. "Malinchismo" is derived from "La Malinche," the native woman who became Hernando Cortés's common-law wife in Mexico; she is seen has having "betrayed" her people by siding with the Spaniards. The truth is more complicated of course. La Malinche was sold into slavery, then given to Cortés. Educated and knowledgeable in several languages, she facilitated Cortés's ability to forge alliances among the various indigenous peoples who hated the Aztecs and fought alongside the Spaniards to end Aztec domination of their societies.

27. Alexis de Tocqueville, *Democracy in America,* New York: Signet, 2001, page 233.

28. Historian Lord Acton saw the concentration of power as the greatest threat to human liberty. His famous statement, of course, is "power tends to corrupt and absolute power corrupt absolutely." For more information, see *The Selected Writings of Lord Acton,* or visit *Acton.org.* "Liberty is not a means to a higher political end," he observed. "It is itself the highest political end."

29. Mexican concerns about the War on Drugs center on how that effort has

been used to undermine human rights in Mexico. "Mexico, of course, has its own human rights problems, inextricably linked to the two other major issues on the Bush-Fox agenda: trade and the war on drugs," Daniel Wilkinson, of Human Rights Watch, wrote in the *Los Angeles Times*. See, "Fox Steps Up to the Plate on Human Rights," by Daniel Wilkinson, *Los Angeles Times*, February 16, 2001.

30.  "Whether the United States is winning the war on drugs is a subjective matter," Jim Oliphant writes. "Those who say the country is doing so point to the decline in hard drug use by Americans over the past 20 years, the drop in drug-related street crime, and the capture or elimination of several notorious drug lords such as Colombia's Pablo Escobar. Critics say that the flow of illegal narcotics into the United States remains as constant as ever and that the social ills that lie at the root of addiction have yet to be addressed." Marshall is quoted in Oliphant's article. See "Heeding the Lessons of the War Against Drugs," by Jim Oliphant, *Legal Times*, October 11, 2001.

31.  An alarming development in the War on Drugs in Colombia is the systematic use of dangerous pesticides. "American officials also said the spraying—using glyphosate, a powerful chemical found in many pesticides—is at least 90 percent effective in first-time use, wiping out fields within a few weeks," Juan Forero reported from Santa Ana, Colombia. There is concern that glyphosate causes health problems to the people who are also exposed to the chemical during aerial spraying. See "No Crops Spared in Colombia's Coca War," by Juan Forero, *New York Times*, January 31, 2001.

32.  In addition to Mexico, Brazil, Ecuador, and Venezuela have expressed concern that, among other things, their environments are being polluted by fungicides used to destroy coca crops in Colombia. See "Mexico Warns of Colombia Drug War Spillover," Jane Perlez, *New York Times*, January 31, 2001. Indeed, Washington authorized the expenditure of $40 million in "social infrastructure" projects in Ecuador. See "Ecuador Afraid as a Drug War Heads Its Way," by Larry Rohter, *New York Times*, January 8, 2001.

33.  "The Corruption of Col. James Hiett," by Bruce Shapiro, July 5, 2000, *Salon.com*.

34.  Ibid.

35.  "General Mart'nez is the sixth Mexican general jailed on charges of being in the pay of the drug lords since 1997," Tim Weiner reported in "Mexico's Image Is Buffed and Tarnished with Military Drug Arrests," *New York Times*, April 7, 2001.

36.  Robert White's remarks to Jeff Stein are quoted in Bruce Shapiro's report.

37.  "Kentucky Journal: Fighting Appalachia's Top Cash Crop, Marijuana," by Francis X. Clines, *New York Times*, February, 28, 2001.

38.  Sgt. Ronnie Ray, as quoted in "Kentucky Journal: Fighting Appalachia's Top Cash Crop, Marijuana," by Francis X. Clines, *New York Times*, February, 28, 2001.

39.  "Drug Suspects Are Arrested, Attesting to a Changing Mexico," by Tim Weiner, *New York Times*, May 28, 2002. Earlier in the year, Mr. Wiener reported, "Bringing down the Arellano Felix dons was the biggest victory in years in a bloody drug war Mexico had been certain to lose." See "New Web of Trust Topples a Mighty Mexican Cartel," *New York Times*, April 26, 2002.

40. "Mexico Is Making Headway on Smuggling," by Elisabeth Malkin, *New York Times,* June 5, 2003.

41. de Tocqueville, *Democracy in America,* page 220.

42. "The Teachings of Don Fernando," by Charles Bowden, *Harper's,* June 2002, page 47.

43. de Tocqueville, *Democracy in America,* page 385.

44. In the same way, firemen achieved the status of heroes in New York after the terrorist attack of September 11, 2001, with many well-heeled New Yorkers lauding the firefighters and rescue workers in ways that blue-collar workers seldom had been admired. In one charming cartoon summing up the sentiment published in the *New Yorker* magazine, one well-dressed woman, pictured having coffee with her daughter, protests, "An attorney or a doctor? Why can't you marry a fireman?"

45. American law enforcement officers are not allowed to carry firearms in Mexico. Having foreign citizens engaged in law enforcement is troubling enough as it is; the possibility of having American agents engaged in street gunfights absolutely terrifies.

46. "Airline Workers Said to Operate Vast Drug Ring," by Rick Bragg, *New York Times,* August 26, 1999.

47. "More Smuggling Arrests at Miami Airport," by Rick Bragg, *New York Times,* September 10, 1999.

48. "At U.S. Ports, Drug Smuggling Is Fast Becoming an Inside Job," by Mireya Navarro, *New York Times,* August 26, 1977.

49. "U.S. Officials Say Mexican Military Aids Drug Traffic," by Tim Golden, *New York Times,* March 26, 1988.

50. "Back in the early 1980s, New York City was regarded as the crime capital of America," Rudy Giuliani said, announcing this assignment. "It was featured on the front cover of *Time* magazine as the rotting apple and much of it was due to the significant levels of crime. Mexico City faces a challenge like that today." See "Firm Run by Giuliani Gets Contract to Advise the Police in Mexico City," by Lydia Polgreen, *New York Times,* October 11, 2002.

51. Figures are from a joint study between the National Autonomous University of Mexico (UNAM) and Georgetown University. See "Resultado de un estudio de expertos de EEUU y Mexico," *Diario de Yucatan,* March 18, 2002.

52. That Americans tend to indulge in linguistic somersaults (employing euphemisms, such as "wrongdoing," "morally bankrupt," and "fraud") and legalistic fictions (Americans can plead the absurd fabrication of "no contest" when they are "guilty") is another reason why Mexico appears more corrupt vis-à-vis the United States.

# Drug Trafficking: An Irrational Prohibition

## EXECUTIVE ABSTRACT

The illegal drug trade continues to undermine the economic growth of the NAFTA nations as it destroys the lives of millions. That Mexico and Canada have not allowed the United States to spearhead a misguided campaign—the so-called War on Drugs—on their territories has created problems for the entire continent, but not for the reasons usually cited. In addition to the devastating human cost of drug addiction, the drug trade negatively impacts companies in all three nations.[1] History, however, offers a successful model for changing misguided approaches in order to arrive at more rational, and sustainable, policies. For American companies involved in business in Mexico, it is imperative that managers are informed about the issue of drugs and drug trafficking, given that legitimate businesses are unwittingly used by drug cartels to further their objectives. This is necessary not only to protect the firms' interests, but also to allow companies to form intelligent public policy positions, and to understand how both Canada and Mexico are developing bilateral drug policies that stand in stark contrast to that of the United States. In the same way that Canada and Mexico undermined Prohibition in the United States, it is almost certain that in the course of the decade ahead, it will be impossible for American drug laws not be modified to reflect the more rational remedies of our neighbors.

## DISCUSSION

The 18th Amendment to the U.S. Constitutions reads, "Section 1. After one year from the ratification of this article the manufacture, sale, or transportation of intoxicating liquors within, the importation thereof into, or the exportation thereof from the United States and all territory subject to the jurisdiction thereof for beverage purposes is hereby prohibited. Section 2. The Congress and the several states shall have concurrent power to enforce this article by appropriate legislation. Section 3. This article shall be inoperative unless it shall have been ratified as an amendment to the Constitution by the legislatures of the several states, as provided in the Constitution, within seven years from the date of the submission hereof to the states by the Congress." The United States, however, was unable to implement these laws successfully, for several reasons. The most important one, of course, is that Americans wanted to drink, and were prepared to break the law in order to do so. That Americans—even law enforcement officials—from all walks of life flaunted the law of the land engendered a certain disrespect for the rule of law. The same applies, of course, in other areas where people are prevented from indulging in their preferences.[2]

"U.S. lawmakers discovered with alcohol in the 1920s that it's difficult to run a successful prohibitionist regime when a neighboring country has more tolerant policies. Now it's the same neighbor and a different drug," H. G. Levine wrote for Pacific News Service.[3] In the 1920s, when the border with Mexico was even more porous than it is today, it was not uncommon for Americans to drive to the border to purchase alcohol, which they then consumed in their homes, whether in Los Angeles or Houston. Organized crime, too, set up operations in Canada and Mexico for bootlegging, and the cumulative impact of this black market in alcohol doomed any prospect that the American experiment in Prohibition would succeed, particularly as violence escalated. "Though public attention focuses on the drugs smuggled from Mexico to the north, officials here are increasingly concerned by an ever more lethal flow of guns south from the United States," Tim Weiner reported, signaling that the same pattern that emerged during Prohibition has reappeared now.[4] What is clear, however, is that current drug policies are similarly not sustainable, and the economic and social consequences of pursuing a failed approach are enormous.

## An American Quagmire

It is clear that Americans have a dysfunctional relationship when it comes to drugs. They bemoan substance abuse as a Biblical plague, often blaming others for a problem created by demand for drugs by Americans. Ignoring the demand for drugs, Americans have concentrated, almost exclusively, on supply. For decades, this War on Drugs has exacted a disproportionate price on countries where drugs are produced or, through happenstance of geography, are used for transit purposes. The annual "certification" process imposed by the U.S. Congress, for instance, has been seen as demeaning by other nations, particularly when there is no similar process to certify that Americans are doing all they should to stop their children, families, and friends from abusing drugs.

One can despair at the current state of affairs, or one can focus on implementing sensible policies. Drug trafficking, in essence, constitutes a challenge and an opportunity for the NAFTA nations to work constructively for the benefit of North America. Indeed, the drug problem should be seen as an opportunity to develop long-term solutions that are sound and further the economic development of what, truthfully, is in a convoluted way, a growth industry. "Part of the recovery process is a commitment to truth, and I began to feel that I was not being truthful," Stephen Gaghan, the screenwriter for *Traffic* told the *New York Times,* days before winning an Oscar. "The stigma and shame of drug addiction is part of what makes it difficult for people to raise their hand and ask for help, and I felt that by not being completely honest I was, in a way, perpetuating that stigma."[5]

The same dishonesty can be seen in the official positions taken by various administrations in Washington, D.C.—from either political party. "There is a place in American policy for efforts to interdict drug shipments overseas, and to prevent the cultivation of crops that are used to make drugs," the *New York Times* opined, leading an increasing chorus of sensible voices calling for a truthful analysis of the drug issue. "Law enforcement programs in the United States must also play a role. But these programs cannot succeed without a more robust effort to curtail demand for drugs at home. The bulk of the federal government's $19.2 billion annual drug-fighting budget is still spent on interdiction and enforcement. Yet the number of hard-core users of cocaine has remained steady over the last decade at around 3.5 million. The number of hard-core heroin users, meanwhile, has risen from 600,000 in the early 1990's to 980,000 today."[6]

Be that as it may, while the greater public policy issues surrounding narcotics—do governments have the right to criminalize activities that adults wish to pursue that do not harm others?—is debated, the fact remains that there is a growing and robust industry surrounding treating chemical dependencies.[7] As it stands, state governments in the United States spent $81.3 billion combating drugs, and, on a federal level, the economic impact of all substance abuse, using 1995 figures, exceeded $227 billion. In a state-by-state analysis of the economic costs of drug abuse titled "Shoveling Up: The Impact of Substance Abuse on State Budgets," published by the National Center on Addiction and Substance Abuse at Columbia University in 2001, it was estimated that total state spending in 1998 was $620 billion, of which more than 13.1 percent went to substance abuse. New York State led the way, spending $8.6 billion, or more than 18 percent of the state's budget, on substance abuse. The District of Columbia led the way in per capita expenditures on substance abuse programs, spending $812 per resident.[8]

Though no value judgment is made on either New York or Washington as being communities that nurture dysfunction that contributes to chemical dependencies, there are ample opportunities emerging in drug prevention and treatment as industries. "We cannot simply arrest our way out of the problem [of substance abuse]. Treatment programs that follow a criminal from arrest to post-release follow-up must be implemented to end the cycle of drug abuse and crime," Edward Jurith, acting director of the White House Office of National Drug Control Policy, said at the time of the report's release.[9]

The drug trade is an instance where a market fails because of misguided intervention. Current drug laws defy common sense; as a result, supply and demand are distorted. One can regret the fact that an unfortunate supply chain exacerbates corruption and unleashes unprecedented violence in Mexico. One can decry the fact that a perverse demand in the United States (and Canada) points to the disintegration of the American family.[10] One would be misguided to dwell on either unhappy thought; it is better to understand that there are opportunities for the business community and offer dispassionate solutions to market conditions complicated and confounded by policy makers.

Indeed, if the drug "problem" could be solved by spending money, it would have been solved already. "Since 1970, the federal anti-drug budget has grown from $1 billion to more than $17 billion a year," Robin Rauzi reported from California.[11] Substance abuse and drug addiction in the United States are so problematic that on his first state visit to Mexico, President George W. Bush acknowledged it: Demand "by millions of Americans, who spend an estimated $63 billion a year on drugs, is the main reason that tons of them are shipped across the border."[12] The American press concurred with the importance of fighting drugs as a matter of public policy. "A closer partnership with Mexico will require reducing tensions over immigration and illicit drugs," the *New York Times* opined, identifying the bilateral priorities from America's perspective.[13]

Illicit drugs constitute a formidable industry, and with so much money, it's not surprising that the organized drug cartels are awash in profits—and the technology they can buy. Consider, for instance, the state-of-the-art technology employed by drug traffickers. South American "cartels are putting their own dark twist on the same productivity-enhancing strategies that other multinational businesses have seized on in the Internet age," Paul Kaihla reported in *Business 2.0.* "Indeed, the $80 billion-a-year cocaine business poses some unique challenges: The supply chain is immense and global, competition is literally cutthroat, and regulatory pressure is intense. The traffickers have the advantages of unlimited funds and no scruples, and they've invested billions of dollars to create a technological infrastructure that would be the envy of any Fortune 500 company—and of the law enforcement officials charged with going after the drug barons. 'I spent this morning working on the budget,' the head of DEA intelligence Steve Casteel, said. 'Do you think they have to worry about that? If they want it, they buy it.' "[14]

To make matters more insidious, domestic drug production in the United States is surging. As discussed in Chapter 11, Kentucky emerged as a leading supplier of marijuana during the 1990s. Illegal Mexican migrants, furthermore, are now involved in the drug trade, which now extends to both sides of the border. This sinister aspect of Mexicans in the United States is evident, for instance, in a small town such as Sunnyside, Washington, an integrated community of 12,000 residents. "The town's population—50 percent Hispanic—demonstrates the confluence that often occurs in meth-prone areas: Working-class whites, who usually cook their own drugs or buy from a close-knit circle of acquaintances, mix with Hispanic workers among whom Mexican drug rings recruit local contacts. High-volume meth production coordinated by drug rings feeds ever-growing demand, while individual cooks remain on the industry's ground floor."[15]

When discussing biases, it is difficult to say anything with certitude; the commingling of reason and irrationality creates ambivalence. "People like [Senator Joseph] Lieberman and [Senator Sam] Brownback may be truly offended by some media content.

But they are remarkably vague about what, exactly, it is that offends them," Marjorie Heins reports. "If you ask them about a particular movie, 'Bonnie and Clyde,' say, or 'Saving Private Ryan,' they all say, 'Well, that's OK. I'm talking about bad violence.' When it comes to artists like Marilyn Manson, or heavy-metal music, these things simply offend them, and they want to believe there is scientific evidence to back up the notion that these things are harmful."[16]

Is it possible in a democracy for lawmakers to legislate personal taste, or personal habits? Of course not, but in the process of enforcing an unenforceable prohibition, temptations are distorted and families—American, Canadian and Mexican—are torn apart. The following story by an anguished mother makes a strong argument for treating the demand side of the drugs equation once her son has been seduced by the allure of the forbidden. Wendy Mnookin described her family's struggle with her son's heroin addiction in *Salon.com* thusly:

> Each time Seth started doing drugs was worse than the time before—the drugs scarier, his dependence more complete. This smart, charming boy, always ready with a story and a promise, couldn't bluff his way through anymore. He lost his job. He couldn't pay his rent. He didn't have money for groceries. The cook at a favorite diner gave him free breakfast, but refused him money. In another diner, he watched for coffee cups people left on the counter so he could get free refills.
>
> No matter how bad things got, Seth refused to enter long-term treatment. He went to detox, but not to rehab. Or he went to rehab, but not the halfway house. He tried therapy, counseling, methadone, acupuncture, medication for depression and anxiety, meditation and biofeedback.
>
> He was an IV heroin user.[17]

The Mnookin family's experience suggests that America's "puritanical" scare tactics employed by Washington bureaucrats backfires.

"In the beginning," Kyle, an Ecstasy user, reports, "I would go to the National Institute on Drug Abuse home page and read what they'd have to say about it and then I'd compare it to my own experience. It's so far off that basically—and I think a lot of kids do this—I lost faith in what the U.S. government had to say about Ecstasy."[18] If Washington was lying about the effect of Ecstasy, then it was lying about all drugs, youngsters conclude, fast becoming cynical of anything government has to say on the matter. This, then, has become, if not an open invitation, then an open rationalization to use and abuse all drugs.

## The Emergence of a Canada-Mexico Bilateral Approach

Canadians, for their part, have had enough. Criminalizing drugs has done nothing to stop people from using drugs. Deceptive propaganda—"This is your brain on drugs" was ridiculed as "This is your brain on propaganda" by American high school students—has alienated youngsters. America's War on Drugs, if not an "Apocalypse Now" for the nations on the frontlines, is an "Apothecary Now"—particularly for America's neighbors.

Mexico and Canada have been subjected to fallout as their nations are ensnarled in the drug trade, both as producers and transit countries. Mexico is a producer and transit country from producer countries in Latin America. Canada is also a producer and transit country for narcotics originating from Europe. The two countries, in keeping with the bilateralism they have cultivated, are now embarking on a course that stands in direct opposition to Washington's position. "It seems like a no brainer," Toronto's *Globe and Mail* opined in August 2001. "Invest a dollar in treating drug addiction . . . and $6 will be saved in other costs to society. . . . So why are we still arguing? Most of those who consume illegal drugs don't need medical help. For the minority who do, why not treat their problem as a health issue rather than a criminal one? Why not end the criminal prosecution of those who buy and take drugs—of all kinds—and concentrate on pursuing the merchants who supply those drugs?"[19]

Canada's *National Post,* a week earlier, called for the legalization of marijuana as the first step in adopting a rational, and effective, drug policy.[20] In the same month, the *Canadian Medical Association Journal* published two articles calling for legalizing "safe" injection sites for drug users as part of a more humane and effective way of reaching addicts with treatment.[21] These reports resulted in a flurry of positive coverage later that month. From the *Winnipeg Sun* ("Injection Rooms Deserve a Shot," by Mindelle Jacob, August 24) to the *London Free Press* ("Safe Shooting Galleries Have Merit," by Lyn Cockburn, August 28), Canadian newspapers reflect increasingly the sea change in Canadians' views on substance use and abuse, and the need for a better alternative to America's failed War on Drugs.

Mexico, for its part, is looking at more rational approaches, including the decriminalization of certain controlled substances. Fox stated that perhaps some drugs should be decriminalized, arguing that "humanity some day will see that it is best [to decriminalize drugs]."[22] In the summer of 2002, Chihuahua Governor Patricio Mart´nez , where the infamous Juárez drug cartel is headquartered, ordered studies into the social and economic consequences of legalizing marijuana.[23] Across the border from Chihuahua, New Mexico Governor Gary Johnson sought to decriminalize marijuana.[24]

As violence and corruption escalate along the border, civic leaders in Mexico are calling for decriminalization as the only reasonable course of action. "It's part of the enormous power of the drug traffickers, and I don't see any possibility of stopping them by the way we are doing things," Andres Cuellar, a respected historian in Matamoros, argued. "The only results have been deaths, which number in the thousands each year, in exchange for nothing."[25] Cuellar, not unlike many in the Mexican medical community, favors legalizing drugs and spending law enforcement money on public health programs to help addicts.

American law enforcement officials are conceding that the Canadian and Mexican approaches might be worth exploring. "The only true solution to a problem like this is demand reduction. I don't know if putting people in jail does a lot for demand reduction," Sioux City, Iowa Police Chief Joe Frisbie argues. Iowa, like Kansas, Missouri, Nebraska, and South Dakota, constitutes what federal authorities have designated as the "High Intensity Drug Trafficking Area," or HIDTA, for the Midwest, which is suffering through an epidemic in methamphetamine use.[26] Challenging the incarceration of drug users is novel for law enforcement officials, but such an approach is also supported by American think tanks, which argue that treating addiction benefits both the addict and society.[27] "Study after study has shown that the best way to reduce drug consumption is to help addicts get treatment," Sebastian Mallaby reported in the *Washington Post.* "The RAND Drug Policy Research Center calculates that spending an extra $1 million on treatment would reduce cocaine consumption 3.5 times more than spending that money on domestic enforcement."[28]

The changes are unnerving to Washington officials, of course. "If you have lax marijuana policies right across the border, where possession of marijuana is not considered criminal conduct, that invites U.S. citizens into Canada for marijuana use, and that will increase the likelihood that both U.S. citizens and Canadian citizens will bring back the Canadian marijuana across the border for distribution and sale," Asa Hutchinson, the Drug Enforcement Agency, argued, as if there was anything inherently wrong with that.[29]

This, however, is precisely what Canada—and Mexico—did when they decriminalized the possession of a dry martini, straight up with a twist—along with every other kind of alcoholic beverage and drink. Failing to grasp how Canada, in the 2000s, is acting as the U.S. did in the 1920s portends how disappointed American officials will be; Canada, a Commonwealth nation, is following in step with Britain, Australia, and New Zealand, among others, in pushing for the decriminalization of drugs. For its part, Mexican officials, galvanized by some American officials, including New Mexico Governor Gary Johnson, are moving to reconsider Mexico's drug laws.

Fox himself best articulated Mexico's desire for a bilateral approach with Canada. "When the day comes that it is time to adopt the alternative of lifting punishment for consumption of drugs, it would have to come all over the world, because we would gain nothing if Mexico did it but the production and traffic of drugs . . . continued here," he said.[30] These remarks caused an uproar among America's War on Drugs warriors. But it was widely reported throughout Canada, to enthusiastic approval.

Fox's attitude reflects that he is cognizant that in Mexico, where alcoholism remains the chemical addiction of grave concern—almost one in five Mexican adults is addicted to alcohol—treatment is a better approach than outright prohibition.[31] For Canadians, there are new issues emerging that stand to strain relations with the United States. "Canada is in the awkward position in which it either must stand up to the United States—and encourage more refugees and asylum applications—or evict people who say they suffer from cancer and other deadly diseases," Clifford Kraus reported. "While general use of marijuana is illegal in both countries, Canada has been far more tolerant of its use for medical purposes."[32] (Americans, fleeing draconian laws, have applied for political asylum in Canada in order to access medical marijuana, creating an unusual problem for both governments.) Moreover, it is clear that Mexico and Canada are laying the foundation for a bilateral program to decriminalize drugs, undermining America's draconian prohibition once again.[33]

## Opportunities in an Unintended Industry

The genius of the market economy is that unexpected opportunities arise. Consider one example of how the private sector created a flourishing market after misguided policy makers ran amok: Mexico's dominance in the "spring break" market. In a failed attempt to curb youthful exuberance, elected officials in Washington passed measures that coerced states into raising the various drinking ages to a uniform one: to drink one must be at least 21 years old.[34] At the same time, officials in Florida came under pressure to do something about the annual pilgrimage to the beaches from Daytona Beach south to Ft. Lauderdale by spring breakers.

These two developments occurred during a time when, because of "open skies" agreements, significant expansion of air routes between Mexico and the United States unfolded. Tour operators in Cancún realized that, given the draconian local ordinances enacted in communities up and down the Florida coast and the new drinking age in effect throughout the United States, college-age American youth represented a potential market during the slower season that preceded the summer months. In a few short years, Cancún emerged as the spring break destination of choice, a de rigeur rite of passage on campuses throughout the United States, aided and abetted by MTV, which began broadcasting from Cancún during spring break.

Consider how differently things might have turned out had policy makers meddled in this industry. Imagine a delegation of Mexican officials arriving in Washington to meet with their counterparts. Imagine the Mexicans proposing that, to circumvent the drinking age in the United States, Americans entrust up to a quarter of a million American youngsters to vacation in Cancún. These youngsters would arrive in Mexico, sans chaperones, and would be permitted to engage in all kinds of activities, from contests for the skimpiest "swim suits" made of whipped cream, to competitions to see who's the last man standing tequila shot after tequila shot. In Cancún, American spring-breakers could, in essence, indulge in every activity that had been banned by Puritan municipal governments in Florida.[35] The reception would have undoubtedly been one of incredulity. It is unlikely that, on an official level, spring break in Cancún would be the success that it currently is, simply because it raises uncomfortable issues, not the least of which is the realization that American youngsters have to leave the United States to have a little fun.

Without any official effort, however, spring break is now a major industry in Mexico—masterfully marketed on college campuses in the United States and Canada. "Local tourism officials say Cancún is popular because of its reputation as a fun, safe place to spend spring break, but many American students are lured by a different slogan: Anything goes," the Associated Press reported. "[E]xperience has taught officials that there are ways to rein in the approximately 80,000 college and high school students who descend on the [Yucatán] peninsula each year, while still reaping the enormous economic benefits they bring during the six-week spring break period."[36]

One could argue that the inability to have a little *harmless* fun in the United States is one reason youngsters resort to having too much *harmful* fun with drugs. One could also point out that Americans in Mexico are less likely to use drugs simply because it is made clear to them that no matter how little it is, and no matter who their parents are, they will spend time in jail—and it is going to take the intervention of American consular personnel and expensive Mexican attorneys to get them out of trouble. Unlike the United States, where some drug offenders, at least white middle-class ones, "enjoy" a revolving-door justice system that empowers drug users, enables drug abuse, and results in recreational use becoming full-blown addiction, things are different in Mexico.

Here, then, is the convergence of misguided laws and a market economy, one that points to a private sector involvement in ameliorating drug use in the United States. Since the mid-1990s, an unintended industry has emerged: boutique resorts throughout Mexico that specialize in drug detox and rehab for Americans. That well-to-do addicts can disappear from their regular lives for months at a time on a Mexican sojourn provides a discreet face-saving cover that many people value. That real estate prices and the salaries paid medical personnel in Mexico are both significantly lower than in the United States is attractive to insurance companies, since they can better manage their costs.

In the same way that in the 1990s spring break in Cancún came of age, in NAFTA's second decade, there are ample opportunities in the drug rehabilitation *industry*. The idea is a natural outgrowth of the experience among Mexican officials and business community leaders in handling the issues that arise when hundreds of thousands of hormone-laden spring-breakers descend on Cancún. "First aid for frisky undergraduates may not seem like medicine's cutting edge, but companies like Phoenix-based AmeriMED are putting Mexico on the U.S. health industry's radar screen," Joel Millman reported of a program launched by Dr. Mark Engelman. "This is what it takes to build a provider network. We're putting down the planks to a bridge to the day Mexico has more to offer,' Mike Hartung, of the Philadelphia-based Highway to Health, Inc.®, was quoted as saying.[37]

Recall the $81.3 billion that state governments alone spend addressing the consequences of substance abuse. Recall the $227 billion that the American economy could save if drug addiction were eliminated. In any cost-benefit analysis, it is clear that there are ample growth opportunities for creating a business model that combines Mexico's lower operating costs and salaries with America's urgent need to make people healthier. Here, furthermore, is an instance where language as a barrier is a good thing. Whereas in the United States, when a patient leaves rehab he or she instantly returns to a circle of friends and circumstances that make relapse too easy, that is not the case in Mexico. One can only wonder if Robert Downey Jr. might not relapse so often and so tragically if he had a different circle of friends.[38] In my own experience, of the Vietnam veterans who have retired in Mexico whom I know, I have sadly witnessed how it is only when their "buddies" visit from the States that they are at risk of relapsing.[39]

For Americans, extended Mexican "sojourns" could inspire health providers on both sides of the border to invest more purposefully into this new market. Of course, if a delegation of American officials were to arrive in Mexico City to meet with their counterparts and propose that Mexico build a system of "resort rehabs" where the United States could send hundreds of thousands of substance abusers, one can imagine the official reaction from politicians and health insurance providers alike.

This, then, is where the unintended market opportunities emerge. If America's addiction to addictive substances continues, it is a symptom of the kind of stress found in American life. "The more aggressively you search for the most profound experience of your life, the more rigid, narrowing, dispiriting and routine it becomes," Matthew Klam reports in the *New York Times*.[40] The problem, however, is that escaping through drugs becomes a self-defeating proposition. "The chief advantage of drugs is that they are quick and effective, producing desired results without requiring effort. Their chief disadvantage is that they fail us over time; used regularly and frequently, they . . . limit our options and freedom," Andrew Weil concludes.[41]

"Detox resorts" in Mexico were a $85 million industry in 2002, and the potential is enormous, particularly since they have higher success rates than American rehab centers. Whereas in the United States, once patients are released, they find themselves back in an environment that encouraged or facilitated drug use, in Mexico, the language and cultural barriers make it more difficult for relapse. The absence of "triggers"—not to mention the threat of being arrested in a country where penalties are higher for drug offenses—promotes success. "Users also must learn to deal with powerful 'triggers' that can start a craving—anything from a specific street corner to a particular friend or a bit of drug paraphernalia," MSNBC reporter Jon Bonne wrote. "'A lot of times, people can get triggered at support meetings when they hear stories about using,' says Dr. Robert Hood, a clinical psychiatrist. Intensive therapy usually lasts about six months, but an addict may need more casual group counseling for several years."[42] Then again, Robert Downey, Jr. is the poster boy for American rehab failure.

Robert Putnam, as we have seen, has a great deal to say about how longer commutes and the stress of pursuing careers have exacted a heavy price on the integrity of American family life, a leading contributor to substance abuse. "No one knows you at a rave [concert]," Matthew Klam wrote in America's newspaper of record, explaining why youth indulges in Ecstasy, the drug of choice among "ravers." "That's the idea. You merge, you're part of the headless horde. You're certainly not talking about your family and your hopes and failures. It's just weird dancing and music endlessly looped in a collective rapture."[43]

That makes for a tremendous market—and market opportunity. More than two dozen "detox resorts," often euphemistically described as "intensive" spas, "medical" retreats, or "private" luxury resorts, are under development along Mexico's Caribbean and Pacific coasts. "Detox as an industry in Mexico is what Cancún was like in the early 1970s—just beginning," Pedro Joaquin Coldwell, Mexico's former Tourism Secretary said. "The potential size of providing rehab services in a resort setting to Americans and Canadians is easily a billion dollar industry. The same way that Americans fly to Costa Rica for plastic surgery, they will soon start coming to Mexico for an 'extended sojourn' to clean themselves up."[44]

Another reason Mexico is fast becoming a health-care leader for the people of North America is found in the problems confronting older Americans. As more older Americans retire in

Mexico, their primary health-care providers are Mexican doctors, clinics, and hospitals; Medicaid and Social Security benefits are available to beneficiaries who live in Mexico. For Americans who remain in the United States, the crisis in making prescription drugs and pharmaceuticals affordable means that many are availing themselves of Mexican Paternalism for their health-care needs.[45] From Tijuana to Cancún, millions of Americans come in with a shopping list of pharmaceuticals and medical products that they need. One official at Imss, the national health-care agency, estimated that Americans spend $350 million a year in Mexico, which "poses a problem because they are buying medicines that are subsidized by Mexican taxpayers; Mexico is subsidizing the U.S. consumer."[46] This, naturally, affects the ability of Mexico to provide health care to its own citizens, which is not without controversy: why should Mexican taxpayers subsidize pharmaceuticals for Americans?[47]

One can bemoan the scourge of substance abuse, or one can be grateful that, through continental integration, Mexico is uniquely positioned to be a constructive contributor in addressing the chemical dependence health crisis confronting the NAFTA nations.[48] Canada, not unlike Mexico, is also confronting a crisis as its socialist medical health-care system comes under strains. "Long heralded for giving all Canadians free health insurance and paying for almost all medical expenses, the health care system founded in the 1960s has long been the third rail of Canadian politics; not to be touched by private hands, nor altered by Parliament," Clifford Krauss informed the American public. "But growing complaints about long lines for diagnosis and surgery, as well as widespread 'line-jumping' by the affluent and connected, are eroding public confidence in Canada's national health care system and producing a leading issue for next year's [2004] national elections."[49]

Mexico, for its part, is aghast as the "invasion" of Americans who are benefiting from its price controls and subsidies to pharmaceuticals. The country is desperate to make its national health-care industry generate revenue. Indeed, it is clear that "detox rehabs"—along with ecotourism—is an industry in which Mexico is well positioned to become a global pioneer, and Mexican officials are ruminating their options. Though not without irony, it is instructive to see how the market finds creative solutions to meeting the needs of consumers across the continent, which heralds the arrival of a "Betty Ford Clinic South" in NAFTA's second decade.

## SUMMARY

1. Prohibition against drugs has failed to curb substance abuse in the NAFTA nations and has strained international relations.

2. The War on Drugs exacts a heavy price on the NAFTA nations, creating distortions in the economy by diverting resources into futile activities and costing legitimate business billions annually in unnecessary expenses and opportunity costs.

3. As a result, Canada and Mexico are moving on a de facto bilateral approach to first decriminalize and second legalize drugs, a policy that would render America's War on Drugs impossible to maintain.

4. One unintended market beginning to emerge in Mexico is "detox resorts," which are estimated to become a significant industry, approximating half a billion dollars by 2007.

## ENDNOTES

1. Some of the more difficult additions to overcome are not narcotics; they are prescription drugs. "Vicodin detox is harder than heroin detox," says Harold Owens at MusicCarres. "It stays in your system longer." See, "Return to the Valley of the Dolls," by Jeane Macintosh, *Details*, March 2001.

2. It was, after all, rather sublime to see John F. Kennedy smoke Cuban cigars, since he was the one who imposed an embargo on Cuban products. And this disregard for the law was passed on to his son; JFK, Jr. smoked Cohibas, his Cuban cigar of choice.

3. "Blame Canada—Northern Neighbor's Pot Policy Irks U.S. Drug Warriors," by H. G. Levine, Pacific News Service, *Pacificnews.org*, July 25, 2002.

4. "U.S. Guns Smuggled into Mexico Feed Drug War," by Tim Weiner and Ginger Thompson, *New York Times*, May 19, 2001.

5. What finally motivated Stephen Gaghan to turn his life around was stunning bad luck in his chain of supply. "Over one long, five-day weekend, I had three separate heroin dealers get arrested. My dealer, my backup dealer, and my backup-backup dealer. I was left alone, and I just hit that place, that total incomprehensible demoralization. That was the end of it; up five days straight, locked in the bathroom, convinced there was nowhere else to go, I had to kill myself, I'm going to kill myself. I just couldn't take another minute of it," he said. See "The Screenwriter for 'Traffic' Says He Drew on His Past of Drug Use," by Rick Lyman, *New York Times*, February 5, 2001.

6. "Adjusting Drug Policy," *New York Times* editorial, February 27, 2001. The editorial included the fundamental truth in any demand vs. supply

analysis of the drug issue to the point of becoming a mantra: "Studies have consistently shown that treatment programs for addicts are far more cost-effective than enforcement and interdiction in reducing drug use." The *New York Times* was not alone in making this case. "Study after study has shown that the best way to reduce drug consumption is to help addicts get treatment," Sebastian Mallaby opined in the *Washington Post*. "The RAND Drug Policy Research Center calculates that spending an extra $1 million on treatment would reduce cocaine consumption 3.5 times more than spending that money on domestic enforcement." See "Addicted to a Failing War on Drugs," by Sebastian Mallaby, *Washington Post*, January 8, 2001.

7. In value-neutral discussions, why should alcohol and tobacco be legal while other vices are not? Societies have the right to structure their moral and legal codes as they choose, such as preventing married individuals from having sexual relations with others with impunity, or preventing minors from making decisions about their sexuality. There are, however, basic questions about the wisdom of continuing to criminalize narcotics. "When the day comes that it is time to adopt the alternative of lifting punishment for consumption of drugs, it would have to come all over the world because we would gain nothing if Mexico did it but the production and traffic of drugs . . . continued here," Vicente Fox said, raising eyebrows around the world, suggesting that Mexico was prepared to contemplate solving the problem of illegal drugs by making drugs legal. Mr. Fox's comments were reported by the Associated Press on March 19, 2001.

8. "Substance abuse and addiction is the elephant in the living room of state government, creating havoc with service systems, causing illness, injury and death and consuming increasing amounts of state resources," said Joseph Califano, Jr., the center's president at a news conference when the report was issued on January 29, 2001. A copy of the report is available from Columbia University's National Center on Addiction and Substance Abuse in New York.

9. "U.S.: Report on State Drug Abuse Costs," *Tribune-Herald* (Waco, TX), June 29, 2001.

10. The disintegration of American society, of course, has been greatly commented upon, and not just by social critic Tom Wolfe. In fact, unintended chronicles of this dysfunction are evident, whether in fiction (Carl Hiaasen's *Basket Case*) or non-fiction (Susan Orleans' *The Orchid Thief*). A strong argument can be made that *Vanity Fair*, under Tina Brown and Graydon Carter, documents the decline of American civility and, with it, American civilization.

11. "Itinerary: The War on Drugs," by Robin Rauzi, *Los Angeles Times*, January 11, 2001.

12. "Annual Drug Report Shows Coca Growth Increase," by Christopher Marquis, *New York Times*, March 1, 2001.

13. "Reaching Across the Río Grande," Editorial, *New York Times*, January 25, 2001.

14. "The Technology Secrets of Cocaine Inc.," by Paul Kaihla, *Business 2.0*, July 2002.

15. See "Lab-Busting in the Northwest," by Jon Bonne, *www.msnbc.com/news/510820.asp* and "Drug Labs in Valley Hideouts Feed Nation's Habit," by Evelyn Nieves, *New York Times*, May 13, 2001.

16. Interviewed in "Banning Censorship," by Amy Benfor, *Salon.com,* June 11, 2001.

17. "My Son, the Junkie," by Wendy Mnookin, *Salon.com,* August 27, 1999.

18. "Experiencing Ecstasy," by Matthew Klam, *New York Times,* January 21, 2001.

19. "To Decriminalize the Use of Drugs," *Globe and Mail,* August 22, 2001.

20. "Decriminalizing Pot," *National Post,* August 16, 2001. Later that month, the *Saint John Times Globe* urged reforming how alcoholism is treated under the law. See "Room for Improvement in Response to Alcohol," August 29, 2001.

21. See "Hospital Utilization and Costs in a Cohort of Injection Drug Users," by A. Palepu, M. W. Tyndall, J. Muller, M. V. O'Shaughnessy, M. T. Schechter, et al; and "Unsafe Injection Practices in Cohort of Injection Drug Users in Vancouver: Could Safer Injecting Rooms Help?" by E. Wood, M. W. Tyndall, P. M. Spittal, T. Kerr, R. S. Hogg, et al. Both in *Canadian Medical Association Journal* 2002; 165 (4).

22. "That's right, that's true, that's true," Fox said when asked about his call for the eventual legalization of drugs. See "Fox Talks Drug Legalization," by John Rice, Associated Press, March 19, 2001. In Latin America only Uruguay president Jorge Batlle has called for the immediate legalization of all drugs, including cocaine, to the condemnation of American officials.

23. "Chihuahua Considers Legalizing Pot," by Sonny López , *The Dallas Morning News,* June 1, 2002.

24. For the ambitious policy objectives of this Republican, see *Governor.state.nm.us.*

25. "Mexico Officials Worry About Drug Violence," by Julie Watson, *The Brownsville Herald,* June 23, 2001.

26. "Scourge of the Heartland," by Jon Bonne, *www.msnbc.com/news/510819.asp.*

27. "Even for moderate users, meth has a steep addiction curve: It's remarkably easy to get hooked and painfully hard to get off it. Almost as soon as the high begins, users start to fear the crash, especially the tweaking and paranoia. When a user finally comes down, his or her surroundings seem bleak," Jon Bonne reports in "Hooked in the Haight," *www.msnbc.com/news/512127.asp.*

28. "Addicted to a Failing War on Drugs," by Sebastian Mallaby, *Washington Post,* January 8, 2001.

29. Asa Hutchinson is quoted in "Blame Canada—Northern Neighbor's Pot Policy Irks U.S. Drug Warriors," by H. G. Levine, Pacific News Service, July 25, 2002.

30. "Mexican President Quoted Suggesting Eventual Legalization of Drugs," Associated Press, March 19, 2001.

31. The National Addictions Council, or Conadic, reports that 4.6 percent of the adult population is addicted to alcohol. For comparison purposes, Mexico ranked 43rd in the world in terms of alcohol consumption, with 3.2 liters consumed per capita. Figures are for 1998, the latest year available. "There is no tried and true, 'state-of-the-art' treatment of choice for alcohol problems. Rather, the state of the art is an array of empirically supported treatment options," Hester Reid and William Miller write. See Reid K. Hester, William R. Miller, editors, *Handbook of Alcoholism Treatment*

*Approaches: Effective Alternatives.* 2nd Ed. Allyn & Bacon, 1995, page 9. An interesting discussion of the "state" of rehab in the United States is found in *Hooked: Five Addicts Challenge Our Misguided Drug Rehab System,* by Lonny Shavelson, New York: The New Press, 2001. Shavelson asks himself, "Does drug rehab work for those who are most disastrously addicted?" His answer? "I still don't know. In the two years of this investigation I rarely saw rehab done well enough to learn if it might work. What we today call drug rehab does not provide consistent and coherent help to the majority of addicts who come seeking it. It may well be that the nature of the beast of addiction makes effective treatment of addicts a pie-in-the-sky dream, even with the best that rehab could offer. Or it may be that the frustratingly unimpressive treatment results we see today with those most intensely addicted are merely what happens in a rehab system that is as ill as the addicts themselves."

32. "Ill Americans Seek Marijuana's Relief in Canada," by Clifford Krauss, *New York Times,* September 8, 2002.

33. In a bizarre example of the entrepreneurial spirit, some New York nightclubs began to hire private ambulance companies in a bid to whisk patrons who overdose to emergency rooms, without having to resort to calling the 911 emergency system—and thus avoid unwanted police attention. See "Nightclubs Hire Ambulances for Overdoses, Skipping 911," by Jennifer Steinhauer, *New York Times,* April 20, 2001.

34. The threat of loss of federal dollars for highway projects was the "stick" that coerced state legislatures to dance to Washington's tune on the matter.

35. It should be noted that officials in Cancún take extraordinary measures to ensure that the enclave of hotels where the spring-breakers arrive coordinate their security and supervision. For instance, free shuttles are provided for youngsters; car rental agencies will not rent vehicles to those under the age of 21; and hotels coordinate activities to create an orderly unfolding of "events." Upon arriving in Cancún, interestingly, Mexican officials make spring breakers sign a pledge of good conduct, reminding them that they are in a foreign country and that their vacation package does not include reimbursing hotels or restaurants for breaking things. The results are impressive: of the quarter million American and Canadian youth that participate in spring break in Cancún, those injured or who engage in criminal conduct are statistically insignificant.

36. "This year, for the first time, the government, hotels, discos, bars and transportation providers all joined together to launch the 'Be Cool While in Cancún' campaign. Arriving students are given fliers containing a list of dos and don'ts that advise them to 'Enjoy Cancún and be careful,'" the Associated Press reported. It worked; by Spring 2002, more than 210,000 American and Canadian spring-breakers made their way to Cancún, and without the incidence of problems that characterize spring break in Florida resorts, from Daytona Beach to South Beach. See "Cancún Equated with Spring Break," the Associated Press, March 11, 2001.

37. "Another key selling point for Mexican clinics is cost, with able staff recruitable at a fraction of what doctors make in the U.S.," Joel Millman reports. See "Spring-Break Revelers Help Bridge Health-Care Gap," by Joel Millman, *Wall Street Journal,* April 11, 2001.

38. "The war on drugs is really a war on people—on anyone who uses or

grows or makes or sells a forbidden drug," Ethan Nadelmann opined in the *New York Times.* "What has the war on drugs done for Darryl Strawberry and Robert Downey Jr? Are they better off or worse off?" See "An Unwinnable War on Drugs," by Ethan Nadelmann, *New York Times,* April 26, 2001.

39.  A friend who served in Vietnam, and was a recovering alcoholic suffering from Post Traumatic Stress Disorder, led a healthy existence in Mexico for the most part. Only when he had visitors from the States and they headed off to Cancún did he begin to drink again. At times it was horrific, having the police call up in the middle of the night after they were all in trouble. On one occasion, two of his friends were deported, lest they face being charged with a crime, after an episode of binge drinking that ended in their being reduced to drinking rubbing alcohol in Coca-Cola.

40.  "Experiencing Ecstasy," by Matthew Klam, *New York Times,* January 21, 2001.

41.  From *The Natural Mind,* by Andrew Weil, quoted in "Experiencing Ecstasy," by Matthew Klam, *New York Times,* January 21, 2001.

42.  "Hooked in the Haight," by Jon Bonne, *www.msnbc.com/news/512127.asp.* This view is supported by medical research. "A strong and consistent finding in research on motivation is that people are most likely to undertake and persist in an action when they perceive that they have personally chosen to do so. One study, for example, found that a particular alcohol treatment approach was more effective when a client chose it from among alternatives than when it was assigned to the client as his or her only option. . . . Perceived freedom of choice also appears to reduce client resistance and dropout. . . . When clients are told they have no choice, they tend to resist change. When their freedom of choice is acknowledged, they are freed to choose change," Reid Hester and William Miller report. See Reid K. Hester, William R. Miller, editors: *Handbook of Alcoholism Treatment Approaches: Effective Alternatives.* 2nd Ed. Allyn & Bacon, 1995, page 93.

43.  "Experiencing Ecstasy," by Matthew Klam, *New York Times,* January 21, 2001.

44.  Private communication, March 2002. After consulting with individuals in the medical and mental health industries, the consensus is that in 2003, "detox resorts" will be an $83 million industry in Mexico, with an expected market potential to exceed $500 million annually by 2007.

45.  The conflict is a partisan one. Republicans favor providing government subsidies to private insurers. Democrats favor expanding Medicare benefits. Neither plan has managed the necessary bipartisan support to ensure its passage.

46.  "My husband is now 69," Della Leyva, of Los Angeles, said in an interview. "He is taking a diuretic and steroids and drugs for his ulcer. It's really cutting into our money. He is on inhalers and oxygen. But what was happening was I was running out of his inhalers before the end of the month. If I needed to start on the next month's supply, I could not get the reimbursement so I had to pay the full price, $95. . . . Then we found out that a friend could get the same inhalers for $10 in Tijuana, Mexico, about a three-hour drive from here. He gets two or three, to keep us ahead of the game. We didn't tell our doctor at first, and when we did, he

was concerned, but he can't do anything about it. I need the backup. I
need more than two inhalers a month." In addition, all kinds of other
Americans avail themselves of Mexican pharmacies, from high school
bodybuilders who want anabolic steroids, to stressed out middle-aged
women who want valium, to others in search of everything from
tetracycline to Retin-A to Halcyon. Limiting the role of money in an
economy has unintended consequences, one of which is the transfer of
purchasing power from the Mexican state to Americans under medical
care. See "Some Retirees Look Abroad for Prescription Drugs," by Randi
Hutter Epstein, *New York Times*, September 24, 2002.

47. Pharmaceuticals, unhappy about the price controls and restrictions they
face in Mexico and Canada, have begun to prevent American consumers
from purchasing medicines in either of these two countries. This, in turn,
pits the pharmaceuticals against insurance companies who want more
affordable medicines for everyone. "Drug makers have been concerned
for some time that Americans leave the U.S. to take advantage of lower-
cost medications available in Canada, Mexico and other places," Thomas
Burton and Sarah Lueck reported. "Congress has been debating whether
to make it explicitly legal for people to do so. Meanwhile, busloads of
seniors and other Americans with high prescription drug costs continue
to cross the border into Canada and Mexico in search of cheaper
medicines. Dozens of Internet pharmacies have sprouted up in Canada,
where the weak currency and government price caps make brand-name
prescription drugs relatively cheap for U.S. residents." See "Insurer to
Cover Drugs Bought Outside U.S.," by Thomas Burton and Sarah Lueck,
*Wall Street Journal*, October 11, 2002.

48. Despite how it was portrayed in the Hollywood film *Born on the Fourth of
July*, many Vietnam veterans have received medical care on an ongoing
basis at Mexican hospitals and medical facilities.

49. "Long Lines Mar Canada's Low-Cost Health Care," by Clifford Krauss,
*New York Times*, February 13, 2003.

# Conclusion

One trillions dollars' worth of investment opportunities in Mexico over the course of NAFTA's second decade have been identified. Though an astounding figure, funding, over the course of a decade, is achievable. "I will attempt to redress the age-old poverty and inequality that, despite economic gains in several regions, still plague too many Mexicans," Vicente Fox declared in an Op-Ed essay in the *New York Times,* after his election win in 2000. "We must accelerate economic growth, promote local and regional development and above all ensure better distribution of income. Strengthening civil society, democratizing the labor movement, giving women a greater voice and defending minorities are all steps in this direction."[1]

These ambitions were derailed by the September 11th terrorist attacks. It is almost impossible to imagine that the week before these events, Fox addressed a joint session of U.S. Congress—and it seemed that the U.S. and Mexico would reach an immigration agreement on a "fast track" basis. The stunning reversal showed the vulnerabilities of the Fox administration, less than a year in office and without a majority in the Congress. What is of concern, however, is the failure of the Fox administration to move forward in the areas in which it does not need either the United States or the Mexican Congress.

Four areas are ripe for unilateral action by the Fox administration. Foremost is increasing the nation's working capital—more than $300 billion—by implementing the recommendations of Hernando de Soto and titling hitherto untitled assets. "First among the traditional economic weaknesses is Latin America's dependence on foreign capital. This lies at the heart of its vulnerability to outside events," the London *Economist* reported, with compelling prescience. "Although the region's economies were

slightly less volatile in the 1990s than in previous years, the insta-
bility continues. It contributes to a vicious circle, in which uncertainty discourages long-term planning by business and politicians
alike."[2] The multiplier effect of making "dead" assets into working capital cannot be stressed enough, and it would provide an internal source of capital to rival several decades' worth of direct
investment.

Of equal importance, Fox can define the terms under which
private investment in the wastewater treatment industry can unfold. Indeed, the sustained development of some of Mexico's
tourist resources has begun to suffer from the lack of adequate
wastewater treatment.[3] Tens of billions of dollar are waiting to
pour into Mexico once the rules are defined and terms established. The fracas involving Metalclad underscores the need to
make governing rules for this industry, and make them in a fair,
timely, and definite manner that creates a level playing field and
protects the interests of all parties. Indecision has proved to be
worse than bad decisions; Mexico has incurred tremendous opportunity costs and is falling further behind with each passing day.

Third, there are certain constitutional allowances in place
that offer Mexico the opportunity to become a leader in electric
power generation.[4] Though constitutional authorities are in dis-
agreement over the possibility of allowing foreign firms to produce electric power for the domestic market, what is not in dispute is the insatiable demand for electricity by California, the
American Southwest, and Texas. InterGen's operations near Mexicali, if accompanied by a defined program to upgrade Mexican
environmental standards to meet those of the United States, represents a model for significant development of electric power
generation along the border region. In addition, the possibility of
joint ventures in the exploration and development of oil resources is more complex, but there are precedents for Pemex entering into mutually beneficial arrangements in Campeche Bay
Sound. The Fox administration needs to dedicate itself to working within the existing constitutional framework, which stands to
attract tens of billions of dollars in direct foreign investment.

Lastly, a nationwide campaign to get every Mexican to open
a bank account—which would include the issuing of ATM cards,
facilitating remittances—would both increase the nation's capital
by billions and get an estimated $1 billion into the hands of the
poorest members of society.[5] It would also spare millions of Hispanics living in the United States from being exploited by loan
sharks, or falling prey to consumer financial fraud.[6]

As NAFTA concluded its first decade, the greatest danger stems from the failure to forge ahead in the areas that offer the most spectacular opportunities. That these areas are not immediately apparent—and because many are not glamorous—but without mature leadership, economic growth within North America will stagnate. As the summit in Monterrey held in March 2002 concluded, for instance—though there was a consensus that the wealthy nations of the world had surprised their worst critics by honestly describing their failure to do more to alleviate poverty—when it came to U.S.-Mexico relations, there was a somewhat hollow feeling. "The relationship seems high on concept, low on content," is how Ginger Thompson described Vicente Fox and George W. Bush's friendship.[7] The "ambitious" agenda that both leaders had praised had made little progress in reality; creating a "smart border" to help commuters and the movement of trade was a modest accomplishment considering the breathtaking harmony that the European Union had achieved.[8] Thompson noted the meager results by observing laconically that after "[p]resenting dozens of ideas about the kinds of laws, programs and amounts of money needed, Mr. Fox pressed the United States to achieve the dream by [the end of 2001]."[9]

It is a fair criticism to point out that Mexico has focused too much on its foreign agenda to the detriment of certain domestic opportunities that were long neglected by the PRI, given that the United States is consumed by terrorism.[10] In his 2002 State-of-the-Union speech, Fox noted that the "nation faces challenges beyond the power of any one political force to solve them. People hope for more than democracy. They are impatient with discord. They want a democracy that works, fundamental social change and a just economic order."[11] This theme was reiterated in September 2003. This suggests that Mexico should work more closely with Canada on expanding their bilateral alliance, specifically creating the kind of immigration and drug reform laws that can become a prototype for the whole of North America at some date in the near future.

A day after the first anniversary of the September 11th attacks, Fox spoke of Mexico's frustration that NAFTA's priorities had been derailed by the "war" on terror. "There are feelings on my part that I would not describe as frustration or resentment, but I feel strongly that we need to deal with bilateral matters. I constantly make it known to the American government that we need the same kind of attention for Latin America," Fox told the *New York Times*.[12] True enough, but Fox would do well to remember the observation made by Pierre Lemieux. "If you want free trade, just trade," Lemieux points out. "Much of the pre-World War I free trade was, indeed, due to Britain's unilateral free-trade policies. Trade agreements are only helpful to the extent that they help tame domestic producers' interests, support the primacy of consumers, and lock-in the gains of trade."[13]

Mexico—and Fox—is more in control of its destiny that it realizes. Denise Dresser summed up the promise of Fox this way: "Will he be a Reagan Cowboy or a Mexican Mandela?"[14] Whichever description will best characterize the Fox administration, what is clear is that establishing a good working relationship with Tony Garza, the American ambassador named by the Bush White House in the summer of 2002, is a prerequisite. "The U.S. and Mexico share not only a border, but a rich history of common economic and cultural interests," Bush said at the time of the appointment.[15] Thus, the overriding humanitarian concern continues to be the disenfranchisement of millions of people who live in the United States in violation of their human, civil, and labor rights, as well as their right to move across the continent. Of equal importance is how Canada and Mexico can create bilateral programs that would allow citizens of the three NAFTA nations to exercise their right to medical, if alternative, treatment.

As NAFTA enters its second decade, there are unexpected challenges. This is not new; NAFTA began with a devastating devaluation of the Mexican peso and the Zapatista uprising in Chiapas. In 2004, the challenges are isolationist backlash in American foreign policy in response to the terrorist attacks of September 11, 2001, and the inability of the Fox administration to become proactive in the face of the global economic slowdown. "That is because Mexico, probably more than any other country in the world, needs United States growth to jump-start its own sluggish economy," Elisabeth Malkin reported. "Under the North American Free Trade Agreement, Mexico's export industries have become deeply integrated into United States manufacturing and are the country's most dynamic. About 90 percent of what Mexico sells abroad goes north of the border."[16]

This economic dependency is unhealthy, for it links Mexico's future to the United States, an unreliable political ally and a disingenuous economic partner. "When Mexican corn farmers tramp through their fields behind donkey-drawn plows, they have one goal: to eke out a living. Increasingly, however, they find themselves saddled with mountains of unsold produce because farmers in Kansas and Nebraska sell their own corn in Mexico at prices

well below those of the Mexicans," the *New York Times* opined, after an increase in farm subsidies exposed American duplicity before the world. "This is not primarily due to higher efficiency. The
Americans' real advantage comes from huge taxpayer-provided
subsidies that allow them to sell overseas at 20 percent below the
actual cost of production. In other words, we subsidize our farmers so heavily that they can undersell poor competitors abroad.
And just to make sure, we have tariff barriers in place that make
it extremely hard for many third world farmers to sell in the
United States. The same is true for their efforts to sell in Europe
and Japan. The world's farming system is rigged in favor of the
rich."[17]

The problems Mexican farmers faced exacerbated tensions
between the U.S. and Mexico—but it also aligned Mexico and
Canada, since both nations' farmers were adversely affected by
American farm subsidies. "The problems of rural Mexicans are
echoed around the world as countries lower their import barriers,
required by free trade treaties and the rules of the World Trade
Organization," Tina Rosenberg explained. "When markets are
open, agricultural products flood in from wealthy nations, which
subsidize agriculture and allow agribusiness to export crops
cheaply. European farmers get 35 percent of their income in government subsidies, American farmers 20 percent. American subsidies are at record levels, and last year, Washington passed a farm
bill that included a $40 billion increase in subsidies to large grain
and cotton farmers. It seems paradoxical to argue that cheap food
hurts poor people. But three-quarters of the world's poor are
rural. When subsidized imports undercut their products, they
starve. Agricultural subsidies, which rob developing countries of
the ability to export crops, have become the most important dispute at the W.T.O. Wealthy countries do far more harm to poor
nations with these subsidies than they do good with foreign
aid."[18]

These are also issues, of course, for developed trading partners. The Canadians, who are hardly "developing," also joined the
chorus decrying the simple fact that these subsidies constituted
an intervention in the marketplace that undermined free trade.
Canadian farmers, though not affected as adversely as their Mexican counterparts, also faced unfair competition from subsidized-
American agricultural products.[19] Critics of the United States in
Mexico lashed out at Fox for refusing to challenge this American
subterfuge, one more complaint against Fox, who, by 2003, was
seen as an ineffective leader. To its credit, however, Canada has

been able to insulate itself from the American business cycle, if not completely, then to a reassuring degree. "Economists note that when Canada did not follow the United States into a recession after the Sept. 11 attacks, it was the first time in 25 years that the country had been able to avert being tugged into an American tailspin," Clifford Krauss reported. "Low interest rates, the construction boom, surges in car and truck production and higher prices for the oil and gas that Canada produces have enabled the country to go on thriving, at least so far."[20]

Mexico must assert its economic independence similarly. This perception was, to a large degree, a consequence of America's bellicose response to the terrorist attacks of September 11th, one in which the American economy was neglected as the Bush administration pursued military action against Iraq. "Because of the sputtering United States economy, Mexico's economic performance during Fox's first two years in office has been bleak," Elisabeth Malkin wrote. "The economy shrank 0.3 percent in 2001, and analysts expect that the figures from last year will show growth of just over 1 percent."[21]

The economy of North America, however, has grown more complex: the U.S. recession made the Mexican peso and Canadian dollar both appreciate, creating a different set of challenges. "The higher the peso rises in value against the dollar, the more expensive and less competitive Mexican exports become in the United States, by far the country's most important foreign market," Bernard Simon reported. "America buys nearly 90 percent of Mexico's exports. High oil prices in the spring poured dollars into Mexico's central bank. Mexico's foreign currency reserves, an important bulwark against financial crises, now stand [as of May 2003] at a healthy $53.7 billion."[22] Indeed, there were many in Mexico and around the world who shuddered at envisioning Mexico without the PRI. Fox's election challenged Mexicans to think of how their nation—and its place in the world—would change after the PRI's "Reign of Error."

It would be tragic for the Mexican nation, then, to realize that an opposition candidate was elected in Mexico and *nothing* happened, in the worst sense of the phrase: stagnation.[23] To be sure, Vicente Fox entered office with great expectations, and it appeared that in George W. Bush he had found an American leader willing to push for greater economic integration and implement a viable guest-worker program, as Mexico and Canada have done. It is clear that the September 11 attacks on New York and Washington derailed the Bush-Fox agenda. A week prior to these terrorist attacks, Fox addressed a joint session of the U.S. Congress and it appeared that a general agreement on immigration reform would be completed within a matter of months. "Presidents Vicente Fox and George W. Bush both took office two years ago promising to forge a new partnership bridging the Rٞo Grande, one marked by a once-unimaginable level of cooperation on a number of fronts. It hasn't happened, and as a result Mexico's enlightened foreign minister, Jorge Castañeda, has resigned," the *New York Times* published, an inauspicious beginning to 2003. "The centerpiece of the new relationship was to have been a new accord on immigration. That encountered early resistance on Capitol Hill, and the terrorist attacks of Sept. 11, 2001, rearranged the White House's priorities. Washington has since failed to recognize that an immigration deal that serves American economic needs and diminishes the population living illegally in this country can be compatible with heightened security."[24]

For Fox, it has been an embarrassing disappointment to see precisely how Mexico defines itself by the United States. "Mexico has shown a willingness to work on drugs," Interior Minister Santiago Creel said, expressing his government's frustrations. "Mexico has shown a willingness to work on security. But when Mexico asks the United States to work on migration, we have not seen the same willingness."[25] Fox's domestic and international agenda are in such disarray as to be nonexistent.[26] This is not surprising, since the White House—regardless of which party is in power—is quick to resort to protectionism and betray its free-market principles for domestic political consumption.[27]

There are many proactive avenues Mexico can pursue, however. If the United States is consumed by a campaign to exact vengeance on its enemies under the guise of defending its national interests, the analysis offered in this book identifies concrete measures that Mexico can take to strengthen its economy and reposition itself for growth, regardless of where the White House's attention lies. "Mexico could be one of the two or three most dynamic places on the globe," Gray Newman, senior Latin America economist for Morgan Stanley, told Elisabeth Malkin. "Where else do you have the largest capital market on one side and a huge labor market next door?"[28]

Where does one also find so much unrealized potential than in Mexico?

It is imperative for Fox to realize that immigration reform will more likely be the crowning achievement of his administration, which means there have to be other accomplishments of substance before 2006. These include:

- Implementing the "De Soto Program" to title hitherto untitled assets, bringing more than $300 billion in capital assets to the economy.
- Banking reforms in which all Mexicans have access to the formal financial banking system, not only to put more in the pockets of Mexicans who receive remittances from abroad, but to increase the nation's working capital.
- The failure to define the "rules of play" for the wastewater management industry continues to deprive Mexico of tens of billions of fresh investments in this crucial industry.
- If reform at Pemex proves a formidable task, there are significant opportunities in using existing "loopholes," such as electric power generation for export markets and licensing oil exploration and development in the Gulf of Mexico, to permit technical Pemex oversight over efficient foreign-investing oil companies.

"Political reform in Mexico is seeping into all structures of the federal government and out to the state and local levels," Fox wrote, explaining how changes in Mexico offered new opportunities for North America, one week before September 11th. "The way political power is exercised has begun to change dramatically. The relationship between government and Mexican society is being rebuilt on the basis of accountability and the rule of law. Relations between the government and the media are based on greater transparency and openness. Our government is guided by a system of checks and balances between the different branches of government that curtails presidential power."[29] It is time to pick up where the United States and Mexico left off before the violent events of September 11th.

When I return to my home in New York, I am emboldened by defiance: one looks up and the towers aren't there, but that doesn't mean the World Trade Center is truly gone. They were once there, and their presence made the world a better place. There are obstacles that we, as individuals and societies, face, but we can rise above them, to persevere and prevail. A certain patient, nonjudgmental generosity towards each other is in order as Americans, Canadians, and Mexicans continue this grand experiment that continental integration is in fact. "Companies are doing good when they do what they do responsibly, whether it's Ford making cars or Exxon producing oil," John R. Boatright, author of *Ethics and the Conduct of Business,* argued eloquently.[30]

For corporate America and corporate Canada, there are "action items" that require them to join corporate Mexico to work together to ensure that the breathtaking opportunities of NAFTA's second decade come to fruition. Foremost is to lobby the federal officials in Washington, Ottawa, and Mexico City to work together. Friedman's definition of the proper role of government bears repeating: "A government which maintained law and order, defined property rights, served as a means whereby we could modify property rights and other rules of the economic game, adjudicated disputes about the interpretation of the rules, enforced contracts, promoted competition."[31] It is clear that the governments of the NAFTA nations have, by focusing on the "War on Terror," abdicated their responsibilities to the urgent task at hand. The entire continent, for instance, needs to embark on a comprehensive program to rebuild and expand its infrastructure. The entire continent must work to create a viable "North American Security Perimeter" that can safeguard all the people who live in North America. Other areas, from integrating financial services, to creating zones of opportunity in the business of environmentalism, to creating a viable immigration reform, all require proactive leaders in the business community to petition officials.

Left to their own devices, politicians oftentimes do what is more expedient but not what is necessary. NAFTA's continued success, however, requires vision—and hard work. As we embark on NAFTA's second decade—and the over a *trillion* dollars' worth of opportunities—there is much we can teach, and learn from, each other as we work purposefully towards creating more perfect societies for everyone, everywhere.

This book represents three years of ongoing analysis of the impact, economic and social, of NAFTA on the economies of the three nations of North America. I have thoroughly enjoyed writing this book and am delighted to offer an ambitious vision of what North America can realistically become as this century unfolds. Our success, individually and collectively, depends on our doing what we do right, ethically and consistent with what our fellow *continental* citizens expect of responsible corporate citizens, especially in light of the tremendous opportunities that lie before us. There has never been a better time to live and work in North America, for there have never been as many promising business opportunities as there are at the dawn of NAFTA's second decade.

# ENDNOTES

1. "A New Kind of Neighbor," by Vicente Fox, *New York Times*, August 25, 2000.
2. "The Slow Road to Reform," the London *Economist*, December 2, 2000.
3. "This was paradise," Tim Weiner reported of Ixtapa. "But a sewer runs through it. Mexico's environmental protection agency sampled the water in Zihuatanejo's beautiful bay back in September [2002]. The results were not pretty: the agency said sewage from the city's wastewater plant had tainted one of the nation's loveliest harbors." See "For All to Read: A Mexican Resort's Dirty Secret," by Tim Weiner, *New York Times*, February 13, 2003.
4. "At InterGen, John Foster, a senior vice president, said his company had been 'honest and straightforward.' He said InterGen might even retrofit its plant to comply completely with California standards, assuming consumers would help pay the added cost of up to $20 million," Tim Weiner reported. "He said the key to building more plants in Mexico to serve the United States—'a great idea'—was to harmonize the two nations' environmental laws." See "U.S. Will Get Power, and Pollution, from Mexico," by Tim Weiner, *New York Times*, September 17, 2002.
5. If the average fees and exchange-rate manipulation in sending $300 US to Mexico constitute $30, or 10 percent, then it follows that the cumulative purchasing power of $10 billion U.S. in annual remittances would be $1 billion. Western Union, American Express MoneyGram, and the U.S. Postal Service profit handsomely by the disenfranchisement of millions people who, quite simply, lack bank accounts. It is time such social injustices were eliminated throughout the continent.
6. "[W]hen Juan Luis needed $10,000 to pay a tax bill on what remained of his business, he telephoned two of his most reliable loan sharks, bargained for the best interest rate and arranged for a drop at one of the 10 chicken stands in the city that he still owned," Dexter Filkins reported. "This is banking for thousands of Latinos in immigrant neighborhoods in New York and across the country, where loan sharking and other unregulated lending is thriving, often within sight of commercial banks. Unlike the loan sharks of yesteryear, with links to the mob and reputations for brutality, the 'prestamistas,' as they are known here by the Spanish term for moneylender, often constitute a mainstream institution, financing everything from bodegas to discos for the poor and the middle class alike." See, "In Some Immigrant Enclaves, Loan Shark Is the Local Bank," by Dexter Filkins, *New York Times*, April 23, 2001.
7. "U.S.-Mexico Relations: Alliance Meets Boundaries," by Ginger Thompson, *New York Times*, March 23, 2002.
8. With dozens of borders, languages and centuries of historic conflict, how Europe was able to establish the "borderless" euro zone is the more remarkable. By comparison, Mexico and the U.S. continue to struggle with simple goals, such as creating a mechanism by which guest workers are accommodated and how nation-states handle natural human migration.
9. "U.S.-Mexico Relations: Alliance Meets Boundaries," by Ginger Thompson, *New York Times*, March 23, 2002.
10. George W. Bush was taken to task by the *New York Times* as well. Admonishing him for "his failure to advance the hemispheric agenda,"

the newspaper of record took the President's March 2002 trip to Latin America as an opportunity to point out that the protectionism undermined his credibility. "The administration's broader trade agenda, including the proposed Free Trade Area of the Americas, suffered a severe blow earlier this month when President Bush decided to impose new tariffs on steel imports," the editorial stated. See "Mr. Bush Looks South," *New York Times,* March 23, 2002.

11. State of the Union address, Mexico City, September 1, 2002.
12. "After 9/11, Fox Still Waits for U.S. Moves on Mexico," by Ginger Thompson, *New York Times,* September 13, 2002.
13. "Free Trade Doesn't Require Treaties," by Pierre Lemieux, *The Wall Street Journal,* April 24, 2001.
14. "Fox: Un Reagan ranchero o un Mandela mexicano?," by Denise Dresser, *El Universal,* July 26, 2000.
15. "I cannot think of a more qualified person," Senator Kay Bailey Hutchinson, Republican of Texas, said at the time of the appointment. "Tony Garza is going to be someone who will represent our country and represent the views of our country very well, but from the perspective and experience and knowledge on both sides of the border that I have never seen before in a nominee." See "Garza Picked as Ambassador to Mexico," Associated Press, July 16, 2002.
16. "Mexico Keeps Eye on U.S. Indicators," by Elisabeth Malkin, *New York Times,* January 25, 2003.
17. "The Hypocrisy of Farm Subsidies," *New York Times* Editorial, December 1, 2002. That this betrayal of Mexico came at a time when American negotiators fanned out across Latin America to convince these nations to enter into a "free" trade agreement that would encompass the entire hemisphere spoke volumes of the bravado with which the United States acts at times.
18. "Why Mexico's Small Corn Farmers Go Hungry," by Tina Rosenberg, *New York Times,* March 3, 2003.
19. Consider the socioeconomic dislocation exacerbated by American farm subsidies to Mexican farmers. "Although agriculture represents less than 5 percent of the gross domestic product, about one in five working Mexicans are directly or indirectly involved in it," Ginger Thompson reported. "The overwhelming majority are poor subsistence farmers, who work plots as small as two acres. However, midsized farmers are also being devastated. . . . Some 700,000 people are expected to lose jobs in farming and other food industries [in 2003 as a consequence.]" See "NAFTA to Open Floodgates, Engulfing Rural Mexico," by Ginger Thompson, *New York Times,* December 19, 2002.
20. Canadian Prime Minister Jean Chrétien boasted that Canada had become the "new Northern Tiger," evidence of how sovereignty can be maintained even as economic integration unfolds. Mexico, too, must look to Canada to reduce its dependence on America's business cycle. See "Canada Economy Grows Where Others Falter," by Clifford Krauss, *New York Times,* October 8, 2002.
21. "Mexico Keeps Eye on U.S. Indicators," by Elisabeth Malkin, *New York Times,* January 25, 2003.
22. "Dollar's Neighbors Feeling Uneasy," by Bernard Simon, *New York Times,* May 14, 2003.

23. "After the attacks, nothing happened," Ginger Thompson and Tim Weiner reported from Mexico City. "Scrambling to salvage his hallmark foreign policy project [on immigration reform], Mr. Fox urged Mr. Bush to consider legalizing immigrants as part of a hemispheric security strategy. But that got little reaction from a White House looking far beyond the Mexican border and eager to avoid a potentially divisive issue in an election year." See "Mexico Struggles for the Attentions of a Preoccupied U.S.," by Ginger Thompson and Tim Weiner, *New York Times,* October 13, 2002.

24. "Backtracking on Mexico," *New York Times* Editorial, January 11, 2003. "Mr. Castañeda and Mr. Fox formed one of Mexico's unlikelier political unions," Tim Weiner wrote when reporting Mr. Castañeda's resignation. "Mr. Castañeda is an intellectual who came out of the left wing, a political scientist by trade. Mr. Fox was a conservative provincial politician, a former Coca-Cola executive, when Mr. Castañeda joined his political crusade to topple 70 years of one-party rule in Mexico." See "Mexican Official to Quit, Frustrated by U.S.," by Tim Weiner, *New York Times,* January 9, 2003.

25. Quoted in "Mexico Struggles for the Attentions of a Preoccupied U.S.," by Ginger Thompson and Tim Weiner, *New York Times,* October 13, 2002.

26. Mexico's position on "regularizing" the status of illegal immigrants is a matter of human rights. "Mexico has long insisted that it is one thing to have a person cross the border in search of work," Deputy Foreign Minister Enrique Berruga told reporters, "and it is another to have that person be subjected to attacks by authorities. We are most interested in preventing people from being hurt simply because they have crossed the border, and this is a very important advance." See "Measures Aim at Violence Along Border," by Eric Schmitt, *New York Times,* June 24, 2001.

27. "Among those who believe Bush puts political expedience above principle, there is no more damning evidence than his decision in March [2002] to slap punitive tariffs on steel imports, and his condoning of similar anticompetitive favors to the farm and textile industries," Bill Keller wrote in the *New York Times Magazine.* "The Republican faithful were scandalized by how readily the man who preaches free trade was willing to pander to protectionist sentiment." The Clinton White House notoriously protected sugar growers and refused to comply with NAFTA requirements on allowing Mexican trucking companies access. Whether Republican or Democrat, Americans seek four objectives when they put politics above principles. First, Americans demonstrate how self-serving their commitment to free trade is in fact; as long as they have a competitive advantage, they support free trade. Second, Washington politicians are prepared to subsidize inefficient American producers, mostly in the agricultural and textiles industries, simply to curry favor with voters. Third, the United States is unconcerned about the vast distortions that ripple through the global economy. Fourth, while the United States (through the World Bank and the International Monetary Fund) is first to criticize any nation that subsidizes its domestic industry, Americans subsidize failed companies—most recently in its domestic airline industry—giving inefficient companies an unfair competitive advantage vis-à-vis foreign competitors. This is not to pass judgment on American policies, but simply to point out that Mexican government

officials need to be cognizant of how American behavior diverges from American rhetoric. For Keller's article, see "Reagan's Son," by Bill Keller, *New York Times,* January 26, 2003.

28.  "Mexico Keeps Eye on U.S. Indicators," by Elisabeth Malkin, *New York Times,* January 25, 2003.

29.  "More Trust on Both Sides of the Border," by Vicente Fox, *New York Times,* September 4, 2001.

30.  Personal communication, May 2002.

31.  Milton Friedman, "The Role of Government in a Free Society," in *Private Wants and Public Needs,* Edmund Phelps, Editor, New York: W. W. Norton, 1965, pages 115. First published in *Capitalism and Freedom,* by Milton Friedman, University of Chicago Press, 1962.

# Index

European Union, 3, 66, 85, 90, 219
Europe, New World ties with, 49, 160

**F**
Farmers. *See* agriculture
Financial services. *See also* banking industry
  assets, titling untitled, 90, 97–99, 110, 275, 282
  currency, stability of, 89, 90
  poverty, relieving, 148–149
Fishing industry, 13, 173–177, 190, 191, 219
Flores, Robert, 80
Foreign investment
  attitude toward, 31–32
  Canadian-Mexican relations, 53
  education and, 136
  electric power generation, 126
  environmentalism, 170
  in infrastructure building, 71–72, 88
  Mexican banks, ownership of, 56, 89, 91–94, 107–108
  Mexican companies north of border, 42–43
  oil industry, 114, 117, 122–123, 125, 128–129
  reducing dependence on, 275
Fox, Vicente
  banking programs, 99–101, 275–276, 282
  Catholic Church and, 211
  corruption crackdown, 245–246
  education, 141, 142
  energy companies, 117–118, 119, 125, 128, 129, 282
  environmental programs, 166–167, 184–185, 282
  NASP and, 14
  paternalism and, 26, 28, 30–31, 42, 55, 57
  relationship with George W. Bush, 133–134, 275, 277–278, 280–281
Frank, Robert, 26, 137–138, 158, 200, 201, 226, 235
Friedman, Milton, 173
Frisbie, Joe, 262
Fuentes, Carlos, 216–217

**G**
Gaghan, Stephen, 257
Gap, 161–162
García, Rolando, 80
Garment factories. *See* clothing manufacturers
Garza, Tony, 278
Gasoline, refining, 125
Gates, Bill, 159
Gender. *See* women, role of
Germany, 34
Gibson, Ken, 153
Gilmore, David, 237–238
Giraldi, Antonio, 105
Goldsmith, Stephen, 120
Government social welfare programs. *See* paternalism, Mexican
Gramlich, Edward M., 72–73
Guatemala, 148
Guilbault, Rose del Castillo, 102–103
Guzman Montalvo, José, 246

**H**
Haiti, 162
Hamilton-Paterson, James, 146–147
Hank González, Carlos, 236–237, 238
Harken Energy Corp., 34
Health care
  addiction treatment, 258–259, 265–267, 271–273
  in El Paso, 215–216
  insurance in U.S., 207–209
  for senior citizens, 267–269
Hiett, Col. James and Laurie Ann, 244–245
Highway system
  goals, 77–78
  importance, 9–10, 87
  objectives, 70–73
  social costs, 78–79
  timetable, 65–66
Hinojosa, Gilberto, 171
Hood, Robert, 267
Housing
  construction and traffic congestion, 77–79
  low-income development, 83–84
  middle class development, 79–83
  under paternalism, 73–74
  shortage, 63–64, 73
  suburbs, pros and cons of, 74–77
Houston, Stephen D., 129
Hufbauer, Gary, 206
Humphries, Bill, 149
Huntington, Samuel P., 240
Hutchinson, Asa, 263

**I**
Immigration
  Canadian "guest worker" program, 52
  drugs and, 249–250
  employers' view of, 156–157
  financial services for Mexican expatriots, 89, 91–92, 99–104
  illegal in U.S., 58, 60
  reform proposals, 44, 281–282, 286
Infonavit, 73–74, 81
Infrastructure
  airports, 65–69, 67–69
  government role, 86–87
  highway system, 70–73
  goals, 77–78
  importance, 9–10, 87
  objectives, 70–73
  social costs, 78–79
  timetable, 65–66
  housing, 73–84
  railroads, 65–66, 69–70
  repair costs, 19, 63–65
  seaports and airports, 66–69
Investment, foreign. *See* foreign investment

**J**
Jackson, Kenneth, 83–84
Johnson, Gary, 262, 263
Jurith, Edward, 258
Justice system
  guilt and innocence, 229